VĀSAVADATTĀ

A SANSKRIT ROMANCE

VĀSAVADATTĀ

A SANSKRIT ROMANCE

BY

SUBANDHU

TRANSLATED, WITH AN INTRODUCTION AND NOTES, BY

LOUIS H. GRAY, PH.D.

MOTILAL BANARSIDASS
DELHI :: VARANASI : PATNA
1962

MOTILAL BANARSIDASS
Bungalow Road, Jawahar Nagar, Delhi-6
Nepalikhapra, Varanasi-1. U. P.
Bankipore, Patna, Bihar.

Publication of this book was made possible by a grant from the U. S. Information Service.

PRINTED IN INDIA BY SHANTILAL JAIN, SHRI JAINENDRA PRESS, BUNGALOW ROAD, JAWAHAR NAGAR, DELHI-6 AND PUBLISHED BY SUNDARLAL JAIN, MOTILAL BANARSIDASS BUNGALOW ROAD, JAWAHAR NAGAR, DELHI-6.

TO PROFESSOR A. V. WILLIAMS JACKSON

MY DEAR GURU—That you consented, on one of the many occasions that I have been privileged to be your guest, to accept the dedication of this translation of India's oldest formal romance, has ever been to me a source of keenest joy. It is to you that I owe my knowledge of India and her sister land, Iran; and to you I am indebted, as to a *guru* indeed—that word which no tongue can truly translate—for so much that makes for true manhood, without which, as without charity, mere knowledge is but 'as sounding brass, or a tinkling cymbal.' I have tried to make my work, here as always, worthy both of you and of Columbia, to which we are each so loyal. Generously you have helped me, even when your leisure was most limited, and gratefully I acknowledge your aid; for of you I can say with all my heart, as the Irish host of legend cried to their hero, Cáilte, *Adrae buaid ocus bennachtain; is mor in fis ocus in faillsiugud firinde doberi duind ar cach ní fiarfaigther dít*, 'Success and benison attend thee; great is the lore and the disclosure of truth which thou givest us upon all that is asked of thee!'

L. H. G.

PREFACE

THE precept of Horace, *nonum prematur in annum*, has been more than obeyed in this volume, for it was on November 3, 1901, that I began the translation of the *Vāsavadattā*. From that day Subandhu's romance has never been long absent from my thoughts, although many practical exigencies, some of them not wholly agreeable to a scholar, have forced me again and again to lay the task aside, often for six months at a stretch. Yet these clouds, too, have had their silver lining, for not only has my work thus had time to ripen, but much has appeared bearing on the novel during these intervals, or has been called to my attention by friends. The first draft of the translation was, for example, almost completed when, in March, 1903, Dr. George C. O. Haas noted for me an entry in a catalogue of Stechert, of New York, which enabled me to purchase a copy of the edition of the *Vāsavadattā* printed in Telugu script at Madras in 1862. This necessitated a renewed study of the text in comparison with the edition of Hall, and ultimately led me to include a transliteration of the 'southern' recension in my work, together with the variants of all the other editions. Some of these would have been inaccessible to me, had it not been for the courtesy of the India Office, which, at the instance of Mr. F. W. Thomas, its librarian, most generously loaned me the texts I needed, so that I might use them at leisure in my own study.

Excepting the blank-verse renderings of the few Sanskrit stanzas of the *Vāsavadattā*, I have sought to make the translation as literal as the English language would permit, and throughout I have spared no pains to facilitate reference to the original text, as well as to explain each allusion that I could elucidate. In the latter regard I have considered others than professed Sanskritists, for I have ventured to hope that some copies of the work may fall into the hands of students of literature, who may here find points of similarity to, or divergence from, the writings to which their special attention may be directed. I dare not flatter myself that I have invariably hit the true meaning of the original, for there are passages which repeated study, through these eleven years, has failed to solve to my own complete satisfaction. But even for this I scarcely grieve, for, like Propertius, I feel,

Quod si deficiant uires, audacia certe
Laus erit: in magnis et uoluisse sat est.

And if the *cruces* that have baffled me shall be solved by other minds, none will feel greater joy in their success than I.

It is with a feeling almost akin to regret that I lay down my pen. Perhaps to me the *Vāsavadattā* has deeper associations than to almost any one else who has laboured on it. In hours of bitterness and sorrow it has helped me to forget; and it has heightened the pleasure of happy days. With all its faults, I love it; possibly I have even been so blind as to reckon its failings virtues; possibly, too, the innate Anglo-Saxon sympathy for the 'under dog' has made me only the more determined in its praise. Is it worth while, or not? As the Arabs say, *Allāhu a'lamu*, 'God best knows (and man can't tell).'

I am happy to have had, in my work, the assistance of many friends—Mr. Thomas and Dr. Haas, to whom I have already alluded; others to whose courtesies reference will be made in the course of the book—Dr. George A. Grierson, Professor Theodor Zachariae, Mr. Richard Hall; Professor Washburn Hopkins, whose notes aided in introducing me to the mysteries of Grantha script; Professor Charles R. Lanman, who enabled me to use the Harvard copy of Hall's edition until I could procure my own—a courtesy which had already been accorded me for a year previous by the library of the Deutsche Morgenländische Gesellschaft; Mr. T. K. Balasubrahmanya, who replied in full to my queries concerning the 'southern' text; and Mr. G. Payn Quackenbos, who called my attention to the reference to Subandhu in the *Subhāṣitaratnabhāṇḍāgāra*, while to Dr. Charles J. Ogden I am indebted for a number of helpful suggestions and corrections, particularly in the Introduction. In a very special way my thanks are due also to Mr. Alexander Smith Cochran, whose interest in the Columbia University Indo-Iranian Series has rendered possible the printing of this particular volume.

My gratitude to my friend and teacher, Professor A. V. Williams Jackson—here editor as well—is more fittingly expressed elsewhere within these covers. Suffice it to say that he read with me word by word the second of the three drafts of this translation, and that wellnigh every page bears some token of his careful scholarship. And to one other—my wife—my deepest obligations are due for whatsoever may be best in my work. She has subjected every line to a most minute and unsparing revision, besides taking upon herself the arduous task of preparing my manuscript for the press. Her interest in the work has never faltered, and to her criticism, at once most kindly and most severe, I owe more than I can tell.

LOUIS H. GRAY.

NOVEMBER 25, 1912.

CONTENTS

ABBREVIATIONS

ad loc	= (*ad locum*), on the passage.
apud	= in.
bis	= twice.
cf.	= compare.
EI.	= Epigraphia Indica.
H.	= Hall's edition of the Vāsavadattā.
IA.	= Indian Antiquary.
Introd.	= Introduction.
JAOS.	= Journal of the American Oriental Society.
JASBe.	= Journal of the Asiatic Society of Bengal.
JRAS.	= Journal of the Royal Asiatic Society.
JRASBo.	= Journal of the Royal Asiatic Society, Bombay Branch.
KZ.	= Zeitschrift für vergleichende Sprachforschung auf dem Gebiete der indogermanischen Sprachen, ed. A. Kuhn and others.
l.c.	= (*loco citato*), at the place previously cited.
M.	= edition of the Vāsavadattā in Telugu script printed at Madras in 1862.
No.	= number.
n. p.	= no place of publication given.
op. cit.	= (*opus citatum*), the work previously cited.
pp.	= pages.
S.	= edition of the Vāsavadattā printed at Srirangam in 1906–1908.
sqq.	= (*sequentes*), following.
s.v.	= (*sub verbo*) under the word.
SWAW.	= Sitzungsberichte der Wiener Akademie der Wissenschaften.
Tel. ed.	= edition of the Vāsavadattā in Telugu script printed at Madras in 1862.
Tel. ed. 61	= edition of the Vāsavadattā in Telugu script printed at Madras in 1861.
v.	= verse.
WZKM.	= Wiener Zeitschrift für die Kunde des Morgenlandes.
ZDMG.	= Zeitschrift der Deutschen Morgenländischen Gesellschaft.

= when prefixed to a word or meaning in the lexicographical appendix, such word or meaning is cited by the St. Petersburg lexicons only on the authority of native Sanskrit lexicographers.

= when prefixed to a word or meaning in the lexicographical appendix, such word or meaning is entirely omitted by the St. Petersburg lexicons; elsewhere it denotes the omission of words or parts of words to be supplied from the context.

‹ › = single paronomasia.

« » = double paronomasia.

⋘ ⋙ = triple paronomasia.

( ) = when placed around or in words of the transcribed text, the enclosed portions differ from the text of Hâll; when placed around numerals in the translation and transcription, these refer to the pages of the Madras edition of 1862.

[ ] = when placed around or in words of the transcribed text, the enclosed portions, though contained in Hall's edition, are entirely omitted by the Madras edition of 1862; when placed around numerals in the translation and transcription, these refer to the pages of Hall's edition.

INTRODUCTION

Title. The title of the *Vāsavadattā* of Subandhu, the oldest romantic novel in India, seems to be derived from that of a long lost drama by Bhāsa,[1] the *Svapnavāsavadattā*, or 'Dream-Vāsavadattā' (for compounds of this type cf. Wackernagel, *Altindische Grammatik*, 2. 1. 244–245, 250–253, Göttingen, 1905). The dream as a novelistic device in India first occurs in Subandhu (see below, p. 28); though in the drama it is found in the first act of the *Viddhaśālabhañjikā* and the third of the *Karpūramañjarī* (both written by Rājaśēkhara, who was acquainted with Bhāsa's work), as well as in the first of Viśvanāthabhaṭṭa's *Śṛṅgāravāṭikā* (*Catalogue of the Sanskrit Manuscripts in the Library of the India Office*, 7, 1618, London, 1904). In the fifth act of Bhāsa's *Svapnavāsavadattā* the hero, King Vatsarāja, sleeping, dreams of his love Vāsavadattā, who enters, disguised as an attendant of the queen, but who, he thinks, has been burned to death at Lāvānaka (cf. *svapnavāsavadattasya dāhakō*, 'the conflagration of the "Dream-Vāsavadattā"' [Rājaśēkhara, cited in the *Sūktimuktāvalī* (see Peterson and Durgāprasāda, *Subhāṣitāvali of Vallabhadēva*, Introd., p. 81, Bombay, 1886)], and Bhāsa's epithet *jalaṇamitta*, 'friend of fire,' in *Gaüḍavaha*. v. 800), this being employed both in the famous fire-scene in the fourth act of the *Ratnāvalī* (first half of the seventh century) and in the *Tāpasavatsarāja* (before the second half of the ninth century; see the analysis by Hultzsch, in *Nachrichten von der königlichen Gesellschaft der Wissenschaften zu Göttingen*, 1886, pp. 224–241). Not only was the fire-scene thus borrowed from Bhāsa by later dramatists, but from him, it may be conjectured, came, at least in literary form, the entire story of Vāsavadattā and Udayana, or Vatsarāja, as given in the *Ratnāvalī*, *Priya-*

[1] On Bhāsa, see, in general, Hall, 'Fragments of Three Early Hindu Dramatists,' in *JASBe*. 28. 28–29; Lévi, *Théâtre indien*, 1. 157–160, 2. 31–32, Paris, 1890.

darśikā, and *Tāpasavatsarāja*,[1] the ultimate source probably being the lost *Bṛhatkathā*. With the Vāsavadattā of these latter works Subandhu's heroine has only her name in common, nor is any other story concerning her known to exist in Sanskrit literature (cf. Krishnamachariar, Introd., pp. 48–50; Lacôte, *Essai sur Guṇāḍhya et la Bṛhatkathā*, pp. 15–16, Paris, 1908). Though sleeping on the stage is forbidden by Sanskrit dramaturgy, the hero of the *Svapnavāsavadattā* dreams of the heroine, an episode imitated, I would suggest, by Rājaśēkhara in his *Viddhaśālabhañjikā* and *Karpūramañjarī*. In similar fashion Subandhu seems to have derived from this play[2] both the dream-episode and the name of his heroine, who was indeed a 'dream-Vāsavadattā'; and it would then appear that he invented the remainder of the romance. This is also the opinion of Krishnamachariar (Introd., pp. 48, 50), who suggests, however, that Subandhu may have adapted some old wives' tale.

Author. The author of the *Vāsavadattā* was the only Subandhu to win for himself a name in Sanskrit literature, unless exception be made in favour of Subandhu, son of Gōpāyana or Lōpāyana, who, according to the *Sarvānukramaṇī* (ed. Macdonell, p. 19, Oxford, 1886), was one of the four authors of *Rig-Veda* 5. 24 (cf. the legend concerning him in *Bṛhaddēvatā*, 7. 84–102, ed. and tr. Macdonell, Cambridge, Mass., 1904). The name, however, occurs with tolerable frequency in Sanskrit (cf. Böhtlingk and Roth, *Sanskrit-Wörterbuch*, 7. 1086, St. Petersburg, 1875), and it would even seem to be found, under the form Šu-ba-an-di, or Šu-ba-an-du, in one of the Tell-el-Amarna Tablets, dating approximately from the fourteenth or fifteenth century B. C. (Winckler, *Thontafeln von Tell-el-Amarna*, Nos. 224–229, Berlin, 1896).

[1] To this list Krishnamachariar (Introd., p. 37) adds the lost drama *Udayanacarita* (cf. Lévi, *Théatre indien*, 1. 92; 2. 39, Paris, 1890; Schuyler, *Bibliography of the Sanskrit Drama*, p. 90, New York, 1906).

[2] In May, 1910, the *Svapnavāsavadattā* and nine other dramas of Bhāsa were discovered near Padmanābhapura by Gaṇapati Śāstrī, who later found another manuscript containing, among other plays, a second copy of the *Svapnavāsavadattā*. These dramas were edited, after this introduction was already in type, in the *Trivandrum Sanskrit Series*.

Sanskrit References to Subandhu. References in Sanskrit literature and inscriptions to *our* Subandhu (whose date is discussed below, pp. 8–11) are but scanty. By far the most important allusion is contained in the eleventh stanza of Bāṇa's introduction to his *Harṣacarita* (seventh century):

kavīnām agalad darpō nūnaṃ vāsavadattayā
śaktyē "va pāṇḍuputrāṇāṃ gatayā karṇagōcaram,

'verily, the pride of ‹poets› melted away through the « *Vāsavadattā* coming to their ears » even as the pride of the ‹sages› melted away through the Pāṇḍavas' « Indra-given spear coming nigh Karṇa ».'[1] Bāṇa is also supposed to allude to the *Vāsavadattā* when, in the twentieth stanza of his introduction to his *Kādambarī*, he declares his new work to be *iyam atidvayī kathā*, 'this story surpassing the two,' these being, according to the commentator, the *Vāsavadattā* and the *Bṛhatkathā*. About a century later Vākpati, the author of the Prakrit historical poem *Gaüḍavaha*, wrote (v. 800), in describing himself:

bhāsammi jalaṇamittē kantīdēvē a jassa rahuārē
sōbandhavē a bandhammi hāriyandē a āṇandō,

'in Bhāsa—the friend of fire—in the author of the *Raghu* (*vaṃśa*)—that lord of beauty—in Subandhu's work, and in that of Haricandra is his delight.' In Kavirāja's *Rāghavapāṇḍavīya*, which dates from about 1200 A. D., occurs the stanza (1. 41):

subandhur bāṇabhaṭṭaś ca kavirāja iti trayaḥ
vakrōktimārganipuṇāś caturthō vidyatē na vā,

'Subandhu, Bāṇabhaṭṭa, and Kavirāja—these three be skilful in the path of ambiguity[2]; a fourth there is not found.' The

[1] This verse is interpolated at the end of the *Vāsavadattā* by the Telugu and Grantha editions, and Krishnamachariar (Introd., pp. 38–39) implies that it may have been written by Subandhu and later have found its way into the *Harṣacarita*. His theory is to me untenable. On the use of the signs ‹ ›, etc., see p. 17.

[2] On *vakrōkti* see *Sāhityadarpaṇa*, No. 641; Appayyadikṣita, *Kuvalayānandakārikā*, 1. 158–159; *Kāvyaprakāśa*, tr. Jhā, pp. 181–182, Benares, 1898; Bernheimer and Jacobi, in *ZDMG.* 63. 797–821; 64. 130–139, 586–590, 751–759; 65. 308–312. Subandhu is also mentioned immediately before Bāṇa in the *Sarasvatīkanthābharaṇa* according to Müller, *India, What can it Teach us?*, p. 331, note 5, London, 1883, but I have not been able to find the reference.

twelfth-century *Śrīkaṇṭhacarita* of Maṅkha contains the stanza (2. 53):

mēṇṭhē svardviradādhirōhiṇi vaśaṃ yātē subandhāu vidhēḥ
śāntē hanta ca bhāravāu vighaṭitē bāṇē viṣādaspṛśaḥ
vāgdēvyā viramantu mantuvidhurā drāg dṛṣṭayaś cēṣṭatē
śiṣṭaḥ kaścana sa prasādayati tāṃ yadvāṇisadvāṇinī,

'Mēṇṭha having mounted the elephant of the sky [i.e., having died], Subandhu having yielded to the will of destiny, Bhāravi, alas, being at rest, and Bāṇa being broken, let the reason-reft glances of the sorrow-stricken goddess of speech [Sarasvatī] quickly find repose; for any one left that bestirreth himself doth win her, to whose voice she is a goodly dancer.' Two centuries later, Śārṅgadhara, quoting Rājaśēkhara (cf. above, p. 1), who flourished about 900 A. D., in his *Paddhati* (cf. Aufrecht, 'Ueber die Paddhati von Çārṅgadhara,' in *ZDMG*. 27.77; *Śārṅgadhara-paddhati*, ed. Peterson, 1. No. 188, Bombay, 1888), made the citation:

bhāsō rāmilasāumilāu vararuciḥ śrīsāhasāṅkaḥ kavir
mēṇṭhō bhāravikālidāsataralāḥ skandhaḥ subandhuś ca yaḥ
daṇḍī bāṇadivākarāu gaṇapatiḥ kāntaś ca ratnākaraḥ
siddhā yasya sarasvatī bhagavatī kē tasya sarvē 'pi tē,

'Bhāsa, Rāmila, Sāumila, Vararuci, the poet Sāhasāṅka, Mēṇṭha, Bhāravi, Kālidāsa, Tarala, Skandha, and Subandhu, Daṇḍin, Bāṇa, Divākara, Gaṇapati, and the charming Ratnākara,—what are all they to him by whom the exalted Sarasvatī is possessed'? Rājaśēkhara also refers to Subandhu in the following stanza quoted by Aufrecht (*ZDMG*. 36. 366) from the *Saduktikarṇāmṛta* (cf. also Peterson and Durgāprasāda, *Subhāshitāvali of Vallabhadeva*, Introd., p. 57, Bombay, 1886; Krishnamachariar, Introd., p. 41):

subandhāu bhaktir naḥ ka iha raghukārē na ramatē
dhṛtir dākṣīputrē harati haricandrō 'pi hṛdayam
viśuddhōktiḥ śūraḥ prakṛtimadhurā bhāravigiras
tathā "py antarmōdaṃ kam api bhavabhūtir vitanutē,

'in Subandhu is our delight; who rejoiceth not in the author of the *Raghu*(*vaṃśa*)[1]? satisfaction delighteth in the son of Dākṣī[2]; even Haricandra joyeth the heart; of faultless diction is Śūra[3]; the words of Bhāravi are delightsome in theme; Bhavabhūti doth infuse an inward pleasure.' Krishnamachariar also cites an allusion to the author of the *Vāsavadattā* in Abhinavabhaṭṭabāṇa's *Vīranārāyaṇacarita* (*l. c.*):

pratikavibhēdanabāṇaḥ kavitātarugahanaviharaṇamayūraḥ
sahṛdayalōkasubandhur jayati śrībhaṭṭabāṇakavirājaḥ,

'victorious is the noble Bhaṭṭabāṇa, king of poets, an arrow [or, "a Bāṇa"] for piercing hostile poets; a peacock [or, "a Mayūra"] for wandering through the forest of the trees of poetry; a goodly kinsman [or, "a Subandhu"] for all connoisseurs.' An anonymous citation in the modern anthology *Subhāṣitaratnabhāṇḍāgāra* (ed. Parab, 3 ed., p. 56, Bombay, 1891) runs:

māghaś cōrō mayūrō muraripur aparō bhāraviḥ sāravidyaḥ
śrīharṣaḥ kālidāsaḥ kavir atha bhavabhūtyāhvayō bhōjarājaḥ
śrīdaṇḍī ḍiṇḍimākhyaḥ śrutimukuṭagurur bhallaṭō bhaṭṭabāṇaḥ
khyātāś cā 'nyē subandhvādaya iha kṛtibhir viśvam āhlādayanti,

'Māgha, Cōra, Mayūra, Mura's second foe (Murāri), Bhāravi in climax learned, Harṣa, Kālidāsa, and also the poet named Bhavabhūti, Bhōjarāja, Daṇḍin (hight "the Drum"), Bhallaṭa weighty with the diadem of fame, Bhaṭṭabāṇa, and other renowned ones, such as Subandhu, here on earth rejoice the universe with their compositions.'

In the latter part of the sixteenth century, Ballāla, in his *Bhōjaprabandha*, which he set forth as a history of Bhōja, who ruled at Dhārā (the modern Dhār) in the eleventh century, mentioned Subandhu, according to some manuscripts, as one of the thirteen principal members of the host of five hundred *literati* who graced the royal court (cf. Wilson, *Works*, 5. 174, London, 1865; Hall, Introd., p. 7, note 1); but the list varies so extremely in the different manuscripts of the *Bhōjaprabandha*

[1] Kālidāsa. [2] Pāṇini.
[3] See Aufrecht, *Catalogus Catalogorum*, 1. 660, Leipzig, 1891.

that little stress can be laid upon it, especially in view of the legendary character of the work as a whole. Finally, mention should also be made, for the sake of completeness, of an apparent allusion to the *Vāsavadattā* in Daṇḍin's *Daśakumāracarita* (ed. Godabole and Parab, p. 110, lines 11–12, Bombay, 1898): *anurūpabhartṛgāminīnāṃ ca vāsavadattādīnāṃ varṇanēna grāhayā 'nuśayam*, 'and make her repent by a description of Vāsavadattā and others who gained suitable husbands.' This clearly refers, however, to the well-known story of Vāsavadattā and Udayana (see above, p. 2); and it is equally impossible that the *vāsavadattām adhikṛtya kṛtō granthaḥ* mentioned in the *Vārttika* (probably third century B.C.) on Pāṇini, 4. 3. 87, should be connected in any way with Subandhu's romance.

It should also be noted that Narasiṃha Vāidya, one of the glossators of the *Vāsavadattā*, says: *kavir ayaṃ vikramādityasabhyaḥ. tasmin rājñi lōkāntaraṃ prāptē ētan nibandhaṃ kṛtavān*, 'this poet [Subandhu] was a retainer of Vikramāditya. When this king attained the other world, he [Subandhu] composed this work' (Hall, Introd., p. 6, note). Hall's manuscript D, moreover, which belongs to what I may tentatively call the 'South Indian recension' of the *Vāsavadattā* (see below, p. 38), terms Subandhu 'the son of Vararuci's sister' (*śrīvararucibhāginēya*), Vararuci himself being, as is well known, one of the 'nine gems' of Vikramāditya's court, flourishing at least later than the fifth century (Bloch, *Vararuci und Hemacandra*, p. 13, Gütersloh, 1893; cf. Macdonell, *History of Sanskrit Literature*, p. 324, London, 1900). Hall denies that Subandhu was Vararuci's nephew (Introd., pp. 6–7), but it is possible that the tradition contains a larger element of truth than is often supposed (cf. Wilson, *Works*, 5. 177, London, 1865). It is, at all events, echoed by the *Bhōjaprabandha*,—whatever be the value assigned to such testimony—which associates Subandhu and Vararuci in the passage already referred to.

Inscriptions of India mention Subandhu only once to my knowledge. This single instance is a Canarese record of 1168 A.D., found at Balagāmi (Rice, *Mysore Inscriptions*, p. 111,

Bangalore, 1879), which contains the words: 'In *śabda* a Pāṇini paṇḍita, in *nīti* Bhūṣaṇācārya, in *nāṭya* and other *bharata śāstras* Bharatamuni, in *kāvya* Subandhu, in *siddhānta* Lakulīśvara, at the feet of Śiva a Skanda adorning the world, thus is Vāma Śaktiyati truly described.' The only additional information thus gained is that by the twelfth century his fame had spread to southern India.

Subandhu's Allusions to Sanskrit Literature. If Subandhu is thus recognised but sparingly and indefinitely in the literature and epigraphy of his native land, he is himself most generous in alluding to the productions of other authors. The majority of his references, however, cast little light upon his date, for no real conclusions can be drawn from his mention of the *Bṛhatkathā* (ed. Hall, pp. 110, 147), the *Kāmasūtra* (ed. Hall, p. 89), the *Chandōviciti* section of the *Bhāratīyanāṭyaśāstra* (ed. Hall, pp. 94, note, 119, 235), the *Mahābhārata* and *Harivaṃśa* (ed. Hall, pp. 21, 27, 93, 234, 254; on Subandhu's indebtedness to the *Mahābhārata* see Cartellieri, 'Das Mahābhārata bei Subandhu und Bāṇa,' in *WZKM*. 13. 57–74), the *Rāmāyaṇa* (ed. Hall, p. 234), the *Upaniṣads* (ed. Hall, p. 235), and the Mīmāṃsā and Nyāya philosophies (ed. Hall, pp. 93, 235, 297), any more than we can derive any definite conclusions from his general and hostile mention of the Buddhists (ed. Hall, pp. 144, 179, 235, 255, 297 *bis*) and Jains (ed. Hall, pp. 93, 187, 297; cf. on these allusions to the Buddhists and the Jains Telang, 'Subandhu and Kumārila,' in *JRASBo*. 18. 150–159).[1]

It has been held, on the basis of Śivarāma's commentary, that the words *bāuddhasaṅgatim ivā 'laṃkārabhūṣitām*, 'decked with ‹adornments› as an assembly of Buddhists is decked with the ‹*Alaṃkāra*›' (ed. Hall, p. 235), refer to the *Bāuddhasaṅgatyalaṃkāra* of Dharmakīrti (cf., in general, on Dharmakīrti, Pathak, 'Dharmakīrti and Śaṁkarāchārya,' in *JRASBo*. 18. 88–96, and

[1] Reference should also be made, in this connexion, to the allusions collected in Krishnamachariar's Introduction, received after these lines were written, to other Sanskrit literature, especially the *Mahābhārata* and *Rāmāyaṇa*, as well as to religion and philosophy (pp. 22–24, 27–28).

the criticism of Telang, *ib.* 18. 148–150). Since, however, Dharmakīrti is described by I-Tsing, who travelled in India in 671–695 A.D., as among those 'of late years' (*Record of the Buddhist Religion*, tr. Takakusu, p. 181, cf. p. lviii, Oxford, 1896); and since Tāranātha (*Geschichte des Buddhismus in Indien*, tr. Schiefner, pp. 184–185, St. Petersburg, 1869) makes him a contemporary of the Tibetan king, Srong-btsan-sgam-po, who died about 650 A.D. (Duff, *Chronology of India*, p. 53, Westminster, 1899), Lévi ('La Date de Candragomin,' in *Bulletin de l'École d'Extrême-Orient*, 1903, p. 18; cf. Kern, *Manual of Indian Buddhism*, p. 130, note 11, Strassburg, 1896) is doubtless right in denying that Subandhu makes any allusion to Dharmakīrti's activity (for an opposing view see Krishnamachariar, Introd., p. 32).

This leaves but a single literary allusion in the *Vāsavadattā* which can in any way be construed as casting light on the date of the romance. The reference in question is *nyāyasthitim ivō 'ddyōtakaraśvarūpām*, '‹revealing her beauty› as the permanence of the Nyāya system has its ‹form from Uddyōtakara›' (ed. Hall, p. 235). Since we know that Uddyōtakara wrote his *Nyāyavārttika* to refute the heterodox (i.e., Buddhist) views of Dignāga, who flourished between 520 and 600 A.D. (Kern, *op. cit.* p. 129; Müller, *Six Systems of Indian Philosophy*, p. 477, London, 1899), it is obvious that Uddyōtakara, to whom Subandhu so unmistakably refers, can not have lived before the latter part of the sixth century. It is, therefore, certain that the *Vāsavadattā* can not be prior to the late sixth century of our era.

The Date of Subandhu. There is but one allusion in Subandhu's romance itself which can be interpreted as referring to a historical event. This is the tenth introductory stanza:

sā rasavattā vihatā navakā vilasanti carati nō kaṃ kaḥ[1]
sarasī 'va kīrtiśēṣaṃ gatavati bhuvi vikramādityē,

'‹moisture› is destroyed, «cranes sport not», ⋘the heron fares not forth⋙; yea, ‹eloquence› is destroyed, «new-comers make

[1] The theory of Mazumdar (*JRAS.* 1907, pp. 406–408), that the *kaṃ kaḥ* of this stanza involves an allusion to a Kaṅka dynasty, must be regarded as not proven.

disport», «who devours not whom»?—for Vikramāditya, like a lake, hath passed away on earth.' This has been taken, particularly by Hall (Introd., p. 6), to imply that Subandhu 'lived long posterior to the great Vikramāditya of Ujjayinī.' Although some deny that this monarch, about whom cluster so many legends, ever existed (see, for example, Macdonell, *History of Sanskrit Literature*, pp. 323–324, London, 1900), such a view can scarcely be supported, and there is good reason to believe him to be identical with Candragupta II, who reigned from about 374 to 413 (Smith, *Early History of India from 600 B.C. to the Muhammadan Conquest*, 2 ed., pp. 275–283, Oxford, 1908). It would be most tempting, so far as the special problems of the *Vāsavadattā* are concerned, could one accept the view, argued with great learning by Hoernle ('Some Problems of Ancient Indian History,' in *JRAS.* 1903, pp. 545–570, and 'The Identity of Yaśodharman and Vikramāditya, and some Corollaries,' *ib.* 1909, pp. 89–144; against this Fleet, 'Dr. Hoernle's Article on Some Problems of Ancient Indian History,' *ib.* 1904, pp. 164–166, and Smith, 'The Indian Kings named Śilāditya, and the Kingdom of Mo-la-p'o,' in *ZDMG.* 58. 787–796), that Yaśōdharman (on whom see also Smith, *op. cit.* pp. 301–302), whom he identifies with the great Vikramāditya, 'founded his Mālava empire about 533 A.D., and reigned up to about 583 A.D.' Hoernle accordingly dates Subandhu in the second half of the sixth century, and holds that the *Vāsavadattā* was written before 606–612, the latter year being that of Harṣa's coronation. Attractive as is this hypothesis, I am compelled to admit that it can scarcely be used to determine the date of Subandhu, the whole evidence of Indian history being against it.

The period following the death of Vikramāditya is described in the stanza quoted above as one of degeneration, and there may be a covert allusion to the same (or a similar) evil state of affairs in the phrase *navanṛpaticittavṛttibhir iva kulyāpamānakāriṇībhir*, 'as the disposition of new monarchs causes dishonour to the honourable' (ed. Hall, p. 220). Hoernle, holding that Vikramāditya's successor was his son Śīlāditya, who was dethroned by his enemies (probably about 593 A. D.), being 'replaced in the kingdom of his father' (probably before 604 A. D.) only by the aid of the Hun, Pravarasēna II of Kashmir (*Rājataraṅgiṇī* 3. 330), has evolved a most ingenious theory which I was long inclined to adopt. Śīlāditya is, on this hypothesis, described as not only unfortunate, but cruel, as evidenced by his execution of the Māukharī Grahavarman, king of Kanauj, and the brutal fettering and imprisonment of the dead monarch's young wife, Rājyaśrī (*Harṣacarita*, tr. Cowell and Thomas, p. 173, London, 1897); and as unpatriotic, this being shown by his acceptance of assistance from non-Aryan Huns. Despite his restoration by Pravarasēna, the reign of Śīlāditya, who, Hoernle maintains, succeeded his father, Vikramāditya, about 583 A. D., came to a disastrous end in 606 (or 605), when he was utterly defeated by Rājyavardhana II, the brother of the famous Harṣavardhana who is the hero of the *Harṣacarita*. Harṣavardhana himself succeeded to the throne of Thāṇēsar in 606, when Rājyavardhana was treacherously slain by the Gāuḍa king, Śaśāṅka, and reigned until 648 (on Harṣavardhana, in general, cf. Ettinghausen, *Harṣa Vardhana, empereur et poète de l'Inde septentrionale*, Paris, 1906).

While holding this theory, I gave to it the pleasing embellishment of an hypothesis, without real basis, that the dynasties to which Vikramāditya and Harṣavardhana belonged were rivals, and that Bāṇa was the faithful eulogist of Harṣavardhana exactly as Subandhu was loyal to Vikramāditya. Since, moreover, Bāṇa's monarch had been victorious over the degenerate son of Subandhu's royal patron, I deemed that Bāṇa had deliberately set out to surpass Subandhu, so that Harṣavardhana's court might excel Vikramāditya's in literature as well as in arms. Thus, there would have been a deeper motive for Bāṇa to write the *Harṣacarita* than the mere incentive of literary emulation which is generally ascribed to him.

History does not sustain this elaborate figment, which I have recorded mainly to keep others from possible pursuit of a false clue. Not only was Vikramāditya not identical with Yaśōdharman, as already noted, but Śīlāditya was the very reverse of a cruel monarch (Smith, *Early History of India from 600 B.C. to the Muhammadan Conquest*, 2 ed., p. 306, Oxford, 1908). If one were to stress the theory of rivalry both in letters and in war, one might suppose that Subandhu was a courtier either of Śaśāṅka of Gāuḍa or of Dēvagupta of Eastern Mālava (cf. Ettinghausen, *op. cit.* pp. 36–38, 148), both of whom were ignoble in character. But of this there is not the slightest evidence; and even if the name of the father of either of them was Vikramāditya (a most improbable hypothesis), that would give little point to Subandhu's stanza, which plainly alludes to the famous Vikramāditya, and is, therefore, only a conventional harking back to happy times long past. In determining the date of the *Vāsavadattā* I am forced to consider the lines under discussion as utterly valueless.

While the sole known basis for assigning a *terminus a quo* to the composition of Subandhu's romance is, as we have seen, the allusion to Uddyōtakara, who probably flourished in the latter half of the sixth century, the *terminus ad quem* is almost certainly the date of Bāṇa's *Harṣacarita*. This romance, which was left unfinished by its author, ends abruptly with the rescue of Rājyaśrī, the sister of Harṣavardhana and widow of Grahavarman (i. e. 607, or 606), though Harṣa had reigned several years when Bāṇa wrote (*Harṣacarita*, tr. Cowell and Thomas, pp. 75–76, London, 1897). The precise date of composition of Bāṇa's second romance, the *Kādambarī*, is unknown; but, as Bāṇa died before completing it (*Kādambarī*, tr. Ridding, p. 182, London, 1896), it must have been written considerably after the *Harṣacarita*. It may also be regarded as certain that Subandhu lived later, probably by at least a century (cf. p. 12), than Daṇḍin, the author of the picaresque *Daśakumāracarita* (Weber, *Indische Streifen*, I. 311–315, 353, 372, Berlin, 1868; *Daśakumāracarita*, tr. Meyer, pp. 120–127, Leipzig, 1902; Collins, *The Geographical Data of the Raghuvaṃśa and Daśakumāracarita*, p. 46, Leipzig, 1907, places Daṇḍin's literary activity before 585 A. D.).

The Place of Composition of the Vāsavadattā. The question next arises as to the place of composition of the *Vāsavadattā*.

Here the answer must be still more vague.[1] It is obviously impossible that the romance was written at the court of Bhōja, as some manuscripts of the *Bhōjaprabandha* would imply, for that ruler did not reign at Dhārā until the eleventh century; nor does there seem to have been any Bhōja reigning in the latter part of the sixth century at whose court Subandhu might have been, thus being confusedly located by Ballāla in the train of the famous Bhōja of Dhārā. One might, indeed, by reckless theorising, allege that Subandhu, thus being placed at Dhārā in Mālava, had actually been a courtier either of Dēvagupta of Eastern Mālava or of Śīlāditya of Mo-la-p'o (Western Mālava); but the real reason for this wild statement by the author of the *Bhōjaprabandha* (or, more probably, by one of his interpolators) was obviously the identification, occasionally made by Sanskrit authors (cf. Weber, *Akademische Vorlesungen über indische Literaturgeschichte*, 2 ed., pp. 218–219, Berlin, 1876; Rajendralala Mitra, 'Bhoja Rájá of Dhár and his Homonyms,' in *JASBe.* 32. 93), of Bhōja and Vikramāditya, an equation too absurd to require refutation.

To sum up the discussion, we can say with reasonable certainty only that the *Vāsavadattā* was written by Subandhu at a place unknown, probably between 550 and somewhat after 606 A.D., the *terminus a quo* being the circumstance that Uddyōtakara cannot have flourished until at least the middle of the sixth century, and the *terminus ad quem* by the date of composition of the *Harṣacarita*, early in the seventh century.[2]

[1] Absolutely no clue is given by the purely conventional geography of the romance, on which see Weber, *Indische Streifen*, I. 385, Berlin, 1868.

[2] Krishnamachariar devotes a long section of his Introduction (pp. 30–48) to a discussion of Subandhu's date, which he places after Bāṇa and before Vāmana, the author of the *Kāvyālaṃkāravṛtti*, whom tradition makes a minister of Jayāpīḍa of Kashmir (779–813; cf. Duff, *Chronology of India*, pp. 68, 70–71, Westminster, 1899). He rightly argues that the various references in Sanskrit authors to Subandhu and Bāṇa allow of no conclusion as to the priority of the *Vāsavadattā*; but some of his hypotheses, as that Subandhu's dislike of Buddhism proves him to be later than Bāṇa (p. 45), as well as his general implication that the difference between the two writers is due to degeneration of style (cf. pp. 14–18), are, in my judgment, certainly untenable; nor does he touch with sufficient depth upon what evidence may be drawn from Indian history.

Data Concerning Subandhu's Life. Our knowledge of Subandhu is most meagre. In the thirteenth stanza of his introduction to the *Vāsavadattā* he terms himself *sujanāikabandhu*, which Hall (Introd., p. 24), following the commentator, Śivarāma, renders 'an intimate of none but the virtuous,' although the word should rather be translated 'Sujana's only brother.'[1] The tradition that Subandhu was the nephew of the Prakrit grammarian, Vararuci, has already been mentioned (see above, p. 6), though with disapproval; and there seems also to have been a legend that he was, by birth, a Kashmirian Brāhman (Weber, *Indische Streifen*, 1. 371, Berlin, 1868, quoting Cunningham, in *JASBe*. 17. 98–99).[2]

Subandhu is not known to have written anything besides the *Vāsavadattā*. Citations are made from him in the *Śārṅgadharapaddhati*, *Subhāṣitāvalī*, *Padyāvalī*, and *Sūktikarṇāmṛta* (Aufrecht, *Catalogus Catalogorum*, 1. 726, Leipzig, 1891); but the quotations in the first two anthologies, which alone are thus far edited [by Peterson (Bombay, 1888) and by Peterson and Durgāprasāda (Bombay, 1886), respectively], are drawn exclusively from the *Vāsavadattā*. Hall (Introd., p. 48, note), it is true, found in the still unedited *Padyavēṇī* of Vēṇīdatta, compiled about the reign of Shāh Jahān (early 17th century), the following distich then supposed to have been written by Subandhu:

akṣamālāpavṛttijñā kuśāsanaparigrahā
brāhmī "va dāurjanī saṃsad vandanīyā samēkhalā,

'an assembly of scoundrels, knowing ‹how to live by disparaging speeches›, accepting «evil teachings», and ⋘wicked to the just⋙, should be honoured even as an assembly of Brāhmans knowing

[1] Cartellieri, 'Das Mahābhārata bei Subandhu und Bāṇa,' in *WZKM*. 13. 72, translates the stanza thus: 'Durch eine Gnadengabe, die Sarasvatī ihm verliehen, hat Subandhu — d. h. der edle Freunde hat — dieses Buch gemacht; obzwar Subandhu — d.h. der hundert Freunde hat — hat er doch nur den Edlen zum einzigen Freund; eine wahre Schatzkammer ist er in der Kunst, Silbe für Silbe doppelsinnige Dichtungen zu verfertigen.' On Sujana as a proper name see Aufrecht, *op. cit.* 3. 149, Leipzig, 1903.

[2] It is interesting to note, in this connexion, that Krishnamachariar holds that Subandhu was a Vāiṣṇavite and an adherent of the Mīmāṃsā philosophy (Introd., pp. 23, 28).

‹the end of their rosaries›, accepting «seats of *kuśa*-grass», and ««girt with their girdles»».' The distich was not, however, written by Subandhu, but by Trivikrama Bhaṭṭa, the author of the *Damayantīkathā*, or *Nalacampū* (1. 7; cf. Böhtlingk, *Indische Sprüche*, 2 ed., No. 52, St. Petersburg, 1870–1873), who flourished about 915 A.D. (Duff, *Chronology of India*, p. 85, Westminster, 1899).[1]

The Vāsavadattā a Kathā. The *Vāsavadattā* is expressly stated by many manuscripts (cf. Hall's ed., p. 300, note 7, and Śivarāma *ad loc.*) to be an *ākhyāyikā*, or 'tale,' this being very possibly influenced by the reference to some work entitled, from the name of its heroine, *vāsavadattākhyāyikā* in the *Vārttika* on Pāṇini 4. 3. 87 (cf. also the *Vārttika* on 4. 2. 60, and see Krishnamachariar, Introd., pp. 36–37). The *ākhyāyikā*, according to Sanskrit rhetoricians (cf. Regnaud, *Rhétorique sanskrite*, pp. 76–77, Paris, 1884), is a division of *gadya*, or poetical prose; and the classical example is the *Harṣacarita* of Bāṇa, who himself seems to intimate that the *Vāsavadattā* likewise belongs to this category by using the term *ākhyāyikākārā*, 'authors of *ākhyāyikās*,' immediately before his allusion to Subandhu's romance, in the tenth stanza of his introduction to the *Harṣacarita*. The classic description of the *ākhyāyikā* is given in the following passage of the *Sāhityadarpaṇa* (ed. Roer, No. 568, Calcutta, 1851):

ākhyāyikā kathāvat syāt kavēr vaṃśādikīrtanam
asyām anyakavīnāṃ ca vṛttaṃ gadyaṃ kvacit kvacit
kathāṃśānāṃ vyavacchēda āśvāsa iti badhyatē
āryāvaktrāpavaktrāṇāṃ chandasā yēna kēnacit
anyāpadēśēnā "śvāsamukhē bhāvyarthasūcanam,

'the *ākhyāyikā* should be as the *kathā*. (There should be) in it an account of the lineage of the poet and of other poets; poetry

[1] Krishnamachariar (Introd., pp. 39–40) calls attention to a number of passages in the *Nalacampū* (ed. Bombay, 1885; new ed., 1903) in which he holds that Trivikrama Bhaṭṭa imitated Subandhu. He likewise notes parallels between the *Vāsavadattā* and the *Jīvandharacampū* of Haricandra (p. 52), who wrote after 897 A.D. (p. 44), *Śiśupālavadha* (p. 53), *Rāmāyaṇa* (p. 64), *Mēghadūta* (p. 54), *Vikramōrvaśī* (pp. 62. 64), and *Mālatīmādhava* (pp. 61–62), as well as the *Harṣacarita* (pp. 53–57), and *Kādambarī* (pp. 52, 53, 55, 57, 63).

in some places (and) prose in others (should be employed); divisions, called "sighs," are used for the divisions of the story; at the beginning of the "sighs" (there should be) an intimation of the theme, under the guise of something else, by any metre whatsoever of the *āryā*, *vaktra*, or *apavaktra* (classes).'

The *kathā*, or 'story,' best represented by Bāṇa's *Kādambarī*, is described by the *Sāhityadarpaṇa* (No. 567) as follows:

kathāyāṃ sarasaṃ vastu padyāir ēva vinirmitam
kvacid atra bhavēd āryā kvacid vaktrāpavaktrakē
ādāu padyāir namaskāraḥ khalādēr vṛttakīrtanam,

'in the *kathā* a theme with poetic sentiments is represented even with poetry; in it there should be the *āryā* metre in some places, (and) the *vaktra* and *apavaktra* metres in other places; at the beginning (there should be) homage in verse (to a divinity, also) a description of the character of knaves and the like.' The older, and in my judgment the better, definition of this type of Sanskrit literature, however, is given by Daṇḍin, the author of the picaresque *Daśakumāracarita*, who says (*Kāvyādarśa* 1. 23–25, 28):

apādaḥ padasantānō gadyam ākhyāyikā kathā
iti tasya prabhēdāu dvāu tayōr ākhyāyikā kila
nāyakēnāi "va vācyā "nyā nāyakēnē 'tarēṇa vā
svaguṇāviṣkriyā dōṣō nā 'tra bhūtārthaśaṃsinaḥ
api tv aniyamō dṛṣṭas tatrā 'py anyāir udīraṇāt
anyō vaktrā svayaṃ vē "ti kīdṛg vā bhēdalakṣaṇam
....
tat kathākhyāyikē "ty ēkā jātiḥ sañjñādvayāṅkitā
atrāi "vā 'ntarbhaviṣyanti śēṣāś cā "khyānajātayaḥ,

'prose is a series of words without strophes; its two classes are the *ākhyāyikā* (and) the *kathā*. Now, the *ākhyāyikā* should be spoken by the hero, the other (the *kathā*) by the hero or another. A revelation of one's own personality, if he narrates facts, is no fault here. Nevertheless, the lack of fixed distinction is seen from the story being told by others even there (in the *ākhyāyikā*). Whether another (is) the speaker, or one's self, is a sorry standard of discrimination........Therefore the *kathā* (and) *ākhyāyikā* are one category marked with a double name; and here, too, will be comprised the other categories of stories.'[1]

In support of this statement of Daṇḍin, it may be noted that the *Vāsavadattā*, though termed, as we have seen, an *ākhyāyikā* lacks the necessary divisions into 'sighs'; in its opening stanzas it (like a *kathā*) describes 'the character of knaves and the like' (introductory stanzas 6-9); and it contains a long episode spoken by another than the hero—the conversation of the *maina* with his mate concerning the heroine of the story. The manifest resemblance of the *Vāsavadattā* to the *Kādambarī*, which is considered to be a *kathā*, together with its unlikeness to the *Harṣacarita*, whose technique it should share, were it really an *ākhyāyikā*, also serves to confirm the views of Daṇḍin rather than those of the *Sāhityadarpaṇa*. One need have little hesitation, therefore, in regarding the *Vāsavadattā* as technically a *kathā*.[2]

The 'Style' and Rhetorical Embellishments of the Vāsavadattā. The *rīti*, or 'style,' of the *Vāsavadattā* is the *Gāuḍī*, which the *Sāhityadarpaṇa* (No. 627) defines as follows (cf., in general, Regnaud, *Rhétorique sanskrite*, pp. 253–255, Paris, 1884):

> *ōjaḥprakāśakāir varṇāir bandha āḍambaraḥ punaḥ*
> *samāsabahulā gāuḍī,*

'the *Gāuḍī*, moreover, is a resonant arrangement (of words) with sounds expressing strength, (and) abounds in compounds.' Vāmana, in his *Kāvyālaṃkāravṛtti* (I. 2. 12), describes this 'style' as 'consisting of strength (*ōjas*) and grace (*kānti*),' while avoiding 'sweetness' (*mādhurya*) and 'softness' (*sāukumārya*). According to the *Kāvyādarśa* (I. 44a, 46a, 54a, 92a), moreover, the *Gāuḍī* especially affects alliteration, etymologising, and hyperbole.[3] When it is added that, as the *Kāvyādarśa* (I. 14–29) also

[1] It may be mentioned in passing that Ānandavardhana's *Dhvanyālōka*, 3. 8 (tr. Jacobi, in *ZDMG*. 56. 789), states that compound words are longer in the *ākhyāyikā* than in the *kathā*.

[2] I am glad to note that my conclusion in this respect is confirmed by Krishnamachariar (Introd., pp. 8–9).

[3] Krishnamachariar (Introd., pp. 28–29) notes the prevalence in the *Vāsavadattā*

states, an *ākhyāyikā*, *kathā*, or other form of narrative should, like poetry in general, include descriptions of battles, cities, oceans, mountains, seasons, sunrise, moonrise, and the like (each and all of which may be exemplified from the *Vāsavadattā*), we see at once how closely Subandhu was restricted in the composition of his romance, and how faithfully and minutely he discharged his self-imposed task.

The slender thread of narrative in the *Vāsavadattā* is embellished with many forms of literary adornment, which, indeed, constitute by far the major portion of the work. First and foremost among these embellishments stands the *ślēṣa*, or 'paronomasia,' and with good reason Subandhu declares himself to be 'a repository of cunning skill in arranging a series of paronomasias in every syllable' (*pratyakṣaraślēṣamayaprabandhavinyāsavāidagdhyanidhir*, introductory stanza 13). The *ślēṣa* is well defined by Daṇḍin, in his *Kāvyādarśa* (2. 363; cf. Regnaud, *Rhétorique sanskrite*, pp. 227–229, Paris, 1884; *Sāhityadarpaṇa*, No. 705; *Kāvyaprakāśa*, tr. Jhā, pp. 188–197, 217–218, Benares, 1898; *Kuvalayānandakārikā*, 1. 62), as follows:

ślēṣaḥ sarvāsu puṣṇāti prāyō vakrōktiṣu śriyam
bhinnaṃ dvidhā svabhāvōktir vakrōktiś cē 'ti vāṅmayam

'the paronomasia generally enhances the beauty in all equivocations; the phraseology (is) divided in two parts: the natural meaning and the equivocal meaning.' Examples of the *ślēṣa*, usually intimated in the *Vāsavadattā* by *iva*, 'as' (and indicated in this translation by ‹ › or, when double and triple, by « », ‹« »›), abound in Subandhu's romance. As a single specimen may be cited *vānarasēnām iva sugrīvāṅgadōpaśōbhitām*, 'adorned with a

of *utkalikāprāya*, or style of long compounds and words containing alliteration (Regnaud, *Rhétorique sanskrite*, p. 75, Paris, 1884), and of the *vṛtti ārabhaṭī*, or 'violent manner' of scenes of awe and conflict (Lévi, *Théatre indien*, 1. 92–93, Paris, 1890). The 'manner' is also sometimes *madhyamakāiśikī* (according to Vidyānātha, the author of the *Pratāparudrayaśōbhūṣana* [cf. Regnaud, *op. cit.*, pp. 377–378], quoted by Krishnamachariar, *mṛdvarthē 'py anatiprāuḍhabandhā madhyamakāiśikī*, 'not conjoined with excessive dignity in a gentle theme'), and the style is mostly *nārikēlapāka* (according to Vidyānātha, *sa nārikērapākaḥ syād antargūḍharasōdayaḥ*, 'the rising of hidden flavour'), although sometimes *āmrapāka* (for which no definition is given).

‹beautiful throat (*sugrīva*) and with armlets (*aṅgada*)› as the army of monkeys was adorned by ‹Sugrīva and Aṅgada›' (ed. Hall, pp. 63–64).[1]

The figure next in frequence to the *ślēṣa* in the *Vāsavadattā* is the *virōdha*, or 'antithesis,' where the superficial meaning is self-contradictory, while the paronomasiac reading renders the phrase consistent, and even intensifies it. This rhetorical embellishment is defined as follows in the *Kāvyādarśa* (2. 333; cf. *Sāhityadarpaṇa*, No. 718; *Kāvyaprakāśa*, tr. Jhā, pp. 233–235, Benares, 1898; *Kuvalayānandakārikā*, 1. 74):

> *viruddhānāṃ padārthānāṃ yatra saṃsargadarśanam*
> *viśēṣadarśanāyāi "va sa virōdhaḥ smṛtō yathā,*

'when there is an apparent union of antithetical objects simply to show the distinction (between them), it is called *virōdha*.' The conventional sign of the *virōdha* in the *Vāsavadattā* is *api*, as *iva* is indicative of the *ślēṣa*. As an example of the countless instances of the *virōdha* in Subandhu's romance, mention may be made of *agrahēṇā 'pi kāvyajīvajñēna*, 'which ‹has no planets (*a-graha*)› yet knows «Venus (*kāvya*=Śukra=the planet Venus) and Jupiter (*jīva*=Bṛhaspati=the planet Jupiter)», for it is ‹free from theft (*a-graha*)› and knows «the essence (*jīva*) of poetry (*kāvya*)»' (ed. Hall, pp. 113–114).

Besides these two rhetorical devices, Śivarāma, in his commentary on the *Vāsavadattā*, enumerates a long series of *alaṃkāras*, or 'adornments,' which will now briefly be considered.

The *parisaṅkhyā*, or 'special mention,' usually combined with the *ślēṣa* in the *Vāsavadattā*, is an affirmative statement with the implied negation of the paronomasiac meaning of the phrase, and is thus defined by the *Sāhityadarpaṇa* (No. 735; cf. *Kāvyaprakāśa*, tr. Jhā, pp. 245–246, Benares, 1898; *Kuvalayānandakārikā*, 1. 112):

[1] On Subandhu's fondness for paronomasia see, further, Krishnamachariar, Introd., pp. 18–20, who also calls attention to repetitions of paronomasia on the same word (p. 27) as well as to the frequent repetition of the same phrase in the romance (pp. 25–26).

praśnād apraśnatō vā "pi kathitād vastunō bhavēt
tādṛganyavyapōhaś cēc chābda ārthō 'thavā tadā
parisaṅkhyā,

'if there is either an expressed or implied exclusion, whether with or without an interrogation, of a thing similar to (but) other than the object mentioned, then it is a *parisaṅkhyā*.' An example from the *Vāsavadattā* is *nētrōtpāṭanaṃ munīnāṃ*, '‹roots (*nētra*)› were plucked out only in the case of «wormwood-trees (*munīnāṃ*)» (for «ascetics (*munīnāṃ*)» did not pluck out their ‹eyes (*nētra*)›)' (ed. Hall, p. 19).

The *mālādīpaka*, or 'garland elucidator' ('verkettete Klimax,' according to Böhtlingk, *Sanskrit-Wörterbuch in kürzerer Fassung*, s. v., St. Petersburg, 1879–1889), is a rhetorical repetition of words in a sequence so as to heighten the effect, and is thus defined by the *Kāvyādarśa* (2. 108; cf. *Kāvyaprakāśa*, tr. Jhā, p. 226, Benares, 1898; *Kuvalayānandakārikā*, 1. 105):

pūrvapūrvavyapēkṣiṇī
vākyamālā prayuktē "ti tan mālādīpakaṃ matam,

'a conjoined series of words, each of which refers to the one preceding, is considered a *mālādīpaka*.' As an example may be cited *bhujadaṇḍēna kōdaṇḍaṃ kōdaṇḍēna śarāḥ śarāir ariśiras*, 'by his staff-like arm the bow, by the bow the arrows, by the arrows his foeman's head' (ed. Hall, p. 41).

The *utprēkṣā*, or 'poetic fancy,' usually indicated, like the *ślēṣa*, by *iva*, 'as,' in the *Vāsavadattā*, and one of Subandhu's favourite rhetorical devices, is thus concisely defined by the *Sāhityadarpaṇa* (No. 686; cf. *Kāvyādarśa*, 2. 221; *Kāvyaprakāśa*, tr. Jhā, p. 211, Benares, 1898; *Kuvalayānandakārikā*, 1. 30):

bhavēt sambhāvanō "tprēkṣā prakṛtasya parātmanā,

'poetic fancy would be the imagining of an object under the character of something else.' Examples of this figure abound in the *Vāsavadattā*, as in the following description of the moon: *dadhidhavalē kālakṣapaṇakagrāsapiṇḍa iva niśāyamunāphēnapuñja iva mēnakānakhamārjanaśilāśakala iva*, 'while he was white, as it were, with the curds which constitute a morsel of food for (Buddhist) ascetics at their mealtime, and was like a mass of Yamunā's foam by night, and resembled a fragment of stone for the polishing of Mēnakā's nails' (ed. Hall, p. 44).[1]

The *yamaka*, 'repetition' or 'chiming,' is the repeating of words or parts of words of similar sound but divergent meaning, which the *Kāvyādarśa* (1. 61; cf. 3. 1–37; *Sāhityadarpaṇa*, No. 640; *Kāvyaprakāśa*, tr. Jhā, pp. 185–188, Benares, 1898; *Kuvalayānandakārikā*, 4. 6) describes as

āvṛttiṃ varṇasaṅghātagōcarāṃ yamakaṃ viduḥ,

'a repetition consisting of a combination of sounds they know as *yamaka*.' This is illustrated by the following passage from the *Vāsavadattā*: *āndōlitakusumakēsarē kēśarēṇumuṣi raṇitamadhuramaṇīnāṃ ramaṇīnāṃ vikacakumudākarē mudākarē*, '(when there blew a wind that) rocked the filaments of the flowers and removed their pollen from the hair of damsels wearing delightsomely tinkling jewels, whilst it had an abundance of expanded white lotuses, and caused pleasure' (ed. Hall, pp. 52–53).

The *prāuḍhōkti*, or 'pomposity,' is thus defined by the *Kuvalayānandakārikā* (1. 124):

prāuḍhōktir uktā 'rthāhētōs taddhētutvaprakalpanam,

'in the absence of a cause for a thing, the invention of a cause for it is called *prāuḍhōkti*.' It is exemplified in the *Vāsavadattā* by the passage describing the heroine's lip as *mukhacandrasannihitasandhyārāgēṇa dantamaṇirakṣāsindūramudrānukāriṇā*, 'which had the glow of eventide in close proximity to her moonlike face; which had what seemed to be a minium seal as a guard for the jewels of her teeth' (ed. Hall, p. 58).

The *rūpakātiśayōkti*, or 'hyperbolical metaphor,' is merely an exaggerated form of the preceding *alaṃkāra*. It is thus defined in the *Kuvalayānandakārikā* (1. 34):

rūpakātiśayōktiḥ syān nigīryādhyavasānataḥ,

'identification so that (the object identified) should be swallowed

[1] On the similes in the *Vāsavadattā* see also the examples collected by Krishnamachariar, Introd., pp. 20–22.

up (and thus completely disappear) would be *rūpakātiśayōkti*'; and as an example may be cited, from the description of Vāsavadattā just quoted, the passage *vilōcanēndīvarabhramarapaṅktibhyāṃ mukhamadanamandiratōraṇābhyāṃ rāgasāgaravēlābhyāṃ yāuvananartakalāsikābhyāṃ bhrūlatābhyāṃ virāiamānāṃ*, 'adorned with delicate brows which were clusters of bees about her blue-lotus eyes; portals of her face that formed the abode of Love; the shores of Passion's sea; wantoning in youthful dancing' (ed. Hall, p. 61).

The *akramātiśayōkti*, or 'fused hyperbole,' is closely akin to the preceding rhetorical figure, of which it is merely an intensification. It receives the following definition in the *Kuvalayānandakārikā* (I. 39):

akramātiśayōktiḥ syāt sahatvē hētukāryayōḥ,

'*akramātiśayōkti* would be in the unity of cause and effect.' Śivarāma cites but one instance of the figure in the *Vāsavadattā*, this being *samaṃ dviṣāṃ dhanuṣāṃ ca jīvākṛṣṭiṃ yōdhāś cakruḥ*, 'the warriors drew at once the ‹lives (*jīva*)› of their foes and the ‹strings (*jīvā*)› of their bows' (ed. Hall, p. 295).

Two other forms of hyperbole are mentioned by Śivarāma as occurring in Subandhu's romance. The first of these is *bhēdakātiśayōkti*, or 'hyperbole of differentiation.' It is defined as follows in the *Kuvalayānandakārikā* (I. 36):

bhēdakātiśayōktis tu tasyāi "vā 'nyatvavarṇanam,

'*bhēdakātiśayōkti* is the description of that (which is the subject under discussion) by means of differentiation,' and it is exemplified in the *Vāsavadattā* by *pṛthur api gōtrasamutsāraṇavistāritabhūmaṇḍalaḥ*, 'Pṛthu ‹levelled the earth by banishing the mountains› (but Cintāmaṇi ‹covered the earth by sending forth his offspring›)' (ed. Hall, p. 22).

The remaining form of hyperbole in the *Vāsavadattā* is *sambandhātiśayōkti*, or 'hyperbole of connexion,' which is thus defined in the *Kuvalayānandakārikā* (I. 37):

sambandhātiśayōktiḥ syād ayōgē yōgakalpanam,

'*sambandhātiśayōkti* would be the invention of connexion when connexion is absent,' as when Subandhu describes trees as being *anūrukarakaśābhighātaparavaśaravirathaturagagrāsaviṣamitapallavāis*, 'with shoots made uneven by the feeding of the horses of the chariot of the sun which are obedient when lashed by the whip in the hands of Anūru' (ed. Hall, p. 120).

The *ratnāvalī*, or 'jewel necklace,' is defined as follows in the *Kuvalayānandakārikā* (1. 139):

kramikāprakṛtārthānāṃ nyāsaṃ ratnāvalīṃ viduḥ,

'an arrangement of objects serially irrelevant they know as *ratnāvalī*,' and is exemplified in the *Vāsavadattā* where the heroine is described as *vikacēna nētrakamalēna śanāiścarēṇa pādēna tamasā kēśapāśēna grahamayīm iva*, 'she seemed to be made of planets: of ⟨Venus⟩, for she had ⟨wide-open⟩ lotus eyes; of ⟨Saturn⟩, for she had ⟨slow-moving⟩ steps; of ⟨Rāhu⟩, for she had ⟨dark⟩ heavy hair' (ed. Hall, p. 64).

The *kāvyaliṅga*, or 'poetic reason,' is thus defined by the *Sāhityadarpaṇa* (No. 710; cf. *Kāvyaprakāśa*, tr. Jhā, pp. 238–239, Benares, 1898; *Kuvalayānandakārikā*, 1. 120):

hētōr vākyapadārthatvē kāvyaliṅgaṃ nigadyatē,

'*kāvyaliṅga* is applied to the implication of a cause in a sentence or word,' and finds exemplification in the *Vāsavadattā* in the passage *khalāḥ punas tad aniṣṭam anucitam ēvā 'vadhārayanty aniṣṭōdbhāvanarasōttaraṃ hi khalahṛdayaṃ*, 'the wicked, on the other hand, make it (thy conduct) out to be undesirable and indecorous; for the heart of the wicked man finds its highest delight centred in bringing to light what is undesirable' (ed. Hall, p. 70).

The *mīlita*, or 'vanished,' denotes a complete loss of distinction between two objects because of their superficial resemblance, as is expressed by the definition of the *Kuvalayānandakārikā* (1. 145; cf. *Kāvyaprakāśa*, tr. Jhā, pp. 253–254, Benares, 1898; Ruyyaka's *Alaṃkārasarvasva*, ed. Durgāprasāda and Parab, p. 167, Bombay, 1893):

mīlitaṃ yadi sādṛśyād bhēda ēva na lakṣyatē,

'if, because of similarity, a distinction is not observed, it is *mīlita*.' As an example from Subandhu I may cite *mādhurya-*

śāityaśucitvasantāpaśāntibhiḥ payaḥ paya ivē 'ti, 'fancying that "water is as milk because of its sweetness, coolness, purity, and healing of distress"' (ed. Hall, p. 80).

The *anuprāsa*, or 'alliteration,' a rhetorical figure found with considerable frequency in Subandhu's romance, is thus defined by the *Sāhityadarpaṇa* (No. 633; cf. *Kāvyādarśa*, 1. 55; *Kāvyaprakāśa*, tr. Jhā, pp. 182–184, Benares, 1898; *Kuvalayānandakārikā*, 4. 2–5):

anuprāsaḥ śabdasāmyaṃ vāiṣamyē 'pi svarasya yat,

'*anuprāsa* (is) a similarity of sound, despite a dissimilarity of the vowel.' As an example from the *Vāsavadattā* may be cited these two adjectives descriptive of the River Rēvā: *madakalakalahaṃsasārasarasitōdbhrāntabhāḥkūṭavikaṭapucchacchaṭāvyādhūtavikacakamalakhaṇḍavigalitamakarandabindusandōhasurabhitasalilayā*. . . . *upakūlasañjātanalanikuñjapuñjitakulāyakukkuṭaghaṭāghūtkārabhāiravatīrayā*, 'whose waters were perfumed by the abundance of the drops of liquid which had fallen from the fragments of full-blown lotuses shaken by many monstrous tails of *bhāḥkūṭa*-fish that had been terrified by the notes, indistinct for passion, of geese and herons; . . . . . whose banks were strident with the screams of multitudes of wild cocks whose nests thronged the bowers of reeds that had sprung up near its shores' (ed. Hall, pp. 95, 98).

The *sama*, or 'equal,' is thus defined in the *Kāvyādarśa* (1. 47; cf. *Sāhityadarpaṇa*, No. 618; *Kāvyaprakāśa*, tr. Jhā, pp. 175–176, Benares, 1898):

samaṃ bandhēṣv aviṣamaṃ tē mṛdusphuṭamadhyamāḥ
bandhā mṛdusphuṭōnmiśravarṇavinyāsayōnayaḥ,

'*sama* is not uneven in collocations (of words); these collocations, smooth, rough, (and) middling, depend on the arrangement of smooth, rough, and mixed (sounds).' It is illustrated by the passage *kāmadāruṇa madāruṇanētrāsmaramayaṃ ramayantaṃ tvām adayaṃ madayantī param akam itāraṃ param akamitāraṃ vāñchati*, 'what gentle-eyed woman who fervently delighteth thee, that art not inflamed with passion, (but art) the essence of love, delightsome, (and) a most excellent lover, desireth another that is no lover [cruel with passion! red-eyed with lust! alas, an unlovely dame desireth thee, the essence of lovelessness, hot, pitiless, absolutely no lover, (and) bound for utmost woe!]' (ed. Hall, pp. 213–214).

The *vidhi*, or 'rule,' is defined as follows by the *Kuvalayānandakārikā* (I. 167):

siddhasyāi "va vidhānaṃ yat tad āhur vidhyalaṃkṛtim,

'what (is) a precept of a thing well established, that they call the *vidhi* adornment,' and is exemplified by *kuraṅgikē kalpaya kuraṅgaśāvakēbhyaḥ śaṣpāṅkuraṃ kiśōrikē kāraya kiśōrakēbhyaḥ pratyavēkṣāṃ*, 'Kuraṅgikā, prepare a blade of young grass for the antelope fauns! Kiśōrikā, have the young colts looked after'! (ed. Hall, pp. 230–231).

The *sambhāvana*, or 'supposition,' is thus defined by the *Kuvalayānandakārikā* (I. 125):

sambhāvanaṃ yadī 'tthaṃ syād ity ūhō 'nyasya siddhayē,

'*sambhāvana* is a conjecture for the attainment of something else with the thought, "if it were so."' It is illustrated in the *Vāsavadattā* by the passage *tvatkṛtē yā "nayā vēdanā "nubhūtā sā yadi nabhaḥ patrāyatē sāgarō mēlānandāyatē brahmāyatē lipikarō bhujagarājāyatē kathakas tadā kim api katham apy anēkāir yugasahasrāir abhilikhyatē kathyatē vā*, 'the pain that hath been felt by this maiden for thy sake might be written or told in some wise or in some way in many thousands of ages if the sky became paper, the sea an ink-well, the scribe Brāhma, (and) the narrator the Lord of Serpents' (ed. Hall, pp. 238–239).

The *kāraṇamālā*, or 'chain of causes,' is given the following definition in the *Kuvalayānandakārikā* (I. 103; cf. *Kāvyaprakāśa*, tr. Jhā, p. 246, Benares, 1898):

gumphaḥ kāraṇamālā syād yathāprakrāntakāraṇāiḥ.

'a series (made) by causes proceeding one after the other is a *kāraṇamālā*,' and an example is seen by Śivarāma in the description of Vāsavadattā's palace as *ajñātataṭasphāṭikapaṭṭasukhaniṣaṇṇanidrāyamāṇaprāsādapārāvatābhiḥ*, 'with palace doves sleeping comfortably (because) perched on slabs of crystal from shores unknown' (ed. Hall, pp. 217–218).

The *udātta*, or 'exalted,' is thus defined in the *Sāhityadarpaṇa* (No. 752; cf. *Kāvyaprakāśa*, tr. Jhā, p. 240, Benares, 1898; *Kuvalayānandakārikā*, 1. 162–163):

lōkātiśayasampattivarṇanō "dāttam ucyatē
yad vā "pi prastutasyā 'ṅgaṃ mahatāṃ caritaṃ bhavēt,

'the portrayal of extraordinary prosperity is called *udātta*, or it would even be the deeds of the great, (if they form) part of the subject in hand.' An illustration of this figure is found in another portion of the description just quoted: *karpūrapūraviracitapulinataṭaniviṣṭaninadānumīyamānarājahaṃsībhir*, 'with flamingoes whose noise would imply that they had settled near the sand bank formed by the stream of camphor' (ed. Hall, p. 218), only one of extreme wealth being able to possess such a river.[1]

The *kāitavāpahnuti*, or 'false concealment,' is defined by the *Kuvalayānandakārikā* (1. 28) as follows:

kāitavāpahnutir vyaktāu vyājādyāir nihnutēḥ padāiḥ,

'*kāitavāpahnuti* (consists) in the manifestation of concealment by words of pretext and the like,' and finds exemplification in the *Vāsavadattā* in the passage *ativēganipītajaladhijalaśaṅkhamālām iva balākācchalād udvamann adṛśyata jaladaḥ*, 'the cloud seemed to vomit forth, like a crane, what appeared to be a series of ocean shells that had been drunk down too hastily' (ed. Hall, pp. 283–284).

The *lōkōkti*, 'popular expression,' is thus defined by the *Kuvalayānandakārikā* (1. 156):

lōkapravādānukṛtir lōkōktir iti kathyatē,

'the imitation of a popular colloquialism is called *lōkōkti*,' and finds an illustration in Subandhu's romance in the exhortation *tad adhunā yadi tvaṃ sakapāṃśukrīḍanasamaduḥkhasukhō 'si*

[1] Śivarāma rightly notes that this passage also contains the rhetorical figure ***anumāna***, or 'inference' (cf. *Kāvyaprakāśa*, tr. Jhā, pp. 243–244, Benares, 1898; *Kuvalayānandakārikā*, 2. 10).

tadā mām anugaccha, 'now, therefore, if thou didst share the sorrows and joys of our playing together in the dust, then follow me' (ed. Hall, p. 82).

The *svabhāvōkti*, or 'natural description,' receives the following definition in the *Kuvalayānandakārikā* (1. 160; cf. *Kāvyaprakāśa*, tr. Jhā, p. 235, Benares, 1898):

svabhāvōktiḥ svabhāvasya jātyādisthasya varṇanam,

'*svabhāvōkti* is the description of inherent nature consisting of characteristics and the like.' As an example from the *Vāsavadattā* may be cited:

paśyō 'dañcadavāñcadañcitavapuḥ paścārddhapūrvārddhabhāk
stabdhōttānitapṛṣṭhaniṣṭhitamanāgbhugnāgralāṅgūlabhṛt
daṃṣṭrākōṭiviśaṅkaṭāsyakuharaḥ kurvan saṭām utkaṭām
utkarṇaḥ kurutē kramaṃ karipatāu krūrākṛtiḥ kēsarī,

'lo, with his bending body bending up and bending down, now with his hind quarters and now with his fore quarters, with the tip of his tail slightly bent along his hard, arched back, with his cavernous mouth monstrous with the tips of his fangs, making his mane huge, (and) with his ears erect, the horrible lion doth make attack upon the lord of elephants' (ed. Hall, p. 103).

The *kāvyārthāpatti*, or 'poetic inference,' is defined as follows in the *Kuvalayānandakārikā* (1. 119):

kāimutyēnā 'rthasaṃsiddhiḥ kāvyārthāpattir iṣyatē,

'an *a fortiori* attainment of a matter is regarded as *kāvyārthāpatti*.' It is exemplified by Subandhu in his heroine's letter to Kandarpakētu:

pratyakṣādṛṣṭabhāvā 'py asthirahṛdayā hi kāminī bhavati
svapnānubhūtabhāvā dṛḍhayati na pratyayaṃ yuvatiḥ,

'a loving maid is of unsteady heart even when she hath seen the feelings (of her lover) with her eyes; a girl who hath learned his feelings only from a dream hath no assurance' (ed. Hall, p. 164).

Literary and Ethical Merit of the Vāsavadattā. The *Vāsavadatta* apparently being written to display its author's skill in rhetoric, rather than his inventive powers in fiction, we are naturally led to consider what literary value we may assign to it. Here the 'personal equation' must inevitably play a part, and here the fundamental difference between Oriental and Occidental concepts must be duly recognised. In the West the subject-matter comes first in nearly every form of literary composition; and the more tense and nervous the people, the more simple and direct is the style. In the East, on the contrary, the form is often more important than the matter, especially in periods of hyper-civilisation, such as was that during which Subandhu wrote. We must, therefore, consider the *Vāsavadattā* from the luxuriant atmosphere of the land of its author, not from the 'practical' point of view of the West. To me, at least, there is true melody in the long, rolling compounds, a sesquipedalian majesty which can never be equalled save in Sanskrit; and the alliterations have a lulling music all their own to ears weary of the blatant discords of vaunted modern 'progress.' There is, on the other hand, a compact brevity in the paronomasias, which are, in most cases, veritable gems of terseness and twofold appropriateness, even though some are manifestly forced and are actually detrimental to the sense of the passages in which they occur. Yet in judging Subandhu for his faults, it must be remembered that he created, at least so far as we now know, a new literary *genre* in India; and if this fact be borne in mind, his blemishes appear to be marvellously few. In estimating his literary merits special stress should be laid on his descriptions. These are, it must be confessed, cloying from their abundance. They form the preponderating part of the entire romance, and the slender framework of the story is wellnigh lost beneath them. Yet despite this tropical luxuriance, the descriptions are not without beauty and appropriateness, whether they set forth the charms of mountain, forest, and stream, or portray the rāja's valour and the loveliness of the heroine herself. The entire romance may, in a sense, be likened to India's own architecture, where the whole structure is so overlaid with minute detail that the eye forgets the outlines of the building in amazement at the delicate traceries which cover it.

Nor does it seem to me that the ethical standard of the *Vāsavadattā* can be objectionable to one of healthy mind. True, the East is not as the West; and there are personal descriptions more detailed than would be desirable in Occidental literature, together with evident approval of relations and ideals which the less sensual Western mind rightly condemns. There are passages, too, which I would gladly have omitted, had I felt that a faithful translator could do so. And yet, despite all this, I find in the romance no evidence of delight in uncleanness, such as nauseates, for example, in Petronius or in Martial. It is not pornographic; it is, at worst, unmoral, though its rigid adherence to all conventions, both in letter and, I think, in spirit, renders even unmorality almost too harsh an accusation. From an Indian point of view, unlightened by the radiance of Christianity and the morality which it inculcates, I should not hesitate to term the *Vāsavadattā* a moral work, especially in view of the conditions of life in mediæval India. Its atmosphere, luxuriant though it be, has never seemed to me to be debasing.

It is by no means impossible that some will dissent from the views here expressed regarding the literary and moral quality of Subandhu's romance. If so, they may turn from the first Western translator of the *Vāsavadattā* to the first Western editor of the romance, Fitzedward Hall, who, in his Introduction, has unsparingly condemned the entire production both in its literary and in its ethical aspects—a precedent followed by Krishnamachariar in his sarcastic critique of the whole plot of Subandhu's work (Introd., pp. 50–66).

Outline of the Plot of the Romance. The outline of the story of the *Vāsavadattā* is as follows: A king named Cin āmaṇi had a son Kandarpakētu, who was, like his father, the embodiment of all virtues. Once upon a time toward dawn, when true dreams come, the young prince saw in his sleep a vision of a maiden of some eighteen years, whose loveliness could not be surpassed. Jealous sleep forsook Kandarpakētu, who, with his friend Makaranda, left the city in his love-longing for the unknown princess. In their wanderings the pair came to the

Vindhya mountains, and there, in the watches of the night, the sleepless prince overheard the conversation of two birds perched on a branch of the tree beneath which he lay. To the story of the husband-bird, trying to explain his late hours to his suspicious wife, Kandarpakētu listened, and was richly rewarded by what he heard. In the city of Pāṭaliputra on the Ganges, so the *maina* recounted, reigned the mighty monarch Śṛṅgāraśēkhara, who had an only daughter named Vāsavadattā. In the spring she, too, had met her fate in a dream—a youth of matchless beauty, whose name was Kandarpakētu. The confidante of the princess at this juncture was her maid, Tamālikā, who had volunteered to seek Kandarpakētu and bear to him a missive from the princess telling of her love. The lovers were now soon united at Pāṭaliputra, where Kandarpakētu was informed that Śṛṅgāraśēkhara, dismayed at his daughter's unwedded state, had determined to marry her the very next day to the Vidyādhara prince Puṣpakētu. Kandarpakētu and Vāsavadattā accordingly returned almost immediately, by means of a magic steed, to the Vindhyas; but when the prince awoke in the morning, his beloved was no longer in the bower. Mad with sorrow, he was restrained from suicide only by a voice from heaven which promised him reunion with the princess. After many months of weary searching and waiting, he found Vāsavadattā turned to stone. His touch gave the statue life again, and she told him how, while two armies destroyed each other to gain her for their leaders, she had unwittingly intruded in the garden of a hermit, who laid upon her the curse of petrification until her lover should come. Thus, at last, the woes of the lovers were over, and returning to Kandarpakētu's capital, delight was theirs ever afterward (for other summaries see Hall, Introd., pp. 29–43; Stréhly, *Revue politique et littéraire*, 44. 305–308; Krishnamachariar, Introd., pp. 9–14; and the references given in the bibliography, below, pp. 197–199).

From this brief outline of the plot of the *Vāsavadattā* it will be seen that Subandhu alludes to several incidents widely found in literature and folk-tales, such as talking birds, magic steeds, and transformation. To all these I have sought to give parallels, especially from modern Indian folk-tales, in footnotes to the passages in which they occur. There seems to be no parallel, however, to the story of the *Vāsavadattā* as a whole, and, as already stated (p. 2), Subandhu evidently invented the slender plot of his own romance (cf. also Hall, Introd., pp. 1–6).

Sanskrit 'Estilo Culto' Previous to Subandhu, and in Later Epigraphy. This allusion to comparative literature brings us to possible quasi-parallels to the style of the *Vāsavadattā*. The commingling of prose and verse which is characteristic of the *ākhyāyikā*, *kathā*, and other forms of *gadya*, or poetical prose (cf. Regnaud, *Rhétorique sanskrite*, pp. 74–77, Paris, 1884), was by no means an innovation of Subandhu. It is found, for instance, in the *Pañcatantra* and the *Jātakas*, as well as in the *gāthās* of the *Brāhmaṇas* and the Northern Buddhists, even though these latter be more archaic than the prose in which they are set.

Obscure as is the date of the beginning of the *kāvya* style in India, a flood of light has been cast on its early history by Bühler in his 'Die indischen Inschriften und das Alter der indischen Kunstpoesie,' in *SWAW*. 122, Abhandlung 11. There he has shown that the eulogy of Vatsabhaṭṭi, preserved in an inscription in the Temple of the Sun at Maṇḍasōr, and dated 473–474 A.D., contains descriptions of cities, natural phenomena, and the like, together with compound words of inordinate length, and the rhetorical devices of *anuprāsa*, *upamā*, *utprēkṣā*, *rūpaka*, and (possibly) *virōdha*, all of which even fulfil the requirements laid down, for instance, by Daṇḍin in his *Kāvyādarśa*. The term *kāvya* itself occurs at least as early as 375–390 A.D. in Hariṣēṇa's panegyric on Samudragupta, inscribed on a pillar at Allāhābād, which also contains long compounds and the rhetorical figures of *varṇānuprāsa*, *rūpaka*, *upamā*, and *ślēṣa*. The *kāvya* style is carried back to the early second half of the second century A.D. by the Girnār inscription of Rudradāman, which has long compounds and numerous *anuprāsas*, together with two *upamās* and one *utprēkṣā*. It is thus clear that a fairly developed *kāvya* was known in India as early as the second century of our era, not forgetting that the epic of the *Rāmāyaṇa* contains many approximations to the *kāvya* style (Jacobi, *Das Râmâyaṇa*, pp. 119–126, Bonn, 1893).

In the course of time *kāvya* inscriptions became more elaborate, particularly in their use of the *ślēṣa*. Mention can here be made only of the *ślēṣas* and *virōdhas* in the Valabhī grant of Dhruvasēna III, dated in 653–654 A.D. (Hultzsch, *EI*. 1. 85–92); the Balōda plates of Tīvaradēva, of the middle of the eighth century (Hultzsch, *ib*. 7. 102–107); a grant of Indrarāja III, dated in 915 A.D. (Bhandarkar, *ib*. 9. 24–41); the Cambay plates of Gōvinda IV, dated in 929–930 A.D. (Bhandarkar, *ib*. 7. 26–47); and the Dēvulapalli plates of Immaḍi Nṛsiṃha, dated in 1504 (Ramayya, *ib*. 7. 74–85); though allusion should also be made to the general style of such an inscription as the Kaḍaba plates of Gōvinda III, dated in 812–813 A.D. (Lüders, *EI*. 4. 332–349). In the inscriptions of the Vāillabhaṭṭasvāmin temple at Gwaliar, dated in 874–875 A.D. (Hultzsch, *EI*. 1. 154–162), which abound in *virōdhas*, Kielhorn (*apud* Hultzsch, *EI*. 1. 157, note 23) has already called attention to a possible reminiscence of the *dhanadēnā 'pi pracētasā*, 'which is ‹Kubēra›, yet «Varuṇa», for it is ‹generous› and «wise»,' of the *Vāsavadattā* (ed. Hall, p. 111) in the *dhanadō 'pi na pramattō*, 'he was ‹Kubēra›, but not «Varuṇa», for he was ‹generous› and not «inattentive»' (line 6). Kielhorn, moreover, in his edition and translation of the Rādhanpur plates of Gōvinda III, dated in 807–808 A.D. (*EI*. 6. 239–251), expressly declares (p. 240) that 'an examination of the language and general style of most of these verses can leave no doubt that their author or authors are greatly indebted for their expressions and poetical devices to such works as Subandhu's *Vāsavadattā* and Bāṇa's *Kādambarī* and *Harṣacarita*.' There is no need here to repeat the parallels which Kielhorn has drawn between the inscription in question and the romances of Subandhu and Bāṇa (*EI*. 6. 247–250), nor is it necessary to make more than a passing allusion to the fact that a close examination of Indian epigraphy would probably reveal many more parallels to the *Vāsavadattā* and other productions of the same *genre*. It would by no means follow, however, that such resemblances necessarily imply borrowing from the romances of Subandhu and Bāṇa, for the same research would, in all probability, show an equal, or even greater, affinity with *kāvya* literature in general. The *kāvya* of the inscriptions must, therefore, be regarded as an integral part of the vast mass of artificial Sanskrit literature, its development being attained by a process of natural growth.

The Commingling of Prose and Verse and Paronomasia Outside the Vāsavadattā. Outside of India the commingling of prose and poetry in the same composition is found in the Chinese romance *P'ing Shan Lêng Yen* (tr. Julien, *P'ing-Chan-Ling-Yen, Les Deux Jeunes Filles lettrées*, 2 vols., Paris, 1860); in Sa'dī's *Gulistān*; in *The Thousand Nights and One Night*; in the Old Picard *Aucassin et Nicolette*; in Norse Sagas and in Middle Irish tales and histories (cf. Windisch, *Irische Texte*, 3. 447–449, Leipzig, 1891–1897); and in Boccaccio's *L'Ameto*; as well as in the *Saturæ Menippeæ* of Varro; Petronius; the author of the *Historia Apollonii regis Tyri*; and among Basutos and Eskimos (cf. MacCulloch, *Childhood of Fiction*, London, 1905, pp. 480–481; Teuffel-Schwabe, *Geschichte der römischen Literatur*, 5 ed., pp. 43–44, Leipzig, 1890). In like manner, the elaborate paronomasias which are so essentially a part of the style of the *Vāsavadattā*, and which later led to such productions as Kavirāja's *Rāghavapāṇḍavīya*, which in identical words celebrates the deeds of the Raghu princes by one reading and those of the Pāṇḍava heroes by the other reading, or Rāmacandra's *Rasikarañjana* (ed. and tr. Schmidt, Stuttgart, 1896), which may be read as a laudation either of asceticism or of eroticism, were in vogue, as we have seen, long before the time of Subandhu.[1] They also occur in the Chinese romance *Ch'in P'ing Mei* (cf. Giles, *History of Chinese Literature*, p. 309, London, 1901) and in the writings of Lyly.

[1] To this list Krishnamachariar (Introd., p. 18) adds Dhanaṃjaya's *Dvisandhānakāvya* (ed. Bombay, 1895 = *Kāvyamālā*, No. 49) and the *Rāghavayādavapāṇḍavīya*, or *Kathātrayīvyākhyāna*, of Cidambara and his son Anantanārāyaṇa, which gives the substance of the *Rāmāyaṇa*, *Mahābhārata*, and *Bhāgavatapurāṇa*. Another literary curiosity of this general type is the elegy of Leon of Modena on his teacher, Moses Bassola, which may be read either in Hebrew or in Italian (cf. *Jewish Encyclopedia*, 2. 576, New York, 1902).

Subandhu and Lyly. It is Lyly, indeed, with whom Subandhu may perhaps best be compared for a general parallel with the style and spirit of the *Vāsavadattā*. Neither the *Euphues* nor Subandhu's romance is concerned so much with the matter as with the form, although the English author manifests a didactic purpose which finds no counterpart in the Sanskrit writer. Like the *Vāsavadattā*, the *Euphues* and its continuation contain episodes, or stories within stories, as the tale of Callimachus (Lyly, ed. Arbor, pp. 227–245, Birmingham, 1868), which itself contains the story of Cassander the hermit (pp. 235–239), thus parallelling the arrangement not only of the *Vāsavadattā* and the *Kādambarī*, but also of the *Pañcatantra*, *Śukasaptati*, *Vētālapañcaviṃśati*, *The Thousand Nights and One Night*, *Decameron*, and other similar works.[1] Lyly's romance is curiously like Subandhu's in yet other respects. Here I may note particularly from his *Euphues* the use of paronomasia, alliteration, antithesis (corresponding respectively to Subandhu's employment of *ślēṣa*, *anuprāsa*, and *virōdha*), and learned allusions. From the mass of possible citations under each category I quote but two of each. (1) Paronomasia: 'and though they be commonly in a great cholar that receiue the mate, yet would I willingly take euery minute tenne mates to enioy Liuia for my louing mate' (Lyly, ed. Arbor, p. 66, Birmingham, 1868); 'did not Iupiters egge bring forth as well Helen a light huswife in earth, as Castor a light Starre in heauen?' (p. 208).[2] (2) Alliteration: 'these subtill shiftes, these painted practises (if I wer to be wonne) would soone weane me from the teate of Vesta to the toyes of Venus' (p. 76); I am Philautus no Italian lady, who commonly are woed with leasings, and won with lust, entangled with deceipt, and enioyed with delight, caught with sinne, and cast off with shame' (p. 360). (3) Antithesis: 'how curious were we to please our Lady, how carelesse to displease our Lorde? Howe devout in seruing our Goddesse, how desperate in forget-

[1] For a charming modern imitation see Bain, *Digit of the Moon* (London, 1899).

[2] It is well known that paronomasia occurs not infrequently in Shakespeare (e.g. *Julius Caesar*, 1. 2. 155; *Merchant of Venice*, 4. 1. 123; *Taming of the Shrew*, 2. 1. 190; *Richard II*, 2. 1. 74); and it seems to have been a favourite device of Ben Jonson (e.g. *Mermaid ed.*, 1. 15–16, 20, 68, 106, 344; 2. 91; 3. 178, 402, London, n. d.).

D

ting our God'? (p. 106); 'thou weepest for the death of thy daughter, and I laugh at the folly of the father, for greater vanitie is there in the minde of the mourner, then bitternesse in the death of the deceased. But shee was amiable, but yet sinful, but she was young and might haue liued, but she was mortall and must haue dyed. I but hir youth made thee often merry, I but thine age shold once make thee wise. I but hir greene yeares wer unfit for death, I but thy hoary haires should dispyse life' (pp. 182–183). (4) Learned allusions: 'the filthy Sow when she is sicke, eateth the Sea-Crab, and is immediatly recured: the Torteyse hauing tasted the Viper, sucketh Origanum and is quickly reuiued: the Beare ready to pine licketh vp the Ants, and is recouered: the Dog hauing surfetted to procure his vomitte, eateth grasse and findeth remedy: the Hart beeing perced with the dart, runneth out of hand to the hearb Dictanum, and is healed. . . . . Ah well I perceiue that Loue is not unlyke the Figge tree, whose fruite is sweete, whose roote is more bitter then the clawe of a Bitter: or lyke the Apple in Persia, whose blossome sauoreth lyke Honny, whose budde is more sower then Gall' (p. 61); 'Loue knoweth no laws: Did not Iupiter transforme himselfe into the shape of Amphitrio to embrace Alcmæna? Into the forme of a Swan to enioy Læda: Into a Bull to beguile Iò: Into a showre of golde to winne Danae: Did not Neptune chaunge himselfe into a Heyfer, a Ramme, a Floud, a Dolphin, onely for the loue of those he lusted after? Did not Apollo conuert himselfe into a Shephearde, into a Birde, into a Lyon: for the desire he had to heale his disease'? (p. 93).

Parallels such as these might be multiplied indefinitely, not only between the *Vāsavadattā* and the *Euphues*, but between Subandhu's romance and many other productions both of the East and of the West.[1] Here, however, it must suffice to note that Dunlop, in his *History of Prose Fiction* (ed. Wilson, London, 1896), records the following incidents and *motifs* which may now

[1] For parallels in the *Vāsavadattā* and Bāṇa's romances with *The Thousand Nights and One Night* see Gray, 'Literary Studies on the Sanskrit Novel,' in *WZKM.* 18. 39–48.

be compared with those in the *Vāsavadattā*: story within story (1. 30, 37; 2. 389, 405, 409, 416, 436, 438); love from a dream (1. 253, 258–259, 380); magic steeds (1. 339, 342, 375); love letters (2. 382–383; cf. Schlegel, 'Feuilles d'arbre comme lettres d'amour,' in *Mélanges Charles de Harlez*, pp. 271–274, Leiden, 1896); and birds playing a part in *affaires de cœur* (2. 482). It should also be observed that Dunlop repeatedly alludes to Indian parallels with Occidental literature (1. 12, 64–65, 74, 76, 109–110, 210, 306, 318, 413, 459–461; 2. 8, 30, 49, 53–54, 81, 87–88, 90, 118–120, 127–128, 272, 509, 558–559), although the most of these refer to the novel, or 'short story,' and not to the romance.

The Sanskrit Romance Compared with the Greek. The sole national romance literature of the West which has been regarded as connected with that of India is the Greek. The view has been advanced by Peterson (*Kādambarī*, 2 ed., Introd., pp. 101–104, Bombay, 1889, where several parallels are adduced between the *Kādambarī* and Achilles Tatios), Weber (*Sitzungsberichte der Berliner Akademie, phil.-hist. Klasse*, 37. 917), and Goblet d'Alviella (*Ce que l'Inde doit à la Grèce*, p. 136, Paris, 1897) that the Indian romance was a direct importation from Greece. This hypothesis, however, is rejected by Lévi (*Quid de Graecis veterum Indorum monumenta tradiderint*, p. 60, Paris, 1890) with what seems to me to be perfect justice. It is, of course, true that many parallels of incident and even of literary device exist between the Sanskrit and the Greek romance. Among parallels of incident I may note the following, restricting the list to similarities between the Greek romances and the *Vāsavadattā*: falling in love from a dream (story of Zariadres and Odatis as recorded by Athenaios, *Deipnosophistai*, 13. 35; this story is clearly of Eastern origin; cf. Rohde, *Griechischer Roman*, 2 ed., pp. 47–54, Leipzig, 1900, where the parallel with the *Vāsavadattā* is expressly noted; for dreams in general in the Greek romances see Rohde, *op. cit.* pp. 508, 524, 531–533, 547, 561, 566); *svayaṃvara*, or 'self-choice' of a husband (also in the story of Zariadres and Odatis; cf. Rohde, *op. cit.* p. 52); letters between lovers (Achilles Tatios, Τὰ κατὰ Λευκίππην καὶ Κλειτοφῶντα, 5. 18, 20: Niketas Eugenianos,

Τὰ κατὰ Δρόσιλλαν καὶ Χαρικλέα, 2. 169–179, 202–223, 240–277, 284–314; 5. 199–247; Eustathios, Τὸ καθ' Ὑσμίνην καὶ Ὑσμινίαν δρᾶμα, 9. 8; 10. 2; cf. Rohde, *op. cit.* pp. 513, 566); fainting (Chariton, Τὰ περὶ Χαιρέαν καὶ Καλλιρρόην, 1. 4; 2. 7; 3. 6; 4. 5; 8. 1; cf. Rohde, *op. cit.* p. 172, where the parallel with the *Vāsavadattā* is noted); long-winded lamentations (Niketas Eugenianos, 1. 226–257, 289–352; 2. 8–23; 4. 110–150; 5. 131–168, 183–193; 6. 34–94, 204–234, 306–327; 8. 84–130, 196–238; 9. 37–107; cf. Rohde, *op. cit.* p. 566); and threatened suicide (Chariton, 1. 5; 5. 10; 6. 2; 7. 1; 8. 8; cf. Rohde, *op. cit.* p. 527). The following parallels of literary device, similarly restricted, may also be noted: stories within stories and episodes (the adventures of Derkullis and the sub-episode of Astraios in the lost Τὰ ὑπὲρ Θύλην ἄπιστα; the story of Aigialeus in Xenophon Ephesaios, Τὰ κατὰ Ἄνθειαν καὶ Ἀβροκόμην Ἐφεσιακά, 5. 1; and the stories of Knemon in Heliodoros's Αἰθιοπικά, 1. 9–14; 2. 8–10; and of Kalasiris, *ib.* 2. 24–5. 1; 5. 17–33; with the sub-episode of Charikles, *ib.* 2. 29–33); descriptions of nature (Niketas Eugenianos, 1. 77–115; Achilles Tatios, 1. 15; Longos, Ποιμενικὰ τὰ κατὰ Δάφνιν καὶ Χλόην, 4. 2–3); detailed personal descriptions (Achilles Tatios, 1. 1; Niketas Eugenianos, 1. 120–158; cf. Rohde, *op. cit.* pp. 160–166); learned allusions and citations of precedents (Longos, 1. 16; 4. 17; Achilles Tatios, 1. 8; 2. 36–37); and alliteration, *parisoi*, *homoioteleuta*, and similar figures of rhetoric which correspond in a sense to the Sanskrit *anuprāsa* (Achilles Tatios, 1. 1–2; 2. 7; 3. 2, 7; 4. 4; 5. 1, 21; Longos, preface; 1. 18, 30; 2. 35; 3. 3, 24, 33, 34; 4. 18; Eustathios, 1. 4; 2. 13; 4. 1, 3, 12, 21; 5. 11; 7. 13; cf. Rohde, *op. cit.* pp. 552–553, 561), although they often form rhymes (Achilles Tatios, 1. 1, 11; Longos, preface; 2. 26; 3. 13, 23; 4. 17, 28; Eustathios, 1. 9) and strained compounds (Niketas Eugenianos, 1. 133; 2. 143; 3. 121; 5. 341; 7. 48; cf. Rohde, *op. cit.* p. 567).

Yet all these parallels, and many more which might be cited, seem to me to prove nothing. In the first place, a large number of them can be considered parallels only by straining the sense of the term; and in the second place, they are obviously the outworking of independent, though partially similar, processes in the development of Greek and Sanskrit literature respectively, and should be interpreted accordingly. But even were an essential resemblance granted, it would still be difficult, I think, to prove the dependence of the Sanskrit romance on the Greek, the latter being, of course, the earlier. The romances of the two peoples are totally different both in plan and in spirit, as even a cursory reading will show. The least part of the Sanskrit romance is the thread of the story or the adventures of its characters; all the stress is laid on rhetorical embellishment, minute description of nature, detailed characterisation of exploits and of mental, moral, and physical qualities. In the Greek romance, on the other hand, as in Latin (if we may judge from the *Satiræ* of Petronius), the story is everything. The reader is hurried from adventure to adventure, the wilder and more improbable the better; fine writing is practically disregarded; description and appreciation of nature are, to all intents and purposes, non-existent. The only Greek romance, it seems to me, that can, by the utmost stretch of imagination, be compared even superficially with the works of Subandhu and Bāṇa is the Ποιμενικά of Longos; but even there the sole real similarity is a longing for nature rather than for feverish adventure, a longing which may be traced back to Theokritos, Bion, and Moschos on the one hand, and to Bhartṛhari and his congeners on the other. Even the *Daśakumāracarita*, which, as a picaresque romance, one might be tempted to compare with the works of Achilles Tatios, Heliodoros, and Chariton, has a totally different plan from any Greek romance, tracing its 'box arrangement' of stories to the peculiarly Indian scheme which may be seen, for instance, in the *Pañcatantra*, the *Kathāsaritsāgara*, or the *Jātakas*, and which was later carried to Persia, where it was incorporated in *The Thousand Nights and One Night*, ultimately appearing in the Occident in the *Decameron* of Boccaccio.[1] The adventures narrated in Daṇḍin's romance of

[1] For the 'box arrangement' in Egyptian see *King Khufui and the Magicians* (about 2000 B.C.; tr. Maspero, *Contes populaires de l'Égypte ancienne*, 3 ed., pp. 23–42, Paris, 1906); and in Japanese cf. Bakin's *Shichiya no Kura* (1810 A.D.; Aston *History of Japanese Literature*. pp. 359–360, London, 1901).

roguery, moreover, bear no resemblance, either in plot or in episode, to the amorphisms of Eustathios and his fellows. To sum up, the spirit of the Sanskrit and of the Greek romancers is as divergent as the audiences of scholars on the one hand, and of weaklings on the other, for whom they wrote; nor can any real affinity, much less any direct connexion, be traced between the romances of India and of Greece.

The Double Recension of the Vāsavadattā. Like the *Mahābhārata* and the *Rāmāyaṇa*, the *Vāsavadattā* appears to be preserved in two distinct recensions, which I would tentatively call 'northern' and 'southern.' The first of these is represented by the text of Hall (Calcutta, 1859) and the second by the Madras edition of 1862, reprinted as an appendix to the present volume, as well as by Krishnamachariar's text (Srirangam, 1906–1908). The 'southern' text, to which Hall's manuscript D seems also to belong, differs from the 'northern' chiefly in showing a large number of interpolations, particularly *ślēṣas*, *virōdhas*, and other forms of similes appended to the series given by the 'northern' text. The spirit, however, of the 'southern' recension is identical with that of the 'northern.' There is, indeed, one omission of a complimentary allusion to the Buddhists (ed. Hall, p. 235) and of one derogatory reference to the Jains (ed. Hall, p. 297 ; cf. above, p. 7), but the retention of all other depreciatory mentions of both sects shows that the 'southern' redactor was not led to modify his text by any circumstances surrounding him ; nor is there any added allusion in the 'southern' text which seems to be specifically South Indian. It may be regarded as practically certain that the 'northern' text represents Subandhu's original composition more closely than does the 'southern' recension, not only in view of the fact that the author of the romance was, in all probability, a native of northern India, where he almost indubitably wrote (cf. above, pp. 12–13), but also in consideration of the familiar principles of textual criticism that the shorter text is, other things being equal, to be preferred to the longer, and that the more difficult reading is to be preferred to the easier, since the 'southern' recension evidently seeks, by substitution or omission, to avoid many difficulties of word, phrase, or allusion which the 'northern' text boldly retains.

Manuscripts and Editions of the Romance. For the manuscripts of the *Vāsavadattā* and its commentators reference may be made to the catalogues of Sanskrit manuscripts enumerated by Aufrecht (*Catalogus Catalogorum*, 1. 566, 726; 2. 133–134, 224; 3. 120, Leipzig, 1891–1903). The principal commentators on the *Vāsavadattā* have been discussed by Hall (Introd., pp. 44–48), and I myself have written on 'Śivarāma's Commentary on the *Vāsavadattā*' (in *JAOS*. 24. 57–63), so that the problems there treated need not be repeated in this place.

Although the editions of Subandhu's romance will be duly listed in the bibliography (see below, pp. 197–198), a more detailed discussion seems appropriate here. These editions are seven in number. The first and best-known, which represents the 'northern' recension, is that of Fitzedward Hall (Calcutta, 1859), based on eight manuscripts and accompanied by the gloss of Śivarāma Tripāṭhin, who flourished early in the eighteenth century. The introduction to this edition has become a classic among Sanskritists, and the learning which it evinces on every page renders it amply deserving of this honour. Hall's text, however, represents a form really older than any of his manuscripts, being that of Śivarāma, in whose favour the editor repeatedly discarded the united authority of all his manuscripts, a method of textual criticism which may perhaps be considered open to objection. The text of Hall has been reprinted *verbatim* by Jīvānanda Vidyāsāgara (Calcutta, 1874; 3d ed., 1907). The remaining five editions belong to the 'southern' recension. Of these the earliest is one in Telugu script (Madras, 1861), which was reprinted, with a correction of misprints, in Telugu (Madras, 1862) and Grantha script (Madras, 1870). The second of these, duly collated with the India Office copies of the other two, which Mr. F. W. Thomas, librarian of the India Office, London, most kindly placed at my disposal, is transcribed below (pp. 145–195). The text of this 'southern' recension is evidently later than the 'northern', since it abounds in interpolations, especially in the lengthened *ślēṣas* and *virōdhas.* The three editions under consideration contain the same commentary, which has appeared to me to be negligible, and which, according to Mr. J. K. Balasubrahmanyam, the publisher of the Srirangam text (Pref. p. 1) to be mentioned below, 'is traditionally attributed to one Tippa Bhupala, but nothing is certain about it. For instance, just as we were completing this book we got a palm-leaf manuscript of this work containing a commentary said to be by one Ramanatha. On closer examination it turned out to be neither more nor less than the commentary given in the Grantha and Telugu editions.' The same general recension, though with a number of interesting variations, is represented by the edition published at Srirangam in 1906–1908, on the basis of several old palm-leaf manuscripts. It also contains an admirably full, careful, and suggestive modern Sanskrit commentary and an equally noteworthy Sanskrit introduction by the editor, R. V. Krishnamachariar, of which I have most helpfully availed myself. I distinctly consider Hall's and this as the best editions of the *Vāsavadattā* that have yet appeared. The Telugu text is also represented, more closely, by T. V. Srinivasachariar's edition (Trichinopoly, 1906), which, I regret to say, seems to me to offer scope for some improvement. All the divergencies of the Madras, Srirangam, and Trichinopoly editions from the text of Hall will be found duly recorded in the footnotes to the present translation, while the variations of the 'southern' from the 'northern' recension will be indicated by parentheses in the appended transliteration, the portions of the 'northern' text omitted by the 'southern' being there supplied in square brackets. It will be clear that a critical text of the *Vāsavadattā*, which shall take into account all accessible manuscripts, commentaries, and editions, is still a *desideratum.*

The Remaining Sanskrit Prose Romances. Except for a digression on the relation sometimes held to exist between the Sanskrit and the Greek romance (see above, pp. 35–38), this Introduction to the *Vāsavadattā* has thus far purposely been restricted to Subandhu and his work, especially as Meyer (*Daṇḍin's Daçakumāracaritam, die Abenteuer der zehn Prinzen,* pp. 1–139, Leipzig, 1902) and Collins (*The Geographical Data of the Raghuvaṃśa and the Daśakumāracarita considered more especially in their Bearing upon the Date of these Works*, Leipzig, 1907) have devoted admirable studies to Daṇḍin, while Peterson (*Kādambarī*, 2 ed., Introd., Bombay, 1889) has done a similar service for Bāṇa. Moreover, the *Daśakumāracarita*, *Harṣacarita*, and *Kādambarī* are all readily accessible, not only in numerous editions, which need not be enumerated here, but also in excellent translations (the *Daśakumāracarita* by Meyer, *op. cit.*, and by Haberlandt, Munich, 1903; the *Harṣacarita* by Cowell and Thomas, London, 1897; and the *Kādambarī* by Ridding, London, 1896). It may not be amiss, however, to add a brief outline of such other Sanskrit romances as have thus far been analysed, though it must be borne in mind that further investigations and additional and fuller catalogues of Sanskrit manuscripts will, in all probability, add to the sum of *ākhyāna* literature.[1] Omitting *campūs* on Rāma, Kṛṣṇa, Aniruddha, and Nala, as well as *rifacimenti* of the *Mahābhārata* and *Rāmāyaṇa*, and pseudo-histories of Śālivāhana and Mayūravarman, attention may here be called to two late Sanskrit romances. The first of these is the *Yaśastilaka* of Sōmadēva, who completed his romance in 959 A.D. The work has been analysed in detail by Peterson (*Second Report of Operations in Search of Sanskrit Manuscripts in the Bombay Circle*, pp. 33–49, Bombay, 1884) and has been edited by Śivadatta and Parab (*Kāvyamālā*, No. 70, 2 parts, Bombay, 1901–1903). It is a religious romance, treating of the conversion of Māridatta, king of Rājapura, from Brāhmanism to Jainism through the agency of his twin nephew and niece, whom he was about to offer in sacrifice, not knowing who they were, and through the arguments of the Jain sage Sudatta. The familiar device of the story within a story, whereby Māridatta's nephew

[1] Krishnamachariar (Introd., pp. 1–2) notes the paucity of works of this type, but he enumerates the following which would otherwise have escaped my notice: Dhanapāla's *Tilakamañjarī* (ed. Bombay, 1903 = *Kāvyamālā*, No. 85), the Jain romance *Gadyacintāmaṇi* (variously ascribed to Vādībhasiṃha, Pradīpasiṃha, and Siṃhasūri), Abhinavabhaṭṭabāṇa's *Vīranārāyaṇa* and Haricandra's *Jīvandharacampū*, the fragmentary *Śrīkṛṣṇacarita* of Agastyakavi, the lost *Trāilōkyasundarī* of Rudra, and the lost *Taraṅgavatī*. He also attempts to account for this scantiness (pp. 2–8).

tells his uncle all his history, and a series of reincarnations, as in the *Daśakumāracarita* and *Kādambarī*,[1] are both found in Sōmadēva's romance, while learned precedents and, what is still more remarkable, explicit quotations from other poets, including Bāṇa, abound. Altogether, it is clear from Peterson's admirable analysis that the *Yaśastilaka* richly deserves translation, both as belonging to a category of Sanskrit literature of which too few specimens are extant, and as a valuable source for additional knowledge of the tenets of the Jains.

The second romance which should be noted in this connexion is Bāṇēśvara Vidyālaṃkāra Bhaṭṭācārya's *Citracampū*, written in 1744 A.D. in honour of Citrasēna, king of Vardhamāna, and briefly analysed by Eggeling (*Catalogue of the Sanskrit Manuscripts in the Library of the India Office*, 7. 1543–1545, London, 1904). This novel is characterised especially by a long dream, and by an unmistakable inculcation of Vāiṣṇavite Vēdāntism; otherwise it offers but little of interest.

[1] See 'Reincarnation as a Novelistic Device', in *WZKM.* 18. 54–58. For reincarnation in a modern Western novel see Margaret Potter's *Flame-Gatherers* (London, 1904), and Bain's *Descent of the Sun* (London, 1903). The earliest example known is the Egyptian *Tale of the Two Brothers*, written in the nineteenth dynasty (1375–1202 B.C.; tr. Maspero, *Contes populaires de l'Égypte ancienne*, 3 ed., pp. 3–20, Paris, 1906).

[Dr. Ogden draws my attention to a reference to Subandhu in an anthology of a certain Lakṣmaṇa, described by Peterson (*Third Report of Operations in Search of Sanskrit Manuscripts in the Bombay Circle*, p. 35, Bombay, 1887) under the title of *Sūktāvali*. The stanza, whose date is thus far unknown, is as follows (Peterson, *op. cit.*, Appendix, p. 55):

jīyād gadyasudhādhunyāḥ
subandhuḥ prabhavācalaḥ
yad bhaṅgāślēṣaṃ āsādya
bhaṅgaḥ kavibhir āśritaḥ,

'may Subandhu, in strength immovable, prevail over the nectarous stream of prose, for since he gained combination after the breaking (of words into their component parts), the breaking (of words into their component parts) has been employed by poets.']

VĀSAVADATTĀ OF SUBANDHU

[2] Victorious is divine Sarasvatī,
Who aideth bards of keen and nimble wit
To see the world, as 'twere a jujube-fruit,
Lying within the hollow of their hands.

Victorious, too, is Hari, resting now,
The while he smileth on the shepherd lads
Whose upraised arms bend [1] 'neath the awful weight
Of their vast burden; yet cry unto him:
'Ah, weary art thou, let the mountain be;
We will sustain it, Kṛṣṇa, lord of all'!

[3] May he [2] whose waist is girded keep you safe,
Yea, he whose serried furrows brightly shine;
E'en while the zone he hath too tightly drawn
Doth work distraction by its beauteousness.[3]

[4] Victorious is the god [4] whose crescent gleams
Like to a silvern pearl by Umā set [5]
Upon his brow, when from his blazing eye
She gathereth the black collyrium.

[5] How blessèd are those souls beneficent
Who work the weal of others, for to them
The moon that openeth the lotus-buds
Doth give a twofold meed of radiance [6]!

[6] The wise say sooth: 'More loathsome than a snake
Is he whose soul is filled with wickedness':
The serpent ⟨hateth the ichneumon tribe⟩,
But leaves his brethren safe; while knavish folk
With venomed tongues ⟨destroy their nearest kin⟩.[7]

[1] Tel. ed. and Srirangam text, 'arms bent in vain.' [2] Kṛṣṇa.
[3] Tel. ed. interchanges this stanza with the one following.
[4] Śiva. [5] Srirangam text, against the metre, adds 'upon his head.
[6] Translated in Böhtlingk, *Indische Sprüche*, 2 ed., No. 4552, St. Petersburg, 1870–1873.
[7] Böhtlingk, *op. cit.* No. 6214. The stanza is still popular in Mithila (see Grierson,

[7] In evil only are the wicked wise;
Like as the owl is blind, save in the dark.[1]

There is but one eclipse—foul calumny;
Only the clouds that hide the moon are black.[2]

[8] And when with sooty and polluting touch
The man of evil fain would smirch the good,
He doth increase the radiance of the just;
E'en as the ashes in the grinder's hand
Do but enhance the lustrous mirror's sheen.[3]

Yet ‹drought doth rule› o'er all, the «cranes sport not»
Nor doth the ⋘heron seek the azure vault⋙,
For lo, the lake hath left this mortal world;
All ‹joy is fled›, and «strange kings now bear rule»,
Wasting the earth with ⋘fratricidal⋙ strife,
For Vikramāditya hath passed away.[4]

[11] The words of goodly bards rejoice thine ears,
E'en when thou knowest not their wondrous skill;
For in a jasmine wreath thine eyes delight,
Though to thy senses come no perfumes sweet.[5]

The noble gain true knowledge of themselves
By observation of their fellow men;
As on the mirror's polished surface falls
The vision of the soul's own magnitude.[6]

Curiosities of Indian Literature, pp. 8–9, Bankipore, 1895, who says: 'Here *nakuladvēṣī* is a threefold pun. It means either "hating the ichneumon," or "not hating his own race," or "not hating the members of the family of the man he has bitten").' My attention was kindly called to this reference by Professor Zachariae (card of May 2, 1907), and Dr. Grierson very courteously loaned me his personal copy of the little book. It should be noted that the modern proverb reads *mṛṣā na* instead of *na mṛṣā*.

[1] Böhtlingk, *Indische Sprüche*, 2 ed., No. 142, St. Petersburg, 1870–1873.

[2] Böhtlingk, *op. cit.* No. 6126; Tel. ed. and Srirangam text interchange this stanza with the one following.

[3] Böhtlingk, *op. cit.* No. 7376.

[4] For the valuelessness of this stanza as a source to determine the date of the *Vāsavadattā* see Introduction, pp. 8–11.

[5] Böhtlingk, *op. cit.* No. 680.

[6] Böhtlingk, *op. cit.* No. 2148.

[9] Through great Sarasvatī this book was writ
By Sujana's one brother, whom mankind
Doth call Subandhu, skilled full dextrously
To interweave in every word a pun.[1]

[10] There was a king named Cintāmaṇi, whose like had never existed,[2] whose nail-jewelled feet were unscarred, though rubbed by the edge of a touchstone which was the series of the beautiful crest-gems of the circle of all the princes of the earth.

[11] He caused astonishment by ‹gifts of gold, food, raiment, and estates› as Nṛsiṃha caused astonishment by ‹rending the body of Hiraṇyakaśipu›[3]; he gave joy to the ‹divinities by his goods› as Kṛṣṇa gave joy to ‹Vasudēva›; [12] he ‹conquered with ease› the circle of the earth as Nārāyaṇa ‹upheld› the circle of the world by his ‹boar's form›; he produced ‹glorious and blissful› prosperity as Kaṃsa's foe produced prosperity for ‹Yaśōdā and Nanda›; he made ‹poetry honoured› as Ānakadundubhi made ‹Kāvyā afraid›[4]; [13] he had his lotus[5] feet embellished by the rays[6] of the crest-jewels of ‹many serpents› as Sāgaraśāyi had his lotus[5] feet embellished by the rays[6] of the crest-jewel of the ‹cosmic serpent›; he protected ‹unceasingly› as Varuṇa protected the ‹western regions›; he adorned ‹petitions with gifts› as Agastya adorned the ‹southern districts›; he was the lord of a hundred ‹armies› and «habitually levied just taxes» as the ocean is the lord of a hundred ‹rivers› and is the «habitat of fish»; [14] he was followed by a ‹great army› and repulsed «obstacles» as Hara is followed by ‹Mahāsēna› and repulses «Māra»; he was the home of the ‹wise› and the dwelling-place of the «acts of all men» as Mēru is the home of the ‹gods› and the dwelling-place of «Viśvakarman»; he ‹rejoiced in generosity at festal times› and removed sorrow by his «beauty» as the sun ‹loves not the night› and removes the sorrow of «Chāyā»; he

[1] Omitted by Tel. ed. and Srirangam text. Cf. Introduction, p. 13.

[2] Tel. ed., 'of no mean nature.' For a somewhat similar description of a king see *Kādambarī*, pp. 7–14, Bombay ed., 1890 (tr. Ridding, pp. 3–5, London, 1896.

[3] Cf. *Viṣṇupurāṇa*, I. 17–20.

[4] Cf. *Harivaṃśa*, 59.

[5] Tel. ed. and Srirangam text omit 'lotus.'

[6] Tel. ed., 'series.'

gave ‹unimpeded› prosperity and afforded delight in «intercourse» as the God of the Flowery Banner[1] gave prosperity to ‹Aniruddha› and afforded delight to «Rati».

[15] Though a ‹demigod›, he was a «god», for he was a «benevolent» ‹receptacle of wisdom›; though a ‹Dhṛtarāṣṭra›, he was a «friend of Bhīma», for he was a ‹ruler of a kingdom› «who loved virtue»; though ‹come to earth›, he took refuge[2] in the «courts of the gods», for he was ‹filled with patience› and took refuge[2] in «good government»; [16] though a ‹great reed› by nature, he was «smooth» within, for his was the nature of ‹Arjuna›, «upright» within; [17] though born of a ‹buffalo›, he was «begotten by a bull», for he was born of a ‹queen› and was a «producer of government»; though no ‹central gem of a necklace›, he was the «midmost jewel of a throat-band», for he was a ‹fearless›, «mighty leader».

While he ruled the earth, ‹quibblings[3] and fallacies› were practised only in arguments[4] (for there was no need of ‹habitually checking deceit›[5]); [18] there was ‹infidelity› only among materialists (for there was no ‹poverty›); there was employment of a ‹spur› only in executing commands[6] (for there was no employment of ‹petty enemies›); there was ‹picking› [19] only on lutes (for there was no ‹back-biting›); there was association with ‹threshing-floors› only in the case of rice (for there was no association with ‹evil men›); there was capture of ‹snakes› only among serpent-charmers (for there was no need to capture ‹liars›); ‹imposts› were cut only in the receipt of taxes (for there was no amputation of ‹hands›[7]); ‹roots› were plucked out only in the case of «wormwood-trees» (for «ascetics» did not pluck out their ‹eyes›); [20] only lotuses opposed the ‹moon› (for there was no opposition to ‹Brāhmans›[8]); ‹'ruler of the world'› was applied only to the elephant of the north[9] (but not to any man

[1] Kāma. [2] Srirangam text, 'he was the refuge of.'
[3] Srirangam text adds 'futile answers.' [4] Tel. ed., 'only in Nyāya textbooks.'
[5] Srirangam text adds 'and castes.'
[6] Tel. ed. and Srirangam text, 'only in yōga-exercises.'
[7] Tel. ed. and Srirangam text, 'there was hand-cutting only in blossoms.'
[8] Tel. ed. and Srirangam text, 'the king.'
[9] Tel. ed. and Srirangam text, 'only to the world-elephants.'

save the <king>); there were <fire-tests and balance-tests> only in the case of different sorts of gold (for there were no <ordeals by fire or balance>[1]); only jewels were <pierced by needles> (for there was no <disturbance by suggestive movements>); only in child-bearing[2] was there rending with <griping pains> (for there was no rending by <impalement>); [21] <Duḥśāsana was known> only in the *Bhārata*[3] (for there was no <glimpse of evil instruction>); the <sun's rays opened leaves>[4] only in the case of lotuses (for there was no <sawing asunder>[5]).

Though the Great Boar was intent on upholding the <earth>, yet he (Cintāmaṇi) clove <mountains>. Rāghava entered the forest with <Sītā> leaving his native land (but Cintāmani entered the forest having his <native land>). Bharata had affection for Rāma, yet made <Rāma depart> from his kingdom (but Cintāmaṇi made <peace> in his kingdom). [22] When Nala was united to Ḍamayantī it was a <marriage of one already wedded> (but Cintāmaṇi <regained his territory>). Pṛthu <levelled the earth by banishing the mountains>[6] (but Cintāmaṇi <covered the earth by sending forth his offspring>[7]). There was, therefore, no reason to mention former kings.[8]

He, moreover, was another sort of monarch and had humbled all the princes on earth. Thus he was a mountain with a visible exaltation of <peak>, which never ceased to delight the <<Gan-

[1] In the ordeal by balance the accused was twice weighed. If he was lighter at the second weighing than at the first, he was acquitted; but if heavier, he was condemned. In the fire-ordeal the defendant was required to carry a heated metal pot a certain distance, and was adjudged innocent if his hands, which might be bound with leaves as a partial protection, remained unburned (see Jolly, *Recht und Sitte*, p. 145, Strassburg, 1896).

[2] Tel. ed., 'in new (i.e. 'first') child-bearings of young women'; Srirangam text, 'in child-bearings.'

[3] Tel. ed. and Srirangam text, 'in the *Mahābhārata*.'

[4] Tel. ed. and Srirangam text, 'the opening of leaves of lotuses by the rays of the sun was the very utmost decree.'

[5] Cf. the Iranian legend of the sawing asunder of Yima by Spityura (*Yašt*, 19. 46).

[6] Cf. *Mahābhārata*, 7. 69.

[7] This rendering seems justified by the context and by the paronomasiac meanings of the words employed, although the commentary does not allude to the applicability of the passage to Cintāmaṇi.

[8] Tel. ed. adds 'but rather (there was occasion) of blame (of them).'

dharvas who roamed along its slopes»; for he never ceased, with his visible exaltation of ‹majesty›, to delight the «steeds that bore his army». [23] He was a ‹Himālaya›, though not shaken by «snow» nor suited to the birth of «Umā», for he was ‹indeed a lotus› unshaken by «pride» and unsuited for the birth of «deceit». He was a «snowy» ‹bullock›-banner set upon a «hill», for he was «indeed exalted in speech» and set as a banner of ‹justice›.

He was a ‹wind›, ‹bending all the forest down›, ‹a friend of the fire›, ‹eager for the clouds›, and ‹bearing along the flowers›; for he was ‹ever patient›, ‹straightening every crooked way›,[1] ‹foremost of ascetics›, ‹not avid of sensual pleasures›,[2] and the ‹joy of the wise›. [24] He was a mine of gems ‹with no serpents›,[3] exceeding[4] deep its ‹boundaries›, ‹no otter a terror to it›, ever a very refuge for ‹fishes›, ‹filled with water›, ‹bearing ships›,[5] whereto (belonged) the ‹mountain[6] and the crocodile›, ‹the mighty-lord of rivers›, the ‹ocean›; [25] for he was ‹no knave›,[7] exceeding[4] deep his ‹decorum›, ‹no light of his dismaying any›, ever a refuge like the ‹moon›,[8] ‹delightsome›, ‹rich in children›,[9] ‹his serenity unshaken›, ‹great, proud›, and ‹with a signet ring›. [26] As the moon causes joy in the ‹night season›, is the friend[10] of ‹white lotuses›, has his mansion filled with all the ‹digits›, and is ‹unsurpassed by the constellations›; he caused joy in the ‹festivals›, was the friend[10] of ‹pleasure groves on earth›, had his mansion filled with all the ‹arts›, and ‹subdued the excessive might of his foes›. As Sumēru caused the ‹sun to rise›, gave a ‹golden glory›, and had ‹wealth surpassing the (other) mountains›; he caused the ‹prosperity of his friends›, possessed ‹every beauty›, and had ‹good fortune impregnable and abundant›.

[1] Or, 'banishing all famine.' [2] Or, 'eager for the gods.'
[3] Tel. ed., 'with no *timayas*' (glossed as 'a sort of fish,' i.e. 'a whale'); Srirangam text, 'with no fear of serpents.' [4] Tel. ed. and Srirangam text omit.
[5] Tel. ed. and Srirangam text, 'with a good bed.' [6] Māināka.
[7] Tel. ed., 'unbending'; Srirangam text, 'fearing not his subjects.'
[8] Tel. ed., 'ever with a moon-like mind.'
[9] Tel. ed. and Srirangam text, 'receptacle of virtue.'
[10] Tel. ed., 'the one friend.'

[27] Even had Arjuna been ever with them, the ranks of his foes would not have been equal to the ‹combats in the *Mahābhārata*›, for they were not equal to ‹bearing great burdens›. Though ‹Bhīṣma›, he was «unkind to Śāntanu», for he was ‹terrible› and had a «ceaseless desire for glory»; though ‹wandering on the mountains›, «he dwelt not on the hills», for he was ‹accompanied by his attendants› and «needed not the admiration of his family».

[28] And, furthermore, he ‹wavered [1] not from the path of a warrior›, as Triśaṅku [2] ‹wavered [1] in the path of the constellations›; though he was ‹Śiva›, «he drank no poison», for he was a ‹giver of weal› and «not depressed»; though he was a ‹fire›, he was not a «flame», for he was a ‹purifier› and free from «evil habits»; though he was a ‹burner›, he was not a «consumer», for he had a ‹longing for hermitages› and was no «destroyer»; [29] he was no Yama ‹snatching life away suddenly›, for he did not ‹deprive of life without reason›; he was no Rāhu increasing his ‹radiance by swallowing the sun's disc›,[3] for he did not increase his ‹greed by seizing the kingdom of a friend›; he was no Nala crushed [4] by ‹Kali›, for he was not crushed [4] by ‹strife›; he was no Cakri exhilarated by the death of ‹Śṛgāla›,[5] for he was not exhilarated by the death of a ‹craven›; he was attended by ‹glory and generosity› as the cowherd Nanda was attended by ‹Yaśōdā›; he ‹planned peace and war› as Jarāsanda's ‹body was disrupted union› [6]; he possessed ‹generosity and luxury› as Bhārgava ‹ever wandered in the clouds›; [30] he was attended by ‹good friends› and commanded «good counsel» as Daśaratha was attended by ‹Sumitrā› and commanded «Sumantra»; he was ‹devoted to worthy objects of generosity› and protected the «earth» as Dilīpa was ‹beloved by Sudakṣiṇā› and protected

[1] Tel. ed. and Srirangam text, 'fell.'

[2] Srirangam text, 'though Triśaṅku .... for he had triple powers.'

[3] Cf. *Mahābhārata*, 1. 19.

[4] Tel. ed. and Srirangam text, 'having his body conquered'; cf. *Mahābhārata*, 3. 58–61.

[5] Cf. *Harivaṃśa*, 100.

[6] Cf. *Mahābhārata*, 2. 17.

the «cow» [1]; his glory was exalted by his ‹virtuous life› as Rāma's glory was exalted by the ‹birth of Kuśa and Lava›.

He had a son named Kandarpakētu. He was the ‹joy of the hermits› as the coral-tree ‹stands in Indra's garden› [2]; [31] he ‹produced weal› as Himālaya was the ‹birthplace of Śiva›; he was ‹marked by his luxurious pleasures› as Mandara is ‹scarred by the body of the serpent›; his ‹crores were enjoyed by great kings› as Kāilāsa's ‹summit is enjoyed by the Great Lord› [3]; he gave pleasure to many ‹women› as the spring gives pleasure in many ‹gardens›; [32] he made the ‹earth› resound as Mandara, lifted on high in the churning of the ocean of milk, made the ‹water› resound; he ‹took delight in love› as the God of Passion's Bond [4] ‹rejoices Rati›; he was shaken by ‹meditation› as the collected ashes of Śiva are shaken at ‹twilight› [5]; [33] he had a ‹pure heart› and «clung to Viṣṇu's feet» as an autumn cloud has a ‹lurid centre› and «depends from the sky» [6]; he was accustomed to ‹all passion and merriment› as Arjuna was accustomed to be ‹courageous in battle›; [34] he was adorned with a ‹garland of the circle of the earth› as Kaṃsa was adorned with a ‹blue lotus garland›; he gave joy to the ‹humble› [7] and «delighted the wise» as Tārkṣya gave joy to ‹Vinatā› [7] and had «Sumukha for a son»; he ‹clasped› a beautiful form to his «breast» as Viṣṇu ‹changed› his beautiful form into a «boar»; he had ‹time and justice› put into his own power as Śāntanava had ‹Death› put into his own power; [35] he governed ‹full happily› as the host of Kāuravas was led by ‹Suśarman›.

Though ‹Subāhu›,[8] he was a joy to «Rāma», for he had ‹beautiful arms› and gave joy to «women»; though he had ‹two

[1] Cf. *Raghuvaṃśa*, 1–2.

[2] The heaven of Indra, the home of warriors fallen in battle, and the future hope of popular classic Hinduism, is particularly renowned for its wonderful coral-tree, which, according to *Viṣṇupurāṇa*, 5. 30, was produced at the churning of the ocean of milk, and which has golden bark, copper-coloured leaves, and flowers of surpassing fragrance.

[3] Śiva.

[4] Kāma.

[5] An allusion to Śiva's revel dances at nightfall.

[6] Srirangam text, 'he had a ‹pure heart› as an autumn cloud has a ‹lurid centre›; he ‹clung to Viṣṇu's feet› as the moon ‹depends from the sky›.'

[7] Tel. ed. and Srirangam text omit.

[8] Cf. *Rāmāyaṇa*, 1. 30.

eyes›, he was «Śiva», for he was a «great monarch» who ‹gazed on all alike› ; though ‹made of pearls›, his «waist had no central jewel», for he was ‹free from disease› and «virile» ; as a cloud [36] ‹terrifies flamingoes with showers of exceeding purity›, he ‹slew kings terrified by the edge of his flashing sword› ; though a light upon a ‹pole›, his «wick was not consumed», for he was the light of his ‹race› and his «estate was unimpaired».

The noble, resembling oceans with beauteous ‹mountains›, with ‹waters› increased exceedingly, and with ‹contented creatures›, attained their highest growth through him who was, as it were, the moon when its «house has all its digits, removes the distress of night, opens the white lotuses», [37] is a friend to «white lotus groves»,[1] and «adorns a quarter of the sky» ; for the noble, with ‹radiant limbs›, with ‹life› increased exceedingly, and with ‹amiable qualities›, [38] attained their highest growth through him who was the «home of the aggregation of all virtues, delighted in Śiva's way, destroyed his enemies», was a friend of «pleasure groves on earth»,[1] and had his «hopes fulfilled».

And the hearts of women rejoiced at the sight of him who was like the God of the Dolphin Banner, causing ‹Aniruddha› delight, ‹dear to Rati›, and ‹armed with an arrow of flowers› ; for he caused ‹unimpeded› delight, was a ‹friend of wantonness›, and ‹surpassed the Flower-God›. For him who was as the spring with the ‹attendant southern breeze›, with ‹sweet koel-notes›[2] pleasing the ear,[3] expanding the ‹buds›, making the ‹forests bend›, [39] ‹delightsome with fragrant flowers›, with ‹lotuses› easy for all to gather, possessing an abundance of ‹white thorn-apple trees› spread abroad, but passing over the ‹wormwood›, damsels felt attachment, being like creepers of the forest with a thousand «buds», crowded with «bees», charming with «sprigs», and with «sportive birds» ; since he had a ‹continual

[1] Tel. ed. and Srirangam text omit.

[2] The notes of the koel, or Indian cuckoo (*Eudynamis orientalis*, Linn.), though in themselves scarcely pleasant, are hailed with delight as a harbinger of spring, and the bird is, therefore, regarded as a friend of love.

[3] Tel. ed. and Srirangam text, 'the eye and ear.'

income for the attendant nobles›,[1] possessed a ‹sweet koel-voice› pleasing the ear,[2] expanded ‹love›, gave a ‹charming colour to women›, ‹delighted in learned sages›, possessed ‹good fortune› easy for all to gather, spread abroad an abundance of ‹gold›, and surpassed his ‹foes›, while the damsels [40] were filled with a thousand «anxieties», were sought by «lovers»,[3] were charming because of their «coral necklaces»,[4] and were at the «wanton age».

And by his staff-like arm on the field of battle [41] the bow was gained, by the bow the arrows, by the arrows his foeman's head, by this [5] the world,[6] by this [7] a leader such as had never been before, by the leader fame, by fame the seven seas, by the seas the renown of the kings of the Kṛta and other ages, and by that [8] constancy, and by this [9] something marvellous every instant. And the periphery of the bosoms of the lovely wives of his foes, who had been consumed by the fire of his majesty, was deserted by their pearl necklaces, as if terrified by the blows of their hands.

[42] And his sword, as if coloured with lac from the feet of the Goddess of Victory which had been moistened with the blood of slain infantry, elephants, and horses, shone over a sea of conflict whose shores were covered with quantities of pearls [10] fallen from must elephants' [11] frontal lobes which were shattered by sharp arrows, with flying ‹birds›, with hundreds of ‹rivers and white and blue lotuses› whose manifold charms were spread through the ‹beautiful› waters,[12] with [13] ‹dancing waters›, and terrible because of the fierce pride of the ‹*cārubhaṭa*›-fish which

[1] Or, 'was a competency for his retainers, sages, and honourable men.'

[2] Tel. ed. and Srirangam text, 'the eye and ear.'

[3] Or, 'had curls on their foreheads.'

[4] Or, 'because of their long hair.'

[5] Tel. ed. and Srirangam text, 'by the foeman's head.'

[6] Tel. ed., 'by the world unprecedented renown as a leader, and by renown fame.'

[7] Srirangam text, 'by the world.'

[8] Tel. ed. and Srirangam text, 'by renown.'

[9] Tel. ed. and Srirangam text, 'by constancy.'

[10] Srirangam text, 'round pearls.'

[11] The frontal lobe of an elephant is believed to contain a pearl, called *kuñjaramaṇi* or *gajamaṇi*, which is possessed of magic properties (Crooke, *Popular Religion and Folk-Lore of Northern India*, 2 ed., 2. 240, Westminster, 1896).

[12] Tel. ed. and Srirangam text, not alluding to pun, 'with tortoises (clinging) on the feet of elephants coming up from the beautiful water, with lovely white and blue lotuses, with hundreds of rivers.'

[13] Tel. ed. and Srirangam text, 'undulating with.'

were eager to consort with the [43] <*surasundarīs*>; since it shone on a sea of conflict[1] whose shores were covered with quantities of pearls fallen from must elephants' frontal lobes which were shattered by sharp arrows, with flying <darts>, with hundreds of <fleshless, white-umbrellaed armies> whose manifold charms were spread through the <red> waters, with[2] <convulsing corpses>, and terrible because of the fierce pride of <warriors> eager to consort with the <Apsarasas>.

[44] Then, once upon a time, when the night was finished; when the Lotus-Lord of shell-like beauty was sinking with his spouse, the Night, into the western[3] sea; while he was white, as it were, with the curds which constitute a morsel of food for (Buddhist) ascetics at their mealtime, and was like a mass of Yamunā's foam by night, and resembled a fragment of stone[4] for the polishing of Mēnakā's nails, and had the shade of the soma-plant in the centre of his body, and resembled the silvern earring[5] of a head laid softly down on the pillow of the western mount, and seemed to be the goblet of Lady Night containing a remnant of wine; [45] when the bees had their feet caught in the pollen of the white lotuses which had been converted into cold[6] paste by the dew; when by their soft chatter the *mainas* revealed women at their rendezvous; when the huts of the ascetics awoke intent on study; when the streets resounded with poetic tales chanted by mendicants in the *vibhāsa* mode[7]; [46] when the lamps seemed unable, because of their exceeding thinness,[8] to bear the blackness of night[9] which they had entirely

[1] Tel. ed. and Srirangam text, 'in the forefront of battle, as on a sea terrible with the roaring noise of soldiers marching in eagerness to consort with the Apsarasas'—apparently with no attempt to pun.

[2] Tel. ed. and Srirangam text, 'undulating with.'

[3] The distinctly conventional character of Subandhu's romance is well illustrated by his making the moon set in the west because the sun does.

[4] Tel. ed., 'crystalline stone'; Srirangam text, 'fragment of white stone for the polishing.'

[5] Tel. ed., 'the circle of the silvern earring of night, with her head softly resting,' etc.; similarly the Srirangam text.

[6] Tel. ed. and Srirangam text, 'cold, icy water.'

[7] Tel. ed., '*hāsa* mode.'

[8] Or, 'emptiness.

[9] Tel. ed. and Srirangam text, 'mass of nocturnal blackness.

swallowed up, and which they vomited, as it were,[1] under the guise of lampblack, and were exhausted by having stretched their necks a hundred times as if to see the tremulous delights of amorous union,[2] [47] and had been witnesses of manifold ways of wanton sport,[3] seeming to protect the darkness[4] lurking beneath them as if it were a refugee; when they had become ‹dull› because their «oil» had been consumed as knaves[5] become ‹slack› because their «affections» have been consumed; when they had reached the end of their ‹wicks› as the exceedingly aged reach the end of their ‹lives›; when they had only their ‹bowls› left as noble lords reduced in their estate have only their ‹bodies› left; [48] when they were ‹put in the middle of the house› as demons ‹wander abroad at the end and middle of night›; when they had ‹moths› flying about them as the ‹sun› descends on the summit of the western mount; when the gifts of flowers in the boudoirs, that had been noisy with the humming[6] of swarms of bees delighting[7] in the abundance of unceasing drops[8] of honey had withered; [49] when the downy Nepal jasmines had fallen from the tresses; when fair women seemed to be pouring forth teardrops for grief at separation from their lovers[9] and, with bud-like feet[10] tinkling with anklets, delayed, as it were, the departure of their best beloved; when the mist of perspiration[11] had been dried by the wind of the wings of a swarm of bees enamoured of the perfume of the wreaths of half-opened Malabar jasmine[12] in thick tresses dishevelled by weariness of

[1] Tel. ed. and Srirangam text omit 'as it were.'

[2] Tel. ed., 'the quivering of amorous women.'

[3] Tel. ed., 'varied love-joys with delights manifold'; Srirangam text, 'wanton sport with perturbations manifold.'

[4] Tel. ed. and Srirangam text, 'mass of darkness.'

[5] Tel. ed. and Srirangam text, 'the voices of knaves.'

[6] Tel. ed. and Srirangam text, 'sound of the humming.'

[7] Tel. ed. and Srirangam text, 'stupefied with the intoxication of tasting.'

[8] Tel. ed., 'drops fallen unceasingly'; Srirangam text, 'drops falling unceasingly.'

[9] Tel. ed. and Srirangam text, 'best beloved.'

[10] Tel. ed. and Srirangam text add 'when they (the fair women) shone with bud-like feet.'

[11] Tel. ed., 'particles of the mist of perspiration'; Srirangam text, 'particles of perspiration.'

[12] Tel. ed. and Srirangam text, '*mādhavī*.'

intense passion in the waning night; [50] when damsels were tuneful[1] with the jingle of the bracelets on their tremulous, slender arms while they illumined their apartments by the light of the rays[2] of their milk-white teeth, revealed through their sobbing at the pain caused by the loosening of the hair which adhered to the fresh[3] nail-marks[4]; [51] while their attendants, wearied with importunities for another glimpse, saw lovers constantly; while (the damsels themselves) felt bashful just for an instant at the endearing words of the house-parrots who had remembered[5] a hundred shameless speeches uttered in the night[6]; [52] when they (the damsels) had the beauty, as it were, of an autumnal day with <clouds not adorned by sky>,[7] for their <bosoms were adorned by the marks of nails>; when they seemed nigh unto death and had their faces set toward the <city of the Lord of Life>,[8] for their faces were set toward their <lovers' persons>; when they resembled a row of trees in a forest in the spring-tide abounding in <sap>, for they abounded in <anxiety>; when they were embraced by their lovers; when there blew a wind that rocked the filaments of the flowers and removed their pollen from the hair [53] of damsels wearing delightsomely tinkling jewels, whilst it had an abundance of expanded white lotuses, and caused pleasure, and rejoiced in union, and rained down a fire of chaff,[9] as it were, on lonely[10] girls lightly deserted by their lovers, and surrendered them wholly to the burning arrows of love, and carried far [54] the plaint of the Brahminy duck[11];

[1] Tel. ed. and Srirangam text, 'charming.'

[2] Tel. ed. and Srirangam text omit 'rays.'

[3] Tel. ed. and Srirangam text omit 'fresh.'

[4] See Schmidt, *Beiträge zur indischen Erotik*, pp. 478–496, Leipzig, 1902.

[5] Tel. ed., 'who made up speeches of love's shamelessness'; Srirangam text, 'who remembered speeches of love's shamelessness.'

[6] The same embarrassing habit of the parrot is mentioned by Amaru (see Böhtlingk, *Indische Sprüche*, 2 ed., No. 2710, St. Petersburg, 1870–1873).

[7] Their beauty was like the dark massed clouds.

[8] A euphemism for Yama, the God of Death.

[9] A fire of chaff being proverbially sudden and intense; Tel. ed. and Srirangam text, 'powder of a fire of chaff,' also omitting 'rained down.'

[10] Tel. ed., 'lonely, deserted.'

[11] According to the conventions of Sanskrit literature, two indiscreet lovers were transformed into Brahminy ducks (*Cascara rutila*, Pallas) and condemned to pass

then (Kandarpakētu) saw in a dream [1] a damsel [2] about eighteen years of age with her hips girt [3] round with the bond of a girdle [4] which was the gate [5] of the city of delight of her thighs; which was the golden rampart of the great treasure-house of the city of joy [6]; which was a trench for the line of the tendril of down [7];

each night separated by a river, from whose opposite banks they continually call to each other.

[1] Cf. Hall, Introd., pp. 30-31, note; and, for parallels in Sanskrit romances and dramas, as well as in *The Thousand Nights and One Night*, see Gray, 'Literary Studies on the Sanskrit Novel,' in *WZKM.* 18. 40-41, 50. For a more modern parallel, reference may be made to the Panjābī legends of Princess Adhik Anūp Daī, daughter of Rāja Sirkaṭ (a hero of the Rāja Rasālū cycle), and of Jalālī, the blacksmith's daughter (Temple, *Legends of the Panjāb*, 1. 233; 2. 168-169, Bombay, 1884-1900). The same motif is found in early European romances, as in the *Artus de la Bretagne* and *Palmerin de Oliva* (Dunlop, *History of Prose Fiction*, 1. 258-259, 380, London, 1896). See also, for other instances of dreams toward morning, *Harṣacarita*, pp. 136-138, 166, 207, Bombay ed., 1892 (tr. Cowell and Thomas, pp. 105-106, 132-133, 177, London, 1897); *Kādambarī*, pp. 135-136, Bombay ed., 1890 (tr. Ridding, p. 57, London, 1896); *Bṛhatkathāślōkasaṃgraha*, 2. 43 (ed. and tr. Lacôte, Paris, 1908); Natesa Sastri, *Dravidian Nights*, p. 49, Madras, 1886; Frere, *Old Deccan Days*, 2 ed., pp. 68-69, London, 1870. In India, as elsewhere in the East, dreams play an important rôle in divination, and the wide sphere of Sanskrit oneiromancy has been admirably discussed by Julius von Negelein (*Der Traumschlüssel des Jagaddēva*, Giessen, 1912), on the basis of a critical edition and translation of Jagaddēva's *Svapnacintāmaṇi*. It seems generally agreed that dreams toward morning come true (cf. the texts cited by Hall, *loc. cit.*). According to the *Kathāsaritsāgara*, 46. 150, 'the slow or speedy fruitage of it [a dream] depends on the difference of time [when it is beheld]; but this dream, being seen at the end of the night, will give a speedy fulfilment'; and it may be added that the Asura princess Uṣā, to whom Subandhu himself alludes (below, p. 61), first saw her future husband, Aniruddha, in a dream (*Kathāsaritsāgara*, 31. 11-32, tr. Tawney, 1. 276-277, Calcutta, 1880).

[2] This detailed description of the heroine, to which many parallels might be cited in Sanskrit literature, becomes of special interest when compared with the well-known representations of the female form in Indian art, in which the breasts and hips are of exaggerated development, while the waist is correspondingly slender. Vāsavadattā is to be classed, from Subandhu's description, as a *padminī*, having, among other characteristics, a moon-like face, eyes with reddish corners, dark, heavy hair, a line of down on the abdomen, and a slow gait; a *taruṇī*, as being between sixteen and thirty, and a *dēvasattvā*, as being noble in conduct and wealthy (Schmidt, *Beiträge zur indischen Erotik*, pp. 220-224, 243-253, Leipzig, 1902). For similar, but far briefer, descriptions of Oriental beauties, see, for example, Swynnerton, *Romantic Tales from the Panjāb*, pp. 391-392, London, 1903; *The Thousand Nights and One Night*, tr. Payne, 3. 111-112; 4. 295; 7. 147, 210; 8. 103-104, London, 1882-1884.

[3] Tel. ed. and Srirangam text, 'marked out.'

[4] Tel. ed., 'new girdle.'

[5] Tel. ed. and Srirangam text, 'garland of.'

[6] Tel. ed. and Srirangam text, 'the golden rampart of the abode of the treasure of her thighs, Love's great depository.'

[7] Tel. ed., 'zone of the trench for the multiform tendril of down'; Srirangam text also adds 'zone.'

which was a halo for the disc of the moon of her hips; which had a golden inscription consisting of a line of down that proclaimed victory over the triple world[1]; which was the line of the moat of the prison of the hearts of all men; [55] and was as the bar of the chamber of a flock of birds which were the glances of the world.[2]

(She was) adorned with a waist which seemed full of sorrow through failure to see her moon-like face that was hidden by the burden of her swelling breasts; which appeared to be filled with weariness from the oppression[3] of the urns of her bosom and the circlets of her heavy[4] hips; which had apparently conceived a deep resentment for her massy buttocks[5]; [56] which seemed filled with exhaustion from the restraining hand[6] of the Creator who had compressed it exceedingly; and which had become extremely slender, as if on account of its anxious thought: 'Suppose mine own breasts should fall on me like projections from a height'?

(She was) beautified by breasts with golden jewels filled with gems of passion[7]; with nipples for seals; apparently nailed with iron under the guise of nipples through fear of falling because of their vast circumference; [57] accumulations of loveliness, as it were, remaining after the consecration of all her members; the lotuses, so to say, of the pool of the heart; possessed of the beauty of a pillow for the cheek[8] of Love; the fruit of the tendril of the line of down; caskets full of the dust of the lure that

[1] Tel. ed., 'which had Love's golden inscription with a row of letters that proclaimed his victory over the wide triple world'; similarly the Srirangam text.

[2] She attracted and kept captive, like so many birds, the glances of every one. Tel. ed., 'as the golden bar of the chamber of the abode of her thighs for birds which were the glances of the whole world'; Srirangam text, 'as the golden bar of the chamber of the abode of birds which were the glances of the whole world.'

[3] Tel. ed. and Srirangam text, 'the confined oppression on both sides from.'

[4] Tel. ed. and Srirangam text, 'very heavy.'

[5] Because her waist shrank away from them.

[6] Srirangam text, 'as if with pain produced by the seizure of the hand.'

[7] Tel. ed. and Srirangam text, 'golden caskets filled with gems of passion.'

[8] Tel. ed., 'a box of the unguent of Love'; Srirangam text, 'a pillow for the disport of Love.'

increases the pride of passion[1]; heavy with the fall of the hearts of all mankind; the fruits of the mighty tree of existence; the product of the great tree of youth; two Brahminy ducks, charming with necklaces of pearl for lotus-filaments[2]; [58] fruits of the tree of Prayāga, which seemed to stand at the juncture of the line of down with her necklace of pearl[3]; the solitary dwelling[4] of the God of Love when overcome by weariness from the conquest of the triple world.

(She was) beauteous with a bud-like lower lip which had the glow of eventide in close proximity[5] to her moon-like face; which had what seemed to be a minium seal as a guard for the jewels of her teeth; [59] which was coloured, as it were, by the flushing redness of her heart[6]; which was, so to say, a fresh bud[7] of the coral-tree from Passion's sea. (She was) adorned by a pair of eyes which were longer than a very tender screw-pine blossom; with languidly tremulous glances; giving rise to a suspicion that they were the windows of wanton Love abiding in the inner chamber of her heart; causing beatitude by their very passion; [60] with redness in their corners as if for anger at her ears, which hindered their further extension[8]; seeming to whiten all the world; making the sky seem filled with a forest of expanded lotuses; pouring forth, so to say, thousands of oceans of milk; seeming to surpass the loveliness of a garland of downy Nepal jasmine and blue lotus.[9]

(She was) beautified by a nose which was the column[10] of the

[1] Tel. ed., 'dust of the proud nature of passion'; Srirangam text, 'dust that increases the pride of passion.'

[2] Tel. ed. and Srirangam text, 'hidden through their greed of lotus-filaments (which were) pearl necklaces.'

[3] Tel. ed., 'the shores of Prayāga in the guise of the junction of the Ganges and the Jumna, (which were) her pearl necklace and line of down'; similarly the Srirangam text.

[4] Tel. ed., 'the solitary rest-house'; Srirangam text, 'the victory rest-house.'

[5] Tel. ed. and Srirangam text, 'continual close proximity.'

[6] Tel. ed., 'inward redness.'

[7] Tel. ed. and Srirangam text, 'a bit.'

[8] The eyes of an Indian beauty are conventionally supposed to extend to her ears.

[9] Tel. ed., 'surpassing a garland of blue lotuses clinging to downy Nepal jasmine-flowers.'

[10] Tel. ed., 'trunk.'

balance for the jewels of her teeth[1]; [61] the bridge betwixt the oceans of her eyes[2]; a wall, as it were, between two elephants mad with youthful passion. (She was) adorned with delicate brows which were clusters of bees about her blue-lotus eyes[3]; portals[4] of her face that formed the abode of Love; the shores[5] of Passion's sea; wantoning in youthful dancing. She possessed, as it were, the loveliness of the sky in the rainy season [62] with ‹clouds› swelling with beauty, for her ‹breasts› swelled with beauty.[6]

Like one[7] who has gained the cry of Victory she stood on the tip of a trembling ‹balance›,[8] for she had trembling ‹anklets›; she was like Suyōdhana's valour while his eyes rested on ‹Karṇa›, for her eyes extended to her ‹ears›; she seemed to have the sportiveness of the Dwarf[9] in exhibiting his ‹destruction of Bali›,[10] for she revealed her ‹furrowed folds›; she was like the station of the sun in Scorpio ‹after traversing Virgo and Libra›, for she ‹transcended comparison with other damsels›; [63] she rejoiced in ‹unblemished beauty› as Uṣā rejoiced at the sight of ‹Aniruddha›[11]; she had the ‹beauty of lovely eyes› as Śacī ‹delighted in gazing on Indra's pleasure groves›; she had, as it were, the sportful dancing of Śiva with his ‹quivering serpent›, for she had beautiful ‹eyes and ears›; she had lofty dark ‹nipples› as a forest[12] has lofty dark ‹bread-fruit trees›; [64] she was adorned with a

[1] Compare the Euphuistic passage in Ben Jonson's *Cynthia's Revels*, 5. 2: 'You that tell your mistress, her beauty is all composed of theft; her hair stole from Apollo's goldy-locks; her white and red, lilies and roses stolen out of paradise; her eyes two stars, plucked from the sky; her nose the gnomon of Love's dial, that tells you how the clock of your heart goes; and for her other parts, as you cannot reckon them, they are so many; so you cannot recount them, they are so manifest.'

[2] Tel. ed. and Srirangam text, 'the bridge, as it were, betwixt the ambrosial oceans of her eyes.'

[3] The bees being extremely fond of the lotus.

[4] Tel. ed. and Srirangam text, 'garlands of the portals.'

[5] Tel. ed. and Srirangam text, 'currents.'

[6] Tel. ed. and Srirangam text, '‹clouds swelling with rain›' and '‹breasts shining with pearl necklaces›.'

[7] Tel. ed., 'like a king.'

[8] This seems to be introduced merely for the sake of the pun on *tulākōṭi*.

[9] Viṣṇu.

[10] Cf. *Rāmāyaṇa*, 1. 29; *Bhāgavatapurāṇa*, 8. 21–23.

[11] Cf. *Harivaṃśa*, 173–186; *Kathāsaritsāgara*, 6. 31.

[12] Tel. ed. and Srirangam text, 'the Vindhya forest.'

<beautiful throat and with armlets> as the army of monkeys was adorned by <Sugrīva and Aṅgada>.

She seemed to be made of planets [1]: of the <Sun>, for she had a <shining> ornament; of the <Moon>, for she had a <beautiful> round face [2]; of <Mars>, for she had a <rosy> bud-like [3] lower lip; of <Mercury>, for she had a <lovely> appearance; of <Jupiter>, for she had <heavy> round hips; of <Venus>, for she had <wide-open> lotus eyes [4]; of <Saturn>, for she had <slow-moving> steps; of <Rāhu>, for she had <dark> heavy hair.[5]

She was a picture, as it were, on the wall of life [6]; [65] the place of assembly, so to say, of the loveliness of the triple world; apparently the perfect elixir for the Great Ascetic [7] in his youth [8]; seemingly the place of Passion's fancy; the repository, so it would seem, of delight; [66] the flag of conquest over the threefold earth,[9] as it were, of the God of the Dolphin Banner [10]; evidently the manifestation of intellect [11]; the conqueror, it would seem, of Passion [12]; a powder, so to say, to numb the senses [13]; a power, one would think, to bewilder Love; apparently the joyous abode of beauty; the sole sanctuary, as it were, of good fortune [14]; seemingly the place where loveliness had its origin [15]; [67] wellnigh a perfect seduction of the mind [16]; almost a blind [17] of the juggler

1 A similar thought is expressed by Bhartṛhari (Böhtlingk, *Indische Sprüche*, 2 ed., No. 2169, St. Petersburg, 1870–1873). In like fashion a girl is described as made of flowers in *Harṣacarita*, p. 38, Bombay ed., 1892 (tr. Cowell and Thomas, p. 263, London, 1897).

2 Tel. ed. and Srirangam text, 'for she had a smile of <white beauty>.'

3 Tel. ed. and Srirangam text omit 'bud-like.'

4 Tel. ed. and Srirangam text insert, transferring this further down, 'of <Venus>, for she had a <white> pearl necklace.'

5 Tel. ed. and Srirangam text omit.

6 Tel. ed. and Srirangam text, 'like a picture on the life-wall of the theatre of the triple world.'

7 Śiva.

8 Tel. ed., 'the perfect elixir of youth.'

9 Tel. ed. and Srirangam text omit 'over the threefold earth.'

10 Kāma.

11 Tel. ed. and Srirangam text omit.

12 Tel. ed. and Srirangam text, 'the battle-ground, as it were, of Love.'

13 Tel. ed., 'the confusion, so to say, of all the senses.'

14 Tel. ed., 'good fortune's birth-hall, as it were, of friends' disport.'

15 Tel. ed. and Srirangam text, 'rendezvous.'

16 Tel. ed. and Srirangam text, 'wellnigh a perfect spell for the winning of love' (Srirangam text, 'mind').

17 Tel. ed. and Srirangam text, 'almost a mighty drug to bind the eyes.'

Love; a production of the Creator, so to say, for the enchantment of the triple world.

Then, while he drank her in, as it were, with eyes dilated with joy, sleep, which he had long served, became jealous[1] and deserted him. [68] But when he awoke, he was unable to sustain himself, being drowned, so to speak, in a sea of poison, and as if submerged in the words of his enemies. Thus then, for an instant, he embraced the sky, and with outstretched arms[2] cried to his beloved, as if she were painted in the heavens,[3] graven on his eye, and carven on his heart: 'O, dearest one, come! come! where dost thou go'[4]? Then in that very place he passed the day on his bed, with his eyes closed,[5] with all his attendants barred out, with the doors shut, [69] and refusing all enjoyment of food,[6] betel, and the like. Thus, too,[7] he spent the night as well with longings for the coming of the dream.

Then his confidential friend, named Makaranda, somehow gained entrance[8] and thus addressed Kandarpakētu, who was overwhelmed with the wounds of the arrows of Love: 'My friend, [70] why dost thou take to this unwonted course, which is unbecoming to a man of honour? When they behold this conduct of thine, the good are swayed by perplexity, while the wicked, on the other hand, make it out to be undesirable and indecorous[9]; for the heart of the evil man finds its highest delight centred in bringing to light what is undesirable. Who, pray, can discern the true character of such an one?

'Thus, even though a ‹Bhīma›, he is «no foe of Baka»,[10] for he

[1] In like manner life becomes jealous of Mahāśvētā because of her love for Puṇḍarīka in the *Kādambarī*, p. 325, Bombay ed., 1890 (tr. Ridding, p. 128, London, 1896).

[2] Tel. ed., 'stretching out his arms for an instant to the sky to embrace it'; Srirangam text, 'blindly stretching out his arms to the sky to embrace it.'

[3] Tel. ed. and Srirangam text, 'in the heavens and its subdivisions.'

[4] Tel. ed. and Srirangam text, 'O, dearest one, go not! go not'!

[5] Tel. ed. and Srirangam text, 'clinging to his couch.'

[6] Tel. ed. and Srirangam text omit 'food.'

[7] Tel. ed. and Srirangam text add 'somehow or other.'

[8] Tel. ed. and Srirangam text, 'gained entrance and a sight (of Kandarpakētu).'

[9] Tel. ed. and Srirangam text, 'pursue thy (Srirangam text, 'this') indecorous and undesirable course.'

[10] See *Mahābhārata*, I. 159–166.

is ‹horrible› and a «foe of them that praise him»; though a ‹fire›, he is a «wind», for he is a ‹devourer of his own place of refuge› and a «dog in his mother» [1]; [71] though very ‹pungent›, he is of «fine flavour», for he is very ‹cruel› and «utterly insipid»; he does not abandon his ‹bitterness›, though «flattered by clasped hands and prostration at his feet»,[2] even as mustard-oil abandons not its ‹sharpness›, though «caressed with both hands and held to the head»; he is ‹delightful on account of his freedom from faults› (at first), but afterwards is unpleasant and «cruel» even as the fruit of the palmyra-palm tastes ‹pleasant at first›, but is disagreeable and «sharp» at the last; he, when ‹deserted›, wrinkles his brow even as the dust of the feet, when ‹shaken off›, discolours the head.

'He ‹confirms his folly› in proportion as he is «humoured» even as the fruit of the poison-tree ‹strengthens madness› in proportion as it is «honoured»; [72] he has no lack of ‹enemies› with his «bad conduct» even as there is no dearth of ‹water› in «low ground»[3]; he brings distress to the ‹good› with his «great jealousy» even as a summer day brings distress to the ‹flowers› with its «swarms of gnats»; he is cunning in binding ‹sins› together and eager to «destroy the works of all men» even as the darkness is cunning in binding ‹night› together and eager for «sunset».

[73] 'Though ‹Śiva›, he is «Viṣṇu», for he is a ‹prince› of «unseemly conduct»[4]; he is ‹deaf› and «praises not his subjects» even as Indra's horse ‹cried aloud› and «exulted in his birth from the ocean»; he agitates the heart of a good man, even though he is ‹disturbed› and shows «affection», like as the churning-stick agitates the heart of the cream, even though it is ‹separated› and

[1] A false etymological pun on Mātariśvan, an obscure Vedic deity (on whom see Macdonell, *Vedic Mythology*, pp. 71–72, Strassburg, 1897; Hillebrandt, *Vedische Mythologie*, 2. 149–153, Breslau, 1899; and the authorities there cited). The name probably means 'having water as his mother' (Fay, *JAOS.* 16. clxxii–clxxiii), or, less plausibly, 'materiae puer' (Fay, *KZ.* 45. 134–135).

[2] Literally, 'sustained by the head (of his suppliant).'

[3] Tel. ed., 'he has no lack of ‹enemies› even as a dearth of ‹water› is not produced by a river in low ground.'

[4] Tel. ed. and Srirangam text, 'he has ‹unseemly conduct› even as Rudra has ‹abnormal eyes›; he is ‹deceitful› even as Viṣṇu ‹holds a disc›.'

shows «butter»[1]; [74] he is noisy with ‹self-praise› and «garrulous of his wanderings in the world» even as an offering to the Yakṣas is noisy with ‹crows› and «bears evidence of wandering dogs»[2]; his visage is distorted from ‹entire lack of self-control› and his «generosity» is suppressed even as a must elephant[3] fixes his distorted visage on ‹his female› and suppresses his «ichor»; he is ‹not alarmed by fear of God› even as a bull is ‹wearied from union with the cow›.

'He is ‹miserable through his disgrace of his family› and is devoted to «evil ways»[4] even as a paramour is ‹distressed by an error in his name› and is devoted to the «way of the fair»; [75] he causes slowness in ‹softly modulated and excellent› speech even as the disease of indigestion[5] causes slowness in ‹body› (and) speech; he is devoted to the ‹breaking of agreements› and a friend of the «foes of his lord» even as a jackal is devoted to the ‹flesh of a corpse› and delights in the «night»; [76] ‹the sight of him causes distress to his kindred› even as a corpse is ‹deprived of the use of its eyes›; he destroys ‹good fortune› even as the axe cuts the ‹sandal-wood›; he ‹destroys his family› and cuts down «men gifted with patience» even as the spade ‹cleaves the earth› and cuts down the «creatures that share in the soil»[6]; [77] he engages in ‹low actions› even as a dog engaged in ‹venereal acts› makes good folk ashamed; he, for all his ‹charms of hair and face›, has no pleasure in his «lute, skilful though he is» like as a must elephant ‹delights in the forest›, yet has no pleasure in the «spreading greensward, even though he traverses it».[7]

[1] Tel. ed., not expressing 'of a good man,' has 'shows continually.'

[2] Tel. ed. and Srirangam text, 'he ‹wanders about the world› even as an offering to the Yakṣas has ‹flocks of crows›,' etc.

[3] Tel. ed. and Srirangam text, 'as an elephant.'

[4] If *vāmādhvan* be synonymous with *vāmācāra*, this may be an allusion to the infamous 'left hand' Tantra-worship (Hopkins, *Religions of India*, pp. 490–492, Boston, 1895).

[5] See Jolly, *Medicin*, p. 77, Strassburg, 1901.

[6] Trees, according to the commentator Śivarāma.

[7] Tel. ed., 'he has no pleasure in his ‹goodly youth›' (*yavasam + san = saṃvayasam*); Srirangam text, 'he rejoices not in ‹his companions of equal age› even as the elephant ‹continually› rejoices not, . . .' (*yavasam + sa = savayasam*).

[78] 'The shoots of evil vices are born without seed and grow without a stock, and hard they are to uproot; if a particle of iniquity enters into the heart of the wicked, it is a terrible thing. But into the heart of the good it enters not; and if at any time it does enter, [79] it is like quicksilver, unstable for an instant; the virtuous, even as deer, are obedient to the voice of one[1] who knows their pleasure; persons like thee easily capture the heart of a friend[2] as do the wagtails of the autumn-tide; and the wise[3] give no unseemly counsel, while the friendship of the foolish is thrown on the side of profit. [80] And likewise,[4] when milk, fancying[5] that "water is as milk because of its sweetness, coolness, purity, and healing of distress," enters into friendship (with water), destruction is wrought by water itself, when it reflects that "ruin has come in times gone by through the decoction of me myself, increased by union with that (milk)."[6] This conduct is, therefore, extraordinary; follow the course, my friend,[7] which is customary among the upright; [81] the noble themselves go utterly astray by mistaking their direction.'[8]

When he (Makaranda) had said this,[9] and more to the same effect, Kandarpakētu, dominated by the wounds of many[10] arrows

[1] Tel. ed., 'take refuge with one'; Srirangam text, 'the virtuous are not, like deer, obedient to a petty pleasure.'

[2] Tel. ed., 'persons like thee take away pleasure, as do the wagtails'; Sriṛangam text, 'persons like thee obtain the weal of a host of friends.'

[3] Tel. ed., 'the friendly-minded.'

[4] Tel. ed. omits 'and likewise.'

[5] Tel. ed. and Srirangam text add 'from the identity of sound.'

[6] Tel. ed., 'by water, thinking that "ruin has come upon me aforetime in the decoction of milk, which had gained increase from union with myself"'; similarly the Srirangam text. The close union of mingled water and milk becomes, in Sanskrit literature, a type of the truest and most altruistic friendship (cf. Böhtlingk, *Indische Sprüche*, 2 ed., Nos. 2024, 2026, St. Petersburg, 1870–1873). The passage may, perhaps, be partially elucidated by a stanza from Bhartṛhari (*ib.* No. 2026), thus rendered by Tawney (*Two Centuries of Bhartrihari*, pp. 30–31, Calcutta, 1877):

'Milk to the water with it mixed its native virtues gave,
Which, pitying sore its tortured friend, rushed on a flaming grave;
The milk, unwilling to be left, must share its fellow's fate,—
True friendship envy cannot reach, nor fiery pains abate'!

[7] Tel. ed. and Srirangam text omit 'my friend.'

[8] Tel. ed. and Srirangam text, 'the good, though going astray by mistaking their direction, again regain the right path.'

[9] Tel. ed. and Srirangam text, 'his dear friend, Makaranda, having said,' etc.

[10] Tel. ed. and Srirangam text omit 'many.'

of Love, somehow said slowly: 'Good friend, my mind[1] is confused by a ⟨hundred afflictions⟩ as Diti was confused by ⟨Indra⟩.[2] This is no time for advice; my limbs seem to be on fire; [82] my faculties are boiling, so to speak; my vitals feel as if bursting[3]; my breath is almost leaving me; my senses are wellnigh eradicated; and my memory is destroyed.[4] Now, therefore, if thou didst share the sorrows and joys of our playing together in the dust,[5] then follow me.' So speaking he went forth from the city with him, unnoticed by his retinue.

Straightway, after going a distance of several hundred *nalvas*,[6] a great mountain,[7] called Vindhya, was seen with its thousand peaks bowed down to earth,[8] restrained by Agastya's word[9]; [83] with its sides[10] thronged with hundreds of savages eager to slaughter hundreds of female yaks who had been delighted by hearing the songs of pairs of Vidyādharas (then) slumbering peacefully[11] in the bowers within its caves; with its rocky sides cooled by breezes bearing the perfume of trickling yellow sandal-wood[12] broken and dragged down by the trunks of the elephants on its ridges[13]; [84] with the monkeys[14] eager to lick their paws wet with the sap of the palmyra-palm fruit which had been broken by its exceedingly long fall; with its borders fragrant with the

[1] Tel. ed. and Srirangam text, 'the mind of folk like us.'

[2] Cf. *Rāmāyaṇa*, 1. 46.

[3] Tel. ed. omits this clause.

[4] Tel. ed. and Srirangam text, 'is, as it were, destroyed.'

[5] Alluding to their childhood days as playmates. Tel. ed. and Srirangam text, 'Now this is enough of this talk. If thou didst share the joys and sorrows of our laying in the dust, then let it be come together with me.'

[6] A *nalva* is equivalent to 400 cubits. Tel. ed., 'then, having gone with him a journey measured by several hundred *nalvas*'; similarly the Srirangam text.

[7] Tel. ed. and Srirangam text omit 'great.' With this description of the Vindhya Cartellieri ('Subandhu and Bāṇa,' in *WZKM*. 1. 132) compares that given by the *Kādambarī*, pp. 38–43, Bombay ed., 1890 (tr. Ridding, pp. 16–18, London, 1896).

[8] Tel. ed. and Srirangam text, 'to the chasms of the earth.'

[9] Cf. *Mahābhārata*, 3. 103–104.

[10] Tel. ed. and Srirangam text, 'with its sloping sides thronged with hosts of savages eager to slaughter herds of female yaks.'

[11] Tel. ed. and Srirangam text omit 'peacefully,' the latter having 'awakened from sleep.'

[12] Tel. ed. and Srirangam text, 'sandal-wood sap.'

[13] Tel. ed. and Srirangam text, 'elephants come to its sloping ridges.'

[14] Tel. ed. and Srirangam text, 'with hosts of monkeys.'

perfume of the juice of various fruits sipped again and again[1] by pairs of *chickores* dwelling near its overhanging cascades; [85] seeming to sustain a host of stars clinging to its summit since its peak was speckled by pearls[2] fallen from the temples of must elephants which had been cloven by the edges of the sharp claws of thousands of bold lions.

The shadow of its foot was haunted by ‹bears, gayals, griffins, lions, and lotuses› as Sugrīva [86] had the shadow of his feet honoured by ‹Ṛkṣa,[3] Gavaya, Śarabha, Kēsari, and Kumuda›[4]: its ‹peace was disturbed by the exhalations of elephants› as the Lord of Cattle[5] has his ‹ashes disturbed by the hissing of his serpent›; it had a ‹chaplet of beautiful forests› as Janārdana[6] wears ‹beautiful sylvan garlands›; it had ‹*dita*-bark and *syandana*-trees› as the God of a Thousand Rays[7] has a ‹chariot with seven steeds›; [87] it was ‹full of caverns and infested with jackals› as Śiva had ‹Kartikēya near him and was attended by Pārvatī›; it was full of ‹jungles and wastes and was covered with white thorn-apples› as a paramour is filled with ‹petulance and passion for his mistress and is amorous›; it had ‹Arabian jasmine-plants and *Arjuna*-trees› as Śrīparvata has the ‹*Mallikārjuna*› near it; [88] it had ‹Italian panic and bind-weed› as Naravāhanadatta was the ‹husband of Priyaṅguśyāmā›[8]; it ‹formed a place for emblic myrobalan-trees› as a child is ‹held by its nurse›; it had a series of forests[9] rosy with the ‹reddish lustre of ruddle›[10] as the dawn of day makes the series of forests[9] rosy with the ‹radiance of the mountain-born Aruṇa›; it was impenetrable on account of ‹many creeping plants› as the dark lunar fortnight is impene-

[1] Tel. ed. omits ‘again and again.’

[2] Tel. ed. and Srirangam text, ‘massy pearls’

[3] Jāmbavat, the king of the bears.

[4] Tel. ed. and Srirangam text, ‘‹Kumuda and Panasa› . . . ‹lotuses and jack-trees›.’

[5] Śiva.

[6] Viṣṇu. Tel. ed., ‘it had a ‹chaplet of magnificent forests›, as Janārdana wears ‹full-blown sylvan garlands›.’

[7] Sūrya.

[8] See Lacôte, *Essai sur Guṇāḍhya et la Bṛhatkathā*, pp. 213, 228, Paris, 1908.

[9] Tel. ed. and Srirangam text, ‘leafy fore.

[10] Tel. ed. and Srirangam text omit ‘‹ruddle› . . . ‹mountain-born›.

trable on account of its ‹blackness›; it had gifts of a ‹hundred crores› as Karṇa had the gift of ‹Indra's bolt›; [89] it was covered with ‹tail feathers moulted by peacocks› as Bhīṣma was covered[1] with ‹crescent-headed arrows›; it was filled with ‹elephants and was fragrant from the perfume of its jungles› as the *Kāmasūtra* was written by ‹Mallanāga and contains the delight and enjoyment of mistresses›; it was a refuge for the race of ‹deer› as Hiraṇyakaśipu was a refuge for the race of ‹Śambara›.[2]

Because of the guise of its ruddle it seemed to have been employed by Aruṇa to trace the path of the chariot of the sun[3]; [90] it watched, as it were, the journey of Agastya with eyes dilated because the sun and moon had come upon its summit; on account of the old sloughs of snakes it seemed to have a mass of entrails hanging out[4]; as Kumbhakarṇa had a host of monkeys come within his ‹teeth›,[5] it had a host of monkeys come upon its ‹summit›; [91] it had bowers of screw-pines for the rendezvous of the assembled nymphs of Śacī's Lord who marked their pathway with a series of footprints dyed with red henna.

Though of ‹no family›, it was adorned by a «noble ancestry», for it did ‹not cling to the ground› and it was «adorned with beautiful bamboos»; though it was ‹evidently safe›, it yielded the «fruit of death», for it had ‹*hara*-nut trees› and yielded «plantains»; though ‹measured›, it was «measureless», for it had ‹plateaus› and was «immeasurable»; [92] though ‹noisy›, it was «silent», for it had a ‹river› and was «still»; though a ‹Bhīma›, it was a friend of «Kīcaka», for it was ‹terrible› and a friend of «reeds»; though it hid its ‹garments›, it had brilliant «raiment», for it hid the ‹sky› and had brilliant «sunbeams».

[93] It showed, moreover,[6] a ‹malady of many of its com-

[1] Tel. ed. and Srirangam text, 'had his body covered.' Cf. Hopkins. 'Position of the Ruling Caste in Ancient India,' in *JAOS.* 13. 278.

[2] Cf. *Viṣṇupurāṇa*, 1. 19; 5. 27.

[3] Tel. ed. and Srirangam text, 'the sun on high.'

[4] Tel. ed., 'tubular entrails hanging out of chasms cleft by thunderbolts'; similarly the Srirangam text.

[5] Cf. *Rāmāyaṇa*, 6. 67.

[6] Tel. ed. and Srirangam text, 'like a sick man.

ponents› as if by a «great abdominal swelling»,[1] for it indicated a ‹change of many metals› by its «thick bushes»; as a good man shows his ‹greatness› by «habits of mercy», it showed its ‹loftiness› by the «course of the planets on its summit».

As the Mīmāṃsā and Nyāya philosophies conceal the views of the ‹Digambara Jains›, it concealed the view of the ‹quarters of heaven and of the sky›. It also had its vicinage adorned with pools which were delightful on account of the appearance of the ‹blue lotus›,[2] as the *Harivaṃśa* is delightful on account of the appearance of ‹Puṣkara›; [94] that were thronged with ‹pairs of fishes and with crabs› as the Zodiac has ‹Pisces, Gemini, and Cancer›[3]; and that had hosts of ‹birds, elephants, galangal, and young medlar-trees› as the parts of the day have the host of ‹Śakuni, Nāga, Bhadra, and Vālava›.[4] It also showed manifold ‹metrical› charms with «*kusumavicitrās*, *vaṃśapatrapatitas*, *sukumāralalitās*, *puṣpitāgrās*, *śikhariṇīs*, *praharṣiṇīs*, and *latās*»,[5] since it showed manifold charms ‹produced› through its «creepers, lovely on account of their flowers, which had fallen on the bamboo leaves, tender in their grace, tipped with blossoms, crested, and charming».

[95] As if by a very dear mistress with outstretched wavy arms, it was embraced, furthermore, by the Rēvā, whose waters were perfumed by the abundance of the drops of liquid which had fallen from the fragments[6] of fullblown lotuses shaken by many monstrous tails of *bhāṅkūṭa*-fish[7] that had been terrified by the notes, indistinct for passion, of geese and herons; whose waters

[1] See Jolly, *Medicin*, pp. 79–80, Strassburg, 1901.

[2] Tel. ed. and Srirangam text, '‹the blue lotus and the *bedda*-nut tree›, as the *Harivaṃśa* is delightful on account of the appearance of ‹Viṣṇu›.'

[3] Tel. ed and Srirangam text, 'thronged with pairs of ‹fishes, dolphins, and crabs›, as the Zodiac has ‹Pisces, Capricorn, Cancer, and Gemini›.'

[4] See Ginzel, *Handbuch der mathematischen und technischen Chronologie*, 1. 359–361, Leipzig, 1906.

[5] See Weber, *Ueber die Metrik der Inder*, pp. 380, 394, 366, 361–362, 393, 384, Berlin, 1863; Colebrooke, *Miscellaneous Essays*, 2. 144, London, 1873. Srirangam text, like Hall's manuscript D and the commentator, adds 'like the *Chandōviciti*.'

[6] Tel. ed. and Srirangam text, 'fallen from masses of lotuses.'

[7] Tel. ed., 'by monstrous jaws of *utkuṭa*-fish'; similarly the Srirangam text, though the latter has '*bhākūṭa*-fish.'

had been drunk up by the circling navels of beauties of Pulinda kings at their evening ablutions[1]; [96] whose banks resounded with the din of flamingoes noisy with passion[2]; whose waters were curdled with drops of the streams of ichor exuded from the temple lobes of must elephants near its banks[3]; with the gardens on its shores witnesses to the trituration of the tremulous sport of pairs of young deities delightfully ensconced on the sand formed by the abundant dust fallen from the forests of screw-pines that grew along its banks; [97] in whose waters dove the nymphs who dwelt in bowers within bits of rose-apple that had fallen near the forests[4] on its banks; whose environs[5] were lauded by pairs of divinities drawn by curiosity at the sound of the sweet, low notes of the many gallinules that nestled in the creepers of chair-bottom cane growing on its shores[6]; [98] whose banks were strident with the screams[7] of multitudes of wild cocks whose nests thronged the bowers of reeds[8] that had sprung up near its shores; whose soft banks were trodden by the water nymphs[9]; whose tremulous[10] waves were rippled by the breezes from the gardens; [99] whose demi-carp were watched by female herons[11] which had entered the numerous bowers of reeds; whose reed-forests[12] were terrible from supporting paddy birds eager for the shoals of small fish; the water near whose bank was coloured by the shoals of exceedingly quick *rājilas* fleeing from

[1] Tel. ed., 'concealed in the circles of the deep navels of beauties of Pulinda kings bathing at eventide'; similarly the Srirangam text.

[2] This clause is omitted by Tel. ed.

[3] Tel. ed., 'abundance of drops . . . falling from the rounded frontal lobes of the huge must elephants standing near its banks'; Srirangam text, 'must elephants standing near the river-banks.'

[4] Tel. ed. and Srirangam text, 'lotuses fallen in the cavities on its banks.'

[5] Tel. ed. and Srirangam text, 'delightsomeness.'

[6] Tel. ed., 'sound of the abundant amorous sport of the gallinules that nestled in the forests of chair-bottom cane.'

[7] Srirangam text, 'made by.'

[8] Tel. ed., 'screams of wild cocks thronging the bowers of masses of reeds.'

[9] Tel. ed. and Srirangam text, 'whose very soft sands were trodden by water nymphs eager to enjoy the sunshine.'

[10] Tel. ed., 'very tremulous.'

[11] Tel. ed. and Srirangam text, 'evil female herons.'

[12] Tel. ed. and Srirangam text, 'the tendrils of whose reed-forests.'

the sight of the *uddaṇḍapālas* who moved within the circles of its rippling[1] waves; [100] whose shores[2] were dug up by hundreds[3] of barbarians whose greed for getting treasure had been aroused by the sight of the mating of pairs of wagtails.

[101] As if angry, it displayed a <distortion of its face>, for it displayed an <outlet and waves>; drunk, so to say, it had a <tottering gait>, for it had a <winding current>; it was the beauty of the dawn, as it were, that gives <time> increase, for it gave its <shores> increase; it was like unto the place of combat of the Bhāratas with <quivering corpses>, for it had <dancing waters>; it was, one might fancy, the rainy season with <peacocks appearing but serpents hidden>, for its <pools were hid by expanded lotuses>; [102] it seemed to be one who courts a <king> out of desire for gain,[4] for it courted the <mountain>. And also—

Even to-day it seems to call on him[5]
Who from a jar was born, while on its heights
Loud scream the elephants, with temples rent
By tawny lions' fearsome claws and keen.

Then said Makaranda:

[103] 'Behold this lion with his sinewy frame,
Now rising high behind and now before[6];
His curving tail along his archèd back,
His cavernous mouth, and white-tipped fangs agleam:
Yea, and his ears erect,[7] the while he springs
Upon the lordly king of elephants.[8]

'And furthermore—

'His ears erect,[9] in sudden onslaught skilled
His mane astart, and jaws all hideous,[10]

[1] Tel. ed. and Srirangam text omit.

[2] Tel. ed. and Srirangam text, 'uneven shores.' [3] Tel. ed. omits 'hundreds.'

[4] Tel. ed., 'it seemed an amorous woman <courting a king>.'

[5] Agastya; cf. *Rāmāyaṇa*, 7. 57.

[6] Tel. ed. and Srirangam text interchange the order of the epithets.

[7] Tel. ed., 'neck erect.'

[8] The literal translation of this stanza is given above, Introduction, p. 26.

[9] Srirangam text, 'neck erect.' [10] Tel. ed. and Srirangam text, 'cavernous.'

His stiffened tail high-waving in the breeze—
No artist could portray this awful beast
[104] What time he croucheth on the mighty brow
Of some great elephant, shrill trumpeting
Adown the lonely dells of Vindhya's mount.'

Meanwhile, in the cool shade of a rose-apple tree [1] that seemed a paramour conspicuous on account of ‹aphrodisiacs›, since it was conspicuous on account of its ‹*mainas*›,[2] he (Kandarpakētu) rested, after having gone a few steps [3] along the Vindhya forest which abounded in ‹banyans› as a river in a low region abounds in ‹underbrush›; [105] which had ‹great reeds everywhere› as the battlefield [4] of the capture of Uttara's kine had ‹Bṛhannalā appear›; which produced an abundance of ‹camphor› as the entrance of a drum in a dry land produces an abundance of ‹water from the clouds› [5]; which had ‹sap inherent in many trees› as the nectarous converse of the wise has its ‹savour drunk by many a knave›; which continually held ‹plantain trees› as Nalakūbara's desire was to hold ‹Rambhā› continually; [106] which had its paths indicated by ‹*ghaṇṭāravā*-plants› as the course of a must elephant has his path indicated by the ‹sound of his bells›; which had ‹quickly growing *kadambas*› as the worship of the Holy Lord [6] has ‹many fruits growing near by›; which gave joy to hundreds of ‹reeds› as the wealth of Virāṭa gave joy to hundreds of ‹Kīcakas›.[7]

[107] Meanwhile, to the peak of the western mount climbed

[1] Tel. ed. and Srirangam text, 'in the shade under a rose-apple tree.'

[2] Tel. ed. and Srirangam text add, 'like Vikartana, who ‹loved Chāyā›, for it had ‹delightful shade›; like Viṣṇu, who possessed ‹Lakṣmī›, for it possessed ‹beauty›; as a king bent on invasion is adorned with ‹thronging vehicles›, it was adorned with ‹close-set leaves›; as the Veda is bedecked with many ‹schools›, it was bedecked with many ‹branches›; as a group of courtesans has ‹the love of many paramours›; it was ‹bright with many buds›.'

[3] Tel. ed., 'a journey of some length'; Srirangam text, 'a journey of some steps.'

[4] Tel. ed., 'as the land of the capture'; cf. *Mahābhārata*, 4. 36–69.

[5] Tel. ed. and Srirangam text, 'as the drum in the Kuru land brought a host of full mighty men' (i.e., the Kāuravas and Pāṇḍavas). The allusion seems to be to a rain charm.

[6] Śiva. Tel. ed., 'as the worship of the Holy Lord has ‹many fruits gone forth from afar›, it had ‹lofty-growing *kadambas*›.'

[7] Cf. *Mahābhārata*, 4. 14–22.

that very god whose garment is of rays, with his disc red as the eyes of a must buffalo[1] exhausted by heat. Then Makaranda, getting fruits and roots, brought an abundance[2] of pleasing food in some way or other, and himself ate the remainder of what had been enjoyed by Kandarpakētu. Thereupon, placing that most dear one on the tablet of his heart, looking on her as if limned by a pencil,[3] [108] Kandarpakētu, with unshaken resolution, slept on a couch of boughs prepared by Makaranda. Then, when but half a watch of the night[4] had elapsed, Kandarpakētu heard there, on the tip of the rose-apple tree, the chatter of a parrot and a *maina*[5] quarrelling one with the other, and he said to Makaranda: 'Good friend, let us now listen to the chit-chat of this pair'!

[109] Then the *maina*[6] said, in a voice tremulous with anger: 'Wretch! you have gone off courting some other *maina*! How else have you passed this night'? Hearing this,[7] the parrot said to her: 'My dear, an unprecedented story has been heard and witnessed by me[8]; for this reason there has been a loss of time.'

[1] Tel. ed. and Srirangam text, 'forest elephant.'

[2] Tel. ed. and Srirangam text omit 'abundance.'

[3] Tel. ed. and Srirangam text, 'looking on that most dear one as if limned by the pencil of fancy on the tablet of his heart.'

[4] Tel. ed. and Srirangam text, 'when but a watch of the night had elapsed,' also omitting 'there.'

[5] The association of the parrot and *maina* (here called *śārikā*) is a commonplace in both the ancient and the modern literature of India. In this association they convey weighty information in Swynnerton, *Rājā Rasālu*, pp. 105, 115–117, Calcutta, 1884 (where the *maina* is called *śārak*); Knowles, *Folk-Tales of Kashmir*, 2 ed., pp. 65–66, London, 1893 (where it is termed *hār*); Schiefner, *Tibetan Tales*, tr. Ralston, pp. 168–169, London, 1906; Steel and Temple, *Wide-Awake Stories*, p. 139, Bombay 1884; Ram Satya Mukharji, *Indian Folklore*, p. 60, Calcutta, 1904 (where the *maina* is called *sāri*). On talking birds in general in modern Indian folk-tales cf. Knowles, *op. cit.*, pp. 168–169, 198, 231, 434; Steel and Temple, *op. cit.*, pp. 176, 412; Temple, *Legends of the Panjāb*, I. 9–10, Bombay, 1884; Day, *Folk-Tales of Bengal*, pp. 41–42, 134–135, London, 1883; Frere, *Old Deccan Days*, 2 ed., pp. 74–75, London, 1870; Dracott, *Simla Village Tales*, p. 62, London, 1906; Natesa Sastri, *Dravidian Nights*, p. 275, Madras, 1886; O'Connor, *Folk-Tales from Tibet*, pp. 160, 166, London, 1906. On the basis of the belief see MacCulloch, *Childhood of Fiction*, pp. 38, 247, London, 1905.

[6] Tel. ed. and Srirangam text, 'a *maina* in the rose-apple bower, in a voice tremulous with anger, said to a parrot that had come after a long time.'

[7] Tel. ed. and Srirangam text insert 'then.'

[8] Tel. ed. and Srirangam text, 'dismiss your wrath! An unprecedented great story has been witnessed by me.'

Then, being urged[1] by the *maina*, whose curiosity had been aroused, he began to recount the tale.

[110] 'There is a city named Kusumapura,[2] adorned with whitewashed houses[3] that have ‹statues› as the introductions[4] to the *Bṛhatkathā* have ‹heroines›[5]; where ‹children play› even as the ‹*māṇavakakrīḍas*›[6] have metres; that have ‹turrets› as herds of elephants have ‹must beasts›; that have ‹windows› as Sugrīva's army had ‹Gavākṣa›; that are situated in ‹pleasant places› as Bali's abodes are situated in the ‹Sutala-hell›; [111] that is filled with a population which is ‹Kubēra› yet «Varuṇa», for it is ‹generous› and «wise»; which is a ‹goatherd› yet a «deer», for it ‹holds fast to passion› and is «delightful»[7]; which is ‹Priyaṃvada› yet «Puṣpakētu», for it ‹speaks kindly› and is «bedecked with flowers»; which is ‹Bharata› yet «Śatrughna», for it ‹delights in astronomy› and «slays its foes»[8]; [112] which ‹makes the lunar day its highest object› yet «gives no heed to the lunar day», for it is ‹devoted to lovers› and «gives full heed

[1] Tel. ed. and Srirangam text, 'repeatedly pressed.'

[2] With this description of Kusumapura Cartellieri ('Subandhu and Bāṇa,' in *WZKM*. 1. 132) compares that of Ujjayinī in *Kādambarī*, pp. 102–111, Bombay ed., 1890 (tr. Ridding, pp. 210–214, London, 1896). Kusumapura is, of course, synonymous with Pāṭaliputra, the Palibothra of the classics, and the modern Patna (cf. Lassen, *Indische Alterthumskunde*, 1, 2 ed., 167–169, Leipzig, 1867; Hall, Introd., pp. 35–36; M'Crindle, *Ancient India as described in Classical Literature*, p. 42, n. 3, Westminster, 1901).

[3] Tel. ed. and Srirangam text, 'radiant with houses ‹white with auspicious whitewash› as the peaks of Mount Mandara are ‹delightsome with renowned ambrosia›.'

[4] Tel. ed. and Srirangam text, 'sections.' Lacôte (*Essai sur Guṇāḍhya et la Bṛhatkathā*, pp. 220–225, Paris, 1908), adopting the *lambhāir* or *lambhakāir* of Hall's manuscripts D and F and the commentator Jagaddhara, translates 'conquests,' thus bringing the allusion of Subandhu into harmony with the divisions of the *Kathāsaritsāgara* and *Bṛhatkathāmañjarī* (for other interpretations see Speyer, 'Het zoogenaamde groote verhaal (de Bṛhatkathā) en de tijd zijner samenstelling,' in *Verslagen en mededeelingen der Koninklijk Akademie van Wetenschappen, Afdeeling Letterkunde*, 4. 9. 142; Von Mańkowski, *Der Auszug aus dem Pañcatantra in Kshemendras Brihatkathâmañjarî*, Introd., p. 10, Leipzig, 1892).

[5] Lacôte (*loc. cit.*) very plausibly translates *śālabhañjikā* by '*vidyādharīs*' (cf. Jagaddhara's gloss *ad loc.*, *śālabhañjikā vidyādharī*, '*śālabhañjikā* (is the same as) *vidyādharī*').

[6] See Weber, *Ueber die Metrik der Inder*, p. 367, Berlin, 1863.

[7] Tel. ed. and Srirangam text, 'which is ‹Kṛṣṇa› yet «Rāma», for it is ‹eloquent› and «delightful».'

[8] Srirangam text, 'yet «Lakṣmaṇa» . . . and «prosperous».'

to hospitality»; which is ‹unnumbered› yet «numbered», for it is ‹peaceable› and «learned»; which is ‹no arrow› yet an «arrow», for it ‹discloses secrets› and is «valiant»; which is ‹not degraded› yet is addicted to many «liquors», for it is ‹free from repentance› and addicted to many «sacrifices»; which is (Viṣṇu's) ‹disc› yet «no disc», for it is ‹beautiful› and «without guile»; which ‹exudes no ichor› yet is «Supratīka»,[1] for it ‹has no egotism› and is «goodly in figure»; [113] which is ‹no bird› yet is a «flamingo», for it is like ‹Viṣṇu's bird› and «pure»; which shows no ‹diminution of oil› yet is a «household lamp», for it shows no ‹ill consequences of affection› and «illumines its race»; which has no ‹knots› yet is a «bamboo-shoot», for it has no ‹deceit› and is a «scion of its race»; which increases its ‹lustre by justice› as a summer's day increases its ‹glow by Taurus›; which begins ‹asceticism› as the day at the end of Māgha begins ‹Phālguna›[2]; [114] which ‹has no planets› yet knows «Venus and Jupiter», for it is ‹free from theft› and knows «the essence of poetry».

'It is supplied with a population of courtesans who show the ‹marks of tooth-bites› as a day of the rainy season[3] shows ‹broken clouds›; who are adorned with ‹*pravālamaṇi*-bites› as the seashore is adorned with ‹coral and jewels›[4]; who are ‹expert in practising the *indrāṇī*›[5] as the host of Apsarasas are ‹cunning from their association with Indra's wife›; who have their appetites whetted by their ‹paramours› as a wild elephant[6] has his appetite whetted by the ‹young boughs›; [115] who are bred up ‹for strangers› as the koel is bred up ‹by another›; who

[1] The world-elephant of the northeast quarter.

[2] Māgha is the name of a lunar month corresponding to the latter part of January and the first part of February, and is followed by Phālguna. Tel. ed. and Srirangam text add, 'which goes in the path of the ‹good› as the wind goes in the path of the ‹planets›; which is the lord of ‹earth› as the sun is the lord of ‹rays›; which has ‹gold› as the Great Lord (Śiva) has the ‹moon›.'

[3] Tel. ed. and Srirangam text, 'as the autumn.'

[4] Tel. ed. and Srirangam text, 'who are adorned with ‹hair› as the seashore is adorned with ‹coral›.' See Schmidt, *Beiträge zur indischen Erotik*, pp. 502–503, Leipzig, 1902.

[5] See Schmidt, *op. cit.* pp. 530–531, 564, 570.

[6] Tel. ed. and Srirangam text, 'lordly elephant.

are rocked <by Kāma> as a bee is rocked <among the flowers>; who are skilled in drawing <paramours> as a leech is skilled in drawing <blood>; who are bent on <coition> as a sacrificial priest [1] is bent on <divinity>; who have <gay paramours> as the arm of the Great Dancer [2] has the <quivering serpent>; who <inflame the hearts of their gallants> as Garuḍa <causes anguish to the hearts of serpents>; [116] who are <superior to (other) courtesans> as the demon [3] Andha was <impaled on the trident>.

'There, too, dwells the revered Kātyāyanī herself, called Vētālā,[4] whose lotus feet are caressed by the garlands on the crests of gods and demons; [117] who is the forest fire of the great woods [5] of Śumbha and Niśumbha [6]; who is the adamantine cliff of the mountain of the great demon [7] Mahiṣa; whose lotus feet are bathed by the river [8] of Jahnu's daughter falling from the matted locks [9] of Him [10] who holds the Ganges subdued by love.[11]

'And in its environs flows the blessed Ganges, with a stream of fragrance from the lines of pollen of the flowers of the diadems of gods and demons [12]; [118] with a current of the tide of virtue [13] from the ascetic's water-jar of the Great Father [14]; a pure rope [15] for Sagara's hundreds [16] of sons, come [17] to earth, to ascend to the city of the gods [18]; with its waters perfumed by the dripping of the yellow sandal-wood trees [19] on the bank, (trees) shaken by being

[1] Tel. ed. and Srirangam text, 'as one who continually performs sacrifices.'

[2] Śiva. Tel. ed., 'who are <tight in the embrace of their lovers> as the forest of the arms of the Great Dancer has <the marks of the serpent he holds>.'

[3] Tel. ed. and Srirangam text omit 'demon.' For the allusion cf. *Harivaṃśa*, 143-144.

[4] Tel. ed. and Srirangam text, 'Caṇḍā.'

[5] Tel. ed. and Srirangam text add 'of the might of the great demons'; cf. *Mārkaṇḍēyapurāṇa*, 72-73.

[6] Cf. *Mārkaṇḍēyapurāṇa*, 85-90.

[7] Tel. ed. and Srirangam text, 'of the excellent mountain of the demon.'

[8] Ganges.

[9] Tel. ed. and Srirangam text, 'from the pinnacle of the matted locks.'

[10] Śiva.

[11] Tel. ed. and Srirangam text, 'subdued by the strife of love.'

[12] Tel. ed. and Srirangam text, 'pollen of diadem-flowers fallen in the bathing of gods and demons.'

[13] Srirangam text, 'proceeding from.'

[14] Brahmā.

[15] Srirangam text, 'a pure rope-ladder.'

[16] Tel. ed. omits 'hundreds.'

[17] Tel. ed. and Srirangam text, 'fallen.'

[18] Cf. *Mahābhārata*, 3. 106-109.

[19] Tel. ed. and Srirangam text, 'perfumed by the sap dripping from.'

rubbed by the frontal lobes [1] of Āirāvata; with its waves in commotion from their beating by the round hips of wanton Apsarasas; with its current pure because of the perfume of the forest of matted locks of the Seven Sages [2] come down to bathe; winding because of the very purification produced by its revolutions in the terrible cave of the matted locks [3] of Him [4] whose crest is the moon.

'As the earth is capable of the delight of touching the ‹trunk of Sārvabhāuma›, it is capable of the delight of touching the ‹hands of universal sovereigns›; as a pool in the autumn-tide has ‹white lotuses and (other varieties of) white lotuses› submerged [5] by the water but revealed by swarms of bees hovering about and intoxicated with [6] the perfume, so it has ‹Kumuda and Puṇḍarīka›; [119] as the *Chandōviciti* has the ‹*mālinī* (metre)› [7] it has the ‹Mālinī (river)› [8]; though it has its darkness destroyed, it is ‹full of darkness›, for it has the ‹Tamasā›; though it has [9] billows, it is ‹not difficult to cross on account of its billows›, for it is ‹impassable for the Avīci-hell›.

'This city is also adorned in one place and another with trees of pleasure gardens that produce [10] flowers multitudinous as the hosts of stars; [120] that prop up the clouds with shoots [11] made

[1] Tel. ed. and Srirangam text, 'cheek.'

[2] Tel. ed. and Srirangam text, 'forest of pure matted locks of the circle of the Seven Sages.'

[3] Tel. ed. and Srirangam text, 'winding even now as if in the purification produced by its revolution in the cave of the terrible matted locks.'

[4] Śiva.

[5] Tel. ed. and Srirangam text, 'deeply submerged.'

[6] Tel. ed. and Srirangam text omit 'and intoxicated with.'

[7] See Weber, *Ueber die Metrik der Inder*, p. 391, Berlin, 1863. South Indian manuscripts give the name *Chandōviciti* to the sixteenth book of the *Bhāratīyanāṭyaśāstra* (ed. Regnaud, 'La Métrique de Bharata,' in *Annales du Musée Guimet*, 2, Paris, 1881), and Krishnamachariar (Introd., pp. 35-36) likewise discards the old hypothesis that the *Chandōviciti* mentioned by Subandhu was the one written by Daṇḍin.

[8] Tel. ed. and Srirangam text add 'as the series of planets is adorned with ‹Saturn, the moon, and the sun›, it has the ‹Yamunā and flamingoes›; as the beauty of an autumnal day has ‹the sound of yawning Brahminy ducks and Viṣṇu awakened›, it has ‹blazing red lotuses and the eyes of expanded white lotuses›.'

[9] Tel. ed., 'is full of.'

[10] Tel. ed. and Srirangam text insert 'a multitude of flowers, as it were, of the *santānaka*-tree clinging to its pinnacles,' the *santānaka* being one of the five trees of Indra's heaven.

[11] Tel. ed. and Srirangam text, 'tips of shoots.'

uneven by the feeding of the horses of the chariot of the sun which are obedient when lashed by the whip in the hands[1] of Anūru; that show the beauty of an untimely evening by thousands of thick, soft, young shoots[2] produced by sprinkling with quantities of drops of ambrosia adhering to the feet of the gazelle in the moon; that are ‹refuges of joy most excellent› as Bharata's conduct was ‹ever a refuge to Rāma›; that sustain ‹cocoanut palms› as great heroes sustain the ‹wanton sport of women›; that extend wide the ‹*bedda*-nut trees› as raw youths let their ‹eyes› stray wide[3]; that have ‹lofty[4] iron-wood trees› as lions bent on cleaving the frontal lobes of must[5] elephants have ‹bristling manes›; that, though they have ‹omens of approaching death›, are «long-lived», for they indeed have ‹soap-berry trees› and «*saj*-trees»[6]; [121] it (the city) is filled with ‹many temples› as the belly of Aditi is filled with ‹hosts of many gods›; it is adorned with ‹great offerings› and abounds in «gallants» as Hell is adorned by ‹great Bali› and abounds in «serpents»; it is pure even through its ‹drinking haunts›, because of its ‹temples›; it is free from calamities even through its ‹serpents›, because of its ‹wealthy› inhabitants. Where also[7] dwells a king named Śṛṅgāraśēkhara, whose staff-like arms are marked with the impress[8] of the jewelled earrings of sleeping women exhausted by much[9] passion; whose lotus hands are fragrant with the perfume of the garlands of flowers in the hair of the goddess of fortune of his mighty adversaries; [122] who makes ‹the affairs of others prosper in many ways› like a far-famed field which yields ‹great store of grain›. He cleaves the ‹might (of the foe), is pure, rules

[1] Tel. ed. and Srirangam text omit 'hands.'

[2] Tel. ed. and Srirangam text, 'flower-shoots.'

[3] Tel. ed., 'have their faculties of politeness far away.' Tel. ed. and Srirangam text insert here, 'that are devoted to the ‹China rose› as ascetics are devoted to ‹muttered prayers›; that are adorned with ‹purging cassias› as those ornamented are adorned with ‹made garlands›.'

[4] Tel. ed. and Srirangam text, 'blooming.'

[5] Tel. ed. and Srirangam text omit 'must.'

[6] Tel. ed. and Srirangam text add 'though ‹provided with ascetics›, they are «dominated by passion», for they are ‹filled with *muni*-› and «*madana*-»trees.'

[7] Tel. ed. and Srirangam text, 'there.'

[8] Tel. ed., 'edges.'

[9] Tel. ed. and Srirangam text, 'vehemence.'

justly, is free from envy and full of forethought, continually active, a giver of wealth, and a cause of happiness›, being ‹Indra, Agni, Yama, Nirṛti, Varuṇa, Vāyu, Kubēra, and Śiva›; thus, though he has ‹eight forms›, he has «not eight forms», for he indeed has ‹eight qualities›[1] and his «form is indestructible»; as Arjuna had ‹Subhadrā› and «Bhīmasēna», he has ‹good fortune› and a «terrible army»; as[2] Kṛṣṇa had ‹Satyabhāmā› together with «Bala», he has ‹truth, glory, and fortune› together with an «army».

[123] 'One[3] doth ‹protect the gods›, yet ‹drinketh wine›;
The other[4] hath a pure and single heart:
One[3] had a ‹planet[5] for his council-lord›,
And still ‹was taken in iniquity›[6];
The other[4] loveth righteousness alone:
The hand of one[3] doth wield the ‹thunderbolt›,
Yet lusteth after wealth ‹ten millionfold›;
The other[4] giveth all, and by his side
Great Indra's self doth seem but worthless grass!

[124] 'In battle dread our king[4] doth draw his bow,
Launching his arrows at the hostile host;
Yea, dealeth doom unto his enemies
And winneth glory on the blood-dyed field.
On haste the foe, deeming his valour fled,
But swift their headless corpses strew the ground;
And ere our monarch stands amidst the fray,
Death doth abide within the foemen's ranks.[7]

[125] 'While this king, skilled in kingly conduct, the conductor of the world with its girdle of four seas,[8] rules the earth, there is loosing of a ‹bull› in sacrifice[9] to ancestors (but there is no loosing of ‹law›); there is ascent of ‹Virgo and Libra› by the moon

[1] The eight duties of the king are receiving, giving, sending, stopping, pronouncing, overseeing, condemning, and acquitting.
[2] Tel. ed. and Srirangam text transfer these characterisations to the previous sentence.
[3] Indra. [4] Sṛṅgāraśēkhara. [5] Bṛhaspati (Jupiter).
[6] That is, in adultery with Ahalyā, the wife of Bṛhaspati.
[7] Tel. ed. and Srirangam text, 'Unto their doom the foemen's ranks have passed.'
[8] Tel. ed. and Srirangam text, 'girdle of the four oceans.'
[9] Tel. ed. and Srirangam text, 'sacrifices.'

(but there is no ascent of the <balance by girls>) [1]; there is thought of <*śūla* and *vyāghāta*> in yōgas [2] (but there is no thought of <striking with the impaling stake>); there is cessation of <ichor> on elephants' cheeks (but there is no cessation of <generosity>) [3]; there is <employment> of the right and left hands in indicating direction [4] (but there is no <amputation> of right and left hands); there is a <separation of cream> in the case of curds (but there is no <piercing with arrows>); [126] there is a <series of connexions> in sound-composition (but there is no <binding in fetters>); there are <similes and paraleipses> among the adornments of poetry [5] (but there is no <reproach because of carelessness>); there is a <falling off of bits of targets> of arrows (but there is no <cessation in the joy of giving lacs>); there is <entire destruction of *kvips*> [6] (but there is no <destruction of all birds>); there is <closing of buds> in lotus-pools (but there is no <shrinkage of treasure> [7]); there is <loss of caste> among rascals, but there is no <lack of Malabar jasmines> in garlands of flowers [8]; there is cessation of <ichor> in aged elephants, but there is no cessation of <passion> among men; [127] there is <silver> in bracelets [9] and the like, but there is no <bad caste connexion> among fair women; there is <interruption of the *gāndhāra* mode> in the musical scale, but there is no <surrender of minium> among ladies in the city [10]; there is <absence of roughness>

[1] That is, it is not necessary for any maiden to undergo the ordeal by balance (cf. Jolly, *Recht und Sitte*, p. 145, Strassburg, 1896).

[2] 'Die Zeit, welche die Summe der Bewegung in Länge von Sonne und Mond beansprucht, um den Betrag der Ausdehnung eines Mondhauses, d. i. 13° 20′, zu erreichen, heisst ein yoga' (Ginzel, *Handbuch der mathematischen und technischen Chronologie*, I. 361, Leipzig, 1906). The *yōgas śūla* (106° 40′–120° 0′) and *vyāghāta* (160° 0′–173° 20′) correspond to the ninth and thirteenth lunar mansions respectively (*ib.* p. 362). Tel. ed., 'in parturitions there is thought of being struck with pangs'; Srirangam text, 'yōga-exercises.'

[3] Tel. ed. and Srirangam text omit.

[4] Tel. ed. and Srirangam text, 'indications of direction.'

[5] Tel. ed. omits 'of poetry.'

[6] On the grammatical term *kvip* see *Pāṇini*, 3. 2. 61, 76, 87, 177.

[7] Tel. ed. and Srirangam text add 'among the people.'

[8] Tel. ed., 'there is <lack of Malabar jasmines> in garlands, but there is no <loss of caste> in a wicked family'; Srirangam text, 'in families.'

[9] Tel. ed. and Srirangam text, 'earrings.'

[10] That is, none become widows. Tel. ed. and Srirangam text add 'there is knowledge of <intonation> in songs, but there is no knowledge of <fainting> among the people.

among attendants of low rank, but there is no ‹lack of raiment› among retainers[1]; there are ‹dark clouds› in the nights, but there are no ‹dirty robes› among men; [128] there are ‹quaver notes› in songs, but there are no ‹fickle affections› among gallants; there are ‹outpourings of manly vigour› in tremulous delightsomeness, but there is no ‹desertion of justice› among citizens; there are ‹breaks› in changing musical modes, but there is no ‹crookedness› in thoughts; there is lack of ‹limb› in the God of Love, but there is no lack of ‹allegiance› in a retainer; there is an approach of ‹Love› at the appearance of youth, but there is no approach of ‹Death› among subjects; there are ‹wounds by the teeth› in amorous delights, but there is no ‹slaughter of birds› among the people; there is a ‹binding of the girdle› in love's disports, but there is no ‹tying of the tongue› in assent to generosity; [129] there is ‹redness of the lower lip› among young girls, but there is no ‹base inclination› among subjects; there is ‹cutting› in the case of hair, but there is no ‹spinning›[2] among women; there is ‹swordship› of[3] swords, but there is no ‹cruelty› of men[4]; ‹death by the sword› is ordained of warriors,[5] but there is no ‹loss of taxes or children›.[6]

'And set above all the harem is the chief queen,[7] named Anaṅgavatī, who has a ‹host of delighted attendants› as the ichorous streak on the cheek[8] of the world-elephant has a ‹swarm of delighted bees›; [130] who is ‹tender› like Pārvatī ‹with the beautiful Kumāra›.[9] And in some way, by Heaven's will, there was born

[1] Tel. ed., 'there is lack of ‹toil› among attendants of low rank, but there is no lack of ‹silk› in undergarments.'

[2] Cf. Quintus Curtius, 5. 2. 19 'Non aliud magis in contumeliam Persarum feminae accipiunt quam admouere lanae manus.' Even the modern weaver castes of India rank only as 'clean Śūdras' (Bhattacharya, *Hindu Castes and Sects*, pp. 227–236, Calcutta, 1896).

[3] Tel. ed. and Srirangam text, 'in.' [4] Tel. ed. and Srirangam text, 'in minds.'

[5] Tel. ed. and Srirangam text, 'in battles.'

[6] Tel. ed. and Srirangam text add 'among subjects.'

[7] Tel. ed. and Srirangam text add 'of that king thus constituted.'

[8] Tel. ed. and Srirangam text omit 'on the cheek.'

[9] Tel. ed. and Srirangam text, 'who is ‹tender› and adorned with a «golden diadem» as Pārvatī has the ‹beautiful Kumāra› and is adorned with a «digit of the moon»; who is lovely with ‹fresh garlands› and has «her face adorned with a sectarial

to them, after they had reached middle age, a daughter named Vāsavadattā, with a form enchanting the triple world; ‹giving joy to the eyes of thousands› as Pulōman's daughter ‹delighted the God of a Thousand Eyes›.[1] Now, even though she has reached maturity, she, who ‹rejoices her family› as Rāvaṇa's arm ‹made the mountains quake›, has remained averse to marriage in her youth.[2]

[131] 'But once upon a time[3] came Spring, that causes fever in travellers[4] through the soft, low sound of the swarms of bees that settle on the masses of buds of the opening mango-trees; that carries to every quarter the noise of the koels, whose throats are fragrant from tasting the perfume of the flowers of the mango shaken by the gentle Malaya breeze; that makes all[5] the lake resound with the din of the *kalahaṃsas,* intoxicated and clinging to the clusters of expanded lotuses; [132] that wounds the hearts of the wives of absentees with the arrows of the southern breeze,[6] come into contact with quantities of falling drops of showers of sap[7] passing out through holes in the stems[8] of buds

mark» as a stretch of forest is lovely with ‹new Arabian jasmines› and has «groves of *ashoka*-trees»; who has ‹beautiful hair› and a «sweet voice» as the host of Apsarasas has ‹Sukēśī› and «Mañjughōṣā».'

[1] Tel. ed. and Srirangam text add 'with an ‹exquisite form› as the slopes of Mount Mēru have ‹beautiful gold›; with ‹glistening pupils› as an autumn night has ‹glittering stars›; beautified with a ‹row of perfect teeth› as an assembly of good men has a ‹group of faultless Brāhmans›; adorned with ‹garlanded, lovely tresses› as the good fortune of the Rākṣasa race was adorned with ‹Mālyavān and Sukēśa›.' The deity in question is Indra.

[2] Tel. ed. and Srirangam text add 'now, even though she has reached maturity, she has remained averse to marriage in her youth, which ‹rejoices her family› as the forest of Rāvaṇa's arms ‹made the mountains quake›; which is adorned with ‹love› as Mount Vindhya is adorned with ‹*madana*-trees›; which has innate ‹loveliness› as the ocean has innate ‹salinity›; which is beautified with ‹excellent adornments› as Indra's pleasure grove is adorned ‹continually with the *kalpa*-tree› (Srirangam text, 'which is delighted with ‹youths of excellent adornment› as Indra's pleasure grove is delighted ‹continually with the *kalpa*-tree›'); which is ‹charming› as the wind ‹carries off flowers›.'

[3] Tel. ed. and Srirangam text, 'then once upon a time.'

[4] Because the humming of the bees recalls to them the homes that they have been obliged to leave and fills them with the fever of love-longing.

[5] Tel. ed. omits 'all.'

[6] Tel. ed., 'by warding off love in the southern breeze, which has its origin in quantities of drops'; similarly the Srirangam text.

[7] Srirangam text, 'sweet sap.' [8] Tel. ed. and Srirangam text omit 'stems.

of trumpet-flowers cloven by the tips of the claws[1] of koels; that makes medlar-trees horripilate from sprinkling[2] with rum in mouthfuls[3] by amorous girls merry with wine; that has hundreds of *ushoka*-trees delighted by the slow[4] stroke of the tremulous lotus feet, beautiful with anklets, of wanton damsels enslaved by amorous delights[5]; that has countless hundreds[6] of travellers bewildered[7] with listening to festal songs[8] begun by knaves eager to hear songs full of obscenity sung everywhere[9]; [133] that has <red lotuses> as a rascal is <unpleasant to the good>; that has no <Malabar jasmine creepers> as one of low birth has no <origin>; that is honoured with hundreds of <yellowish-red *dhak*-trees> as Rāvaṇa was honoured by hundreds of <demons that had drunk of blood>; that has <sweet breezes> as a great lady-killer has <perfumes>; that has <thriving blue lotuses> as a good king makes the <circle of earth prosper>; [134] that has <full-grown cucumbers> as a realist[10] <increases hope of weal>; that has <overcome winter> as the poetic composition of good poets <possesses *tu*, *hi*, and *na*>[11]; that is <freed from continuous night> as a good man has <no connexion with the bad>; that <has blue lotuses, azure lotuses, and *sal*-trees> as a fisherman <catches *rājīva*-, *utpala*-, and *śāla*-fish>[12]; that dislikes[13] the <cranes of Maru>

[1] Tel. ed., 'hard beaks'; Srirangam text, 'hard nails and beaks.'

[2] Tel. ed., 'attention.'

[3] Tel. ed. and Srirangam text add 'from the lotus mouths.' According to the conventions of Sanskrit literature, the medlar (*Mimusops Elengi*, Willd.) blooms only when sprinkled with mouthfuls of wine from the lips of beautiful girls. In like manner, the *ushoka* (*Jonesia asoca*) blossoms only when touched by a fair girl's foot.

[4] Tel. ed. omits 'slow.'

[5] Tel. ed., 'ardour.'

[6] Tel. ed. and Srirangam text omit 'hundreds.'

[7] Tel. ed. and Srirangam text, 'delighting in.'

[8] Srirangam text, 'beat of festal songs.'

[9] Tel. ed. and Srirangam text, 'sung daily by buffoons full of obscenity.' The allusion is, of course, to the Holi-festival, held in early spring (see Crooke, *Popular Religion and Folk-Lore of Northern India*, 2. 313–322, Westminster, 1896).

[10] Srirangam text, 'as a city man.'

[11] Tel. ed., 'that has no <winter> attached as the poetry of good poets has no <*tu*, *hi*, and *na*> attached'; Srirangam text, 'that has <no fall of winter attached> as the poetry of good poets has <no particles *tu* and *hi* attached>.'

[12] Tel. ed., 'that has <multitudes of blue and azure lotuses> as a fisherman <catches nets of *rājīva*- and *utpala*-fish>.'

[13] Tel. ed., 'displeases.'

as flocks of birds[1] in a beautiful tank dislike[2] the <basil>; [135] that has the beauty of the <*indrāṇī*-plant> as Śakra delights in <Indrāṇī>[3]; that <surpasses the wormwood-tree> as a great hero[4] <subdues his foes>; that has the <beauty of globe-amaranths> as a knave has <unimpaired good fortune>.

[136] 'When spring-tide is far advanced on earth, who is not transformed,[5] since even an <emancipated ascetic beamed>, for the <mango with its creeper bloomed>? Like a <feather-guard>[6] the swarm of bees shone as a <protection>, nestling on the arrow-shaft of the fresh mango-buds[7] of Him whose arrows are flowers. Upon the Arabian jasmine-bud[8] that had come forth from its stem the sweetly[9] humming bee [137] seemed to sound the trumpet-call for Kāma's march[10] to victory over the threefold world. By its fresh shoots the *ushoka*, because of its longing to be touched by a maiden's ankleted foot,[11] red with the dye of new lac, seemed to have assumed that colour.[12] The medlar-tree shone as if, through sprinkling[13] with mouthfuls from amorous girls' lotus lips completely[14] filled with sweet wine, it had assumed its (the wine's) colour[15] in its own flowers. The *ushoka*-cluster, dotted by multitudes of bees that had fallen within it, inflamed the hearts[16] of travellers like the circlet of the half-extinguished pyre of the Mind-Born God. [138] Like a necklace of pearls and sapphires,[17] the beauty of the spring-tide was radiant with rows of blossoming Arabian jasmines and goodly swarms of bees.

[1] Tel. ed. omits 'of birds.' [2] Tel. ed., 'displease.'

[3] Tel. ed. and Srirangam text, 'that is <radiant with the *indrāṇī*-plant> as Śakra is <delightful to Indrāṇī>.'

[4] Tel. ed., 'as one of great wisdom.'

[5] Tel. ed., 'who would not be transformed'?

[6] Tel. ed., 'like the written series of the letters of a name,' without attempt at paronomasia; similarly the Srirangam text.

[7] Tel. ed., 'flowers.'

[8] Tel. ed. and Srirangam text, 'in the hollow of the expanded Arabian jasmines.'

[9] Tel. ed. omits 'sweetly.' [10] Tel. ed. omits 'march.'

[11] Tel. ed., 'a maiden's foot charming with the tinkling of an exquisite anklet.'

[12] Tel. ed., 'that very colour.'

[13] Tel. ed., 'contact.' [14] Tel. ed. omits 'completely.'

[15] Tel. ed. and Srirangam text, 'perfume.' [16] Tel. ed., 'minds.'

[17] Tel. ed. and Srirangam text, 'like a necklace with pearls and sapphires.'

The flower of the iron-wood tree was lovely as the wheel [1] of the God of Flowery Arrows for agitating the hearts of absentees. The trumpet-flower seemed to be the hook of the God of the Flowery Bow to catch the fish which are the hearts of the travellers.[2]

[139] 'The breeze of Malaya blew with odours of great sweetness from the perfumes commingled by being crushed by the braids on the sloping foreheads [3] of Lāṭa damsels, eager for abundance [4] of amorous play; bearing the fragrance of the perfume of saffron-dust on the urn-like bosoms [5] of fair Karṇāṭic beauties, versed in all amorous arts; making the sky re-echo with the sound of the very sweet [6] humming of swarms of bees, collected because of the fragrance inherent in the splendour [7] of the hair of beautiful, artfully expert damsels of Kuntala [8]; skilful in gathering perfumes for marks on lovely cheeks of Kērala girls, tremulous with the passion of young adolescence [9]; [140] cunning [10] to touch the round buttocks of large-buttocked Mālava *ingénues*,[11] versed in all the four-and-sixty arts; cooled by [12] abundant drops of perspiration from the burden of the firm and swelling breasts of Andhra dames, overcome by amorous exhaustion.[13]

[1] Tel. ed., 'round whetstone'; Srirangam text, 'round whetstone for the arrows.'

[2] Cf. the quatrain of Bhartṛhari (Böhtlingk, *Indische Sprüche*, 2 ed., No. 6237, St. Petersburg, 1870–1873) thus translated by Jackson (in *Cosmopolitan Magazine*, 26. 276):

'Angling in life's river,
Cupid drops his line;
On the hook he fastens
Some fair maiden fine.
Men—those silly fishes—
Quick dart up above;
Out he pulls and fries them
In the fire of love.'

[3] Tel. ed., 'perfume of flowers (Srirangam text, 'association of the perfume of medlar-flowers') in the massy braids of hair dishevelled on the sloping brows.'

[4] Tel. ed. omits 'abundance.'

[5] Tel. ed., 'masses of saffron-dust on the pairs of fair, urn-like bosoms.'

[6] Tel. ed. omits 'very sweet.'

[7] Srirangam text, 'swaying.'

[8] Tel. ed. and Srirangam text, 'on account of the delightful fragrance inherent in the tresses of western beauties filled with love-longing.'

[9] Tel. ed., 'lifted up by young adolescence.'

[10] Tel. ed., 'fortunate.'

[11] Tel. ed., 'talkative Mālava damsels.'

[12] Tel. ed., 'cool from.'

[13] On the erotic characteristics of women from the several districts of India see Schmidt, *Beiträge zur indischen Erotik*, pp. 315–338, Leipzig, 1902, and for the 'four-and-sixty arts' see *ib.* pp. 136–146.

'Meanwhile, being informed by Vāsavadattā's maids of honour of her intention [not to wed],[1] Śṛṅgāraśēkhara brought together, for his daughter's self-choice,[2] an assembly of the kings[3] that possess the entire earth. Then Vāsavadattā[4] ascended a dais noisy[5] with the loud murmur of swarms of bees drunken with the fragrance of the perfume[6] of burning aloes; [141] that was whitened by the radiance of the lustre of most vehement laughter[7]; that was thronged with a multitude of suitors skilled in many stories of ridicule of their rivals; [142] that was thronged with swarms of bees from the pleasure groves of the city, attracted by the fragrance of the burning incense[8]; that made the air re-echo with ‹delightful music› as Arjuna's battle made the air re-echo with ‹Nandighōṣa›.[9]

'And there stood[10] princes: some ‹conquered courtesans› as Kalāṅkura ‹had the adornments of his city conquered by the bird›[11]; [143] others were ‹blind, swart, and without teachers› as the Pāṇḍavas were ‹associated with Kṛṣṇa, Drāupadī, and their teachers›; others had ‹hopes of joy›[12] exceeding[13] full blown as

[1] Tel. ed. and Srirangam text, 'his daughter's intention.'

[2] On the 'self-choice' (*svayaṃvara*) of a husband, a special privilege of the warrior caste, see Schmidt, *op. cit.* pp. 649–654; Jolly, *Recht und Sitte*, pp. 50–51, Strassburg, 1896; Post, *Grundriss der ethnologischen Jurisprudenz*, I. 18–19, Oldenburg, 1894–1895; Schiefner, *Tibetan Tales*, tr. Ralston, pp. 282–284, London, 1906; Budhasvāmin, *Bṛhatkathāślōkasaṃgraha*, 5. 80–93; 20. 93–121 (ed. Lacôte, Paris, 1908); and, in modern folk-tales, Knowles, *Folk-Tales of Kashmir*, 2 ed., p. 494, London, 1893; Steel and Temple, *Wide-Awake Stories*, p. 430 (references to further literature), Bombay, 1884; Natesa Sastri, *Dravidian Nights*, pp. 29–31, 61–67, 143, Madras, 1886; Swynnerton, *Indian Nights' Entertainment*, pp. 160–161, 171, 289, London, 1892. The *svayaṃvara* also forms one of the main motifs of the entire *Kādambarī*.

[3] Tel. ed. and Srirangam text, 'princes.'

[4] Tel. ed. and Srirangam text, 'the exquisitely hipped Vāsavadattā.'

[5] Tel. ed., 'whose atmosphere resounded.'

[6] Tel. ed., 'perfume of the smoke.'

[7] Tel. ed., 'perfumed by the fragrance of the abundance of most vehement laughter.'

[8] Tel. ed. and Srirangam text, 'fragrance of the burning perfume materials of bdellium and the like.'

[9] Tel. ed. and Srirangam text add 'with gifts of ‹parched grain› as a monarch's audience-hall has gifts of ‹kings›; beautified with a ‹canopy› as a hermit's abode is beautified with ‹sacrifices›; adorned with ‹flowers› as Indra's heaven is adorned with ‹gods›.'

[10] Tel. ed. and Srirangam text, 'there, for an instant, stood.'

[11] Tel. ed. and Srirangam text, 'some ‹knew courtesans› as Kalāṅkura ‹seized the adornments of the city›.' The bird in question is Garuḍa.

[12] Tel. ed. and Srirangam text omit 'of joy.'

[13] Tel. ed. and Srirangam text omit 'exceeding.'

autumn days have ‹cucumbers›[1] exceeding[2] full blown; others desired the ‹very beautiful girl› as men eager to repel a foe[3] desire ‹their own army›; [144] some listened to ‹Holi-songs› as fowlers listen for ‹birds›; some were intent on the pursuit of ‹(mere) appearance› as hunters are intent on the pursuit of ‹wild beasts›; some destroyed the doctrines of ‹conventionality› as adherents of the teachings of Jāimini destroy the doctrines of the ‹Buddhists›; some showed (only) the ‹returns of the year› as wagtails reveal ‹gain for astrōlogers›; some uttered ‹rather doleful cries› as the borders of Sumēru are ‹made of gold›; [145] some were ‹dazzled at the sight of glorious folk› as pools of expanded[4] white lotuses are ‹closed at the sight of the sun›; [146] some trusted in the delusion[5] produced by the sight of the ‹beauty of the universe› as Duryōdhana trusted in the delusion[5] produced by the sight of ‹Kṛṣṇa›; some, though ‹haughty within themselves through the consciousness of their elephants›, had goodly «steeds», for they were indeed ‹powerful in their knowledge of self-defence› and had goodly «arms»; some, though desiring to ‹seize the hands (of their foes)›, thought «to give life», for indeed, desiring ‹to wed (Vāsavadattā)›, they thought «of a thing not easy to do»; [147] some, though ‹subdued›, were «stalwart», for they were indeed ‹dejected› and «motionless»; some had their ‹peace› taken away on account of their ignorance of the mysteries of their «senses» as the Pāṇḍava princes had their ‹lands› taken away on account of their ignorance of the mysteries of the «dice»; some were ‹Guṇāḍhyas›, authors of «*Bṛhatkathās*», for they were ‹rich in hunting-nets› (and) authors of «great stories»[6]; others were ‹winds› with «sweet breezes», for ‹they went in crooked ways› (and) «bore perfumes»[7];

[1] Tel. ed. and Srirangam text, 'quarters of the sky.'
[2] Tel. ed. and Srirangam text omit 'exceeding.'
[3] Tel. ed. and Srirangam text, 'eager for attack.'
[4] Tel. ed. and Srirangam text omit 'expanded.'
[5] Tel. ed. and Srirangam text, 'marvels of the delusion.'
[6] Tel. ed., 'some followed after ‹great stories› as Guṇāḍhyas follow after ‹*Bṛhatkathās*›'; similarly the Srirangam text.
[7] Tel. ed. and Srirangam text, 'others bore ‹perfumes› as winds bear ‹sweet breezes›.'

[148] some manifested hopes on account of ‹crows› as the troops of the Kurus manifested hopes on account of ‹Drōṇa›[1]; some were unable to bear the ‹glory of heroes› as white lotus groups are unable to bear the ‹rays of the sun›. And[2] having regarded them one by one, [149] the princess retired from the dais with loveless heart.

'Then in a dream[3] that very night she saw a youth adorned with an ‹armlet› as Vāli was adorned by ‹Aṅgada›; ‹with pearls about his neck› as the koel ‹has a sweet note›; skilful in attracting the ‹fair› as the golden gazelle was skilful in attracting ‹Rāma›; [150] rejoicing ‹the ears of his elders› by his nectarous words as Jayanta rejoiced ‹Indra›; ‹to whom gave he not joy› as Kṛṣṇa ‹gave no joy to Kaṃsa›?; with ‹swift-moving hands› as a great cloud has ‹glittering hail›[4]; the elemental root of the tree of beauty[5]; the hill of ascent for the jewel of passion[6]; the mountain of origin of streams of delightful stories[7]; the spring-tide month of the mango of dexterity; the mirror of the face of nobility[8]; [151] the elemental seed of the tendrils of knowledge; the chosen spouse of glory[9]; the rival house to Lakṣmī and Sarasvatī[10]; the original abode of proficiency in virtue; the

[1] Tel. ed., 'some showed ‹a knowledge of crows› as the troops of the Kurus showed ‹the teaching of Drōṇa›.'

[2] Tel. ed. and Srirangam text, 'and immediately.'

[3] Tel. ed. omits 'in a dream.' For instances in modern folk-tales of the heroine falling in love with the hero from a dream see Frere, *Old Deccan Days*, 2 ed., p. 119, London, 1870; Temple, *Legends of the Panjāb*, 2. 278–279; 3. 370–371, Bombay, 1884–1900; Swynnerton, *Indian Nights' Entertainment*, pp. 248–251, London, 1892 (where, as in the *Vāsavadattā*, both the hero and the heroine dream of each other).

[4] Tel. ed. adds 'with ‹great truthfulness and glory› as the ocean has ‹great beasts and the (Vāḍava) fire›; composed, as it were, of pure rivers—his hair the ‹Mālinī›, for it was ‹garlanded›; his nose the ‹Tuṅgabhadrā›, for it was ‹aquiline and graceful›; his lip the ‹Śōṇa›, for it was ‹red›; his voice the ‹Narmadā›, for it ‹gave pleasure›; his arm the ‹Gōdā›, for it ‹gave the earth›; and his fame the ‹Ganges›, for it ‹sustained the heavens›.' So also the Srirangam text, except for the omission of '‹with great truthfulness›' and '‹great beasts›.'

[5] Tel. ed. and Srirangam text, 'love.'

[6] Tel. ed. and Srirangam text, 'for the multitude of jewels of all the qualities.'

[7] Tel. ed. and Srirangam text, 'streams of stories of delightsome love.'

[8] Tel. ed., 'the mirror of beauty.'

[9] Tel. ed., 'Sarasvatī.'

[10] Tel. ed., 'glory and Lakṣmī.

treasury, as it were, of great loveliness[1]; with a form seductive[2] in the threefold world. And he is named Kandarpakētu, the son of a king named Cintāmaṇi. And even in sleep she heard his name and the like.[3]

'Straightway (she thought): "O Prajāpati! This I consider perfection in the creation of beauty! [152] He has been formed by the Lote-Born God,[4] who, with his mind eager to behold the loveliness of his own skill,[5] took the atoms of beauty inherent in the threefold world[6]! Otherwise, how is there possibly such perfect grace in him? In vain did Damayantī endure the hardship of dwelling in the forest[7] for Nala's sake. [153] Uselessly did Indumatī, even though a queen, become enamoured of Aja.[8] Fruitlessly Śakuntalā suffered the curse of Durvāsas for Duṣmanta's sake. To no purpose Madanamañjarī loved Naravāhanadatta.[9] [154] In vain was Rambhā, whose thighs surpassed the plantain,[10] enamoured of Nalakūbara. Fruitlessly did Dhūmōrṇā long for Yama among the thousands of Gandharvas, Gaṇas, and many gods[11] who came to her self-choice."[12]

[155] 'Thus meditating in many ways, as if she had ascended the midst of the fire of separation, as if she were swallowed up by the flame of the Vāḍava fire,[13] as if she were devoured by the awful fire of the flame of the Last Day,[14] as if she had entered

1 Tel. ed. and Srirangam text, 'the treasury of the wealth of great loveliness.'

2 Tel. ed. and Srirangam text, 'delightful.'

3 Tel. ed. and Srirangam text, 'even in sleep she heard his name and the like, that "he is Kandarpakētu, the son of a king named Cintāmaṇi."'

4 Tel. ed. and Srirangam text, 'formed by the Creator.'

5 Tel. ed. and Srirangam text, 'with his mind eager to behold his skill all at once.'

6 Tel. ed., 'beauty of the totality of the threefold world.'

7 Tel. ed., 'endure hardship in the forest.'

8 See *Raghuvaṃśa*, 6. 8.

9 This legend is apparently now lost.

10 See *Rāmāyaṇa* 7. 26. Tel. ed., 'who surpassed the plantain on the slopes of Mount Mēru by the massiness of her thighs.'

11 Tel. ed. and Srirangam text, 'among the hosts of gods.' The allusion is apparently based on *Rig-Veda* 10. 10.

12 Tel. ed. and Srirangam text add 'vainly Ṛddhi found Kubēra among the Gandharvas and Yakṣas. Fruitlessly the mind of Pulōman's daughter clave to the Lord of the Gods (Indra).'

13 Tel. ed. and Srirangam text, 'flame of the fire of love.'

14 Tel. ed. and Srirangam text, 'as if seized by the fire of Spring, as if devoured by the awful flame of the southern breeze.'

into the caverns of hell[1]; thinking of Kandarpakētu as if he were carven on her heart, which was emptied of all its faculties,[2] as if he were engraved there, inlaid, riveted, swallowed up, joined by strongest cement,[3] entered into the frame of her bones, within her vitals, flecked with her marrow's pith, enveloped in her breath, placed in her inmost soul, [156] liquefied in her sheltering[4] blood, distributed through her flesh; as if mad,[5] as if deaf, as if dumb, as if listless, as if abandoning all her faculties, as if swooning, as if blasted by a planet, as if surrounded by a series of the billows[6] of the sea of youth, as if enveloped by the bonds of love, as if pierced by Kāma's flowery arrows, as if reeling from the venom of the thought of love,[7] as if shaken[8] by the arrows of the contemplation of beauty, as if bereft of life by the winds of Malaya (she exclaimed): "Dear friend Anaṅgalēkhā, put thy lotus hand upon my heart! The pain of separation is hard to bear! Foolish Madanamañjarī, [157] sprinkle sandal water[9]! Simple Vasantasēnā, bind my heavy hair! Fickle Taraṅgavatī, scatter the screw-pines' pollen[10]! *Gauche* Madanamālinī, fan me with bits of *śāivala*[11]! Trivial Citralēkhā,[12] trace in a picture[13] the thief of my thoughts! Noble[14] Vilāsavatī, scatter an abundance of pearl-dust[15]! Passionate Rāgalēkhā, cover my bosom with a quantity of lotus leaves! Dear[16] Kāntimatī, gently[17] wipe away my tear-

[1] Tel. ed. and Srirangam text, 'into the house of the hell of madness.'

[2] Tel. ed., 'as if emptied of all her faculties; thinking of Kandarpakētu as if he were carven on her heart.'

[3] Tel. ed., 'adamant.'

[4] Tel. ed. and Srirangam text omit 'sheltering.'

[5] Tel. ed. and Srirangam text add 'as if blind.'

[6] Tel. ed. and Srirangam text, 'rolling billows.'

[7] Tel. ed. and Srirangam text, 'from the poisonous fluid of the thought of love.'

[8] Tel. ed. and Srirangam text, 'pierced.'

[9] Tel. ed. and Srirangam text, 'sprinkle my limbs with sandal water'!

[10] Tel. ed. and Srirangam text, 'scatter the screw-pines' pollen on my limbs'!

[11] Tel. ed., 'with a bunch of *śāivāla*': Srirangam text, 'make a bracelet with a bunch of *śāivāla*'!

[12] Tel. ed., 'Citrarēkhā.'

[13] Tel. ed. and Srirangam text, 'on a tablet.'

[14] Tel. ed. and Srirangam text, 'beautiful.'

[15] Tel. ed. and Srirangam text add 'on my limbs.'

[16] Tel. ed. and Srirangam text, 'most dear.'

[17] Tel. ed. and Srirangam text, 'very gently.'

drops[1]! [158] Come, good Sleep! Be kind to me! Alas! what is the use of my remaining faculties? Only too truly my other members were not made an eye by the Creator! Lord of the Flowery Weapons, this the supplication to thee: 'Attend thou upon a man of such a sort'[2]! [159] Breeze of Malaya, that teacheth to behold the woe[3] of love, blow as thou wilt; my life is gone"! Thus speaking in phrases manifold, she[4] swooned, together with her friends.

'Straightway, having her life revived by the exertions of her servants, now[5] upon the strand of the bank of a river[6] of exceeding cool camphor water, now on the shore of a stream of most chill sandal-wood water, now in the shade of trees[7] on the banks of pools covered with forests of lotuses,[8] [160] now in plantain groves whose leaves were swayed by the wind, now on couches of flowers,[9] now on beds of lotus-leaves,[10] with her body burned by the fierce separation-fire of the collection of the rays of the twelve suns arisen at the time of the world's destruction, excessively emaciated, and, as it were, lifeless[11] (she cried): "His lotus mouth with its lote-like lower lip overspread with a smile white as the lustre of the tremulous waves of the milk-ocean agitated by mighty, trembling Mandara[12]! [161] His pair of eyes enamoured of his <ears> as a company of Brāhmans is enamoured of <Holy Writ>! The beauty of his straight nose which is spread full[13] far abroad, as if eager to breathe the innate perfume of his fragrant mouth! His row of teeth lovely as a digit of the

[1] Tel. ed. adds 'Yūthikā, jasmine-adorned, agitate the damp winds with a fan of bits of plantain'!; Srirangam text, 'bits of reed.'

[2] Tel. ed. and Srirangam text, 'be thou obedient to one like me'!

[3] Tel. ed. and Srirangam text, 'great joy.'

[4] Tel. ed. and Srirangam text, 'Vāsavadattā.'

[5] Tel. ed. and Srirangam text add 'led by her attendants.'

[6] Tel. ed. and Srirangam text, 'on the bank of a river filled with.'

[7] Tel. ed. and Srirangam text, 'sandal-wood trees.'

[8] Tel. ed., 'with very red *dhak*-trees, lotuses, and *kadambas*'; similarly the Srirangam text.

[9] Tel. ed. and Srirangam text, 'shoots of flowers.'

[10] Tel. ed. and Srirangam text add 'now on rocks cooled by masses of camphor.'

[11] Tel. ed. adds 'devoid of strength.'

[12] Tel. ed., 'very greatly agitated.'

[13] Tel. ed. and Srirangam text omit 'full.'

moon freed from blemish and white as a mass of foamy milk[1]! His beauty never seen before, surpassing Kāma[2]! Those blessèd places and people, the pure letters of his name, [162] and the righteous things which have been adorned by him"[3]!

'Over and over thinking thus, as if he were painted on the quarters and sub-quarters[4] (of the sky), as if he were engraved on the cloud, as if he were reflected in her eye, she painted him in a picture as if he had been seen before, and kept gazing here and there.[5] Then her confidante, named Tamālikā, having regarded her together with her friends, was sent to observe the feelings of Kandarpakētu; [163] and she came with me and is standing right here beneath the tree.'[6]

So speaking, he (the parrot) ceased. Then Makaranda, rising joyfully, told Tamālikā of the affair; and she, courtesying, presented an epistle to Makaranda.[7] Then he[8] read it himself:

[164] 'E'en when her eyes behold her lover true,
A maiden wavereth 'twixt hope and fear;
But when she only dreameth of his troth,
Ah, then, what fond assurance can she have'[9]?

[1] Tel. ed., 'white as the foam of delicate nectar from a collection of the digits'; Srirangam text, 'beautiful as a collection of the digits.'

[2] Tel. ed., 'his beauty, surpassing Kāma in visible form'!

[3] Tel. ed. and Srirangam text, 'those blessed places, those pure people, the lucky letters of his name, the things adorned by him'!

[4] Srirangam text omits 'sub-quarters.'

[5] Tel. ed., 'she kept looking for him here and there as if he were painted on the sky, reflected in her eye, or seen before in a picture'; similarly the Srirangam text.

[6] Cf. Gray, 'Literary Studies on the Sanskrit Novel,' in *WZKM*. 18. 43–45, 48–49, for paintings of beloved objects; and for instances of love letters and confidantes as love messengers in modern Indian tales see Temple, *Legends of the Panjāb*, 1. 237; 2. 280–283, 295–297; 3. 372–375, Bombay, 1884–1900; Knowles, *Folk-Tales of Kashmir*, 2 ed., p. 68, London, 1893; Swynnerton, *Romantic Tales from the Panjāb*, p. 389, Westminster, 1903, and *Indian Nights' Entertainment*, pp. 171, 252, London, 1892. Cf. also Cimmino, *L'Uso delle didascalie nel dramma indiano*, pp. 35–36, Naples, 1912.

[7] Tel. ed. and Srirangam text, 'then Kandarpakētu, rising joyfully and calling Tamālikā, made known the state of affairs. She, courtesying, presented him an epistle.'

[8] Tel. ed., 'then Makaranda, taking it, read it himself'; Srirangam text, 'then Makaranda, taking and untying the epistle, read it himself.' For the confidant not only reading the heroine's love letter to the hero, but also writing one to her for him, see Swynnerton, *Indian Nights' Entertainment*, pp. 171, 252, London, 1892.

[9] The literal translation of this stanza is given above, Introduction, p. 26.

Hearing this, Kandarpakētu, being above all joy [1] as if plunged in the ocean of ambrosia, rising slowly [2] with both his arms outstretched, embraced Tamālikā. Then, asking her [3] the entire story of Vāsavadattā,—'What does she do? What does she say? How is she'? and the like—Kandarpakētu set forth, having passed the night there, and likewise the day.[4]

[165] Meanwhile even that Blessed One whose garland is rays had descended to the middle world as if to tell the [5] story. Then into the water of the western sea sank the jewel of day, having the form of the disc in the crest of the cock of day; moving slowly, as if because of the grief brought upon multitudes [6] of Brahminy ducks; charming with clusters of the flowers of the coral-tree [7]; possessed of the loveliness of the frontal lobes of Indra's elephant, splashed with red lead [8]; with a circlet like unto an earring of the jewel in the hood of the monstrous Vāsuki, undulating beneath the bond of the mass [9] of tangled locks of Śiva, shaken by the impetuous motion of his revel dance; [166] delightful as a mass [10] of succulent barley to a bulling cow at evening [11]; with the beauty of a ruddy [12] jewelled earring of a courtesan of the west [13]; formed like the rounded shoulder of the buffalo of day, cloven by the sword of blackness [14]; [167] the Black Ascetic's begging-bowl, as it were, filled with honey [15]; seeming to be the beauty of the clouds with clusters of unfading

[1] Tel. ed. and Srirangam text, 'deeming himself, as it were, above all joy.'

[2] Tel. ed. and Srirangam text, 'very slowly.'

[3] Srirangam text, 'and then, sitting with her, he asked her.'

[4] Tel. ed. and Srirangam text, 'Kandarpakētu, with her and his friend, set forth from that place, having passed the day exactly there.'

[5] Tel. ed. and Srirangam text, 'this.' [6] Tel. ed. and Srirangam text, 'hearts.'

[7] Tel. ed. and Srirangam text, 'coral-tree of the western mount.'

[8] Tel. ed. and Srirangam text, 'coloured with a line of red lead.'

[9] Tel. ed., 'in the hood of monstrous undulating Vāsuki, bound in the diadem of the mass'; similarly the Srirangam text.

[10] Srirangam text, 'dish.'

[11] Tel. ed., 'delightful as a moist line of lac to a woman at evening.'

[12] Tel. ed. omits 'ruddy.'

[13] Srirangam text, 'earring of Varuṇa's darling.'

[14] Is there here a covert allusion to the victory of Kālī (Durgā) over the demon Mahiṣa?

[15] Tel. ed. and Srirangam text, 'the skull, filled with sweet honey, of the Celestial Ascetic.'

flowers; like unto a cluster[1] from the *ushoka*-tree of heaven; the golden mirror, so to say, of a wanton of the west[2]; with the aspect of a branch of a coral-tree shaken by the motion of the tossing waves.

And[3] gradually, [168] when the trees had their tops melodious with the soft notes of multitudes of sparrows, free from quarrels with each other[4] and desirous of their nests after having rolled in the dust and flown up again; when the crows were eager for home; when the inner apartments[5] gave forth the fragrance of the incense of aloes burning constantly; when the old men were angered at interruptions[6] from the confused murmur of young folks eager to hear the poetic[7] tales begun by the sages seated on the banks of the Taṭinī, adorned with millet-grass; when the children longed for slumber, soothed with very light hands by old women[8] who told them stories[9] with tongues tremulous in the lullaby; [169] when the courtesans had assumed the insignia of passion; when the sages had entered upon their evening devotions, disgusted at hearing manifold obscene words[10] from harlots possessed by their paramours[11]; when the forest regions had the surfaces of the very soft sites of cow-stalls occupied by herds of

[1] Tel. ed. and Srirangam text, 'clusters of flowers.'

[2] Tel. ed. adds '‹going toward the west› and «red» as Bhadra was ‹addicted to brandy› and was «amorous»; abandoning ‹its rays› and «cloudy» as a foolish man abandons ‹his wealth› and is «dejected»; with red ‹rays› as a Buddhist mendicant has red ‹garments›; possessed of ‹understanding› as the sun was possessed of ‹Saṃjñā›'; so also the Srirangam text, except 'mighty Bhadra' for 'Bhadra' and 'poor man' for 'foolish man.'

[3] Tel. ed., 'then'; Srirangam text, 'and then.' This entire sentence is translated and compared with *Harṣacarita*, Jamnu ed., 1879, pp. 30, 2–36, 4 (tr. Cowell and Thomas, pp. 67–68, London, 1897), by Cartellieri, 'Subandhu and Bāṇa,' in *WZKM.* I. 118–124.

[4] Tel. ed. omits 'with each other.'

[5] Tel. ed., 'interstices in the lattices of the inner apartments.'

[6] Tel. ed., 'filled with anger at the sound of'; Srirangam text, 'desirous of the cessation of the sound of.'

[7] Tel. ed. and Srirangam text omit 'poetic.'

[8] Tel. ed., 'when the children, longing for slumber, were attended by old women who were pleased at being patted by very light hands'; similarly the Srirangam text.

[9] Tel. ed. and Srirangam text, 'many stories.'

[10] Srirangam text, 'had their ears disgusted by hundreds of obscene words.'

[11] Tel. ed., 'when fair women were disgusted . . .; when the sages had entered upon their evening devotions.'

antelopes slowly ruminating; when the thick woods[1] had nests filled with multitudes of sleepy crows[2]; [170] when the trees of the hermitages[3] had[4] families of monkeys without their monkey tricks[5]; when the flocks of owls that dwelt in huts within the hollows of aged trees were eager to set out; when the lamplight flashed forth[6] as if the tips[7] of the rays of the sun had burst into a flame, going forth to affright the darkness; when He[8] whose banner is a fish, who steals the mind of all the world,[9] and who hath a resonant bow, was unceasingly[10] raining a shower of arrows; [171] when the courtesans, lovely in their attire of passion's task[11] and devoted to bawdy talk, were arranging their adornment; when women had their hips resonant with girdle-zones[12] bound on by their attendants; [172] when the courtyards had people hurrying to go to the houses of many folk[13] who were continuing their narration of interrupted tales[14]; when the pleasure gardens[15] were inhabited by the cocks; when the peacocks had ascended their perches; when the householders had performed the duties of eventide; when the swarms of bees were reposing[16]

[1] Tel. ed. and Srirangam text, 'clumps of village trees.'
[2] Tel. ed. and Srirangam text, 'ravens awakening from sleep.'
[3] Srirangam text, 'trees in the gardens.'
[4] Tel. ed. and Srirangam text, 'were filled with.'
[5] Tel. ed. adds 'when the trees in the gardens had flocks of cranes devoid of their noisy cries.'
[6] Tel. ed. omits 'forth.'
[7] Tel. ed. and Srirangam text, 'branches.'
[8] Kāma.
[9] Tel. ed. and Srirangam text, 'all things living.'
[10] Tel. ed. and Srirangam text omit 'unceasingly.'
[11] Tel. ed., 'charming and lovely in passion's attire.'
[12] Tel. ed., 'girdle-adornments.'
[13] Tel. ed. and Srirangam text, 'houses of tellers of tales.'
[14] On the popularity of telling stories at night in India see Steel and Temple, *Wide-Awake Stories*, pp. vii, 2–3, Bombay, 1884; Swynnerton, *Rājā Rasālu*, p. 152, Calcutta, 1884; Day, *Folk-Tales of Bengal*, p. 176, London, 1883. According to some Oriental traditions (Rohde, *Griechischer Roman*, 2 ed., p. 593, Leipzig, 1900), telling stories at night was imported from Greece to India by Alexander the Great. But the custom prevails widely, being found, for instance, among the natives of Guiana (Im Thurn, *Among the Indians of Guiana*, p. 216, London, 1883), the North American Indians (Waitz, *Anthropologie der Naturvölker*, 3. 234–235, Leipzig, 1862), the Micronesians (*ib.* 5. 2. 81, Leipzig, 1870), the Africans (Nassau, *Fetichism in West Africa*, p. 330, London, 1904; Struyf, 'Aus dem Märchenschatz der Bakongo (Niederkongo),' in *Anthropos*, 3. 742), and in Europe generally (MacCulloch, *Childhood of Fiction*, p. 2, London, 1905). It should also be noted that the entire story of the parrot in the *Kādambarī* (pp. 101, 614–615, Bombay ed., 1890 (tr. Ridding, pp. 46, 203, London, 1896)) is told at night.
[15] Tel. ed. adds 'of the Kirātas'; Srirangam text, 'of Kirāta houses.'
[16] Tel. ed. and Srirangam text add 'in crooked beds.'

in huts within the hollows of lotus-buds, narrow because the tips of their filaments were bent up and down [1] in their contraction [2]; —then, with the thought: 'By this path the lordly shining (sun) must go'! the lordly twilight was seen, as if with raiment of all manner of cloth [3]; as if a continuous tessellated pavement of jewels made by Ocean [4]; [173] as if containing the blood of the buffalo of day, cloven by blackness [5]; as if a coral-creeper of the great ocean of the sky [6]; as if the red lotus of the pool of the heavens; as if the golden bridge [7] of the progress [8] of Kāma; as if the madder-hued, ruddy banner of the palace of the sky; with a yellow ‹sky› as at her self-choice Lakṣmī chose Him [9] of the yellow ‹robes›; devoted to the ‹stars› and with a red «atmosphere» as a female (Buddhist) ascetic is devoted to ‹Tārā› and wears red «garments».[10]

And straightway [11]—while the courtesans seemed to be pupils [12] of the twilight skilled in ‹arrangements of pleasure-giving (musical) modes›, for they were skilled in ‹amorous tricks of night› [13]; [174] while the sky seemed to be a street of shops devoid of ‹them that hold the balance›, for it was devoid of ‹the sustainers [14] of Libra›; while the lotuses had the folds of their buds tightly [15] closed; while bees [16] wandered here and there over

[1] Tel. ed., 'bent high up.' [2] Srirangam text, 'instantaneous contraction.'

[3] Tel. ed., 'with raiment of cloth on every side'; similarly the Srirangam text.

[4] Tel. ed. and Srirangam text, 'made by Ocean for the sun.'

[5] Tel. ed. and Srirangam text, 'cloven by the sword of blackness.' Is there here a covert allusion to the victory of Kālī (Durgā) over the demon Mahiṣa?

[6] Tel. ed. and Srirangam text, 'creeper of the western ocean.'

[7] Tel. ed. and Srirangam text, 'golden banner.'

[8] Tel. ed. and Srirangam text, 'chariot.' [9] Viṣṇu.

[10] Tel. ed. adds '‹reddened with buds› as a courtesan is ‹addicted to paramours›; with ‹liver-red clouds› as a beautiful woman has ‹her breasts copper-coloured with saffron›; with reddish ‹stars› as an ichneumon has reddish ‹eyes›'; so also the Srirangam text, except 'fair faced dame' for 'courtesan.'

[11] Tel. ed. and Srirangam text, 'then straightway.'

[12] Srirangam text omits 'pupils.'

[13] Tel. ed., 'when the courtesans were skilled, as it were, in nightly amours; when the flashing lamplights seemed to be pupils of the twilight'; with no attempt at paronomasia.

[14] The moon, etc., according to Śivarāma.

[15] Tel. ed. omits 'tightly.'

[16] Tel. ed. and Srirangam text, 'swarms of bees.'

the lotus-pool as representatives of the darkness[1]; [175] while the lotuses, love-lorn through separation from the sun, seemed to wail under the semblance of the cries[2] of distressed female ospreys[3]; while the early evening seemed an astrologer <pointing out the houses>, for it <revealed the constellations>—there spread darkness like the blackness of the column[4] of Śiva's throat; [176] with most goodly <stars> as the army of the demons had the most goodly <Tāraka>[5]; increasing the outcry of the <owls> as the combat of the Bhāratas increased the outcry of <Ulūka>[6]; dulling the glory of the <crows> as the prowess of Dhṛṣṭadyumna dulled the glory of <Drōṇa>; with <owls> moving about as Indra's pleasure garden had <Indra> moving about; <hiding all the quarters of the sky> as fire[7] <consumes all its fuel>; [177] resting its belly, as it were, on the mountain slopes with their very close fragments of stone[8]; with its eye, so to say, on peaks that were red with lustre[9] from the light of the eyes of sleeping lions[10]; seeming to have life through the fire-flies; apparently increased by the columns of smoke from oblations; made dense, as it were, by masses of aloes-wood smoke[11] in adorning the heavy tresses of amorous girls; [178] seeming to be illumined by spray from the stream of ichor from[12] elephants' temples blackened by swarms of bees clustering right closely together[13]; heaped, if one might say so, in the shadows of clumps[14] of dense *tamāla*-trees; apparently

[1] Tel. ed. and Srirangam text, 'repelled by the darkness.'

[2] Srirangam text, 'notes.'

[3] Tel. ed. and Srirangam text add 'while the lotuses, standing in water coloured by the reflected hue of twilight, seemed filled with fire through the pain of their hearts at the destruction of their spouses.'

[4] Tel. ed. and Srirangam text omit 'column.'

[5] Tel. ed. and Srirangam text, 'revealing the <stars> as the army of the demons revealed <Tāraka>.'

[6] Srirangam text, 'of Ulūka and Śakuni'; cf. *Mahābhārata*, 5. 161.

[7] Tel. ed. and Srirangam text, 'the flame of fire.'

[8] Tel. ed., 'rough with their very close stones.'

[9] Tel. ed. and Srirangam text, 'splendour of the lustre.'

[10] Tel. ed. and Srirangam text, 'lions awakened from sleep.'

[11] Tel. ed. omits 'aloes-wood' and 'heavy'; Srirangam text omits 'aloes-wood.'

[12] Srirangam text, 'dripping ichor fallen from.'

[13] Tel. ed., 'seeming to be illumined by very thick swarms of black bees; blackened, as it were, by the spray of dripping ichor fallen from elephants' temples.'

[14] Tel. ed. and Srirangam text, 'forest clusters.'

lurking in the hoods of serpents, swart as lampblack; the mantle, as it were, of a woman who keeps an assignation by night; the remedy, if it might so be termed, for the gray hair of an aged courtesan[1]; the offspring of life, one might say; the friend, as it were, of the iron age; [179] the comrade, in all seeming, of a rogue's heart[2]; ‹concealing› manifest objects as Buddhist doctrines ‹deny› manifest objects. It was darkness which seemed to delight in the enchanting round lobes of absolutely must elephants[3]; which apparently yielded fruit in forests of clusters of wide-spreading *tamāla*-trees with exceedingly close and numerous leaves[4]; which trembled, as it were, in the masses of very[5] heavy tresses of dearest sweethearts; which apparently was mingled with rays of sapphire gems[6]; [180] which was like the exceeding dense blackness in pits, on river-banks, and in forests[7]; which was proud, it would seem, of swarms of bees, manifestly cunning, huge, and evidently strong, drunkenly dancing on the boughs of the *conessi*-bark trees[8]; gleaming with the hoods of serpents, destructive[9] with very thick venom; broken[10] with menacing flashes from the teeth of tuskers, mad with their burden of ichor.[11]

[181] And at the time of the rising of the moon with its blackness of night, bowing low, as it were, with folded hands under the

[1] Tel. ed. and Srirangam text, 'courtesans.' [2] Tel. ed., 'rogues' hearts.'

[3] Tel. ed., 'in the lobes of must elephants'; Srirangam text, 'in the enchanting lobes of herds of must elephants.'

[4] Tel. ed., 'in swarms of bees, manifestly cunning, huge, and evidently strong, hidden in the calyxes of great expanded flowers on the boughs of many trees in the forests of clusters of wide-spreading *tamāla*-trees with exceedingly close and numerous leaves.'

[5] Tel. ed. omits 'very' and 'dearest'; Srirangam text omits 'very.'

[6] Tel. ed. and Srirangam text omit 'gems.'

[7] Tel. ed. and Srirangam text omit 'forests.'

[8] Tel. ed. omits this description; Srirangam text, 'swarms of bees, manifestly cunning, huge, and strong, with their feet hidden in the calyxes of great expanded flowers on the boughs of many trees.'

[9] Srirangam text, 'destructive to elephants.'

[10] Tel. ed., 'utterly broken.'

[11] Tel. ed., 'burden of ichor; with the ‹zone of earth› folded up as the commencement of sunrise has ‹blue lotuses› folded up; concealing ‹every fissure› as the high estate of the wicked conceals ‹all character›; bowing, as it were, with folded hands under the guise of closing blue lotuses to the night which had come'; similarly the Srirangam text.

guise of closing blue lotuses, immediately[1] the stars shone forth, scattered like drops of the stream of water of Jahnu's daughter wandering in the winding hollows of[2] the mass of matted locks of Śiva, shaken by the fury of his twilight dance; showers[3] of drops, one might say, shed from the trunks[4] of the herd of terrible must[5] world-elephants bowed with the burden of bearing[6] the earth, hard to sustain[7]; [182] masses of foam, as it were, poured out by the steeds[8] of day, weary of wandering in the far distant sky; giving rise to the suspicion that they might be a grove of white lotuses[9] in the great ocean of the heavens; like ciphers[10] because of the nullity of metempsychosis, scattered[11] in the sky as if on the ink-black skin rug of the Creator who reckoneth the sum total with a bit of the moon for chalk; parched grain, it would seem, sown by the hand of Rati, (the wife) of Him whose banner is a dolphin,[12] and who setteth forth to conquer[13] the threefold world; [183] like globules[14] on the pearly arrows of Him of the flowery bow[12]; masses[15] of foam, as it were, in the ocean of the sky; handfuls of cosmetic, so to say, prepared by Rati in the courts[16] of heaven; multitudes[17] of pearls, one might fancy, in the necklace of the Lakṣmī of the heavens; fragments of the bones of Kāma, in all seeming, scattered by the wind's impulse[18] from the circle of the pyre of the moon[19]; [184] like the semblance of

[1] Tel. ed. and Srirangam text, 'then immediately.'

[2] Tel. ed. and Srirangam text, 'wandering in her devious roamings in.'

[3] Tel. ed. and Srirangam text, 'wide-spread showers.'

[4] Tel. ed., 'cheeks.'

[5] Tel. ed. and Srirangam text omit 'must.'

[6] Tel. ed. and Srirangam text, 'bowed with bearing.'

[7] Tel. ed. and Srirangam text, 'hard to bear.'

[8] Tel. ed. and Srirangam text, 'broad masses of foam on the edges of the cavities of the mouths of the steeds.'

[9] Tel. ed. and Srirangam text, 'mass of white lotuses.'

[10] Literally 'points' (cf. the form of the null sign in the Bakhṣāli Manuscript). On the importance of this passage for the history of the Arabic (properly, Hindu) numerals see Bühler, *Indische Paläographie*, p. 78, Strassburg, 1896; cf. also Smith and Karpinski, *Hindu-Arabic Numerals*, pp. 51–54, New York, 1911.

[11] Tel. ed. and Srirangam text, 'painted.'

[12] Kāma.

[13] Tel. ed. and Srirangam text, 'in desire of conquest over.'

[14] Tel. ed. and Srirangam text, 'scattered globules.'

[15] Tel. ed., 'wide-spread masses.'

[16] Tel. ed., 'in the delimitation of.'

[17] Tel. ed., 'torn-off multitudes of pearls'; Srirangam text, 'old multitudes of pearls.'

[18] Tel. ed. and Srirangam text, 'entrance.'

[19] Tel. ed., 'from the circle of the pyre of Kāma, burnt by the Destroyer's (Siva's) fire'; similarly the Srirangam text.

parched grain [1] roasted in the pan [2] of the vast surface [3] of the sky, that was excessively heated by the evening breeze and smoky with the smoke [4] of rising dusk.

With them the sky shone as if turned to a leper.[5] Exceedingly distressed [6] was the pair of *cakravākas*, filled with a series of ‹deep [7] sighs› and skilled in the joining of «bills in delightful contact» as the diction of a good poet [8] is filled with a series of ‹long [9] chapters› and skilled in the joining of «delightful paronomasias and *vaktra* metres».[10] [185] Separated was the pair of Brahminy ducks, whose feet were variegated by swarms of bees delighted and intoxicated by the honey-drops that adhered from their course through the clusters [11] of lotuses, and who were parted by the incarnate curse [12] of darkness as if by the noose [13] of Death. [186] The pair of Brahminy ducks was parted like the heart of a lotus, distressed by separation from the sun. A swarm of bees was seen moving beside a lotus as if they were the messengers of the husband moon about to come. Under the guise of stars [14] the quarters of the sky made lamentation with great drops of tears,[15] as if in grief for the departed Lord of Day.[16] Under the guise of its series of new filaments the lotus burned within the heart of its bud like a fire of chaff [17] at separation from its shining love.

1 Tel. ed. and Srirangam text, 'parched grain bursted.'

2 Tel. ed., 'kitchen.'

3 Srirangam text omits 'vast surface.'

4 Tel. ed. omits 'with the smoke.'

5 According to a reading recorded by Śivarāma, 'with them the sky shone as if spotted.'

6 Srirangam text, 'then exceedingly distressed.'

7 Tel. ed., 'very deep.'

8 Tel. ed., 'good poetry.'

9 Tel. ed., 'very long.'

10 See Weber, *Ueber die Metrik der Inder*, p. 199, Berlin, 1863; Tel. ed., 'paronomasias, *vaktra* metres, and *cakras*' (the latter being a *carmen figuratum* in the form of a disc; cf. *Kāvyaprakāśa*, tr. Jhā, p. 197, Benares, 1898; *Vidagdhamukhamaṇḍana*, 3. 12–15, ed. Haeberlin in his *Kāvyasaṅgraha*, pp. 290–291, Calcutta, 1847).

11 Tel. ed. and Srirangam text omit 'clusters.'

12 Tel. ed. and Srirangam text, 'being parted as if by the curse.'

13 Yama, the god of death, is believed to draw the souls of the dying from their bodies by means of a noose or cord.

14 Tel. ed., 'under the guise of drops of water from the eyes of the stars'; similar the Srirangam text.

15 Tel. ed. and Srirangam text omit 'with great drops of tears.'

16 Tel. ed. and Srirangam text, 'the departed beloved of the Lord of Day.'

17 Tel. ed. and Srirangam text, 'the chaff fire of the flame of grief burned in the heart of the lotus.'

[187] Forthwith[1] black darkness spread like a mass of collyrium from the forest of the sky, reduced to ashes by the rays[2] of the sun; blotting out ‹the heavens and the sky› as the words of revelation blot out ‹the doctrines of the Digambara Jains›[3]; a molten *rājapaṭṭa* gem,[4] as it were; and as the surge of the ocean.[5] And[6] straightway the Lord of Night ascended with the ruddy disc of his arising; the ball[7] of the princess Night; the[8] golden mirror of Kāma; like to a cluster of young red coral-flowers on the eastern mount; round as drops of saffron on the foreheads of eastern damsels[9]; [188] like a golden earring of the beautiful sky; a mass of henna, as it were, dropped from the hands of tiring-maids of celestial brides; a golden jar, it would seem, in the stucco of the heavens; a golden[10] dish in motion, it might be termed, for the progress of the God of the Dolphin Banner, setting forth for the conquest[11] of the threefold world; stealing the beauty of the top of Kāma's golden quiver; possessed of the colour of the China roses that grow on the topmost peak of the eastern mount; a dish, as it were, filled with a ball of pellucid saffron belonging to a wanton of the night; [189] even as a single[12] jar-like breast, tawny with saffron, of a fair dame of the east[13]; ‹occupied by a gazelle› as the milk ocean[14] is ‹ruled by Viṣṇu›;

[1] Tel. ed. and Srirangam text, 'then.'

[2] Tel. ed. and Srirangam text, 'by the forest conflagration of the rays.'

[3] Tel. ed. and Srirangam text add 'though ‹Kṛṣṇa›, it concealed the distinctive characteristics of «Viṣṇu», for it was ‹black› and concealed the distinctive characteristics of «all forms».'

[4] An inferior sort of diamond.

[5] Tel. ed. and Srirangam text, 'as running streams of cloth of molten silver.'

[6] Tel. ed. and Srirangam text, 'then.'

[7] Tel. ed. and Srirangam text, 'like a patchwork garment.'

[8] Tel. ed. and Srirangam text, 'like the.'

[9] Tel. ed. and Srirangam text, 'round as sectarial marks of *bandhūka*-flowers fastened to the forehead as adornments of eastern damsels.'

[10] Tel. ed. and Srirangam text, 'auspicious.'

[11] Tel. ed., 'seeking to conquer.' Tel. ed. omits the two adjectives following; the Srirangam text omits the second only, having for the first 'like the mouth of Kāma's golden quiver.'

[12] Tel. ed. omits 'single.'

[13] Srirangam text adds 'a cage, so to say, for the pleasure birds of the female *Vidyādharas* that wander in the sky; the lute-gourd, wrapped in red cloth, one might fancy, of a pair of *kinnaras* resting on the summit of the eastern mount.'

[14] Tel. ed. and Srirangam text, 'Garuḍa.'

with distinctive marks› as Rāma was ‹attended by Lakṣmaṇa›[1]; the lord of the ‹stars› as Sugrīva was the lord of ‹Tārā›[2]; with a ‹red disc› as a good monarch has a ‹devoted circle (of attendants)›.[3]

Then[4] the glow brought close to night went to destruction as if entered into the heart of a loving woman; as if drunk by the cups of the ēyes[5] of female *chickores*[6]; [190] as if licked up by masses of red lotuses.

Straightway the Lord of Planets[7] ascended like a cake of butter[8] exhibited by the neatress Night; a mirror, it would seem, bearing the beautiful face of Him whose banner is of flowers[9]; the white umbrella, as it were, of Him whose banner is a dolphin; the round ivory hilt, it might be termed, of the great sword of night; the white chowry, one would fancy, of the mighty King of Passion; [191] like to the sandy shore[10] of a Yamunā of the night; the crystal linga, so to speak, of the Great Ascetic of the heavens; the egg of a black serpent, in all seeming; a shell, as it were of the great celestial sea[11]· a monument. one might call it, to Him whose banner is a dolphin and who was consumed by the Foe of Love[12]; like to the circle of the pyre, marked with charcoal in dark spots, of Him who was born of fancy; apparently a white lotus of the Ganges coursing in the heavens; a mass of

[1] See *Mahābhārata*, 3. 276.

[2] Tel. ed. and Srirangam text, 'with ‹reddened stars› as the Lord of the Monkeys had ‹Tārā's love›; dear to ‹Rōhiṇī (the fourth lunar mansion)› as a bull is dear to the ‹cow›.'

[3] Tel. ed., 'with a ‹red disc› and accompanied by «soft rays» as a good monarch has a ‹devoted circle (of attendants)› and is accompanied by «light taxes»'; similarly the Srirangam text.

[4] Tel. ed. and Srirangam text omit 'then.'

[5] Tel. ed. and Srirangam text, 'pairs of eyes.' According to the conventions of Sanskrit literature, the eyes of the *chickore* (*Caccabis chukor*, Gray) become red at the sight of poison. It is also supposed to live only on moonbeams (see below, p. 108).

[6] Tel. ed. and Srirangam text, 'female *cakravākas*.'

[7] Tel. ed. and Srirangam text, 'the blessed Lord of Stars, with his radiance destroyed.'

[8] Tel. ed. and Srirangam text, 'fresh butter.'

[9] Tel. ed., 'bearing the reflexion of a gazelle.'

[10] Tel. ed. and Srirangam text, 'new shore.'

[11] Srirangam text adds 'the crystalline water-pot, so to say, of the Ascetic of the sky.'

[12] Tel. ed., 'a monument, one might call it, marked with charcoal in dark spots, to Him who was born of fancy and was burnt by the fire from Śiva's eye.'

foam, as it were, of the mighty ocean of the sky; a quicksilver ball, one might imagine, of the dark metallurgist[1]; a silver jar, so to say, spangled with shoots of millet-grass[2]; [192] lovely as the wheel of Kāma's chariot[3]; the dove, it might be termed, of the palace of the heavens; even as the beauteous crest-jewel of the eastern mount[4]; like unto Āirāvata's frontal lobe when deprived of its minium[5]; resembling a fragment of the head of an old and broken-horned cow belonging to the field of heaven with its white wheat of stars; a silver vessel,[6] as it were, yellowish with balls of sandalwood, fallen from the hands of a divine maiden. [193] And it was the white lotus of the bees of the eyes[7]; like to[8] the sand bank bed of the geese[9] of the mind; the crystalline fan of the fires of separation; the round white whetstone of Kāma's arrows.

[194–195] Meanwhile there were equivocal and jealous[10] conversations, full of innuendoes and broken with emotion,[11] (delivered by the lips) of female messengers sent to sweethearts by hosts of women anxious for a rendezvous. [196] As for example[12]: 'Beware of evil women's wiles, beloved! Thou dost not truly know thyself! [Beware, destroyer of bliss! Truly thou knowest not that thou art made a wretched woman!]'; [197–198] 'Thou art a lover,[13] (even though) not one among them that draw and kiss (women and) make (them) run! [Thou utter rascal! Thou art

[1] Tel. ed., 'the celestial metallurgist.'

[2] Tel. ed. and Srirangam text add 'for the anointing of the Mind-Born God (Kāma).'

[3] Tel. ed. and Srirangam text, 'the white wheel, as it were, of Kāma's chariot.'

[4] Tel. ed. and Srirangam text, interchanging this adjective with the one preceding, 'even as the crest-jewel of the serpent-king of the eastern mount.'

[5] Tel. ed., 'laved in the river of heaven'; similarly the Srirangam text.

[6] Tel. ed. and Srirangam text, 'fan.'

[7] Tel. ed. and Srirangam text, 'the eyes of the world'

[8] Tel. ed. and Srirangam text omit 'like to.'

[9] Tel. ed. and Srirangam text, 'flamingoes.'

[10] Tel. ed. and Srirangam text omit 'jealous.'

[11] Tel. ed., 'displacements (of words).'

[12] The passage following is certainly the most difficult in the entire *Vāsavadattā*, and only the most probable of the many interpretations suggested by Śivarāma and Krishnamachariar have been adopted. The renderings here given do not attempt, therefore, to exhaust all the possibilities. The reproachful translation is placed in brackets.

[13] Ironical.

hard as a rock! Thou art magnetite, (even though) not one among loadstones, touchstones, (and) magnets!]'; [199] 'Thou art like a rower, devoted to other than the functions of his duty, drawing his sword in vain! [Thou that hast the reward of duty[1]! Thou art devoted to another (woman) and gifted with excessive speech to no purpose!]'; 'Distressedly, as it were, thou thinkest in thy mind of one[2] hard to win! [Good friend,[1] thou thinkest of one[2] hard to win[3] as if she were thine own wife!]'; [200] 'He goeth in the ways of truth who standeth[4] filled with delight at the swords of his foes! [He is insipid in his ways who standeth without initiative before his co-wives!]'; [201] 'He is a hero indeed who brings from the conflict the elephants of the foe! [He is filled with delight who brings the wife of a rival to old age through (amorous) struggle!]'; [202] 'Holding a massy, broad sword, and suddenly assailing the foe, he obtains great glory through the conflict! [Holding the thighs, hands, and hair (of his beloved), he obtains an excellent position with his body, uniting at the supreme moment!]'; [203] 'Set free from passion, thou art beautiful indeed, and friendly to mankind! [Thou passionate man, bereft of lordship! Thou art assuredly not lovely, and art deserted!]'; [204] 'Thou adornment of the earth! Bold[5] (is she), white like the autumn clouds, with a clear sense of her own greatness, able to ward off the jealousy of revellers,[6] with firmness and timidity in her mind, and world-wide truth in her speech! [Thou wise one,[1] thou utter destruction of the earth, not white like the autumn clouds, untransparent, selfish, jealous as a reveller! "Patient (am I), loving to think of the adornment of the world, (but) in his mind is cowardice, and world-wide falsehood in his speech"[7]!]'; [205–207] 'She, the receptacle of bliss, surpassing

[1] Ironical. [2] Tel. ed. and Srirangam text, 'a woman.'

[3] The wife of another.

[4] Tel. ed. and Srirangam text, 'he whose thoughts are on the ways of truth (or, on insipid ways) standeth.'

[5] Tel. ed., 'with her boldness vanished.'

[6] Tel. ed. and Srirangam text, 'able to defend the magnitude of her own evident thoughts of greatness.'

[7] The supposed address of the woman in love

Lakṣmī with her gentle smile,[1] (though herself) unsurpassed; yielding unto thee; with her heart spotless as a mirror; transcending the tendrils with her lotus hand; with coquetry in her sportful fingers[2]; peering perturbedly[3] through the interstices of the bars of her windows;—she suffereth distress at eventide,[4] being lonely without thee, her ram: for, O lord of life! who here depend not for life upon some happy man[5]? [Thou lord of violence! She, the receptacle of bliss, surpassing Lakṣmī with her gentle smile,[1] (though herself) unsurpassed; yielding unto thee; with her heart spotless as a mirror; transcending the tendrils with her lotus hand; with coquetry in her sportful fingers[2]; peering perturbedly[3] through the interstices of the bars of her windows;—she laugheth not, (but) suffereth distress at eventide,[4] being lonely without thee, her ram: for, O destroyer of life! who here depend not for life upon some happy man[5]?]'; [208] 'Let other women be! I suffer slavery before thee! Therefore be there love because of love! [Thou that art cast off by other (women)! Thou speechless one! Thou slave (even) in the presence of the base! I[6] go to her! Therefore let hatred arise from love!]'; [209] 'Straightway thou art mightily beloved; why dost thou not perform the lovely rites of love, especially since death standeth immediately near[7]? [Thou art straightway utterly devoid of love, why dost thou not perform the lovely rites of love, especially since death standeth immediately near[7]?]'; [210] 'Thou purifier of them that have the minds of false lovers! Thou glorious one! By love is she[8] to be won, great and noble,[9] with large eyes, with sidelong glances; then her attendants will show

[1] Tel. ed. and Srirangam text, 'she by whom the lotus-dwelling Lakṣmī is surpassed with smiling laughter.'

[2] Tel. ed. and Srirangam text, 'her fingers sportful, as it were. with coquetry.'

[3] Tel. ed. omits 'perturbedly.'

[4] Tel. ed. and Srirangam text, 'she suffereth distress (even) without (an ascetic's) curse, having her destruction prevented by her folk.'

[5] Tel. ed. and Srirangam text, 'on what happy man doth she not depend'?

[6] The messenger.

[7] Tel. ed. and Srirangam text, 'since stern death is immediately near.'

[8] Tel. ed. and Srirangam text, 'this unparalleled maid.'

[9] Tel. ed. and Srirangam text, 'accompanied by Lakṣmī.'

their slavery! [Thou false lover! Thou effacer of thoughts! Thou inglorious one! Alas, sir! By love is she[1] to be won, great and noble,[2] with large eyes, with sidelong glances; then her attendants will show their slavery!]'; 'By thee, who art like to a lotus, the fabulous riches of thy foes and the faces of their women are blackened! [By thee the faces of women like unto Lakṣmī are blackened, not the lotus faces of thy foes!]'; [211] 'Having inspired confidence of all, attended by Lakṣmī, departing from the rules (of decorum), having obtained one to be obtained,[3] wavering an instant,[4] slow for modesty, with love violently born through pain among the flowers of Him whose shafts are flowers,[5] she fainteth limblessly, Limbless God[6] (saying): "Bliss thou bringest me, thou that art devoted to songs of many measures"! [Having inspired confidence of all, attended by Lakṣmī, (but) with her youth departed, obtained in a way she should not be obtained,[3] wavering an instant,[4] slow for modesty, with love violently born through pain among the flowers of Him whose shafts are flowers,[5] she fainteth limblessly, Limbless God[6] (saying): "Woe thou bringest me, thou that art devoted to songs of many measures"!]'; [212–213] 'What woman was (ever) abandoned by thee that bearest love's burden, with thy beautiful lips, with thy sectarial mark characterised by a streak of dust,[7] with thy moon-like face, (when once she had) clung to thy heart[8] with her soft-formed hand, with her breast, holding the water of drops of sweat, moving on thy broad bosom, being overcome by thy unblemished lustre? [What woman was (ever) released by thee,

[1] Tel. ed. and Srirangam text, 'this unparalleled maid.'

[2] Tel. ed. and Srirangam text, 'accompanied by Lakṣmī.'

[3] Tel. ed. and Srirangam text, 'having obtained to-day a covenant of all the world for some time, she, attended by Lakṣmī [having inspired an agreement of all, a woman who should not be obtained hath been obtained for some time].'

[4] Tel. ed., 'just for an instant.'

[5] Kāma.

[6] Tel. ed. and Srirangam text omit 'limblessly, Limbless God.' The 'Limbless God' is Kāma.

[7] Tel. ed. and Srirangam text, 'characterised by Kāma [characterised by lovelessness].'

[8] Srirangam text, 'what woman with beautiful lips that bear love's burden, with a sectarial mark characterised by Kāma, (and) with a lotus face hath clung to thy heart [what woman with hideous lips that bear love's burden, characterised by lovelessness, devoid of auspicious signs, and with a moon-like face (!) hath clung to thy heart].'

with thy hideous lips, vile for love's burden, marked with streaks of dust, devoid of auspicious signs, with thy moon-like face,[1] (when once she had) clung to thy heart [2] with her soft-formed hand, with her breast, holding the water of drops of sweat, moving on thy broad bosom, being won by gold unalloyed ?] '; [214] 'What gentle-eyed woman who fervently delighteth thee, that art not inflamed with passion, (but art) the essence of love, delightsome, (and) a most excellent lover, desireth another that is no lover, with her breast a ravishing opponent, charming with an eye that steals [3] the light of the gazelle's eye? [Cruel with passion! Red-eyed with lust! Alas, an unlovely dame with hostile breast, gaining (thee) with an angry eye that steals [4] the light of sight, desireth thee, the essence of lovelessness, hot,[5] pitiless, absolutely no lover, (and) bound for utmost woe!].'

Straightway the world rejoiced as if it had entered [6] the ocean of milk, as if it had entered a house of crystal; as if it enjoyed the blessedness of habitation in the White Islands.[7] [215] And [8] in due course Kandarpakētu, accompanied by Tamālikā and Makaranda, went to the city of Vāsavadattā's father,[9] while, like the sighing of the night, most gently blew the evening breeze [10] with far horizons tuneful with the murmur of swarms of bees intoxicated and delighted by many drops [11] of nectar in calyxes of forests of white lotuses with unfolded petals of their buds; with its coming greeted by amorous *chickores* sluggish from copious draughts of moonbeams; bewitching because of beads of perspiration on the fair brides of the Pulinda king, wearied with the exhaustion [12] of excessive love.

[1] Ironical. [2] See note 8, p. 107.

[3] Tel. ed. and Srirangam text, 'and with an eye that steals.'

[4] Tel. ed. and Srirangam text, 'and with an angry eye that steals.'

[5] Tel. ed., 'lustful.' [6] Tel. ed. and Srirangam text, 'plunged into.'

[7] Tel. ed. and Srirangam text, 'as if it had settled in the White Islands.' On the White Islands see Hopkins, *The Great Epic of India*, p. 116, New York, 1901.

[8] Tel. ed. and Srirangam text, 'and then.'

[9] Tel. ed. and Srirangam text, 'to the city of Vāsavadattā.'

[10] Srirangam text adds 'removing the heat.'

[11] Tel. ed. and Srirangam text, 'swarms of bees delighted with intoxication from the flavour of the abundant dripping of many drops.'

[12] Tel. ed. omits 'exhaustion.'

[216] Then[1] he, whose power was that of Śiva's joy, saw the mansion of Vāsavadattā surrounded[2] by an encircling wall; with its cloud-touching crest built in a quarter of the capital; white with stucco; with bits of gold,[3] pearls, emeralds, and rubies inserted one after the other like a host of deities staying to see Vāsavadattā[4]; [217] adorned with banners that seemed to mock the beauty of the ocean[5] of the sky as if with clusters of the flowers of the cloud-tree disporting in the wind; adorned with very numerous[6] streams flowing through courts with slabs of golden stone, (these streams) bearing the savour of water perfumed with[7] camphor, saffron, cardamom, and cloves, and with palace doves sleeping[8] comfortably perched on slabs of crystal from shores unknown[9]; [218] with waters full of the blossoms of the trees near the crumbling banks[10]; with seats[11] bedewed by masses of spray moving at the striking of[12] the firm buttocks of wanton[13] damsels incessantly plunging and emerging; with flamingoes whose noise would imply that they had settled near the sand bank formed by the stream of camphor[14]; [219] revealing the Brahminy ducks' sudden dread of darkness because of the groves of expanded blue lotuses[14]; <containing goodly waters> as young women <have goodly breasts>; bathing the <lips of the

[1] Tel. ed. and Srirangam text, 'then, having entered.' Cartellieri, 'Subandhu and Bāṇa' in *WZKM.* I. 132, compares with this Candrāpīḍa's first meeting with Kādambarī (*Kādambarī*, pp. 182 sqq., Bombay ed., 1890 (tr. Ridding, pp. 143 sqq., London, 1896)).

[2] Tel. ed. omits down to 'adorned with banners.'

[3] Srirangam text, 'seeming to have gold.'

[4] Tel. ed., 'the mansion of Vāsavadattā.'

[5] Tel. ed. and Srirangam text, 'city.'

[6] Tel. ed. omits 'very numerous'; Srirangam text, 'numerous.'

[7] Tel. ed. and Srirangam text, 'bearing the perfume of.'

[8] Tel. ed., 'white doves of the palace born and sleeping'; Srirangam text, 'curious white doves of the palace sleeping.'

[9] Tel. ed. and Srirangam text, 'slabs of crystal near the banks.'

[10] Tel. ed. and Srirangam text, 'trees on the crumbling banks.'

[11] Tel. ed. and Srirangam text, 'seats on the banks.'

[12] Tel. ed. and Srirangam text, 'upheaved by striking against.'

[13] Tel. ed. and Srirangam text omit 'wanton.'

[14] Tel. ed. and Srirangam text, 'that they had perched on the sand bank of the stream of camphor.'

[15] Tel. ed., 'revealing the terror of ducks and *cakravākas* at the darkness because of the expanded blue lotuses.'

pitchers in water› as the battle arts[1] of Sugrīva bathed ‹Kumbhakarṇa in blood›; ‹sprinkled with dust from the feet of fair women› as the shores of the sea are ‹variegated with the colours of beautiful trees›; [220] ‹causing contempt for canals› as the disposition of new monarchs[2] ‹causes dishonour to the honourable›[3]; adorned with palaces that seemed to bear aloft, under the guise of the strings of pearls placed on their pinnacles, a host of stars come in curiosity[4] to behold the damsels of the city; [221] made brilliant with flocks of peacocks lurking in the vicinity; presenting the semblance of crystal pitchers; on one side[5] showing the rising[6] of untimely clouds by masses of the smoke of aloes burning constantly; on the other side having peacocks dancing joyously,[7] called by the exceeding[8] deep roll of drums; with the ‹descent of the eyes of the world›[9] as the even-tide has the ‹setting sun›; with ‹charming women, filled with love-longing›, as Janaka's place of sacrifice[10] had ‹Rāma longing for his wife›; [222] ‹delighting in love's union› as multitudes of mankind[11] ‹honour divinity›[12]; the repository, as it were, of delightsomeness; the home, so to say, of love; the palace, it might be termed, of wanton sport[13]; [223] the place of assembly, it would seem, of loveliness.

Kandarpakētu, as well as Makaranda, was astonished at hearing[14] the chatter of the maidens, tender in their affection

[1] Tel. ed., 'battle deeds'; Srirangam text, 'tendency toward battle'; cf. *Rāmāyaṇa*, 6. 67.

[2] Is there here a possible covert allusion to the recent accession of a new king inferior to his predecessor (cf. p. 9 above)?

[3] Tel. ed. and Srirangam text, '‹with elephants going to the canals› as the rule of monarchs has ‹honourable men, income, respect, and taxes›.'

[4] Tel. ed. and Srirangam text omit 'in curiosity.'

[5] Tel. ed. omits 'on one side.'

[6] Tel. ed. and Srirangam text, 'warlike preparation.'

[7] Tel. ed. and Srirangam text, 'having intoxicated peacocks.'

[8] Tel. ed. and Srirangam text omit 'exceeding.'

[9] Namely, to see its beauty.

[10] The Daṇḍaka forest, where Sītā was carried off from Rāma.

[11] Tel. ed. and Srirangam text, 'humanity.'

[12] Tel. ed. and Srirangam text add 'adorned with many ‹walls› as a forest is adorned with many ‹*sal*-trees›.'

[13] Tel. ed. and Srirangam text, 'of all wanton sports.'

[14] Tel. ed., 'Kandarpakētu, entering that palace with Makaranda, hearing . . ., saw

one for the other[1]: 'Thou runnest successfully in thy running, Nigalitā[2]! Capalā standeth unsteadily! What of her? [224] Here is the cluster of flowers fallen from thine own ear'! 'Surēkhā, thou, whose beauty is entreated by the gods, art filled with wine (and) drunken'! 'Kalahā,[3] thou dost wellnigh summon love by the soft tinklings of the bond of thy golden girdle'! 'Malayā, by thy very glance thou hast learned the will of Him who overcame Śiva'[4]! [225] 'Kalikā, loosen that noisy girdle, the banner of strife; we hear the faint, sweet sound of the lute'[5]! 'My girdle is not the nuisance; it is thou, with thy irrumation[6] and noisiness'[7]! 'This silly Avantisēnā is afraid lest she fall there in offering flowers'[8]! 'Enough of thy tricks, Lavaṅgikā! Thy tremor[9] betrayeth thy state of mind.' [226] 'Thy languid form seemeth to bear the wounds of Love's arrows, Anaṅgalēkhā! The mighty wave of anxiety is indeed concealed to thy advantage! Speak, doth the moon itself reach comparison in thy face, whose loveliness should be drunk in by the eyes'[10]? [227] 'Somebody apparently dwelleth in thy heart, Satīvratā! Thy words are felt in a hundred ways as

Vāsavadattā,' omitting 'was astonished'; Srirangam text, 'Kandarpakētu, hearing . . ., entered that palace with Makaranda.'

[1] For similar series of exclamations, see *Kādambarī*, pp. 173–174, 357, Bombay ed., 1890 (tr. Ridding, pp. 68–69, 144–145, London, 1896); *Harṣacarita*, pp. 177–178, 277–278, Bombay ed., 1892 (tr. Cowell and Thomas, pp. 144–145, 247–248, London, 1897).

[2] Tel. ed. and Srirangam text, '(though) not addressed,' the Srirangam text adding 'fair maid'!

[3] Tel. ed. and Srirangam text, 'Surēkhā, with fair streak of wine on thy cheek, thou art a Lakṣmī wooed by the gods! Drunken Kalahā.'

[4] Tel. ed. and Srirangam text, 'perform the will of Him (Kāma) who overcame Śiva; thou hast learned it just with a glance.'

[5] Tel. ed., 'we hear this faint, sweet sound of the lute, the banner of strife,' omitting 'loosen this noisy girdle.'

[6] See Schmidt, *Beiträge zur indischen Erotik*, pp. 546–550, 593, Leipzig, 1902.

[7] Tel. ed. and Srirangam text, 'with thy noisiness and roughness.'

[8] Tel. ed. and Srirangam text, 'there, in offering *nāga*-flowers, this trembling maid feareth that "I may fall".'

[9] Tel. ed. and Srirangam text, 'tremor filled with sighs.'

[10] Tel. ed. and Srirangam text, 'thy form seemeth to bear the wounds of love's arrows, Anaṅgalēkhā, and thy pearl necklace is arranged at thy behest! Speak, Utkalikā, doth the moon reach comparison in thy face, filled with anxiety, (despite) the beauty of the lotuses in thine eyes'?

having the hardness of the hundred edges (of Indra's thunderbolt)'! 'This braid of hair of thine, Kuntalikā,[1] is like a bit of black cloud with a mass of hail with its garland[2] of lovely expanded Arabian jasmines'! 'Near the city gate, Kēralikā, the sounds of song are heard! What, pray, dost thou purpose'? [228] 'Instantaneously, even in the twinkling of an eye, Muralikā, thou dost distress thy host of girl friends, trembling and anxious for a kind word! Because of thy lover thou art abandoned by thy husband, who remembereth the bliss, driving away love's fever, that was gained by him, raging aloud as he thudded thy breast! Why art thou distracted? Thy lover longeth for a greater thing than a feast; (and) thy husband [229] hath remembered thy favour, with its delightsomeness of passion'! 'Doth not the wound of nails, sharp from fresh paring, cause pain by night in an amorous woman, Kurutā'? 'Why is not he moon, the place for the eyes of all happy people to gaze on, drunk in by thy shining eyes? [230] Dear friend Madanamālinī, with thy caprices of union and abandonment cause thou distraction by contact with thy ruddy lip! Shining with his rosy crest, he (the moon) is like the cheek of a Mālava maid flushed with intoxication; what is the difference between thee and a creeping plant'[3]? [231] 'Kuraṅgikā, prepare a blade of young grass for the antelope fauns'! 'Kiśōrikā, have the young colts looked after'! 'Taralikā, put in motion the mass of smoke from the

[1] Tel. ed., 'beautiful Kēralikā'; Srirangam text, 'Kēralikā.'

[2] Tel. ed., 'delightful with its garland.'

[3] Tel. ed., '"Kuntalikā, (thou art) adorned with thy tresses, and no sounds of song are heard near the city gate! What dost thou purpose? Instantaneously, even in the twinkling of an eye, thou hast thy host of girl friends trembling and anxious for a kind word"! "Suratā, by whom art thou now deserted that raged aloud in amorous sport, remembering the bliss, driving away love's fever, that he won in thudding thy breast? What is said? Thy lover hath been mindful of a greater thing than a feast, (even) thy favour, with its delightsomeness of passion? In the night, with unseemly noise, he hath inflicted on an amorous woman the pain of his nails, sharp from fresh paring. Why is not the moon, the place for the eyes of all successful people to gaze on, drunk in by thy shining eyes?" "Dear friend Madanamālinī, cause not discontent in the bee, with his desire to approach and leave thy ruddy lip! What is the difference between thee and a creeping plant with its abundance of quivering petals, soft as the cheek of a Mālava maid flushed with intoxication"?'; similarly the Srirangam text.

aloes'! 'Karpūrikā, whiten[1] the burden of thy breasts with camphor-dust'! 'Mātaṅgikā, have the begging[2] of the young elephants borne in mind'! 'Śaśilēkhā, draw a digit of the moon[3] on thy broad forehead'! 'Kētakikā, note the longing of the bower of screw-pine'! [232] 'Śakunikā, give food to the pet birds'! 'Madanamañjarī, festoon the plantain house as a bower for meeting'[4]! 'Śṛṅgāramañjarī, prepare the arrangements[5] of love'! 'Sañjīvikā,[6] give a sprig of pepper to the pair of *chickores*'! 'Pallavikā, make the artificial grove of screw-pine blossom with camphor-powder'! 'Sahakāramañjarī, produce the perfume of the mango by the breeze of thy fan'[7]! 'Madanalēkhā, write a love-line of the wind of Malaya'! [233] 'Mṛṇālikā,[8] give a blade of lotus-fibre to the young flamingoes'! 'Vilāsavatī, make the young peacock sport'! 'Tamālikā, perfume the palace court[9] with sandal water'! 'Kāñcanikā, scatter liquid musk in the gold pavilion'! 'Pravālikā, sprinkle the grove of young[10] shoots with saffron'!

Entering[11] with these thoughts among others: 'Oh, the exceeding beauty of the mansions! Oh, the wanton blissfulness of love! This pavilion, for instance, made of elephants' tusks, whose beauty is the beauty of the spotless teeth of Mālava's daughters, with wide interstices for the (amorous) sport of their (proper) seasons[12]! [234] This pet parrot confined in a cage of bars made of golden rods'!, he (Kandarpakētu) saw Vāsavadattā brilliant with a pair

[1] Tel. ed., 'dust.'

[2] Tel. ed. and Srirangam text, 'washing.'

[3] A digit of the moon is $\frac{1}{16}$ part of it. The purpose of drawing this emblem, according to the Sanskrit commentator Śivarāma, was to frighten Love away, the moon being described by Subandhu himself (see above, p. 103) as the pyre of Kāma.

[4] Tel. ed. and Srirangam text, 'Madanamañjarī, anklet it to the arbour of creepers! Kadalikā, open the plantain house'!

[5] Tel. ed. and Srirangam text, 'arrangement.'

[6] Tel. ed. and Srirangam text, 'Sañjīvanikā.'

[7] Tel. ed. and Srirangam text, 'efface the drops of sweat by the wind of thy fan with its mango perfume'!

[8] Tel. ed. and Srirangam text, 'Makarikā, adorned by Kāma.'

[9] Tel. ed. and Srirangam text, 'have the court of the palace covered.'

[10] Tel. ed. and Srirangam text omit 'young.'

[11] Tel. ed. omits these meditations of Kandarpakētu; Srirangam text omits the exclamation concerning the pavilion, prefacing the whole with 'and he thought.'

[12] See Schmidt, *Beiträge zur indischen Erotik*, pp. 403–429, Leipzig, 1902.

of legs with ‹reddened feet› as grammar[1] has ‹rubricated *pādas*›; with ‹goodly joints› as the *Bhārata*[2] has ‹a hundred books›; charming with ‹beautiful ankles› as the *Rāmāyaṇa* is charming with its ‹*Sundarakāṇḍa*›; [235] with a glorious ‹slender waist› as the *Chandōviciti* has the glorious ‹*tanumadhyā* metre›[3]; with ‹hands and ears that must be reckoned with› as astronomy has the ‹*hasta* and *śravaṇa*[4] that may be counted›; ‹revealing her beauty› as the permanence of the Nyāya system[5] has its ‹form from Uddyōtakara›; decked with ‹ornaments› as an assembly of Buddhists[6] is decked with the ‹*Alaṁkāra*›; [236] showing the ‹essence of delight› as an Upaniṣad shows him whose ‹being is bliss›[7]; with beautiful ‹feet› as an abode with a family of Brāhmans has beautiful ‹conduct›; with lovely ‹buttocks› as the beauty of the Vindhya Mountains has lovely ‹slopes›; beautified with ‹massy hips› as Tārā[8] was beautified in being the ‹wife of the Teacher›; with a slender[9] ‹waist› that might be grasped by the hand as (Indra's) bolt[10] of a hundred points has a slender[9] ‹middle› that might be grasped by the hand; with a ‹lovely face› as the friend of Priyaṅguśyāmā was ‹Priyadarśanā›[11]; ‹glorious as the moon› as Brahmadatta's queen was ‹Sōmaprabhā›[12]; [237] ‹incomparable› as the female elephant of the (southwest) quarter was ‹Anupamā›; adorned with a ‹sectarial mark› as the seashore

[1] Alluding to the red colophons of the *pādas*, or quarter-divisions, of each book of Pāṇini's grammar.

[2] Tel. ed. and Srirangam text, '*Mahābhārata*.' On the reference see Cartellieri, 'Das Mahābhārata bei Subandhu und Bāṇa,' in *WZKM*. 13. 71.

[3] See Weber, *Ueber die Metrik der Inder*, pp. 365–366, Berlin, 1863, the scheme being — — ⏑ | ⏑ — —.

[4] Two *nakṣatras*, or lunar mansions, corresponding respectively to $\delta, \gamma, \epsilon, \alpha, \beta$ Corvi, and α, β, γ Aquilae.

[5] Tel. ed. and Srirangam text, 'the science of the Nyāya.' On the importance of this allusion for dating the *Vāsavadattā*, see Introduction, p. 8.

[6] Tel. ed. and Srirangam text, 'the composition of the poetry of excellent poets.'

[7] Tel. ed., '‹joyful› as an Upaniṣad has ‹Brahmā›; ‹adorning humanity› as the radiance of the sun ‹lights the world›'; similarly the Srirangam text.

[8] Tel. ed., 'Rōhiṇī.' The 'Teacher' is Bṛhaspati.

[9] Tel. ed. and Srirangam text omit 'slender.'

[10] Tel. ed., 'the form of the bolt'; Srirangam text, 'the stem of the bolt.'

[11] The details of this legend seem to be lost; cf. Lacôte, *Essai sur Guṇāḍhya et la Bṛhatkathā*, p. 213, Paris, 1908.

[12] See *Kathāsaritsāgara*, 17. 114.

is adorned with ‹*tamāla*-leaves›[1]; ‹languid with intoxication› as Aśvatara's daughter was ‹Madālasā›.[2]

Then sudden[3] faintness seized the consciousness of Kandarpakētu as he drank her in with an eye dilated with affection.[4] Beholding him in her turn, Vāsavadattā fainted.[5] Then, with their consciousness restored by the exertions of Makaranda and the attendant maidens, they[6] twain adorned a single settle.

[238] Thereupon a vessel[7] of all confidence named Kalāvatī, dearer than Vāsavadattā's own life (to her), addressed Kandarpakētu: 'Scion of noble parentage! This is no occasion for confidential conversation[8]; therefore thou art told only the least part[9]! The pain that hath been felt by this maiden for thy sake might be written or told[10] in some wise or in some way in many thousands of ages if the sky became paper,[11] the sea [239] an ink-well, the scribe Brahmā, (and) the narrator the Lord of Serpents.[12] By thee[13] a kingdom has been abandoned—what need of more? Thou thyself art brought into peril! When the night shall be near to dawn, against her will[14] this daughter of

[1] Tel. ed., '‹giving joy› and adorned with a «sectarial mark» as the Rēvā is the ‹Narmadā› and is adorned with «*tamāla*-leaves»'; similarly the Srirangam text.

[2] This daughter of Aśvatara is probably identical with the one carried off by Kuvalayāśva (see below, p. 130). The mythology given by Subandhu, however, seems confused, and may be influenced by paronomasiac requirements. No daughter of Aśvatara is thus far known to be mentioned elsewhere, and Madālasā is usually described as the child of the Gandharva Viśvavasu and as abducted by Pātālakētu, a Dāitya prince, from whom she was rescued by Kuvalayāśva, who made her one of his wives. She died of grief when she heard that her husband had fallen in battle. See *Mārkaṇḍēyapurāṇa*, 21-22.

[3] Tel. ed. and Srirangam text omit 'sudden.'

[4] Tel. ed. and Srirangam text omit 'with affection.'

[5] Tel. ed., 'Vāsavadattā fainted after him.'

[6] Tel. ed. and Srirangam text, 'these.' [7] Tel. ed. and Srirangam text, 'a friend.'

[8] Tel. ed. and Srirangam text, 'of confidential conversations.'

[9] Tel. ed. and Srirangam text, 'only the least part is told.'

[10] Tel. ed., 'might be written or not.'

[11] See Köhler, 'Und wenn der Himmel wär Papier,' in his *Kleinere Schriften*, 3. 293-318, Berlin, 1900; Zachariae, 'Und wenn der Himmel wär Papier,' in *Zeitschrift des Vereins für Volkskunde*, 11. 331.

[12] The cosmic serpent Śēṣa.

[13] Tel. ed. and Srirangam text, 'and by thee.'

[14] Tel. ed. and Srirangam text, 'into the peril of her, who has learned that "when the night shall dawn, against her will,"' etc.

our monarch is to be given in marriage by her father, [240] filled with alarm at the sin[1] of her passing youth, to Puṣpakētu, son of Vijayakētu, the supreme lord of the Vidyādharas. Thus she has reflected[2]: "If to-day Tamālikā comes not with that person,[3] then inevitably must I lay me in the fire![4]" Therefore, most fortunate prince, through the power of her good deeds thou art come to this land.[5] Thy highness is criterion, now, of what is fitting here.' With these words she was silent.

Then, as if terribly terrified, as if bathed in the billows of the ocean of the bliss of love,[6] as if anointed to the sovereignty of the threefold world,[7] Kandarpakētu, [241] taking counsel with Vāsavadattā (and) leaving Makaranda there in the city to search for tidings, set forth from the city with her[8] by means of a horse named Manōjava,[9] who <ever faced his course> as a serpent <faces the wind>.[10]

And[11] by degrees—having gone, even in the twinkling of an

1 Tel. ed. omits 'the sin of.' On the seriousness, and even sinfulness, of permitting a daughter to reach the age of puberty without being married, cf. Jolly, *Recht und Sitte*, pp. 54-58, Strassburg, 1896; Schmidt, *Beiträge zur indischen Erotik*, pp. 645-649, Leipzig, 1902.

2 Tel. ed. adds 'having taken counsel with us'; similarly the Srirangam text.

3 Kandarpakētu, whom modesty forbade her to mention by name.

4 Tel. ed. and Srirangam text, 'the fire must be my refuge.'

5 Tel. ed. omits this sentence; Srirangam text, 'and from the power of good deeds the full fortunate (pair) are met.'

6 Tel. ed. and Srirangam text, 'bathed in the billows of the ocean of the ambrosia of the bliss of love.'

7 Tel. ed. and Srirangam text omit 'as if anointed to the sovereignty of the threefold world.'

8 Tel. ed., 'with this Vāsavadattā.'

9 It is, perhaps, worth noting that *manōjava* occurs as an epithet of horses in *Rig-Veda*, 6. 62. 3, as well as in later literature (Böhtlingk and Roth, *Sanskrit-Wörterbuch*, 5. 531, St. Petersburg, 1868).

10 Tel. ed. and Srirangam text add 'who was adorned by <whorls on his neck> as a river-bank [Srirangam text, 'the ocean'] is adorned with <pearl oysters>; who was characterised by <curls on his breast> as the forests of Vindhya are characterised by <*pipul*-trees>; who went like <the mind> as a goose goes in <Mānasa> [Srirangam text adds 'who was adorned with <studs> as a forest is adorned with <rhinoceroses>']; who was decked with <shoulders> as a tree is decked with a <branch>; who had <black about his eyes> as the thunderbolt is the <weapon of Indra>.'

11 Tel. ed. and Srirangam text, 'then by degrees, going a journey of a *gavyūti* [about four miles], departing through the enclosure of a cemetery, . . . going a journey of many hundred leagues even in the space of the twinkling of an eye, he again entered.'

eye, many hundred leagues [1] through the enclosure of a cemetery thronged with flocks of fearless herons assembled in desire of a mouthful of flesh [2]; [242] horrible with the howls of awful goblins that had *kaṭapūtanas* [3] quivering with eagerness for the hideous corpses chilling [4] in the circle of half-burned funeral pyres; repulsive with patches of ground full of swarms of buzzing flies sprinkled with quantities of blood from the amputation of ears and noses of thieves placed on the top of stakes [5]; with the horrible sound of the bursting of human skulls slowly crackling as they were burned by fires of straw [6]; [243] with its contour concealed by rows of skulls, ashes, ‹jackals, fires, goblins›, and serpents as He who holds the trident in his hand [7] has his contour concealed by rows of skulls, ashes, ‹Śivā, the element of fire›, and serpents [8]; frequented by many ‹dogs› as

[1] For instances of the magic horse in modern Indian folk-tales, cf. Steel and Temple, *Wide-Awake Stories*, pp. 425–426, Bombay, 1884; Day, *Folk-Tales of Bengal*, pp. 73, 80, 214–219, 249, London, 1883; Thornhill, *Indian Fairy Tales*, pp. 108–145, London, n.d.; Dracott, *Simla Village Tales*, p. 102, London, 1906; Campbell, *Santal Folk Tales*, p. 86, Pokhuria, 1891; Leitner, 'Historical Legend of the Origin of Ghilgit' (a Dard legend), in *IA.* 1. 88.

[2] Tel. ed., 'for the purpose of a mouthful of human flesh'; similarly the Srirangam text.

[3] Tel. ed., 'horrible with howls from the awful throats of *kaṭapūtanas*.' The *kaṭapūtana* is the ghost of a renegade Kṣatriya (Manu, 12. 71).

[4] Tel. ed. and Srirangam text, 'hideous corpses with the raw odour of their fat chilling.'

[5] See Jolly, *Recht und Sitte*, pp. 126–127, 130, Strassburg, 1896. Impalement was accomplished by 'a stout iron rod with a thin point at the top. The condemned person was made to sit on the top which penetrated into his body slowly and went out by the head' (Ram Satya Mukharji, *Indian Folklore*, p. 129, note, Calcutta, 1904).

[6] Tel. ed., 'noisy with the dancing of horrible demons at the ends of whose hands were skulls resounding with the drip, drip of the fall of quantities of blood fallen from the amputation of noses of thieves placed on the tops of stakes; repulsive with patches of ground filled with the abundant sport of swarms of bees; awful with the bursting of sharply crackling human skulls, burning in fires of straw; filled with fiery fire fired from goblins' open mouths; with the noise of the division of corpses made by hosts of monstrous female fiends with pendants of skulls that had entrails for threads; with funeral fires circumambulated to the right by pairs of demons with auspicious marriage cords formed of wet sinews'; similarly the Srirangam text.

[7] Śiva.

[8] Tel. ed. and Srirangam text, 'with its contour concealed by rows of skulls, ‹jackals›, many fires, ‹serpents, and the moon› as He who holds the trident in his hand has his contour concealed by rows of skulls, ‹Śivā›, many fires, and ‹lordly serpents›.'

the leadership of men is courted by many <kingdoms>[1]—he entered the Vindhya forest,[2] which had a multitude of <bow-string-hemp plants> arising as the Last Day has a multitude of <suns> arising; [244] with <infinite roots> as the existence of the Serpent King[3] is <rooted in Ananta>; with <owls> dwelling at will as the assembly of the gods has <Indra> standing at will; rich in many[4] <Bengal quince-trees> as honour to the noble is rich in <fruit of many[4] blessings>; with <deep-rooted *arjuna*-trees> as the battlefield of the Bhāratas had <Arjuna loftily grown>; with <racemose asparagus plants ever with a thousand roots> as the status of Pulōman's family had <Indrāṇī fit for Him who hath a thousand eyes>[5]; with fruitful[6] <*gaṇikārikās*> as the bent of mind[7] of a keeper of courtesans[8] has a fruitful[6] <recourse to harlots>; [245] with expanded <*ashokas*, *chir*-pines, and *kamala*-trees> as the success of the righteous has <noble men joyous, free from sorrow, and upright>; containing <emblic myrobalan> as the play of children has <pleasure for their nurses>; composed in some places of <pepper-trees> as the bent of mind of the hero of Raghu's line[9] was toward the <princess of Vidēha>; [246] with <*amṛta*-plants> appearing in other places as the time of the churning of the ocean of milk had <nectar> appearing; with <*aparājitā*-plants> at will as the might[10] of Nārāyaṇa was <invincible> at will; revealing <stalks of bitter-apples> in yet

[1] Tel. ed. adds 'dominated by <headless corpses> as the Daṇḍaka forest was dominated by <Kabandha>; surrounded by many <conjurers> as a universal monarch is surrounded by many <kings>; with <crows> moving about as heaven has <Bala's foe [Indra]> moving about'; so also the Srirangam text, except for the omission of the last simile. For the allusion to Kabandha, cf. *Mahābhārata*, 3. 279.

[2] With this description Cartellieri ('Subandhu and Bāṇa,' in *WZKM*. I. 132) compares that given by the *Kādambarī* (pp. 38–43, Bombay ed., 1890 (tr. Ridding, pp. 16–18, London, 1896)).

[3] The cosmic serpent Śēṣa. Tel. ed. and Srirangam text, 'kingdom.'

[4] Tel. ed. and Srirangam text omit 'many.'

[5] Indra.

[6] Tel. ed. and Srirangam text, 'revealing.'

[7] Tel. ed. and Srirangam text omit 'of mind.'

[8] Tel. ed. and Srirangam text, 'Śūrapāla.' The basis of the legend connected with him seems to be thus far unknown.

[9] Rāma.

[10] Tel. ed., 'form'; Srirangam text, '<shining with pellucid water> as the might of Nārāyaṇa was <bright and invincible>.'

other places as the eloquence of Vālmīki revealed the ‹lineage of Ikṣvāku›; filled[1] with many ‹*dhak*-trees› as Lankā was frequented by many ‹demons›; encompassed[1] with clumps of ‹*arjuna*-trees and pen-reed grass› as the army of the Kurus[2] was encompassed with quantities of ‹Arjuna's arrows›; with ‹many beasts›[1] as the form of Nārāyaṇa is ‹manifold›; [247] filled[1] with ‹jack-trees, sandal-trees,[3] white lotuses, and reeds› as Sugrīva's army was attended by ‹Panasa, Candana,[3] Kumuda, and Nala›; adorned[1] with ‹*sindūras* and glory-trees›, and decked with ‹fresh buds› as an unwidowed woman is adorned with a ‹sectarial mark of minium› and is decked with ‹long hair›; [248] occupied[1] by ‹owls, crows, and birds, and filled with *dhārtarāṣṭra* geese› as the army of the Kurus was officered by ‹Ulūka, Drōṇa, and Śakuni, and joined[4] by the sons of Dhṛtarāṣṭra›; though adorned with ‹unfaded caste›, it had a «lineage of no family»,[5] for it was adorned with ‹globe-amaranth and Malabar jasmine› and had «no bamboos clinging to the earth»[5]; though revealing ‹no terror›, it was «full of terror», for it revealed ‹*hara-nut* trees› and was «full of reeds»; though ‹always in perfect health›, it had a «great abdominal tumour»,[6] for it ‹ever contained negroes' olive-wood trees› and had «high-grown thickets»; [249] though filled with ‹dice›, it was «unmolested by men», for it was filled with ‹bees› and was «rich in elephants' ichor»; though adorned with families of ‹Brāhmans›, it had a «lineage of no honourable family», for it was adorned with families of ‹birds› and had «no bamboos clinging to the earth».

Immediately[7] the night passed with slumber of them twain. And by degrees,[8] when, like a mass of live carp, the host of stars

[1] Tel. ed. and Srirangam text add 'in places.'

[2] Tel. ed. and Srirangam text, 'the army of Dhṛtarāṣṭra's sons.'

[3] Tel. ed. and Srirangam text omit 'sandal-trees' and 'Candana.'

[4] Tel. ed. and Srirangam text, 'adorned.'

[5] Tel. ed. and Srirangam text, 'it had a ‹hateful lineage›, . . . for it had ‹bamboos laden with birds›.'

[6] See Jolly, *Medicin*, pp. 79–80, Strassburg, 1901.

[7] Tel. ed. and Srirangam text, 'meanwhile.'

[8] Tel. ed., 'and then by degrees'; Srirangam text, 'then by degrees.'

had been removed by the black fisherman casting his net[1] of darkness in the great ocean of the sky; [250] when the mendicant expanded lotus grove, wearing vestments of red robes[2] (and) bearing a book of a hundred leaves with reed threads of unevenly growing delicate lotus-fibres, seemed to pronounce his laws by the soft and very deep sounds of the bees,[3] intoxicated by their heavy draughts in milking the drops of honey; when, like seeds of blackness, the bees were sown by the darkness, as by a husbandman, in the white lotuses with their fields of flowers, with their masses of pollen made mud by the juice of their honey, with their petals touched by the clouds under the guise of bees[4]; [251] when the lotus[5] offered to the Lord whose garland is of rays[6] a mass of[7] incense, as it were, in the semblance of high-stalked white lotuses thronged with swarms[8] of bees with their pollen fire; when the moon[9] resembled a mortar whose interior had been destroyed by blows of the pestle of rising dawn, shaken by the two palms of his consort Night; when the hosts of stars had vanished like grain scattered in the threshing mortar; when the hosts of stars seemed to have flowers[10] expanded for the quarters of heaven that were bent like branches, and when the disc of the moon had fallen like fruit because of the monkey of day that, like the ruddy face[11] of dawn, had climbed the tree of heaven; [252] when the cock of day, with the lovely appearance of the new crest[12] of the glittering Aruṇa, had begun to traverse the court of heaven, variegated with the threshed grain

[1] Tel. ed., 'launching his boat.'

[2] Tel. ed. and Srirangam text, 'red robes of twilight.'

[3] Tel. ed. and Srirangam text, 'by the delightful sounds of the bees.'

[4] Tel. ed. and Srirangam text, 'when, like masses of the seeds of blackness, the bees were sown in the fields of flowers, whose masses of pollen were made mud by the juice of their honey, the folds of whose petals were touched by the clouds.'

[5] Tel. ed. and Srirangam text, 'lotus hermitess.'

[6] The sun.

[7] Tel. ed. and Srirangam text omit 'a mass of.'

[8] Tel. ed. and Srirangam text, 'filled with smoke of swarms.'

[9] Tel. ed. and Srirangam text, 'disc of the moon.'

[10] Tel. ed. and Srirangam text, 'an abundance of flowers.'

[11] Tel. ed. and Srirangam text, 'that, having the ruddy face.'

[12] Tel. ed. and Srirangam text, 'appearance of the crest of rays.'

of the host[1] of stars; when the district of Indra[2] seemed to say with a laugh: 'This Lord of the Twice-Born,[3] increased by concourse with me, will fall[4] through union with the district of Varuṇa'[5]; when to his rising had climbed the sun,[6] with his disc red, as it were, with streams of blood from the lordly elephant of darkness slain by the stroke of the paw[7] of a ruddy lion; as if with streams of ruddle laved by the cataracts on the summit[8] of the mountain of the dawn; with the lustre,[9] so to say, of rubies cloven by the hard hoofs of lofty steeds[10]; [253] flowing with blood, one might imagine, dripping from the heads of must elephants slain by the claws of lions[11]; with the beauty, to all appearance, of the China rose growing on the summit of the peak of the hill of dawn; seemingly with the delightsome flavour of Him who gives prosperity[12] to the affairs of the threefold world; as if with his hand outstretched to seize the white lotuses[13] of the stars; tawny with the saffron colour of a wanton beauty of the east[14]; the jewel in the hood of the lordly serpent of the eastern mount; the golden[15] bud in the sapphire-tree of heaven; [254] the golden urn in the rampart[16] of the city of the sky; like to a jar of molten iron; a drop of safflower extract on the forehead of the east[17]; the single flower of the forest[18] creeper of

[1] Tel. ed. omits 'of the host.' [2] The east. [3] The moon.

[4] Tel. ed. and Srirangam text, 'is falling.'

[5] The west, with a punning allusion to Lakṣmī, the wife of Varuṇa.

[6] Tel. ed. and Srirangam text, 'the blessed sun.'

[7] Tel. ed., 'by the fall of the hard claws.'

[8] Tel. ed., 'streams from cataracts of ruddle on the summits.'

[9] Srirangam text, 'dust.' [10] Tel. ed. and Srirangam text, 'galloping steeds.'

[11] Tel. ed. and Srirangam text transpose this after the following clause and make it read, 'flowing with streams of blood, one might imagine, dripping from the heads of must elephants slain by the claws of lions of the eastern mount.'

[12] Tel. ed., 'red, as it were, with colour eager to prosper'; similarly the Srirangam text.

[13] Tel. ed. and Srirangam text, 'the forest of the white lotuses.'

[14] Tel. ed. and Srirangam text, 'with rays tawny as saffron; the golden mirror, as it were, of a wanton beauty of the east.'

[15] Tel. ed. omits 'golden.'

[16] Tel. ed. and Srirangam text, 'an urn full of gold in the eastern door.'

[17] Tel. ed. and Srirangam text, 'a drop forming a sectarial mark of saffron set on the forehead of a damsel of the east.'

[18] Tel. ed. and Srirangam text, 'young.'

dawn; like to a thread of cloth, red with Bengal madder, woven with threads of the colour of the dawn; seeming to be the disc of a golden dinar of the east; the magic globe, so to say, of the Vidyādhara of day; even as the foot of a world-elephant, red with the colour of ruddle; the thief of the darkness of night[1]; when the young dawn was arising ruddy as a bit of fresh[2] coral; like a chowry, dyed with Bengal madder,[3] on an elephant of the quarters; seeming to emit the blood of the battleground[4] of the *Mahābhārata* on the plains of Kuru; [255] anointed, as it were, with the beauty of the bow of the Lord[5] of the Gods among them that split[6] the clouds; simulating the red cloth in the huts[7] of Buddhist hermitages; like to the colour of safflower in the streamers of banners; the ripening of fruit, so to say, among the jujubes; beauteous as a mass[8] of the saffron of[9] the courtyard of the mighty palace of the sky; like the red entrance-curtain of the actor[10] Time; and[11] when the multitude of the rays of him whose rays are heat had suddenly become hot, as if from taking the burning grief of the hearts[12] of the Brahminy ducks that were tremulous with gentle talk; from the entrance, so to say, of majesty commingled with flame[13]; from union, in all seeming, with the fire which is[14] the beauteous jewel of the lord of day;—

[1] Tel. ed., 'like a ball of madder cloth; the disc of a golden dinar, as it were, in the girdle of a beauty of the east, fastened with the ruddy threads of twilight; ‹gathering the stars together› as Kumāra ‹destroyed Tāraka›; with beautiful ‹lotuses› as the Lote-Born God [Viṣṇu] had beautiful ‹Padmā [Lakṣmī]›; beloved of ‹Chāyā› as a traveller ‹delights in shade›; being the ‹sun› as Indra is ‹Gōpati›; even as the foot of a world-elephant, red with the colour of the ruddle of the eastern mount; the thief of the darkness of dawn'; similarly the Srirangam text.

[2] Tel. ed. omits 'fresh.'

[3] Tel. ed., 'like a mass of Bengal madder.'

[4] Tel. ed. and Srirangam text omit 'of the battleground.'

[5] Tel. ed. and Srirangam text omit 'of the Lord.'

[6] Tel. ed., 'hid.' The reference is, of course, to the victory of Indra over the cloud-demons.

[7] Tel. ed., 'branches'; Srirangam text, 'branches of the trees.'

[8] Tel. ed. and Srirangam text omit 'mass of.'

[9] Tel. ed. and Srirangam text, 'in.' [10] Tel. ed., 'great actor.'

[11] Tel. ed. and Srirangam text omit 'and.'

[12] Tel. ed., 'as if from taking the grief from the treasury of the hearts.'

[13] Tel. ed., 'from the entrance, so to say, of burning splendour.'

[14] Tel. ed. and Srirangam text omit 'the fire which is.'

(then,) unconscious because of the condition of his body, which was empty of food[1] in consequence of his wakefulness all the night, wearied by roving over many hundred *yōjanas*,[2] [256] (and) with every sense benumbed, Kandarpakētu, being seized by slumber which came at that time,[3] fell asleep together with Vāsavadattā, who was in the same condition, in a bower of creepers which was delightful with the hum of bees flitting about, infatuated and greedy[4] for the perfume of the flowers swayed by the gentle breeze.

Thereupon, when the sun had climbed to noon,[5] displaying the ‹sky› as a merchant displays his ‹cloth›; ‹lighting up every quarter of heaven› as a mighty forest fire ‹kindles all its fuel›,[6] Kandarpakētu,[7] perceiving, in some way or other, that the bower of creepers lacked his beloved, and starting up and [257] gazing here and there, now on the bushes,[8] now between the creepers, now on the tree-tops, now in the hidden wells,[9] now on the heaps of dry leaves, now on the sky, now on the quarters of heaven and[10] the spaces between them, made lamentation as he wandered about with his heart ceaselessly burning with the fire of separation[11]: 'O beloved Vāsavadattā! Let me behold thee! [258] Hast thou disappeared in jest[12]? Thou knowest what pains are suffered by me[13] for thy sake! Dear[14] Makaranda! Behold the[15] sorry sport of fate with me! What meritorious deed hath not

[1] Tel. ed., 'which was subject to emptiness of food.'

[2] Tel. ed. and Srirangam text, 'a road of many hundred *yōjanas*.'

[3] Tel. ed. and Srirangam text, 'easy to gain at that time.'

[4] Tel. ed. and Srirangam text, 'noisy, infatuated, and greedy.'

[5] Tel. ed. and Srirangam text, 'to the middle of the sky.'

[6] Tel. ed. and Srirangam text add '‹purifying every region› as the tree of paradise ‹accomplishes every wish›.'

[7] Tel. ed. and Srirangam text add 'awakening.'

[8] Tel. ed. and Srirangam text, 'trees.'

[9] Tel. ed. and Srirangam text, 'now in the deep wells, now on the tops of the lofty trees.'

[10] Tel. ed. and Srirangam text, 'and now.'

[11] Tel. ed. omits 'with the fire of separation.'

[12] Tel. ed. and Srirangam text, 'enough of jesting! Thou hast disappeared'!

[13] Tel. ed. and Srirangam text omit 'by me.'

[14] Tel. ed. and Srirangam text, 'dear friend.'

[15] Tel. ed. and Srirangam text, 'this.'

been done by me[1]? Alas, my destiny of evil fruitage[2]! Alas, the course of Time, hard to overcome! Alas, the planets' most cruel glance[3] askance! Alas, the unjust fruition[4] of my elders' blessings! Alas, the result of my evil dreams and ill omens! Is there no escaping destiny in any way? [259] Have not the sciences[5] been sufficiently studied? Have not my teachers been duly honoured? Have not the (sacred) fires been revered? Have the gods on earth[6] been insulted[7]? Have not the kine been circumambulated? Hath not fearlessness been inspired in refugees'?

[260] Thus lamenting in ways manifold,[8] passing forth from the forest toward the south and going[9] for a considerable distance[10] along the great ocean's lagoon with[11] its new reeds, spikenard, lotuses, *niculas*, tamarisks,[12] rattan-canes, and medlars[13]; with its borders overgrown with many *poonga*-oil plants, Bengal quinces, leaf hermitages, and *conessi*-bark trees[14]; with its fair Madagascar potato groves eagerly tasted by the great bees; [261] with swarms of bees clustering on the stems of young *varuṇa*-trees which covered over the wide-spreading masses of rattan creepers[15]; with its trees smeared with liquid showers from

[1] Tel. ed. and Srirangam text, 'what unholy deed hath aforetime been done by me'?

[2] Tel. ed. and Srirangam text, 'alas, the evil fruitage of destiny'!

[3] Tel. ed. and Srirangam text, 'fall.'

[4] Tel. ed., 'discrepancy.'

[5] Tel. ed., 'hath not science.'

[6] The Brāhmans.

[7] Tel. ed. omits this question.

[8] Tel. ed. and Srirangam text add 'desirous of death.'

[9] The passage 'going . . . he (then) saw' is compared with *Harṣacarita*, pp. 262–264, Bombay ed., 1892 (tr. Thomas, pp. 233–235, London, 1897), and translated by Thomas, 'Subandhu and Bāṇa,' in *WZKM*. 12. 21–27.

[10] Tel. ed. and Srirangam text, 'a journey of considerable distance.'

[11] Tel. ed., 'abounding in.'

[12] Tel. ed. omits 'tamarisks.'

[13] Srirangam text, 'abounding in new reeds, spikenard, lotuses, *niculas*, tamarisks, *vañjulas*, and *chir*-pines, and with multitudes of *poonga*-oil plants and Bengal quinces Tel. ed. adds '*poonga*-oil plants and Bengal quinces.'

[14] Tel. ed. and Srirangam text, 'with many leaf hermitages variously built and with *conessi*-bark trees.'

[15] Tel. ed., 'with swarms of bees clustering on the branches of the *varuṇa*-trees which covered over the wide-spreading masses of mango creepers that were eagerly tasted by female bees.'

masses of honey from dripping hives, broken open by monkeys [1]; [262] dense with palmyra-palms, marsh date-palms, betel-nut palms, *kamila*-trees, and iron-wood trees [2]; impenetrable with clumps of camphor-trees, Arabian jasmines, screw-pines, mountain ebony, coral-trees, citrons, basil, and rose-apple trees [3]; [263] with bowers of river reeds filled with the cries of unhampered gallinules [4]; with twigs of luxuriant [5] mangoes inhabited by koels [6] with their massed, sharp notes; with spreading boughs [7] pressed by families of cocks in their swaying nests [8]; with rows of globe-amaranth horripilated with hosts of buds; with its ten quarters anointed with the beauty of the red *ushoka* twigs; with masses of dust [9] from quantities of the pollen of full-blown iron-wood trees [10]; producing delight for mankind by the sweet humming of bees maddened by clusters of flowers tawny with pollen [11]; horribly [12] scratching the temples of fearless elephants rubbed by the boughs of the trunks [13] of the wingseeds that were darkened with ichor [14]; [264] with hollow trunks of *conessi*-bark trees turned into homes for the silk-cotton trees [15] which are propagated

[1] Tel. ed., 'with the spray of liquid showers of masses of dripping honey broken by monkeys'; similarly the Srirangam text.

[2] Tel. ed., 'with lofty cocoanut-palms, betel-nut palms, palmyra-palms, *tamāla*-trees, marsh date-palms, *kamila*-trees, iron-wood trees, *nagkassar*-trees, and camphor-trees'; similarly the Srirangam text.

[3] Tel. ed., 'impenetrable with bushes of Arabian jasmines, screw-pines, mountain ebony, bowstring-hemp, rose-apple trees, citrons, and basil; with branches of many jack-trees rubbed together by the wind'; similarly the Srirangam text.

[4] Tel. ed., 'with numbers of bowers on the river-banks filled with the cries of gallinules'; similarly the Srirangam text.

[5] Tel. ed. and Srirangam text omit 'luxuriant.'

[6] Tel. ed., 'by thronging, eager bees.'

[7] Tel. ed. and Srirangam text, 'with many spreading boughs.'

[8] Tel. ed. omits 'in their swaying nests.'

[9] Tel. ed. and Srirangam text, 'with its edges made gray.'

[10] Tel. ed., 'pollen of the expanded flowers of iron-wood trees'; similarly the Srirangam text.

[11] Tel. ed., 'bees glittering from the *sinduvāra*-trees, tawny with masses of pollen; with cloves, *champaks*, *mahwa*-trees, purging cassias, wingseeds, and *kadambas*'; similarly the Srirangam text.

[12] Tel. ed. omits 'horribly.'

[13] Tel. ed. and Srirangam text omit 'of the trunks.'

[14] Tel. ed. and Srirangam text, 'scraping the ichor-darkened cheeks.'

[15] Tel. ed., 'with crooked, hollow trunks of silk-cotton trees.'

within a few days; with delightful sounds made by the tremulous, twittering hen-sparrows mating with the cock-sparrows; famed for clever [1] *chickores* renowned for going with [2] their mates; with young hares [3] resting comfortably on the surfaces of very smooth [4] mountain rocks; [265] with hosts of lizards dwelling fearlessly in holes in the roots of the *indrāṇīs*; with undismayed antelopes [5]; with the sport of hosts of [6] unmolested mungooses; with opening mango buds surrounded by flocks of sweet koels; with herds of yaks chewing their cuds in the mango forest; having for its drum [7] the flapping of the ears of herds of elephants, slow with slumber from [8] the roar of the waterfalls, sportful and delightsome to hear, on the mountain slopes; with herds of deer delighted by the notes of the songs [9] of *kinnarīs* close by [10]; [266] with the edges of the snouts of young boars shining with the flow of crushed greenish-yellow turmeric [11]; with multitudes of *jālakas* humming about masses of coral-bead plants [12]; filled with shells of pink insects split open by the tips of the nails of young monkeys that had been angered by their bites [13]; with multitudes of lions illumined with beautiful heavy manes smeared with quantities of blood [14] from must elephants' frontal-lobes split open by terrible blows from masses of claws sharp as the tips of the thunderbolt [15]; he (then) saw the ocean skilfully imitating, by the

[1] Tel. ed. and Srirangam text omit 'clever.'

[2] Tel. ed. and Srirangam text, 'eager to consort with.'

[3] Tel. ed. and Srirangam text, 'with multitudes of young hares.'

[4] Tel. ed. and Srirangam text, 'sweet smelling.'

[5] Tel. ed. and Srirangam text, 'herds of antelopes.'

[6] Tel. ed. and Srirangam text omit 'hosts of.'

[7] Tel. ed. and Srirangam text, 'with the drum-noise of.'

[8] Tel. ed., 'slow from the joy of slumber, (yet) anxious to hear'; similarly the Srirangam text.

[9] Tel. ed. and Srirangam text, 'delighting in hearing the song.'

[10] Tel. ed. and Srirangam text, 'neighbouring.'

[11] Tel. ed. and Srirangam text, 'delighted with the noise and the flow of turmeric.'

[12] Tel. ed., 'with litters of wood hedgehogs in many bowers of coral-bead plants'; similarly the Srirangam text.

[13] Tel. ed., 'with multitudes of worms in the cavities of trumpet-flower trees split open by slaps from the paws of young monkeys that had been angered by the bites of wood flies'; similarly the Srirangam text.

[14] Tel. ed., 'ichor.'

[15] Quoted by Vāmana, *Kāvyālaṃkāravṛtti*, 1. 3. 26.

mass of its exceedingly active waves,[1] the God[2] that hath the short axe upraised by his staff-like arm[3] in his revel dance; [267] with its edges charming because of lines of foam that seemed to be the emblems of Ocean's[4] victory; that resembled delightful[5] clusters of sloughs of the family of Śēṣa[6]; masses of atoms, as it were, of the remnants of the moon[7]; streams of cosmetic, in all seeming, for the sport of Lakṣmī; like to bits of the sandal paste of the sea nymphs[8]; a second heaven, so to speak, come down to earth under the guise of a sea; tempting the birds, as with pearls, by masses of drops of rising spray[9]; with its bays filled with mountains of many winged creatures[10] that had come to seek security; dug by hundreds[11] of the sons of Sagara[12]; with uprooted coral-trees[13]; a mine of beautiful gems and jewels; filled with hosts of[14] monkeys and dolphins; [268] with multitudes of crocodiles roving about in their desire for mouthfuls of shoals of *śakulas*[15]; filled with restless *timiṅgilas*[16]; with thickets of *carambolas*, cloves, and citrons swaying in the tide (and) rocked

[1] Tel. ed. and Srirangam text, 'on account of its shore being lashed by an abundance of exceedingly active water.'

[2] Śiva. [3] Tel. ed. and Srirangam text, 'many staff-like arms.'

[4] Srirangam text, 'Varuṇa's.'

[5] Tel. ed. and Srirangam text omit 'delightful.'

[6] Tel. ed. and Srirangam text add 'like consorts of ambrosia; sisters uterine, so to say, of light.'

[7] Srirangam text, 'disc of the moon'; Tel. ed., 'a series of atoms, as it were, of the disc of the moon.' The date of the composition of the *Vāsavadattā* forbids us to see in the mention of the moon (*śaśāṅka*) a reference to the Gauḍa king Śaśāṅka against whom Harṣa made war (*Harṣacarita*, tr. Cowell and Thomas, pp. x, 275, London, 1896; Ettinghausen, *Harṣa Vardhana, empereur et poète de l'Inde septentrionale*, pp. 10, 38, 42, Paris, 1906; cf. also above, Introduction, p. 10).

[8] Tel. ed., 'seeming to hold a mirror.'

[9] Tel. ed., 'like to bits of the unguent of camphor streams on the bosoms of the sea-nymphs.'

[10] Tel. ed. and Srirangam text, 'a second heaven, so to speak, come down to earth; tempting the birds, as with pearls, by masses of spray rising from the pellucid water.'

[11] Tel. ed. and Srirangam text, 'the host.'

[12] Cf. *Mahābhārata*, 3. 106–109.

[13] Tel. ed., 'with coral-trees beautified by the mouths of mussels; Srirangam text, 'with a mass of water going to the submarine fire; with the coral-tree won by Indra.'

[14] Tel. ed. and Srirangam text omit 'hosts of.'

[15] Tel. ed. and Srirangam text, 'flocks of birds.'

[16] Tel. ed. and Srirangam text, 'filled with motionless whales and *timiṅgilas*.'

by the circling mountain of the plantain-trees on its bank[1]; with the young *śāivāla* on the sand banks in its waters[2] trampled by pairs of mermen alarmed by the terrible swaying, produced by wave and wind, of palmyra-palms, marsh date-palms, and *taliera*-palms[3]; with letters on its banks scrawled by the edges of whelks[4] that were distressed because their mouths were torn by tips of coral prongs; with its waters crowded by flocks of birds of Garuḍa's race; seeming to have the completion of its slow churning still unfinished because of its eddying whirlpools; epileptic, as it were, because of its foam[5]; [269] filled with the goodly delights of drink, one might fancy, because of the perfume of the medlars on its banks[6]; angry,[7] so to say, because of its roarings; appearing to be distressed because of its sighings[8]; seamed with frowns, it might be thought, because of its waves; resembling an elephant corral because of Rāma's bridge; the birthplace of ‹salt› as the womb of Kumbhīnasī was the birthplace of ‹Lavaṇa›; ‹lavish in its duties toward the wide-spread[9] rivers that were its spouses› as grammar has ‹abundant comprehensive feminines, *i* and *u* declensions, and gerunds›[10]; showing a great ‹bed› as the retinue of a king shows great ‹ministers›; with ‹hisses› emitted by many ‹serpents› that had come to its ‹waters› as an elephant's place of bondage has ‹trumpetings› emitted by many ‹elephants› that have come to the ‹tying-place›; [270] adorned with ‹*ambhōjacāmaras* and fish› as the series of Viśvāmitra's sons was

1 Tel. ed., 'impenetrable because of the thickets of cardamoms, *carambolas*, cloves, and citrons swaying in the circuit of the plantain forest'; similarly the Srirangam text.

2 Tel. ed. omits 'in its waters'; Srirangam text, 'low-lying, small *śāivāla*.'

3 Tel. ed., 'mermen moving in the forest of *taliera*-palms, terrible, very tremulous, and howling with wave and wind'; similarly the Srirangam text.

4 Tel. ed., 'by the noisy, sharp tips of the whelks'; Srirangam text, 'tips of the sharp nails of the whelks.'

5 Tel. ed. and Srirangam text, 'the masses of its white foam.'

6 Tel. ed., 'possessed of the perfume of drink, one might fancy, because of the perfume of its cardamoms'; Srirangam text, 'because of the perfume of the medlars on its shore.'

7 Tel. ed., 'noisy.'

8 Tel. ed. and Srirangam text, 'exhalations of its serpents.'

9 Tel. ed. and Srirangam text omit 'wide-spread' and 'comprehensive.'

10 See *Pāṇini*, 1. 4. 3; 3. 1. 95.

adorned with ‹lotuses, chowries, and the Matsyas›[1]; the refuge of ‹mountains› as a good man is the refuge of his ‹family›[2]; charming in that it was the ‹abode of Viṣṇu› as a noble man is charming because of his ‹unshaken firmness›; with ‹crocodiles and dolphins ready› as an upright prince ‹promotes the affairs of good folk›; with its ‹surface overflowed by the Karatōyā› as a wrathful man has his ‹face covered with water from his hands›; [271] sprinkled with the water of the ‹Candanā› as one separated (from his beloved) is sprinkled with ‹sandal› water; followed by the ‹Narmadā› as a voluptuary is followed by ‹jesters›[3]; though it had ‹cast forth its venom›,[4] it showed an abundance of «poison», for it ‹raised aloft a mass of dark blue› and showed an abundance of «water»; though it was very ‹old›, «fair women clung about its neck», for it was very ‹great› and its «vicinity was filled with Madagascar potatoes»; though it was the place of origin of ‹the gods›, it was «not ruled by the gods», for it was the place of origin of ‹Surā›[4] and was «ruled by the demons».

[272] And he thought: ‘Ah, me! Kindness hath been shown by Fate even though it hath wrought injury, since this ocean hath been brought[5] within the range of mine eyes! Therefore, abandoning my body here, I shall quench the fire of separation from my love.[6] Even though desertion of the body[7] is not permitted one free from disease, yet it must be done.[8] Doth not every one do deeds which ought to be done or ought not to be done? Thus, what is not done by each one in vain life[9]? [273] As for example[10]: ‹the Lord of the Twice-Born› ravished

[1] Tel. ed. and Srirangam text, ‘adorned with ‹lotuses and beautiful fish› as the series of Viśvamitra's sons was adorned with ‹Ambhōja, Cāru, and Matsya›.’

[2] Tel. ed., ‘with superiority in ‹mountains› as a good man has superiority in ‹family›.’

[3] Tel. ed. and Srirangam text, ‘with ‹fishes and crabs› as the zodiacal signs have ‹Pisces and Cancer›; adorned with many ‹pearls› as a voluptuary is adorned with many ‹courtesans›.’

[4] Namely, at the churning of the ocean by the gods and demons.

[5] Tel. ed. and Srirangam text, ‘hath come.’

[6] Tel. ed. and Srirangam text, ‘therefore I abandon my body here.’

[7] Tel. ed. and Srirangam text, ‘of life.’ [8] Tel. ed. adds ‘by us.’

[9] Tel. ed., ‘every one doth not do everything he should in vain life. What, indeed, is not done by whom?’; similarly the Srirangam text.

[10] A similar list of misdeeds of divine and famous personages is given in the *Daśa-*

his <teacher's wife>[1] and <a most excellent Brāhman> ravished the <wife of his elders>. Pururavas was destroyed because of his greed for the wealth of Brāhmans.[2] Nahuṣa, lusting for another's spouse, became a great <serpent> and became a great <profligate>.[3] Yayāti fell, <having wedded> a Brāhman girl,[4] and <took hold of the hand> of a Brāhman girl [274] Sudyumna <became a woman>,[5] so to say, and was <fond of women>. The cruelty of Sōmaka's murder of <Jantu> was notorious[6] and the cruelty of his murder of <living creatures> was notorious.[6] Purukutsa was despised.[7] Kuvalayāśva carried off[8] <Aśvatara's daughter> and carried off[8] <a young she-mule>. [275] Nṛga became a lizard.[9] <Kali> conquered Nala and <strife> conquered Nala.[10] Śaṁvaraṇa became infatuated with the daughter of <Mitra>[11] and became infatuated with the daughter of <his friend>. [276] Daśaratha died through madness for his beloved <Rāma> and through the madness of a beloved <wife>. Kārtavīrya perished through his

kumāracarita, p. 72, Bombay ed., 1898 (tr. Meyer, p. 209, Leipzig, 1902). This passage of Subandhu is compared with its elaboration in the *Harṣacarita*, pp. 20 sqq., Jamnu ed., 1879 (tr. Cowell and Thomas, pp. 74–75, London, 1897), and translated by Cartellieri, 'Subandhu and Bāṇa,' in *WZKM*. 1. 126–132 (cf. also 13. 68). For other lists of precedents see *Harṣacarita*, pp. 199, 221–224, 288, Bombay ed., 1892 (tr. Cowell and Thomas, pp. 169, 192–194, 258, London, 1897); *Kādambarī*, pp. 166, 339–340, 341, 600, Bombay ed., 1890 (tr. Ridding, pp. 64, 137, 138, 200–201, London, 1896).

[1] The reference is, of course, to the famous rape of Tārā, the wife of Bṛhaspati, by the moon; cf. *Harivaṃśa*, 25; *Viṣṇupurāṇa*, 4. 6.

[2] Cf. *Mahābhārata*, 1. 75.

[3] Tel. ed., 'lusting for Indra's spouse, went to serpenthood (or, 'profligacy')'; similarly the Srirangam text; cf. *Mahābhārata*, 5. 11–17.

[4] Tel. ed., 'the daughter of a household priest'; cf. *Mahābhārata*, 1. 78–86.

[5] See *Rāmāyaṇa*, 7. 87–90.

[6] Tel. ed. and Srirangam text add 'in the world'; cf. *Mahābhārata*, 3. 127–128.

[7] Tel. ed., 'despised, as it were.' The legend to which Subandhu here alludes is uncertain, and is perhaps due simply to a popular etymology of Purukutsa as the 'much despised' (cf. *kutsay*, 'to despise'). Sāyaṇa, however, on *Rig-Veda*, 4. 42. 8 (cf. also Sieg, *Sagenstoffe des Rgveda*, 1. 97, Stuttgart, 1902; Muir, *Original Sanskrit Texts*, 1². 267, London, 1872), mentions an *itihāsa*, or legend, which states that Purukutsa was once imprisoned, so that his realm had no ruler. His chief wife then prayed to the seven Ṛṣis for a son, whereupon, in answer, she gave birth to Trasadasyu.

[8] Tel. ed. and Srirangam text, 'went to'; cf. *Mārkaṇḍeyapurāṇa*, 21–22.

[9] See *Mahābhārata*, 13. 70; *Harivaṃśa*, 171.

[10] Tel. ed. and Srirangam text, 'Nala was conquered by Kali (or, 'by strife').'

[11] See *Mahābhārata*, 1. 173–175.

oppression of ⟨a Brāhman for a cow⟩[1] and through his oppression of ⟨cows[1] and Brāhmans⟩. Yudhiṣṭhira deserted truth in the forefront of battle.[2] Śāntanu wept in the forest on account of excessive affection.[3] Thus no one is immaculate.[4] Therefore, I, too, will abandon my body.'

[277] So thinking, he approached the water of a broad, sandy bank, the hiding places of whose fish were pierced by the tips of the sharp talons of the ospreys; with the scales of shoals of *śakulas* and the excrement of otters[5]; with its margin surrounded by rows of carapaces of horrible crabs that had been abandoned by packs of jackals; with its environs whitened[6] by multitudes of cranes, motionless and intent on devouring shoals of carp that were agitated and wavering because of the exceedingly[7] unsteady flow of the water; which was very cool, being united with the motion of the wind that was generated by quantities of drops[8] of water shaken by the sport of schools of extremely active Gangetic porpoises; [278] with its uneven banks seamed by the tips of very young wild[9] buffaloes' horns that dropped off daily; tuneful with the sweet songs of flocks of continually restless *dhārtarāṣṭra* geese; [279] with the soil along its waters crushed by the repose of mermen and bright with the rays of the sun[10]; delightful with the humming of bees[11] that had settled on hundreds of mighty[12] elephants, whose sloping cheeks were flecked with exceedingly copious ichor; with its circumference filled with multitudes of gems[13] that had fallen in the dance of

[1] Tel. ed. omits 'for a cow' and 'of cows'; cf. *Mahābhārata*, 3. 115-116.

[2] Tel. ed. omits this sentence.

[3] See *Mahābhārata*, I. 100-101.

[4] Tel. ed. and Srirangam text, 'thus, therefore, no one in the world is immaculate.'

[5] Tel. ed., 'filled with broad fish-scales pierced by the tips of the talons of the ospreys; mottled with the accumulated excrement of otters'; similarly the Srirangam text.

[6] Tel. ed., 'much whitened.'

[7] Tel. ed. and Srirangam text omit 'exceedingly.'

[8] Tel. ed. and Srirangam text, 'with its *tamālas* cooled by contact with quantities of drops.'

[9] Tel. ed. omits 'wild.'

[10] Tel. ed., 'with the earth on its banks crushed by the repose of mermen, bright with the rays of the sun, and tuneful with the humming of bees and with beautiful flocks of continually restless *dhārtarāṣṭra* geese'; similarly the Srirangam text.

[11] Tel. ed., 'with swarms of bees'; Srirangam text, 'humming of swarms of bees.'

[12] Tel. ed. and Srirangam text omit 'mighty.'

[13] Tel. ed., 'serpents.'

the mass of the water of the ocean,[1] shaken by the right mobile wind; like [2] a strip of slough cast by the serpent of the ocean [3]; the mirror, as it were, of earth; the crystal pavement, so to say, of Varuṇa.[4]

Then, having bathed and the like,[5] he began to descend to the water [6] to abandon his body. Thereupon, while the sharks were kindly, the fish free from envy, the bees [7] not mean, [280] the tortoises affectionate,[8] the crocodiles not cruel, the dolphins not terrible, (and) the Gangetic porpoises not murderous, there came a heavenly voice [9]: 'Noble Kandarpakētu, again, at no long time, shall there be union of thee with thy beloved. Cease, therefore, from thy resolve to die'! Hearing this, he desisted from death,[10] and eager to get food to sustain his body because of his desire of reunion with his beloved, he went along the shore of the mighty ocean.[11] Then Kandarpakētu [12] passed considerable time wandering here and there, living on fruit and the like in the forest.

Finally, after the lapse of several months,[13] came the rainy season, with <conjoined deep rivers> as he who sings to the *kākalī* has a <continuous low note>; [281] with dancing <peacocks> as the eventide has <Śiva> dancing; producing <much pen-reed grass> as

[1] Tel. ed. and Srirangam text, 'in the breakup of the water.'

[2] Tel. ed. and Srirangam text omit 'like.'

[3] Tel. ed. and Srirangam text, 'a serpent going in the water of the ocean.'

[4] Tel. ed. and Srirangam text add 'with <rubies> as a lotus-grove has a <red colour>; with <branches of coral> as a forest district has <birds and branches of trees>; with <mussels> as a coward has <fear>; attended by many <pearls> as Viṣṇu is attended by many <emancipated ascetics>.'

[5] Tel. ed. and Srirangam text, 'having performed all the duties of bathing and the like.'

[6] Tel. ed. and Srirangam text, 'water of the ocean.'

[7] Tel. ed., 'shoals of fish'; the Srirangam text omits the phrase.

[8] Tel. ed. and Srirangam text, 'devoid of longing.'

[9] Tel. ed. and Srirangam text, 'there came a voice from heaven.' For other instances of intended suicide thus divinely prevented see *Kādambarī*, pp. 332–333, 569–570, Bombay ed., 1890 (tr. Ridding, pp. 133, 195, London, 1896).

[10] Tel. ed. and Srirangam text, 'he desisted indeed from undertaking death.'

[11] Tel. ed. omits this clause; Srirangam text, 'then he went to the forest along the shore, eager to get food to sustain his body because of his hope of reunion with his beloved.'

[12] Tel. ed. and Srirangam text, 'he.'

[13] Tel. ed., 'but finally, after the lapse of several days.'

Kumāra's peacock ‹bears Śarajanman›[1]; quelling the ‹expanse of dust› as a great[2] ascetic quells the ‹tide of passion›; with water-giving ‹hail› as an anchorite has a water-giving ‹pot›; showing a wandering of many ‹ships› as the time of doom shows a wandering of many ‹suns›; with ‹*cātakas* eager[3] because of the clouds› as an unmolested forest district has ‹exceedingly curious[3] gazelles›; [282] ‹giving joy to the husbandman› as Rēvatī's tender hand ‹inspired courage in Balarāma›.[4]

The slender lightning shone like the bejewelled[5] boat of Love in the sky that seemed to be a pleasure pool with a forest of blue lotuses which were the riven clouds[6]; the dancing cord, as it were, of a Caṇḍāla maiden who was the Lakṣmī[7] of the clouds; [283] even as a garland[8] for the gate of the palace of the sky; a row of nail marks upon the cloud, in all seeming, given for remembrance by the departing heat of day[9]; the jewelled[10] girdle strand, one might fancy, of a beauty of the sky; the lovely clustering[11] blossoms, so to say, of the coral-tree of heaven; like to a begemmed stick[12] for cleaning Rati's nails; the jewelled shell, it might be termed,[13] of the God whose banner is of flowers.[14] The cloud[15] seemed to vomit forth, like a crane, what appeared

[1] Tel. ed. and Srirangam text, 'with ‹lofty pen-reed grass› as Kumāra's peacock has ‹Śarajanman mounted upon it›.'

[2] Tel. ed. and Srirangam text omit 'great.'

[3] Tel. ed. and Srirangam text, 'proud.' According to the conventions of Sanskrit literature, the *cātaka* (*Cuculus melanoleucus*) is supposed to live only on the raindrops which it drinks.

[4] Tel. ed. adds '‹loud-resounding› as the lord of Laṅkā [Rāvaṇa] had ‹Mēghanāda›; ‹dark with clouds› as Vindhya is ‹intensely dark›'; so also the Srirangam text, which adds '‹with swollen clouds› as young women have ‹plump breasts›.'

[5] Tel. ed. and Srirangam text, 'golden and bejewelled.'

[6] Tel. ed., 'dark with a forest of riven blue lotuses'; similarly the Srirangam text.

[7] Tel. ed. and Srirangam text, 'dark Lakṣmī.'

[8] Tel. ed. and Srirangam text, 'jewelled garland.'

[9] Tel. ed., 'given, in all seeming, upon the breast of his sky spouse by her dark departing lover, the heat of day.'

[10] Tel. ed. and Srirangam text, 'beauteous.'

[11] Tel. ed. and Srirangam text omit 'clustering.'

[12] Tel. ed., 'stone pick.'

[13] Tel. ed., 'the jewelled lance, as it were, even as the pleasure staff'; Srirangam text, 'the jewelled pleasure staff.'

[14] Kāma.

[15] Tel. ed. and Srirangam text, 'the mass of clouds.'

to be[1] a series of ocean shells that had been drunk down too hastily.[2]

[284] The ⟨rainy season⟩, even the ⟨fate of rain⟩, played,[3] as if with chessmen[4] coloured with lac, with yellow and green frogs[5] jumping in the black enclosures[6] of the irrigated fields. The lightning gleamed like a streak of gold rubbed by the goldsmith bank of clouds on a seeming touchstone that was like a mass of lampblack[7] from the torch of the sun. The screw-pine was beauteous[8] as a saw of the Flower-Weaponed God[9] to cut[10] the hearts of sundered (lovers). [285] The drops of water were as masses of dust shaken off by the violence of the wind from the cloud-tree that was cut by the saw of the slender quivering lightning.[11] The hailstones flashed like pearls[12] from the necklaces of the brides of the several quarters (of the sky); as though they were masses of stars reduced to powder by contact with the cloud grinding-stone that was turned by the violence of the fierce wind[13]; handfuls of grain, so to say, of the setting forth of Him[9] whose banner is a fish, eager to conquer the threefold world.[14]

Straightway at the beginning[15] of autumn, with its wagtails not lame[16]; with the course of the herons unhampered[17]; [286] with

[1] Tel. ed. and Srirangam text omit 'what appeared to be.'

[2] Tel. ed. and Srirangam text, 'drunk in the impulse of excessive thirst.

[3] Tel. ed. and Srirangam text, 'the dark lover of the clouds played with the lightning.'

[4] Tel. ed. and Srirangam text, 'dice'; cf. Thomas, 'The Indian Game of Chess,' in *ZDMG*. 52. 271–272; 53. 364–365; Reinaud, *Mémoire .... sur l'Inde .... d'après les écrivains arabes, persans et chinois*, pp. 131–133, Paris, 1849; al-Bīrūnī, *India*, tr. Sachau, 1. 183–185, London, 1888.

[5] Tel. ed. and Srirangam text, 'young frogs.'

[6] Tel. ed., 'gatherings.'

[7] Tel. ed. and Srirangam text, 'on a touchstone of clouds blackened.'

[8] Tel. ed., 'the rough screw-pine shone'; Srirangam text, 'the screw-pine flower shone.'

[9] Kāma.

[10] Tel. ed., 'made to cut.'

[11] Tel. ed. omits this sentence.

[12] Tel. ed. and Srirangam text, 'masses of pearls.'

[13] Tel. ed., 'whirling from the violence of the wind like masses of stars reduced to powder by contact with banks of clouds.'

[14] Tel. ed. adds 'the new meadow seemed like an upper garment, marked with liquid lac, for the breast of Lady Earth with her cochineal. The maid-servant Rainy Season being departed after bathing the heroine Earth with water from the jars of the clouds, the maid-servant Autumn came, showing bright raiment'; similarly the Srirangam text.

[15] Tel. ed. and Srirangam text, 'very beginning.'

[16] Tel. ed., 'with its wagtails well.'

[17] Tel. ed. omits this clause.

boughs[1] exceedingly noisy with skylarks; with intensely bright dawn; with flocks of wandering parrots in the fields of rice; with flamingoes come as guests[2]; with a sky whose brightness was that of the body of Kaṃsa's foe[3]; with old clouds like goose-down[4]; with the pleasure of dogs whose heat was intensified; [287] with shoots of sweet sugar-cane[5]; with lakes possessed of the quintessence of the delightful sound of the herons; with pools whose banks were dug up by the snouts of boars; delighted by roots of beautiful[6] *kasērus*; with startled *cātakas*[7]; causing joy[8] by the sweet sound of flocks of wandering *matsyaputrikā* birds; with disdained *kadambas*; the foe of conches; with expanded lotuses; with clouds at intervals; [288] with unusually bright stars; with a beautiful moon[9]; with unusually sweet water in th pools[10]; with flocks of motionless cranes swallowing shoals o flashing carp[11]; with multitudes of silent frogs; with shrivelled serpents; with rice[12] yellow with golden particles; with screaming ospreys; with the air delightful with the perfume of fragrant white lotuses; lovely with white lotuses[13]; charming[14] in the moonlight[15]; with moulting peacocks[16]; with murmuring *paddy*-birds; with *dhārtarāṣṭra* geese[17]; with herds of deer delighted by

[1] Tel. ed. and Srirangam text, 'boughs of the trees.'

[2] Tel. ed., 'with flamingoes entering fields of rice that had flocks of wandering parrots'; Srirangam text, 'with fields of rice filled with the noise of wandering parrots.'

[3] Namely, blue as Kṛṣṇa.

[4] Tel. ed., 'with clouds glittering like flocks of geese.'

[5] Tel. ed., 'with the radiance of the moon intensified; with shoots of sugar-cane, the joy of lovers'; Srirangam text, 'with the radiance of the moon intensified; with shoots of sugar-cane crushed by travellers.'

[6] Tel. ed. and Srirangam text omit 'beautiful.'

[7] Tel. ed., 'with startled *cātakas* on the banks of pools dug up,' etc.

[8] Tel. ed. and Srirangam text omit 'causing joy..... expanded lotuses.'

[9] Tel. ed. and Srirangam text, 'with a moon that was the adornment of the west.'

[10] Tel. ed., 'filled with sweet sap'; Srirangam text, 'with exceedingly sweet water.'

[11] Tel. ed., 'with rows of motionless vultures and cranes swallowing flashing carp'; the Srirangam text also omits 'shoals.'

[12] Tel. ed. and Srirangam text, 'wheat and rice.'

[13] Tel. ed., 'lovely with white lotuses that were slightly opened by a wind charming with the perfume of fragrant white lotuses'; similarly the Srirangam text.

[14] Tel. ed. omits from here to 'Kandarpakētu.'

[15] Srirangam text omits this phrase.

[16] Srirangam text, 'with peacocks whose tail feathers had fallen out.

[17] Srirangam text 'with delighted *dhārtarāṣṭra* geese.'

the songs[1] of happy[2] female guardians of the rice; with dead *yūthikā*-jasmines[3]; with faded Malabar jasmine-buds; a kinsman to the *bandhūka*; with beauty born; putting to confusion the bow of Sutrāman[4]; with the ten quarters (of the sky) yellowed by masses[5] of the pollen of the smiling saffron; [289] (and) with blossoming lotuses[6];—(then) Kandarpakētu, wandering about, seeing a stone image, and saying with curiosity, frenzy, and the agitation of grief, 'This is like my beloved,' touched it with his hand.[7]

Then she, simply being touched,[8] again[9] assumed the form of Vāsavadattā, leaving her stony state. Perceiving her, Kandarpakētu, as if plunged in a sea of nectar, asked her, embracing her long: 'Dear Vāsavadattā, tell me what this is'!

Being addressed, and sighing long and fervently, she began to tell[10]: '"Having left his kingdom, alone, (and) like a common man,[11] my lord of great good fortune hath borne woe beyond word or thought for the sake of ill-fortuned me, the undeserving. [290] Now, very emaciated through fasting and the like, my lord maketh his food roots, fruits, and so forth"—thus thinking, I went a distance of some *nalvas* to look for fruit, seeing the trees of a grove.[12] And in an instant I perceived the camp of an army with

[1] Srirangam text, 'by hearing the songs.' [2] Srirangam text omits 'happy.'

[3] Srirangam text omits 'with dead . . . beauty born.'

[4] Srirangam text, 'Śatamakha'; in both cases Indra is meant.

[5] Srirangam text omits 'masses.'

[6] Srirangam text adds 'a kinsman to the *bandhūka*.'

[7] Tel. ed., 'Kandarpakētu, wandering about here and there, (and) seeing a stone image, touched it with his hand'; similarly the Srirangam text. For instances of turning into stone in modern Indian folk-tales see Knowles, *Folk-tales of Kashmir*, 2 ed., pp. 191–196, 401–403 (and literature there cited), London, 1893; Frere, *Old Deccan Days*, 2 ed., pp. 77–78, London, 1870; Natesa Sastri, *Dravidian Nights*, p. 85, Madras, 1886; and for a touch restoring to life see *Kādambarī*, p. 637, Bombay ed., 1890 (tr. Ridding, p. 206, London, 1896). Cf. also Gray, 'Literary Studies on the Sanskrit Novel,' in *WZKM.* 18. 53–54. The fortunes of Vāsavadattā after leaving her home show, it should be noted, a blending of the Bluebeard (violated tabu) and Sleeping Beauty cycles of folk-tales.

[8] Tel. ed., 'simply being seen.' [9] Tel. ed. and Srirangam text omit 'again.'

[10] Tel. ed., 'Kandarpakētu, embracing her tightly, asked: "Dear Vāsavadattā, what is this"? She replied'; similarly the Srirangam text.

[11] Tel. ed., 'like a wanderer.'

[12] Tel. ed. and Srirangam text, '"thou being distressed by thirst through fasting and

its abodes of grass huts being hidden in clumps of trees; its general's house being arranged; [291] the (fodder) bags being put down; its tents being begun; the courtesans' quarters being set up; with hundreds of neighs of horses being heard; with hundreds of drum-skins being beaten for the halt; with a place of sweet water being sought; with multitudes of market flags being displayed.

[292] 'As I thought: "Is this the host of my father come to search for me, or perchance (the army) of my lord"?, the general of the army ran toward me, being informed of events by a scout.[1] Then in like manner there ran up the Kirāta general, who had gone out to hunt followed by an army.[2] Immediately I thought: "If I inform my lord, then he, being alone, will be killed by these; [293] but if I do not inform him, then shall I be slain by them."

'Even at the instant of my thought there arose[3] a battle of the two armies[4] as of two vultures eager for one quarry. Then—on the battle's threshing-floor, where the rays of the sun were removed[5] by the shower-clouds of arrows from the hostile bows[6]; [294] with Vidyādharas wandering about, embracing their opportunities for brave warriors that had been tossed high by pairs of tusks of elephants skilled in deeds of battle[7]; with countless circles of the bards of the gods gathering to witness the

the like, I, awakening before thee at the end of sleep, will fetch fruit, roots, and so forth"—so thinking, I went just a *nalva* [400 cubits] into the forest to seek fruit and the like.'

[1] Tel. ed. and Srirangam text, 'then, as I suddenly saw the camp of an army hidden in a clump of trees and thought: "Is this my father's host come to fetch me or the host of my noble lord"? a Kirāta general, informed of the news from afar by a scout, ran to me.'

[2] Tel. ed. and Srirangam text, 'then in like manner, hearing this, there ran up another Kirāta general, who had gone out to hunt accompanied by a similar army.'

[3] Tel. ed. and Srirangam text, 'then there arose,' omitting Vāsavadattā's reflexions.

[4] Tel. ed. and Srirangam text omit 'armies.'

[5] Tel. ed., 'hidden.'

[6] Tel. ed. omits 'from the hostile bows'; Srirangam text omits 'hostile.'

[7] Tel. ed., 'with female Vidyādharas wandering about, embracing brave warriors that had been cloven by the edges of swords high uplifted by hands skilled in deeds of battle'; similarly the Srirangam text.

conflict[1]; with a welcome appearance caused by headless corpses of bodies occupied by Vētālas[2]; greedy for the adornment,[3] in a she-fiend's ear, of a mortar filled with the foot of an elephant that had been hacked off by the sword of a soldier[4]; [295] with laudations in the excessive din that arose[5]; (and) with timid jackals[6]—the warriors drew at once the ‹lives› of their foes and the ‹strings› of their bows, paying no heed to the bodies as if they were lumps of flesh to be the prey of jackals,[7] or had been bitten by serpents.[8]

'The[9] mighty elephants were like ‹generous› donors that bear not[10] meeting with «beggars», for they ‹shed ichor› and bore not[10] meeting with «arrows»; like fortunate paramours adorned with ‹passion› and with golden «girdles», for they were adorned with ‹minium› and had golden «girths»; like goodly gardens ‹beauteous with plantain-trees› and «filled with birds», for they were ‹bright with banners› and were «attended by elephants»; like nights[11] adorned with garlands of ‹constellations›, for they had garlands of ‹pearls›; like days with ‹blossoming flowers›, for they had ‹lashing trunk-tips›.[12] [296] And[13] the horses seemed like creatures bereft of sense[14] ‹abandoning patience›, for they

[1] Tel. ed., 'with the circle at its doorway formed by the many feet of the bards of the gods that had come to witness the conflict.'

[2] Tel. ed. and Srirangam text omit this clause. The Vētālas are a class of malevolent ghosts who animate corpses and haunt cemeteries. They often enter the body of a living man while his spirit is absent, or may even be spirits of the living which prefer to make their dwelling in corpses (cf. Crooke, *Popular Religion and Folk-Lore of Northern India*, 2 ed., I. 243–244, Westminster, 1896).

[3] Tel. ed. and Srirangam text, 'with the adornment.'

[4] Tel. ed. and Srirangam text, 'foot soldier,' the former adding 'with folk drawn by curiosity.'

[5] Tel. ed., 'with shouts of praise arising'; Srirangam text, 'with laudations in the words spoken by folk drawn by curiosity.'

[6] Tel. ed. and Srirangam text add 'with cowards destroyed; like a conqueror eager for combat.'

[7] Tel. ed. and Srirangam text, 'she-jackals and jackals.'

[8] Tel. ed. and Srirangam text add 'or were wretched fragments of white leprosy.'

[9] Tel. ed. and Srirangam text add 'there.'

[10] Srirangam text omits 'not.'

[11] Tel. ed. and Srirangam text, 'multitudes of nights.'

[12] Tel. ed. and Srirangam text, 'like autumn days with ‹blossoming lotuses›, for they had ‹sparkling drops of water›.'

[13] Tel. ed. omits 'and.'

[14] Tel. ed. and Srirangam text, 'like angry creatures.'

‹left the ground›; like oceans adorned with ‹whirlpools› and with «billows», for they were adorned with ‹whorls (of hair)› and had «swift gaits»; like pleasure parks with ‹*dhārtarāṣṭra* geese›, for they included the ‹*mallikākṣa* breed›; like noble houses charming with very new ‹furniture›, for they were charming with very new ‹harness›[1]; like mines that have the ‹gems of the gods›, for they had ‹curls (on their necks)›; like the Lēkhas that have ‹fortitude together with Indra›, for they ‹sustained most mighty lords›.[2] Long danced the headless corpse as if with joy at the thought: "I am released[3] from the ears that heard detraction of others, from the eyes that beheld the rise of the evil and the fall of the good, and from the head that bowed unworthily."[4]

'Then spread the dust[5] born of battle, hiding the eye as if smiling; concealing the existence of the ear as if afraid of hearing calumny of another; [297] frenzied, as it were, being tossed by the motion of the wind; a cause of grayness, so to speak, to the Apsarasas; a cause of blindness, it might be termed, to the soldiers; the darkness, in all seeming, of the evening of conflict; fallen and cut off from its ‹family›, as it were, since it was cut off from the ‹earth›; resembling the doctrines of the adherents of the Mīmāṁsā that conceal the ‹doctrines of the Jains›, since it concealed the ‹sight of the quarters (of heaven) and the sky›; like unto a good man clinging to ‹Viṣṇu's feet›, since it clung to the ‹zenith›.[6] One assumed an ‹agonising

[1] Tel. ed. and Srirangam text, 'like potters' houses ‹containing very new pots›, for they ‹bore very new harness›.'

[2] Tel. ed., 'like the Lēkhas that ‹have increase with Indra›, for they ‹included *indravṛddha* steeds›; like drunkards ‹living in dramshops›, for they were ‹adorned with defences›'; so the Srirangam text, except 'like the Lēkhas that have increase through the ‹weapons of Indra›, for they had increase through ‹*indrāyudha* steeds›.'

[3] Tel. ed. and Srirangam text, 'thank heaven! I am released.'

[4] Tel. ed. and Srirangam text add 'and from the mouth that praised the unpraiseworthy.'

[5] Tel. ed. and Srirangam text, 'mass of dust.'

[6] Tel. ed. substitutes for the last two similes '‹going in the path of the constellations› as an evil prince ‹goes not in the path of a Kṣatriya›; with the appearance of thick smoke like a quarrel; hiding ‹living creatures› as the quality of passion hides ‹truth›; ‹high-raised› as an ill-bred man is ‹puffed up›; hiding the path of the

posture> as Rāma <bound Rāvaṇa>[1]; another[2] clove <hell> as Kṛṣṇa[3] clove <Naraka>; a third had <hearing, speech, and sight> destroyed as the textbook of the Buddhists <rejects tradition, precept, and doctrine>; a fourth was <surrounded with corpses> as a heretical mendicant is <wrapped with matting>[4]; a fifth, fearing <utter defeat>, plunged into the water[5] as Suyōdhana, fearing the <breaking of his thigh>, plunged into the water[5]; a sixth breathed for a long time on a couch of <pen-reed grass> as Bhīṣma[6] breathed for a long time on a couch of <arrows>; [298] a seventh <lost his strength> as Karṇa, terrified in every limb,[7] <released his spear>.[8] Then, with its banners destroyed, its standards tumbling, its fallen bows and chowries injured, and its swords slipping, the army met destruction.[9]

'Straightway,[10] when the ascetic whose hermitage that was had come with flowers and the like, and had learned of the event, I was cursed by him with the words: "My hermitage hath been broken down because of thee; therefore become stone"[11]! [299] And gradually, perceiving poor me suffering much distress, he[12]

<constellations> as an evil man hides the path of the <good>'; similarly the Srirangam text.

1 Tel. ed. and Srirangam text omit this clause.

2 Tel. ed. and Srirangam text, 'and straightway one.

3 Tel. ed. and Srirangam text, 'Nārāyaṇa'; for the allusion cf. *Harivaṁśa*, 120.

4 Tel. ed. and Srirangam text, 'a fourth had his body <surrounded with corpses> as a heretical mendicant has his body <wrapped with matting>; a fifth, <drunken>, fell like <Surāpa> (Srirangam text, 'the Brāhman Surāpa').' The details of the legend of Surāpa are as yet unknown.

5 Tel. ed. and Srirangam text, 'water of a pool.'

6 Tel. ed. and Srirangam text, 'dying Bhīṣma.'

7 Tel. ed. and Srirangam text, 'with his limbs terrified.'

8 Tel. ed. and Srirangam text add 'another slew <them that caused shouting> as Raghu's scion [Rāma] slew <Rāvaṇa>.'

9 Tel. ed., 'then, with impotent banners, with tumbling standards, and with the daggers of the soldiers of the armies bent, both entire armies mutually proceeded to slaughter'; similarly the Srirangam text.

10 Tel. ed. and Srirangam text, 'and then.'

11 Tel. ed. and Srirangam text, 'had learned of the event through his yōga sight, being angered that "this my hermitage hath been broken down because of thee [Vāsavadattā]," I was cursed with the words: "Become a stone image"!' The folk-tale *motif* is that of the Bluebeard cycle of punishment in consequence of a violation of tabu (see MacCulloch, *Childhood of Fiction*, pp. 306–324, London, 1905).

12 Tel. ed. and Srirangam text, 'then gradually, out of kindness,—"for this unhappy

made the termination of the curse concurrent with the touch of the hand of my noble lord.'

Then Kandarpakētu, together with Makaranda, who[1] had come up, and with Vāsavadattā,[2] [300] went to his own city,[3] and lived[4] enjoying blisses as his heart desired.[5]

girl suffers much distress"—and through pity for my noble lord, this hermit, being entreated.'

[1] Tel. ed. and Srirangam text add 'who had heard of the event.'

[2] Tel. ed. and Srirangam text, 'that Vāsavadattā.'

[3] Tel. ed. adds 'Pāṭalīputra,' which was, however, the old home of Vāsavadattā, not of Kandarpakētu (see above, p. 75).

[4] Tel. ed. and Srirangam text, 'lived much time with them twain.'

[5] Tel. ed. and Srirangam text add '(and) that could scarcely be gained in the world of the gods.' Tel. ed. also adds two stanzas, the first being the thirteenth of Hall's introductory stanzas, and the second being the eleventh introductory stanza of the *Harṣacarita*; the Srirangam text omits the latter interpolation, but here appends the thirteenth introductory stanza of Hall.

శుభమస్తు.

శ్రీమన్నిఖిలసురేంద్రాదివందితపాదకమల

శ్రీవాగ్దేవీదత్తవరప్రసాదేన

సుబంధునామ్నాకవికులసార్వభౌమేన

విరచితః వాసవదత్తాఖ్యః చంపూప్రబంధోయం

ధీమతామర్థపరిజ్ఞానాయ

వ్యాఖ్యానేనసాకం

మధురసుశ్శాస్త్రిణాసంశోధ్యపరిష్కృతః

జ్ఞానసూర్యోదయముద్రాక్షరశాలాయాం

తదధికారిణా॥ భువనగిరి॥ రంగయ్యశెట్టినామ్నా

వైశ్యచూడామణినాముద్రాక్షరై

ర్ముద్రయిత్వా ప్రకటీకృతస్సన్

భువివిజయతేతరాం

౧౮౬౨ సంవత్సరం-యేప్రల్ నెల ౧౯ తేది.

śubham astu

śrīmannikhilasurēṃdrādivaṃditapādakamala-

śrīvāgdēvīdattavaraprasādēna

subaṃdhunāmnā kavikulasārvabhāumēna

viracitaḥ vāsavadattākhyaḥ caṃpūprabaṃdhō 'yaṃ

dhīmatām arthaparijñānāya

vyākhyānēna sākaṃ

madhurasubbhāśāstriṇā saṃśōdhyapariṣkṛtaḥ

jñānasūryōdayamudrākṣaraśālāyāṃ

tadadhikāriṇā bhuvanagiri raṃgayyaśēṭṭināmnā

vāiśyacūḍāmaṇinā mudrākṣarāir

mudrayitvā prakaṭīkṛtas san

bhuvivijayatētarāṃ

1862 saṃvatsaraṃ yēpral nēla 19 tēdı

śrīhayagrīvāya namaḥ.
vāsavadattā savyākhyā.

(1) [2] karabadarasadṛśam akhilaṃ bhuvanatalaṃ yatprasādataḥ kavayaḥ
paśyanti sūkṣmamatayas sā jayati sarasvatī dēvī.
khinno 'si muṃca śāilaṃ bibhṛmō vayam iti vadatsu śithilabhujaḥ
bharabhugnavi(tatha)bāhuṣu gōpēṣu hasan harir jayati.

[4] sa jayati himakaralēkhā cakāsti yasyō 'mayō 't(kayā) nihitā
nayanapradīpakajjalajighṛkṣayā rajataśuktir i(2)va.

[3] kaṭhinataradāmavēṣṭanalēkhāsaṃdēhadāyinō yasya
rājanti valivibhaṅgās sa pātu dāmōdarō bhavataḥ.

[4] bhavati subhagatvam adhikaṃ vistāritaparaguṇasya sujanasya
vahati vikāsitakumudō dviguṇarucim himakar(ad)yōtaḥ.

[5] viṣadharatō 'py ativiṣamaḥ khala iti na mṛṣā vadaṃti vidvāṃsaḥ
yad ayan nakuladvēṣī sakuladvēṣī punaḥ (punaḥ) piśunaḥ.

[6] atimalinē kartavyē bhavati khalānām atīva nipuṇā dhīḥ
timirē hi kāuśikānāṃ rūpaṃ pratipadyatē (dṛṣṭiḥ).

[7] hasta iva bhūtimalinō yathā yathā laṃghayati khalas sujanaṃ
darpaṇam iva tam kurutē tathā tathā nirmalacchāyaṃ.

[6] vidhvastaparaguṇānāṃ bhavati khalānām atīva malinatvaṃ
antaritaśaśirucām api salilamucāṃ malinimā bhyadhikaḥ.

[7] sā rasavattā vihatā navakā (3) vilasaṃti carati nō kaṃ kaḥ
sarasī 'va kīrtiśēṣaṃ gatavati bhuvi vikramādityē.

[8] aviditaguṇā "pi satkavi(phaṇitiḥ) karṇēṣu vamati madhudhārāṃ
anadhigataparimaḷā "pi hi harati dṛśam mālatīmālā.
guṇinām api nijarūpapratipattiḥ parata ēva sambhavati
svamahimadarśanam akṣṇōr mukuratalē jāyatē yasmāt.

[9] [sarasvatīdattavaraprasādaś cakrē subandhuḥ sujanāika-bandhuḥ
pratyakṣaraślēṣamayaprabandhavinyāsavāidagdhyanidhir nibandham].

[10] abhūd (akharvavibhava)sarvōrvīpaticakra[cāru]cūḍāmaṇi(śrēṇi)śāṇa[11]kōṇakaṣaṇa(vi)malīkṛta(pāda)nakhamaṇiḥ nṛsiṃha iva da(4)rśitahiraṇyakaśipukṣētradānavismayaḥ kṛṣṇa iva kṛtavasudēvatarpaṇaḥ [12] nārāyaṇa iva sāukaryasamāsādita-(dharaṇī)maṇḍalaḥ kaṃsārātir iva janitayaśōdānandasamṛddhiḥ ānakadundubhir iva kṛtakāvyā[13]daraḥ sāgaraśāyī "vā 'nanta-bhōgicūḍāmaṇi(śrēṇi)rañjitapāda(ḥ)[padmō] varuṇa ivā "śā(5)ntarakṣaṇaḥ agastya iva dakṣiṇāśāprasādhakaḥ jalanidhir iva vāhinīśatanāyakas samakarapracāraś ca hara [14] iva mahāsēnānu(yātō nirjita[1])māraś ca mērur iva vibudhālayō viśvakarmāśrayaś ca ravir iva kṣaṇadānapriyaś chāyāsantāpaharaś ca kusum-(āyudha) iva janitāniruddhasampad ratisukhapradaś ca vidyādha[15]rō 'pi sumanāḥ dhṛtarāṣṭrō 'pi guṇapriyaḥ (6) kṣamānugatō 'pi [16] sudharmāśritaḥ [2] bṛhannalānubhāvō 'py aṃtassaraḷaḥ mahiṣīsambha[17]vō 'pi vṛṣōtpādī ataraḷō 'pi mahānāyakaḥ rājā cintāmaṇir nāma. yatra ca śāsati (dharaṇī [3])maṃḍalaṃ chalanigrahaprayōgō (nyāyaśāstrēṣu[4]) [18] nāstikatā cārvākēṣu kaṇṭakayōgō [ni]yōgēṣu parīvādō [19] vīṇāsu khalasam(pra)yōgaś śāliṣu dvijihvasaṃ(grahītir ahi)tuṇḍikēṣu karacchēdaḥ (kuṭmala)grahaṇēṣu nētrōtpāṭanam munīnāṃ (7) [dvija]rājaviru[20]ddhatā paṃkajānāṃ sārvabhāumayōgō (diggajānāṃ [5]) [agnitulā-

[1] So also Hall's manuscripts A, B, C, E, F, G, H, and the commentator Narasiṃha.
[2] Tel. ed. 61 and Grantha ed., *āśrayaḥ*.
[3] Tel. ed. 61, Grantha ed., and Srirangam text, *dharāṃ*.
[4] Cf. *nāiyāyikavādēṣu* in Hall's manuscript F ; Trichinopoly ed., *nyāyēṣu*.
[5] So also Hall's manuscripts A, B, C, D, E, F, G, H, and the commentator Jagaddhara.

śuddhiḥ suvarṇānāṃ] (sūci)bhēdō maṇīnāṃ śūlabhaṃgō yuvatī-(navaprasavēṣu agnitulāśuddhis svarṇānāṃ) duśśāsana[21]darśanaṃ (mahā)bhāratē karapatra(vi)dāraṇaṃ jalajānāṃ (param ēvaṃ vyavasthitaṃ). mahāvarāhō gōtrōddharaṇapravṛttō 'pi gōtrōddalanam akarōt. rāghavaḥ pariharann api janakabhuvaṃ janakabhuvā saha vanaṃ vivēśa. bharatō (rāma)darśitabha[22]ktir api rājyē virāmam akarōt. naḷasya damayantyā miḷitasyā 'pi punarbhūparigra(8)hō jātaḥ. pṛthur api gōtrasamutsāraṇavistāritabhūmaṇḍalaḥ. (tad) itthaṃ nā 'sti vāgavasaraḥ (pūrvatanēṣu[1]) rājasu (api tu vacanīyatāyāḥ). sa punar anyō [ēva] dēvō nyakkṛtasarvōrvīpati(cakra)caritaḥ. tathāhi sa parvataḥ kaṭakasaṃcāriṇō gandharvān darśitaśṛṃgōnnatis sukha[23]yan na virarāma. sa himālayō nāvaśyāyōcchalitō nō māyājanmanē hitaś ca. sa himānī giri sthitō vṛṣadhvajaś (ca). (9) (sa) sadāgatiś (cā) 'vadhūtākhilakāntāraḥ pāvakāgrēsarō na [24] bhōgōtsukas sumanōharaś ca. sa ratnākarō 'na(timayō) [katham a]'gādhas sama(10)ryādaḥ nōdrōkō ['py asya] vismayas sadā himakar(ā[25]śayō) 'mṛtamayas (satpātras) tasyā 'calō nakrō 'dhō mahānadīnas samudraś (ca). [26] sa [candra iva] kṣaṇadānaṃdakaraḥ kumudavan(āika)baṃdhus sakalakalākulagṛhaṃ natārātibalaś (caṃdraś ca. sa) mitrōdayahētuḥ kāṃcanaśōbhāṃ bibhrada[27]calādhikalakṣmī-(11)s sumēruḥ [iva]. yasya ca ripuvargas sadāpārthō 'pi na mahābhārataraṇayōgyaḥ bhīṣmō 'py aśāṃtanavēhitaḥ sānucarō 'pi na gōtrabhūṣitaḥ. (12) [28] [api ca] sa triśaṃkur (api) na (nā)kṣatrapatha(cyutaḥ) śaṃkarō 'pi na viṣādī pāvakō 'pi na kṛṣṇavartmā (nā) "śrayāśō ['pi] na dahanaś (ca) nā 'ṃtaka [29] ivā 'kasmād apahṛtajīvanaḥ na rāhur iva mitramaṃḍalagrahaṇa-(saṃ)vardhitarucih na naḷa iva kalivi(jitavigrahaḥ) na cakrī "va sṛgālavadhastutisamullasitaḥ naṃdagōpa iva yaśōdayā ('nvitaḥ[2]) jarāsaṃdha iva ghaṭitasaṃdhivigrahaḥ bhārgava iva sadānabhōgaḥ daśaratha [30] iva sumitrōpētaḥ sumaṃtrādhiṣṭhitaś ca dilīpa iva sudakṣiṇān(vitaḥ[3]) rakṣita(13)guś ca rāma iva janitakuśalavayōrūpōcchrāyaḥ. tasya ca (rājñaḥ) pārijāta ivā "śrita-

[1] Trichinopoly ed. and Srirangam text, *pūrvatarēṣu*.
[2] So also Hall's manuscripts C, E, F, H, and the commentator Jagaddhara.
[3] Cf. *anugatō* in Hall's manuscript C.

naṃdanaḥ himālaya iva jani[31]taśivaḥ maṃdara iva bhōgibhōgāṃkitaḥ kāilāsa iva mahēśvarōpabhuktakōṭiḥ madhur iva nānārāmānaṃdakaraḥ kṣīrōdamathanōdya[32]tamaṃdara iva mukharitabhuvanaḥ rāga(14)(rāja) ivō 'l(lasita)ratiḥ īśānabhūtisaṃcaya iva saṃdhyōcchalitaḥ śaranmēgha ivā 'vadātahṛdayaḥ [33] viṣṇupadāvalaṃbī ca pārtha iva samarasāhasōcitaḥ kaṃsa iva [34] kuvalayāpīḍa(bhūṣaṇaḥ) tārkṣya iva [vinatānandakaraḥ] sumukhanaṃdana(ḥ) [ca] viṣṇur iva krōḍīkṛtasutanuḥ śāṃtanava iva svavaśa[sthāpita]kāla[35]dharmaḥ kāuravavyū(15)ha iva suśarmādhiṣṭhitaḥ [subāhur iva rāmānandī samadṛṣṭir api mahēśvarō muktāmayō 'py ataralamadhyō] jala(dharasamaya) iva [36] vimalataravāridhārātrāsitarājahaṃsa(maṃḍalaḥ [1] subāhur api rāmānaṃdakaraḥ samadṛṣṭir api mahēśvaraḥ muktāmayō 'py ataraḷamadhyaḥ) vaṃśa[pra]dīpō 'py akṣatadaśaḥ tanayō ('bhūt) kaṃdarpakētur nāma. yēna [ca] caṃdrēṇē 'va sakalakalākulagṛhēṇa śarvarītihāriṇā [37] (kāiravavi)baṃdhunā prasādhitāśēna vilōki(16)tā jaladhaya iva (sam)ullasitagōtrās sudūra[vi [2]]vardhitajīvanāḥ prasannasatvās [38] saṃtaḥ parām (ṛddhim) avāpuḥ. yasya [ca] janitāniruddhalīlasya ratipriyasya kusumaśarāsanasya makarakētōr iva darśanēna vanitājanasya hṛdayam ullalāsa. yasmāi cā 'nugatadakṣiṇasadāgatayē (nētra [3])śrutisukha(pradāya) kōmalakōkilarutāya vi(kasita)pallavāya kṛtakā[39]ṃtārataraṃgāya surabhisumanōbhirāmāya sarva[jana]sulabhapadmāya vi(stṛta [4])kana(17)kasaṃpadē atikrāṃtadamanakāya vasaṃtāyē 'vō ('pa)vana[40]latā ivō 'tkalikāsahasrasaṃkulā bhramarasaṃgatāḥ pravālahāriṇyō vilasadvayasas taruṇyaḥ spṛhayāṃ cakruḥ. yasya ca samarabhuvi [41] bhujadaṃḍēna kōdaṃḍaṃ kōdaṃḍēna (bāṇāḥ bāṇāir) ariśiraḥ (ariśirasā) bhūmaṇḍalaṃ (bhūmaṇḍalēnā) 'nubhūta(pūrvanāyakasmaraṇaṃ smaraṇēna ca) kīrtiḥ kīrtyā ca sapta sāgarāḥ sāgarāiḥ kṛtayugādirāja[carita]smaraṇaṃ (smaraṇēna) sthāiryaṃ (sthāiryēṇa) pratikṣaṇam āścaryam āsāditaṃ.

[1] So also Hall's manuscripts C, E, F, G, H, and the commentator Narasiṃha.

[2] Hall's manuscripts B, C, D, G, H also omit *vi*; Trichinopoly ed., *parivardhita*.

[3] So also Hall's manuscripts A, B, C, D, E, F, H, and the commentators Narasiṃha and Jagaddhara.

[4] Cf. *viṣkṛta* in Hall's manuscript D.

yasya ca pratāpānaladagdha(dayitānāṃ) ripusuṃdarīṇāṃ karatala(racita)tāḍanabhītāi[42]r iva muktāhārāiḥ payōdhara(parisarā muktāḥ). yasya ca niśitanārāca(jarjharita)mattamātaṃgakuṃbhasthalavigalitamuktāphala[nikara [1]]daṃturitaparisarē (tarat [2])-patrara(18)thē raktavāri(samuḍḍīyamānadviradapadakacchapē [3] vilasad)utpala(puṃḍarīkē) vāhinīśatasamākulē nṛtyatkabaṃdha-(baṃdhurē) sura(nārī)[43]samāgamōtsuka(carad)bhaṭ(ahuṃ)kāra-(bhāṣaṇarava)bhīṣaṇē (sāgara iva samaraśirasi [4]) bhinnapadātikarituragarudhir(ārdrō) jayalakṣmīpādālaktakarāgaraṃjita iva khaḍgō rarāja. [44] atha kadācid avasannāyāṃ yāmavatyāṃ dadhi(dhavaḷa)kālakṣapaṇaka[grāsa]piṃḍa [5] iva niśāyamunāphēna(stabaka [6]) iva mēnakānakhamārjana(sphaṭika)śilāśakala iva madhucchatrac(chāyā)maṃḍalōdarē paścimācalōpadhānasukhani(ṣaṇṇa)śirasō rājatatāṭaṃka(cakra [7]) iva (śyāmāyāḥ) śēṣamadhubhāji [45] caṣaka iva vibhāvarīvadhvāḥ aparajala(ni)dhipayasi śaṃkhakāṃtikāmuka iva majjati kumudinīnāyakē śiśira(himaśīkara)kardamita(19)kumuda(parāga [8])madhyabaddhacaraṇēṣu ṣaṭcaraṇēṣu kaḷapralāpabōdhit[acakit]ābhisārikāsu śārikāsu prabuddhādhyayanakarmaṭhēṣu maṭhēṣu (hāsa)rāgamukharakārpaṭik[ajan [9]]ōpagīyamānakāvya(kathyāsu) rathyāsu [46] sakalanipīta(nāiśa)timira(saṃghātam [10]) atanīyastayā (sōḍhum [11]) asamarthēṣv iva kajjaḷavyājād udvamat(su) [iva] kāmi(nī)nidhuvanalīlādarśanārtham ivō 'dgrīvikāśatadānakhinnēṣu vividha(vilāsacitrasurata)-[47]sākṣiṣu śaraṇāgatam ivā 'dhō(ni)līnaṃ timira(saṃgham) avatsu durjana(vacanēṣv) iva dagdhasnēhatayā maṃdimānam upagatēṣu ativṛddhēṣv iva daśāṃtam upagatēṣu (ā)pannasadīśva-

[1] Hall's manuscripts C, D, F, H also omit *nikara.*

[2] So also Hall's manuscripts A, B, D, H.

[3] Hall's manuscripts C, E also have *kacchapē* and manuscript A has *kacchapa.*

[4] Hall's manuscript C also has *samaraśirasi*; cf. *samarasarasi* in his manuscripts A, B, E.

[5] Tel. ed. 61 and Grantha ed., *piṇḍaka.*

[6] So also Hall's manuscripts A, B, C, D, E, F, G, H.

[7] So also Hall's manuscripts A, B, D.

[8] So also Hall's manuscripts A, B, C, D, E, F, G, H, and the commentator Jagaddhara.

[9] Hall's manuscripts D, F, H, and the commentator Narasiṃha also omit *jana.*

[10] So also Hall's manuscripts A, B, C, D, E, H, and the commentator Narasiṃha.

[11] So also Hall's manuscripts A, B, E, F, G, H.

rēṣv iva pātramātrāvaśēṣēṣu dānavēṣv iva [48] niśāṃtamadhyacāriṣu astagiriśikharēṣv iva patatpataṃgēṣu pradīpēṣu anavarata(nipatita)makaraṃdabiṃdu(20)saṃdōh(āsvādamadamugdha[1])-madhukaranikuruṃba[2]jhaṃkāra(rava)mukharitēṣu mlānimānam upagacchatsu vāsāgārakusumōpahā[49]rēṣu vigaḷatkuṃdāir aḷakāiḥ priya(tama)virahaśōkāt bāṣpabiṃdūn [iva] (visṛjadbhir[3] iva) priyatamagamananani(rōdham) iva (kurvadbhir[4] vācālita)tulākōṭibhiś caraṇapallavāiḥ (vilasitāsu[5] rajanī)śēṣasurata[bhara[6]]-pariśramavi[50]gaḷitakēśapāśadaradaḷita(mādhavī)mālāparimaḷalubdhamadhukarani(kuruṃba[7])pakṣānila[ni]pītanidāghajalaśīkara(kaṇikāsu) udvēllatbhuja(vallī)kaṃkaṇajhaṇātkāra(subhagāsu[8]) [nava]nakhapada(daṣṭa[9])kēśa(pāśa[10]vi)nirmōka[51]vēdanākṛtasītkāravinirgatadugdhamugdhadaśanakiraṇa[cchaṭā]dhavaḷitabhōgāvāsāsu punardarśanapṛcchāvidhurasakhījanānukṣaṇavīkṣyamāṇapriyatamāsu kṣaṇadāgata(surata)vāiyātyavacana[śata](saṃskāraka[11])gṛhaśukacāṭuvyāhṛtikṣaṇajanitamaṃdākṣāsu śaradvāsaralakṣmīṣv iva [52] nakhālaṃkṛtapayōdharāsu āsannamaraṇāsv iva jīvitēśapurābhimukhī(21)ṣu vasaṃtavanarājiṣv ivō 'tkalikābahuḷāsu priyāir āliṃgyamānāsu kāminīṣu āṃdōḷitakusumakēsarē kēsarēṇumuṣi [53] (rati)raṇita(nūpura[12])maṇīnāṃ ramaṇīnāṃ vikacakumudākarē mudākarē saṃgabhāji priyavirahitāsu rahitāsu (virahitāsu) sukhēna murmura(cūrṇam) iva [varṣati] samaṃtādarpakē darpakēṣudahanasya dūraprasāritakōka[54]priyatamārutē mārutē vahati jaghanamadana(nagaratōraṇasrajā manmatha[13])ma-

[1] Hall's manuscripts B, C, D, E, F, G, H also have *mughda*.

[2] Tel. ed. 61 and Grantha ed., *nikuramba*.

[3] Cf. *utsṛjadbhir iva* in Hall's manuscripts A, B, C, D, E, F, H.

[4] So also Hall's manuscripts D, F, H.

[5] Trichinopoly ed., *vācālatulākōṭibhiḥ caraṇapallavāiḥ priyatamagamananirōdham iva kurvatīṣu.*

[6] Hall's manuscripts C, D, E, F, H also omit *bhara*.

[7] So also Hall's manuscripts A, B, C, F, G, H.

[8] Hall's manuscripts A, B, C, D, F, H also have *subhagāsu*.

[9] So also Hall's manuscripts A, C, D, E, F, H, and the commentators Jagaddhara and Narasiṃha.

[10] So also Hall's manuscripts A, B, D, G, and the commentator Narasiṃha.

[11] Cf. *saṃsmāraka* in Hall's manuscripts A, B, C, D, E, F, G, H, and the commentator Jagaddhara.

[12] So also Hall's manuscript D and the commentator Narasiṃha.

[13] Cf. *manmathamandiramahā°* in Hall's manuscripts A, B, G.

hānidhi(jaghanakōśamaṃdira)kanakaprākārēṇa rōmā(lirūpa)latālavāla(valayēna) jaghanacaṃdramaṃḍalaparivēṣēṇa (vitata)tribhuvanavijayapraśasti(varṇa[1]paṃkti)kanakapatrēṇa (makarakētōḥ) sakalahṛdaya(baṃdījana)nivāsa(gṛha)parikhāvalayēna (22) (sakala)jaga[55]llōcanavihaṃgama(jaghanavāsa)lāsaka(kanaka[2])-śalākāguṇēna [iva] (nava)mēkhalādāmnā pari(kalita)jaghana(sthalāṃ[3]) unnatapayōdharabhārāṃtaritamukhacaṃdradarśanāprāpti(vēdanayē) "va guru(tara)nitaṃbabiṃbapayōdharakuṃbha(niruddhōbhayapārśva[4])pīḍājanitāyāsēnē "va (mama mūrdhni sthitayōr anayōr iyatpramāṇayō stanakalaśayōḥ kathaṃ mayyē "va pātō bhaviṣyatī 'ti ciṃtayē "va gṛhītagurukaḷatrānuśayēnē "va vidhātur atipīḍa[56]yatō hastapāśajanitāyāsēnē "va) kṣīṇataratām upagatēna madhyabhāgēnā 'laṃkṛtām anurāgaratna(pūrita)kanaka(paruvakābhyāṃ) cūcukamudrāsanāthābhyāṃ [atigurupariṇāhatayā patanabhayāt kīlitābhyām iva cūcukacchalēna] (vidhinā) girisārē(ṇē "va cūcukacchalēnā 'tiguruparīṇāhatayā patanabhayakīlitābhyām iva hṛcchayavilēpanacāturikavibhramābhyāṃ) saka[57]lāvayava(nirmiti)śēṣalāvaṇyapuṃjābhyām iva [hṛdayataṭāgakamalābhyām iva hṛcchayakapōlacāturikāvibhramābhyāṃ] rōmāvalīlatāphala(bhūtā)bhyāṃ kaṃdarpa(darpakaśilā)cūrṇapūrṇa(kanaka[5](23)kalaśābhyām iva hṛdayataṭākakamalamukuḷābhyāṃ rōmalatāphalabhūtābhyāṃ[6] hāralatāmṛṇāḷalōbha[58]nilīnacakravākābhyāṃ hāralatārōmāvalīgaṃgāyamunāsaṃgamavyājaprayāgataṭābhyām aśēṣajanahṛdayapatanād iva saṃjātagāuravābhyāṃ) tribhuvanavijayapariśramakhinnasya makarakētōr (viśrama)vijan(āvāsa)gṛhābhyāṃ payōdharābhyāṃ samudbhāsamānāṃ mukhacaṃdra(satata[7])sannihitasaṃdhyārāgēṇa (dvija[8])maṇirakṣāsiṃdūramudrānukāriṇā [59] nis(saradā 'bhyaṃ-

[1] Cf. *varṇarōmāvalī* in Hall's manuscripts A, G; and *rōmavarṇāvalī* in manuscripts B, E, F.

[2] So also Hall's manuscript C.

[3] So also Hall's manuscripts A, B, C, D, E, F, G, H, and the commentators Jagaddhara and Narasiṃha.

[4] So also Hall's manuscripts B, F, G, H.

[5] Trichinopoly ed. omits *kanaka*.

[6] Trichinopoly ed. omits *rōmalatāphalabhūtābhyāṃ*.

[7] Cf. *hitasantata* in Hall's manuscripts A, C, F, G; and *hitasatata* in manuscript D.

[8] So also Hall's manuscripts A, B, C, D, F, G, H, and the commentators Jagaddhara and Narasiṃha.

tara)rāgēṇē 'va raṃjitēna rāgasāgaravidruma(śakalēnē [1]) 'vā 'dharapallavēna [upa]śōbhamānāṃ taruṇa(kāitaka)daḷadrāghīyasā pakṣmalacaṭulālasēna hṛday(āvāsa)gṛhāvasthitahṛcchayavilāsinō gavākṣaśaṃkām (uj)janayatā sarāgēṇā 'pi nirvāṇaṃ [60] (janayatā [2]) gatiprasara(ni)rōdhakaśravaṇakṛta(krōdhēnē) 'vā ('pāṃga)lōhitēna dhavaḷayatē 'va jagada(khilaṃ) utphullakamalakānanasanātham iva gagana(talaṃ) kurvatā dugdhāṃbhōdhisahasrāṇī 'vō'dvamatākuṃda(kusumanilīnām) utpalamālā(m) [lakṣmīm ivō] upahasatā nayanayugaḷēna bhūṣitāṃ daśanaratnatulā(ru[61]ṃḍēnē) 'va nayan(āmṛtasiṃdhu)sētubaṃdhēnē ('va) yāuvanamanmathamattavāraṇa(paraṃḍakēnē) 'va nāsāvaṃśēna pariṣkṛtāṃ vilōcana(kuvalaya [3])bhramarapaṅktibhyāṃ mukhamadanamaṃdiratōraṇa(mālikā(24)bhyāṃ) rāgasāgara(vēṇikābhyāṃ [4]) yāuvananartakalāsikābhyāṃ bhrūlatābhyāṃ vi(rājitāṃ [5]) ghanasama-[62]yākāśalakṣmīm ivō 'llasad(dhāra)payōdharāṃ jaya[śabda]-ghōṣaṇā[6]panna(narapati)mūrtim ivō 'llasattulākōṭipratiṣṭhitāṃ suyōdhanadhṛtim iva karṇaviśrāṃtalōcanāṃ vāmanalīlām iva darśitabalibhaṃgāṃ vṛścikarāśiravisthitim ivā 'tikrāṃtakanyātulāṃ uṣām ivā 'niru[63]ddhadarśanasukhāṃ śacīm iva naṃdanēkṣaṇarucim paśupatitāṃḍavalīlām ivō 'llasaccakṣuśśravasaṃ (viṃdhyā)ṭavīm ivō 'ttuṃgaśyāmalaku(25)cāṃ vānara[64]sēnām iva sugrīvāṃgada[upa]śōbhitāṃ bhāsvatālaṃkārēṇa (śvētarōciṣā smitēna [7]) lōhitēnā ('dharēṇa [8]) sāumyēna darśanēna guruṇā nitaṃbabiṃbēna (sitēna hārēṇa [9]) śanāiścarēṇa pādēna [tamasā kēśapāśēna [10]] (vikacēna lōcanōtpalēna [11]) graha(mayām) iva saṃsārabhitticitra[65]lēkhām iva trāilōkya(raṃgasya) rasāyanasi-

[1] So also Hall's manuscripts A, B, C, D, E, F, H, and the commentator Narasiṃha.
[2] So also Hall's manuscripts A, B, C, D, F, G, H, and the commentator Narasiṃha.
[3] So also Hall's manuscripts A, B, C, D, E, F, G, H.
[4] So also Hall's manuscripts A, B, C, D, F, H, and the commentators Jagaddhara and Narasiṃha.
[5] So also Hall's manuscripts A, B, C, D, E, F, G, and the commentator Narasiṃha.
[6] Cf. *jayaghōṣa* in Hall's manuscripts C, D, F.
[7] Hall's manuscripts C, D, and the commentator Narasiṃha add this after the next phrase.
[8] So also Hall's manuscripts A, B, C, D, E, F, G, H.
[9] Similarly also Hall's manuscripts C, D, and the commentator Narasiṃha.
[10] Hall's manuscripts B, C, E, F, G also omit *tamasā kēśapāśēna.*
[11] So also Hall's manuscripts A, B, C, E, F, G, H.

ddhim iva (yāuvanasya) saṃkalpa(vṛttim [1]) iva śṛṃgārasya (saṃkētabhūmim iva lāvaṇyasya) nidhānam iva [66] kāutukasya [tribhuvana [2]]vijayapatākām iva makaradhvajasya (ājibhūmim) iva [manasō 'bhibhūtim iva] madanasya (sammōhinīm) iva (sarv)-ēṃdriyāṇāṃ mōhanaśaktim iva (madanasya) vihārasthalīm iva sāuṃdaryasya (mitravilāsālaya)śālām iva sāubhāgyasya [utpattisthānam iva lāvaṇyasya] āka[67]rśaṇa(maṃtra [3])siddhim iva (manasijasya) cakṣurbaṃdha(namahāuṣadhīm [4]) iva manmathēṃdrajālinaḥ tribhuvanavilōbhanasṛṣṭim iva prajāpatēḥ [kanyakām] aṣṭādaśavarṣadēśīyāṃ [5] (kanyām) apaśyat [6] svapnē. atha tāṃ prītivisphāritēna caksuṣā pibann iva janitērṣyayē 'va nidrayā ciraṣēvitayā [7] (sa) mumucē. (atha sa prabuddhas [8]) tu viṣasarasī 'va durja[68]navacasī 'va (26) nimagnam ātmānam (ava)dhārayituṃ na śaśāka. tathāhi kṣaṇam (ākāśē tadāliṃganārthaṃ) prasāritabāhuyugaḷaḥ ēhy ēhi priyatamē (mā gaccha mā gacchē [9]) 'tī dikṣu (vidikṣu [10] ca vi)likhitām ivō 'tkīrṇām iva cakṣuṣi nikhātām iva hṛdayē priyatamām ājuhāva. tatas tatrāi "va śayyātalē (nilīnō [11]) niṣiddhāśēṣaparijanō datta(kavāṭaḥ) pari[69]hṛtatāṃbūlā[hārā]disakalōpabhōgas taṃ (divasam) anayat. tathāi "va niśām api svapnasamāgamēcchayā (katham apy) anāiṣīt. atha tasya priyasakhō makaraṃdō nāma katham api labdhapravēśa(darśanaḥ) kaṃdarpasāyakaprahāraparavaśaṃ kaṃdarpakētum uvāca. sakhē kim i[70]dam asāṃpratam asādhujanōcitam (ācāram) āśritō 'si. tavāi "tad[caritam] ālōkya vitarka-(ḍōlāsu) nivasaṃti saṃtaḥ. khalāḥ punas (tvadanucitaṃ aniṣṭam ācāram ācaraṃti). aniṣṭ(ōtpādana)rasōttaraṃ hi (bhavati [12]) khalahṛdayaṃ. kō nāmā 'sya tattvanirūpaṇē samarthaḥ. tathā hi bhīmō 'pi nabakadvēṣī āśrayāśō 'pi mātariśvā ati(kaṭu[71]kō) 'pi

[1] So also Hall's manuscripts A, B, C, F, H.
[2] Hall's manuscripts C, D, H also omit *tribhuvana.*
[3] So also Hall's manuscripts A, D, F, G, H.
[4] Cf. *bandhamahāuṣadhīm* in Hall's manuscripts C, D, G, H.
[5] Tel. ed. 61 and Grantha ed., *varṣīyām.*
[6] Tel. ed. 61 and Grantha ed., *dadarśa.*
[7] Trichinopoly ed., *ciraṃ sēvitayā.*
[8] So also Hall's manuscript D.
[9] So also Hall's manuscript D.
[10] So also Hall's manuscripts A, B, D, E, F, G, H.
[11] So also Hall's manuscripts A, B, C, E.
[12] Cf. *khalahṛdayaṃ bhavati* in Hall's manuscripts C, D, E, H.

mahārasaḥ sarṣapasnēha iva kara(yuga)lālitō 'pi śirasā dhṛtō 'pi na (kāṭavaṃ[1]) jahāti. tālaphalarasa ivā "pāta(27)madhuraḥ (pariṇāmē) virasas tiktaś ca (pādaraja) ivā 'vadhūtō ('pi[2]) mūrdhānaṃ kaṣāyayati. viṣataru(prasūnam) iva yathā yathā 'nubhūyatē tathā tathā mōha[72]m ēva (dṛḍhayati. nīcadēśanadyā iva na vārivirahō 'sya jāyatē). nidāghadivasa iva bahumatsaras (sumanasāṃ saṃtāpaṃ[3]) vahati. aṃdhakāra iva dōṣānubaṃdhacaturaḥ viśvakarmāvalōpanōdyataś ca (rudra iva) virūpākṣaḥ [73] (viṣṇur iva) cakradharaḥ śakrāśva ivō 'ccāiśśravāḥ nadēśajapraśaṃsī ca (sa)śarasyē 'va [vi]bhinnasyā[4] 'pi (satataṃ) snēhaṃ darśa(28)yatō 'pi takrāṭa iva hṛdayaṃ [74] vilōḍayati. yakṣabalir ivā "tmaghōṣamukharō maṃḍala(bhramaṇakaś) ca [matta]mātaṃga iva svavaśālōlamukhō 'dharīkṛtadānaś ca vṛṣabha iva surabhiyānavikalaḥ kāmī 'va gōtraskhalanavi(kalō) vāmādhvā[75]nuraktaś ca [a]jīrṇa(rōga[5]) iva kaḷēbarē vacasi maṃdimānam (ud)vahati. vaṃcaka iva (raktaḥ kaṭapalē) vibhāvarīraktaś ca parē(29)ta iva [76] baṃdhutāpadarśanaḥ paraśur iva bhadraśriyam api khaṃḍayati. kuddāla iva daḷitagōtraḥ kṣamābhājaḥ prāṇinaś (ca) nikṛntati. (rati)[77]kīla iva jaghanyakarmalagnō hrēpayati sādhūn. duṣṭaśūrpaśrutir iva kānanarucir anugatam api yavasaṃ (san)tataṃ nā 'numōdatē. abī[78]jād ēva jāyaṃtē akāṃḍāt[6] [ēva] prarōhaṃti khalavyasanāṃkurā durucchēdā(30)ś (ca[7]) bhavaṃti. asatāṃ [hi] hṛdi praviṣṭō dōṣalavaḥ karāḷāyatē satāṃ tu (hṛdayaṃ) na (pra[8])viśaty ēva yadi (katham api[9] pra-) viśati [79] (tadā[10]) pārada iva (kṣaṇam[11]) api na (tiṣṭhati[12]). mṛgā iva vinōdaviṃdōś (śramagā[13] bhavaṃti sādhavaḥ). sukhaṃ janā

[1] So also Hall's manuscripts B, C, D, E, F, G, H.
[2] So also Hall's manuscripts C, D, E, F, H.
[3] So also Hall's manuscripts A, B, C, D, F, G.
[4] So also Hall's manuscript D.
[5] So also Trichinopoly ed. and Srirangam text; Tel. ed. 61 and Grantha ed., *ajīrṇarōga*.
[6] Cf. *akāṇḍāt prasaranti* in Hall's manuscripts A, B, C, F, G.
[7] So also Hall's manuscript D. [8] So also Hall's manuscripts A, B, F, G.
[9] So also Hall's manuscripts A, B, C, D, F, G, H.
[10] So also Hall's manuscripts C, D, E, F, G, H.
[11] So also Hall's manuscripts A, B, C, D, F, G, H.
[12] So also Hall's manuscripts A, B, C, F, G, H.
[13] So also Hall's manuscript D, and the commentator Jagaddhara.

(hi bhavādṛśāś) śaratsamayā iva [bhavāddṛśā mitrasya hṛdayaṃ[1]] haraṃti na ca (mitra)cētanā visadṛśam upadiśaṃti. acētanānām api māitrī samucitapakṣē nikṣiptā [tathā[80]hi] mādhuryaśāityaśucitvasaṃtāpaśāṃtibhiḥ payaḥ paya (iti[2] śabdasāmyān) mitratām upagatasya (mat)saṃgamād[3] (vṛddhim upagatasya kṣīrasya kvāthē[4] puratō mamāi "va kṣayō yukta) iti (matvē) 'va vāriṇā ["pi] kṣīyatē. tad idam aṣāṃpratam ācaritaṃ [sakhē] gṛhāṇa sādhujanōcitam adhvānaṃ. sā[81]dhavō ('pi) diṅmōhād [param] utpathapravṛttā (api punar gṛhītasatpathā[5]) bhavaṃti. ityādi vadati tasmin (makaraṃdē priyasakhē) katham api smaraśara[nikara]prahāraparavaśaḥ (kaṃdarpakētuḥ) parimitākṣaram uvāca. vayasya ditir iva śatamanyusamākulā bhavaty (asmādṛśajanacitta)vṛttiḥ nā 'yam upadēśakālaḥ pacyaṃ(31)ta iva (mē[6]) 'ṃgāni [82] kvāthyaṃta ivē 'ṃdriyāṇi [bhidyanta iva marmāṇi] nissaraṃtī 'va prāṇāḥ unmūlyaṃta iva vivēkāḥ naṣṭē ('va[7]) smṛtiḥ [tad] adhunā (tad alam anayā kathayā) yadī ('tthaṃ) sahapāṃsu(krīḍā)sama(sukhaduḥkhō) 'si (tan mayā samam āgamyatām) ity uktvā parijanālakṣita (ēva) tēna sahāi ('va purān[8]) nirjagāma. (tatō 'nēka)nalvaśata(mātram) adhvānaṃ gatvā (tēnā) 'gastyavacanasaṃhṛta[83]brahmāṃḍa(khaṃḍa[9])-gataśikharasahasraḥ kaṃdarāṃtar[āl]alatā[10]gṛha(prasupta[11])vidyādharamithunagītākarṇanasukhitacamarī(gaṇa[12])māraṇōt(suka) śabara(kula)saṃbādhakaccha(taṭaḥ) kaṭaka(taṭagata)karikarākṛṣṭabhagnasyaṃdamā[84]naharicaṃdana(rasā)mōda(gaṃdha)-vāhigaṃdhavāhaśiśiritaśilātalaḥ sudūrapatanabhagnatālaphala-

[1] Hall's manuscripts C, D, E, H, and the commentator Jagaddhara also omit *mitrasya hṛdayam.*

[2] So also Hall's manuscripts A, B, C, D, H, and the commentators Jagaddhara and Narasiṃha.

[3] So also Hall's manuscripts A, B, C, D, E, F, H, and the commentator Jagaddhara.

[4] So also Hall's manuscripts C, D, E, G.

[5] Cf. *api punar gṛhītapathā* in Hall's manuscript D.

[6] So also Hall's manuscript D.

[7] So also Hall's manuscript D. [8] So also Hall's manuscripts A, B, C, H.

[9] So also Hall's manuscripts A, C, G, H, and the commentator Jagaddhara.

[10] So also Hall's manuscripts C, D.

[11] Cf. *gṛhasukhaprasupta* in Hall's manuscripts A, C, D, F, G and *gṛhasupta* in manuscript B.

[12] So also Hall's manuscripts A, B, C, F, H.

rasārdrakaratalāsvādanōtsukaśākhāmṛga(kadaṃbakaḥ[1]) pralaṃbamānanirjhar(ōpāṃtani)viṣṭa[2] jīvaṃ(jīvaka) mithuna(lihyamāna)vividhaphala[85]rasāmōda(gaṃdha)surabhitaparisaraḥ sarabhasakēsarisahasrakharanakharadhārāvidāritamattamātaṃgakuṃbhasthalavigaḷita(sthūla)muktāphala(śabaḷa[3])śikharatayā (śikharāva)lagnaṃ tārāgaṇam ivō 'dvahan sugrīva iva [86] ṛkṣagavayaśarabhakēsarikumuda(panasa[4])sēvyamānapādacchāyaḥ paśupatir iva nā(32)ganiśvāsasamutkṣiptabhūtiḥ janārdana iva vi(kaca)vanamālaḥ sahasrakiraṇa iva saptapatrasyaṃdanōpētaḥ virūpākṣa iva [87] sannihitaguhaḥ śivānugataś ca kāmī 'va kāṃtārōṣarasānugataḥ samadanaś ca śrīparvata iva sannihitamallikārjunaḥ naravāhanadatta [88] iva priyaṃguśyāmāsanāthaḥ śiśur iva kṛtadhātrīdhṛtiḥ vāsarāraṃbha ivā [gāirikā[5]]ruṇaprabhāpāṭalita(patra)vanarājiḥ kṛṣṇapakṣa iva bahulatāgahanaḥ karṇa ivā 'nubhū(33)taśatakōṭidānaḥ bhīṣma iva śi[89]khaṃḍimuktāir ardhacaṃdrāir ācita(tanuḥ) kāmasūtravinyāsa iva mallanāga(ghaṭitakāṃtāra)sāmōdaḥ hiraṇyakaśipur iva śaṃbarakulāśrayaḥ gāirikavyājād(upari[6])ravirathamārgamārgaṇārtham ivā 'ruṇēnō 'pāsya[90]mānaḥ śikharagatasūryācaṃdramastayā vistāritalōcanō 'gastyamārgam ivō 'dvīkṣamāṇaḥ (kuliśakṣataraṃdhra)sra(34)stāṃtra(nāḷa[7]) iva jaradajagarabhōgāiḥ kuṃbhakarṇa iva daṃtāṃtarāḷa(gatāir[8]) vānara(vyūhāiḥ[8]) piṃḍā(lakta[91]ka[9]raktapada)paṅktisūcitasaṃ(cāra)śacīpativāravilāsinīsaṃkētakētakīmaṃḍapaḥ akulīnō 'pi sadvaṃśabhūṣitaḥ darśitābhayō 'pi mṛtyuphala(dāyā) saprasthō 'py aparimāṇaḥ sanādō 'pi niś[92]śabdaḥ bhīmō 'pi kīcakasuhṛt pihitāṃbarō 'pi (vi)lasadaṃśukaḥ viṃdhyō (35) nāma [mahā[10]]girir adṛśyata. [93] yaś ca pravṛddhagulmatayā (rōgī 'va) dṛśyamānabahudhātuvikāraḥ. (yaś ca) sādhur

[1] So also Hall's manuscripts D, H.

[2] Cf. *nirjharaśikharōpāntōpaviṣṭa* in Hall's manuscript D.

[3] So also Hall's manuscripts A, B, C, D, H.

[4] So also Hall's manuscript D.

[5] Hall's manuscripts A, B, C, D, F, H, and the commentators Jagaddhara and Narasiṃha also omit *gāirika*.

[6] So also Hall's manuscripts C, D, E, G, H.

[7] So also Hall's manuscripts C, E. [8] So also Hall's manuscripts D, E, G.

[9] Cf. *piṇḍālaktakāṅkita* in Hall's manuscripts A, B, C, D, G, H.

[10] Hall's manuscripts D, E, G, H, and the commentator Jagaddhara also omit *mahā*.

iva sānugrahapracāraprakaṭitamahimā mīmāṃsānyāya iva pihitadigaṃbaradarśanaḥ. yaś ca harivaṃśāir iva puṣkar(ākṣa)prādurbhāvarama[94]ṇīyāiḥ rāśibhir iva mīna(makarakulīramithuna)saṃgatāiḥ karaṇāir iva śakunināgabhadrabālavakulōpētāiḥ (36) dēvakhātāir upaśōbhit(āṃtaḥ[1]). yaś ca kusumavicitrābhiḥ vaṃśapatrapatitābhiḥ sukumāralalitābhiḥ puṣpi[95]tāgrābhiḥ (praharṣiṇībhiḥ śikhariṇībhiḥ) latābhiḥ darśitānēkavṛttavilāsaḥ. yaś ca (samadakala[2])haṃsasārasarasitōdbhrāṃt(ōtkuṭa)vikaṭa(kuṃjakaccha)vyādhūta[vikaca]kamala(ṣaṃḍa)galitamakaraṃdabiṃdusaṃdōhasurabhitasalilayā sāyaṃtana(samayamajjat[3])puḷiṃdarājasuṃdarī [96] (nimna) nābhimaṃḍala(pari)pītasalilayā[madamukhararājahaṃsakulakōlāhalamukharitakūlapulinayā] taṭanikaṭa(sthitavikaṭa[4])mattamātaṃgagaṃḍa(sthalavigaḷan[5])madadhārā(biṃduprakara)stabakitasalilayā tīraprarūḍhakētakīkānana(patitadhūḷīnikuruṃbasaṃjāta)sāikatasukhōpaviṣṭataruṇasura[97]mithunanidhuvanalīlāparimaḷasākṣikūlōpavanayā taṭā(vaṭasthavighaṭitāṃbhōja[6]ṣaṃḍa)maṃḍapāvasthitajaladēvatā(vi)gāhyamāna(payasā) tīraprarūḍhavētasa(vanā[7])bhyaṃtara(ni[8])līnadātyūha(madōtkaṭakēḷi)[98]kuhakuhārāvakāutukākṛṣṭasuramithunasaṃstūyamān(ō(37)pa[9])bhōgayā upakūlasaṃjāta(naḷinapuṃja[10])kuṃjapuṃjita[kulāya]kukkuṭaghaṭāghūtkārabhāiravatīrayā (ātapasēvāsamutsuka)jalamānuṣīmṛditasukumāra(tarapuḷinayā) upavana(pavanā)ṃdō[99]ḷitataraḷa(tara)taraṃgayā (naḷinī)nikuṃjapuṃjaniviṣṭa(duṣṭa[11]bakōṭa)kakuṭuṃbinīnirīkṣyamāṇavṛddhaśapharayā (pōtō)dhānalubdhakōyaṣṭika(skaṃbhana[12])bhīma-

[1] So also Hall's manuscript H, and the commentator Narasiṃha.

[2] So also Hall's manuscripts C, D, and the commentator Narasiṃha.

[3] Cf. *sāyantanasamayōnmajjat* in Hall's manuscripts A, B, C, E, F, G, and *sāyantanasamayamajjana* in manuscript D.

[4] Cf. *taṭanikaṭavikaṭa* in Hall's manuscripts B, D, F.

[5] Cf. *gaṇḍanirgalita* in Hall's manuscripts A, B, D, E, G.

[6] Cf. *taṭāvaṭavighaṭitajambū* in Hall's manuscript D (*vighaṭita* also in manuscript F, *ghaṭita* in manuscript H).

[7] So also Hall's manuscripts A, B, F.

[8] So also Hall's manuscripts A, B, C, E, F, G, H.

[9] So also Hall's manuscripts C, D, E, F, G, H.

[10] Cf. *kuñjapuñjapuñjita* in Hall's manuscript D.

[11] Cf. *naṣṭa* in Hall's manuscripts A, B, and *dhṛṣṭa* in manuscripts C, F; Trichinopoly ed. omits *duṣṭa*.

[12] So also Hall's manuscripts A, E, F, G, and the commentator Narasiṃha.

vētasavana(latayā [1]) [tarala]taraṃgamālā [2]saṃ(tarad)uddaṃḍa-(vāla)da[100]rśanadhāvadaticapalarājilarāji(rājitō [3])pakūlasalilayā (khaṃjarīṭa [4])mithuna(nidhuvana)darśanōpajātanidhigrahaṇakāutukakirāta[śa[101]ta]khanyamāna(sthapuṭita)tīrayā kruddhayē 'va darśitamukha[vi[5]]bhaṃgayā mattayē 'va (skhalad[6])gatyā dinārambhalakṣmyē 'va vardhamānavēlayā bhāratasamarabhūmyē 'va nṛtyatkabaṃdhayā prāvṛṣē 'va vijṛmbhamāṇaśata-(38)patrapihita[102]viṣadharayā (sakāmayē) 'va kṛtabhūbhṛtsēvayā rēvayā priyatamayē 'va prasārita(taraṃga)hastayō 'pagūḍhaḥ. yaś ca

harikharanakharavidāritakuṃbhasthalavikalavāraṇadhvānāṇ
adyā 'pi kuṃbhasaṃbhavaṃ (sam)āhvayatī 'vō 'ccatālabhujaḥ.

(tatrāṃtarē) makaraṃdas tam uvāca

[103] paśyō 'daṃcadavāṃcadaṃcitavapuḥ (pūrvārdhapaścārdha)bhāk
stabdhōttānitapṛṣṭhaniṣṭhitamanāgbhugnāgralāṃgūlabhṛt
daṃṣṭrākōṭiviśaṃkaṭāsyakuharaḥ kurvan saṭāmutkaṭām
(ut)kaṃṭhaḥ kurutē kramaṃ karipatāu krūrākṛtiḥ kēsarī.

api ca

utkarṇō 'yam akāṃḍacaṃḍimapatus sphārasphuratkēsaraḥ
krūrākārakarāḷavaktra(kuharas) stabdhōrdhvalāṃgūlabhṛt
[104] (citrē cā) 'pi na śakyatē (vi)likhituṃ sarvāṃgasaṃkōca-(bhāk [7])
(phīṭ)kurvadgirikuṃjakuṃjaraśiraḥ[8]kuṃbhasthalasthōhariḥ.

anaṃtaraṃ nīcadēśanadyē 'va nyagrōdhōpacitayā uttaragō(grahaṇa)[105]bhūmyē 'va vijṛmbhamāṇabṛhannaḷayā (kuru)dēśa(ḍhak-

[1] Trichinopoly ed., *mālayā*. [2] So also Hall's manuscripts A, B, C, F, H.
[3] So also Hall's manuscript E. [4] So also Hall's manuscripts C, F.
[5] Hall's manuscripts A, B, C, F, H, and the commentators Jagaddhara and Narasiṃha also omit *vi*.
[6] So also Hall's manuscripts C, D, F.
[7] So also Hall's manuscripts A, B, C, D, F, H.
[8] Trichinopoly ed. and Srirangam text, *bṛhat*.

kayē[1]) 'va ghana(39)sārasārthavāhinyā vidagdha[jana]madhu[pāna]gōṣṭhyē 'va nānāviṭapī[106]tāsavayā nalakūbaracittavṛttyē 'va satatadhṛtarambhayā mattamātaṃgagatyē 'va ghaṃṭāravāvēditamārgayā sadīśvarasēvayē ('va) dūrōdgatabahuphalayā virāṭalakṣmyē 'vā "naṃditakīcakaśatayā viṃdhyāṭavyā (katipayadūram adhvānaṃ[2]) gatvā kāmina iva madanaśalākāṅkitasya (vikartanasyē 'va (40) snigdhacchāyasya vāikuṃṭhasyē 'va lakṣmībhṛtaḥ yātrōdyatanṛpatēr iva ghanapatraśōbhitasya vēdasyē 'va bhūriśākhālaṃkṛtasya gāṇikyasyē 'vā 'nēkapallavōjjvalasya[3]) jaṃbūvṛkṣasyā ('dhaś) chāyāyāṃ (sa) viśaśrāma. [107] atrāṃtarē bhagavān api marīcimālī ātapaklāṃta(vana)mahiṣalōcanapāṭalamaṃḍalaś caramācala(śikharam) ārurōha. tatō makaraṃdaḥ phalamūlāny ādāya [kathaṃ] katham[4] api tam abhinaṃditāhāra(m)[paricayam] akārṣīt. svayam (api) tadupabhuktaśēṣam (akarōd aśanaṃ). atha tām ēva priyatamāṃ hṛdayaphalakē (saṃkalpatūlikayā) likhi[108]tām ivā ['va[5]]lōkayan niṣpaṃdakaraṇagrāmaḥ kaṃdarpakētur makaraṃda(viracitē) pallavaśayanē suṣvāpa. atha [ardha]yāmamātrāvakhaṃḍitāyāṃ (yāminyāṃ) [tatra] jaṃbūtaruśikharē (mithaḥ kalahāyamānayōś śukaśārikayōḥ) kalakalaṃ śrutvā kaṃdarpakētur makaraṃdam uvāca. vayasya śṛṇuvas tāvad (anayōr[6]) ālā[109]pam iti. tatō (jaṃbūnikuṃjasthitā[7]) śārikā (kācit cirād āgataṃ śukaṃ[7]) prakōpataraḷākṣaram uvāca. kitava śārikāṃtaram anviṣya [samā]gatō 'si katham anyathā rātrir iyatī tavē 'ti. (atha) tac chrutvā śukas tām avādīt. bhadrē (muṃca kōpaṃ[8]) apūrvā (bṛhat)kathā (pratyakṣīkṛtā mayā) tēnā 'yaṃ kālātipāta (iti). atha samupajātakutūha(41)layā śārikayā (muhur anubadhyamānaḥ kathāṃ[9]) kathayitum ārēbhē. [110] asti (maṃdaragiriśṛṃgāir iva pra-

[1] Cf. *ḍhakkayē 'va* in Hall's manuscript F.

[2] Cf. *katipayam adūram adhvānam* in Hall's manuscript E, *katipayadūram* in manuscript F, and *katipayapadaṃ dūram* in manuscripts A, B.

[3] So also Hall's manuscripts B, C, except *rājāvasathasyē 'va bhūriśālālaṅkṛtasya* instead of *vēdasyē 'va bhūriśākhālamkṛtasya.*

[4] Hall's manuscripts C, D, H also omit the first *kathaṃ.*

[5] Hall's manuscripts C, F, G also omit *'va.*

[6] So also Hall's manuscript F.

[7] So also Hall's manuscript D.

[8] Cf. *mā prakōpaṃ kuru* in Hall's manuscripts B, H.

[9] So also Hall's manuscript C.

śasta[1])sudhādhavaḷāiḥ bṛhatkathā(laṃbāir[2]) iva sālabhaṃjik(ōpaśōbhitāiḥ[3]) vṛttāir iva samāṇavakakrīḍitāiḥ kariyūthāir iva samattavāraṇāiḥ sugrīvasāinyāir iva sagavākṣāiḥ balibhavanāir iva sutalasannivēśāiḥ vēśmabhi[111]r (udbhāsitaṃ[4]) dhanadēnā 'pi pracētasā (gō)pālēnā 'pi rāmēṇa priyaṃvadēnā 'pi puṣpakētunā bharatēnā 'pi śatrughnēna ti(42)thiparēṇā 'py ati[112]thisatkāra-(pravaṇēna[5]) asaṃkhyēnā 'pi saṃkhyāvatā amarmabhēdinā 'pi vīratarēṇa apatitēnā 'pi nānāsavāsaktēna sudarśanēnā 'py acakrēṇa ajāta[113]madēnā 'pi supratīkēna (haṃsēnā 'py apakṣapātinā) aviditasnē(43)hakṣayēṇā 'pi kulapradīpēna agraṃthinā 'pi vaṃśapōtēna (agrahēṇā 'pi kāvyajīvajñēna) nidāghadivasēnē 'va vṛṣa[vi]vardhitarucinā māghavirāmadivasēnē 'va tapasyāraṃbhiṇā [114] (nabhasvatē 'va satpathagāminā vivasvatē 'va gōpatinā mahēśvarēṇē 'va caṃdraṃ dadhatā nivāsi[6])janēnā 'nugataṃ (ghanāpagamēnē[7]) 'va darśitakhaṃḍābhrēṇa vēlātaṭēnē 'va pravāḷa(maṃḍanēna[8]) dēvāṃga(44)nājanēnē 'vē 'ṃdrāṇīparicayavidagdhēna (gajēṃdrēṇē) 'va pallava[115](vardhita)rucinā kōkilēnē 'va parapuṣṭēna bhramarēṇē 'va kusumēṣulālitēna jalāukasē 'va raktākṛṣṭinipuṇēṇa (yāyajūkēnē[9]) 'va suratārthinā mahānaṭabāhu(vanēnē) 'va (baddhabhujaṃgāṃkēna[10]) garuḍēnē 'va vilāsihṛ[116]dayatāpa(kāriṇā aṃdhakēnē) 'va śūlānām uparigatēna vēśyājanēnā 'dhiṣṭhitaṃ kusumapurannāma nagaraṃ. yatra ca surāsuramāuḷimālālālitacaraṇāravimdā śu[117]ṃbhaniśuṃbha-(mahāsurabala[11])mahāvanadāv(ānal[12]a)jvālā mahiṣ[amah]āsuragiri-

[1] Cf. *mandaragiriśikharāir iva praśasta* in Hall's manuscript A, and *mandaraśṛṅgāir iva praśasta* in manuscript C.

[2] Cf. *lambhāir* in Hall's manuscript F, and the commentator Jagaddhara, and *lambhakāir* in manuscript D; Trichinopoly ed., *lambakāir.*

[3] So also Hall's manuscripts C, D, F.

[4] So also Hall's manuscripts A, B, C, D, G, H, and the commentators Jagaddhara and Narasiṃha.

[5] So also Hall's manuscripts C, F, H.

[6] So also Hall's manuscripts A, B, C, F.

[7] Cf. *ghanāpagama* in Hall's manuscripts A, D, and *ghanāgamēnē 'va* in the commentator Jagaddhara.

[8] So also Hall's manuscripts C, F, H, and the commentator Jagaddhara.

[9] So also Hall's manuscript D.

[10] Cf. *baddhabhujaṅgēna* in Hall's manuscripts C, D, H.

[11] Trichinopoly ed. omits *bala.*

[12] So also Hall's manuscript D; cf. *mahāsuravanadāvajvālā* in manuscript H.

(vara[1])vajra[sāra[2]]dhārā praṇaya(kalaha[3])praṇatagaṃgādharajaṭājūṭa(kōṭi[4])skhalitajāhnavījaladhārādhāutapādapadmā bhagavatī kātyāyanī (caṃḍā)bhi(45)dhānā svayaṃ (nivasati). yasya ca parisarē surāsura(majjanagaḷita[5]makuṭa)kusumarajōrājiparimaḷa[118]vāhinī pitāmahakamaṃḍaludharmadravadhārā dharātala(patita)sagarasuta[śata]suranagarasamārōhaṇapuṇyarajjuḥ (āirāvatakapōlagharghaṇa[6]) kaṃpitataṭa(gata)haricaṃdana (syaṃdamānarasa[7])surabhitasalilā salīlasurasuṃdarīnitaṃbabiṃbāhatitaraḷitataraṃgā snānāvatīrṇasaptarṣi(maṃḍalavimala[8])jaṭāṭavīparimaḷapuṇyavēṇī (ēṇī)tilaka(makuṭavikaṭa)jaṭājūṭakuharabhrāṃtijanita(saṃskārē 'vā 'dyā 'pi) kuṭilāvartā dharaṇī 'va sārvabhāumakarasparśōpabhōgakṣamā jaladakālasarasī 'va gaṃdh(a)[āndhō]paribhramad[9]bhramara[119]mālānumīyamānajala(mūla)magnakumudapuṃḍarīkā cchaṃdōvicitir iva mālinīsanāthā (grahapaṅktir iva sūryātmajōpa śōbhitā sarājahaṃsā ca[10] śaratkāladinaśrīr ivō 'jvalatkōkanadā prabuddhapuṃḍarīkākṣā ca hṛtā)ṃdhatamasā 'pi tamasānvitā (vīcīkalilā[11]) 'py (46) (avīcī)durgamā bhagavatī bhāgīrathī (pra[12])vahati. yac[13] ca diśi diśi (saṃtānakatarukusumanikaram iva śikharāvalagnaṃ) tārāgaṇam iva kusumanikaram udvahadbhiḥ utta[120]ṃbhitajaladāiḥ anūru[kara]kaśābhighātaparavaśaravirathaturagagrāsaviṣamit(āgra)pallavāiḥ caṃdracamūrucaraṇasaṃkrāṃtāmṛtakaṇanikarasēkasaṃjāta(bahuḷa)sukumāranava(kusuma)kisalayasahasradarśitākālasaṃdhyā(kāla)vibhramāiḥ bharatacaritāir iva sadārāmāśritāiḥ mahāvīrāir iva nārikēḷīdharāiḥ asaṃskṛtataruṇāir ivā 'tidūrapra(śrayā)(47)kṣāiḥ (tapasvibhir iva japāsaktāiḥ prasādhitāir iva kṛtamālōpaśōbhitāiḥ) [matta]mātaṃgakuṃbhasthala(vi)dāraṇ(ōtsuka)siṃhāir

[1] So also Hall's manuscripts C, F, H.
[2] Hall's manuscripts B, D, E, H also omit *sāra*.
[3] So also Hall's manuscripts A, B, D, F, H.
[4] Cf. *jūṭakūṭa* in Hall's manuscripts A, B, C, F, H.
[5] So also Hall's manuscript C.
[6] Grantha ed., *gargharṇa*; Trichinopoly ed., *gharṣaṇa*.
[7] So also Hall's manuscript D.
[8] Cf. *vimala* in Hall's manuscripts A, B, E, F, G, H.
[9] Trichinopoly ed., *gandhōparibhramad*.
[10] Cf. *grahapaṅktir iva sūryān: gatā sarājahaṃsā ca* in Hall's manuscript C.
[11] So also Hall's manuscript H.
[12] So also Hall's manuscripts A, B, G, H.
[13] Tel. ed. 61 and Grantha ed., *yatra*.

ivō ('tphulla[1])kēsarāiḥ sāriṣṭāir api cirajīvibhiḥ (muniyutāir api madanādhiṣṭhitāiḥ) upavanapādapāi[121]r upaśōbhitaṃ aditijaṭharam ivā 'nēkadēvakulādhyāsitaṃ pātāḷam iva mahābaliśōbhitaṃ bhujaṃgādhiṣṭhitaṃ ca (sasurālayam) api pavitraṃ (bhōgiyuktam) apy (anupadrutaṃ[2]). (tatra[3]) [ca] surata(rabhasa)-khinna(pra)suptasīmaṃtinīratnatāṭaṃka(mukhā)ṃkitabāhudaṃḍaḥ pracaṃḍapratipakṣalakṣmīkēśapāśakusumamālā[122] mōdasurabhitakarakamalaḥ praśastakēdāra iva bahudhānyakāryasaṃpā(48)dakaḥ (pārtha iva subhadrānvitaḥ sabhīmasēnaś ca kṛṣṇa iva satyabhāmānuraktaḥ sabalaś ca) śṛṃgāraśēkharō nāma prativasati. yō valabhit pāvakō dharmarāṇ ṇirṛtiḥ pracētās sadāgatir dhanadaś śaṃkara ity aṣṭamūrti(dhṛd[4]) apy anaṣṭamūrtiḥ [pārtha iva subhadrōpētaḥ sabhīmasēnaś ca kṛṣṇa iva satyabhāmōpētaḥ sabalaś ca].

[123] surāṇāṃ pātāsāu sa punar atipuṇyāikahṛdayō
grahas tasyā 'sthānē gurur ucitamārgē sa nirataḥ.
karas tasyā 'tyarthaṃ vahati śatakōṭipraṇayitāṃ
sa sarvasvaṃ dātā tṛṇam iva (49) (surēṃdraṃ) vijayatē[5].

[124] jīvākṛṣṭiṃ sa cakrē mṛdhabhuvi dhanuṣaḥ śatrur āsīd gatāsur
lakṣāptir mārgaṇānām abhavad aribalē (sad[6])yaśas tēna labdhaṃ
muktā tēna kṣamē 'ti tvaritam aribalāir uttamāṃgāiḥ praviṣṭā
pañcatvaṃ dvēṣi(sāinyāir gatam) avanipatir nā "pa saṃkhyāntaraṃ saḥ.

[125] yatra [ca] ṛājani[7] rājanīticaturē catur(aṃbudhi[8]vēlā)mēkhalāyā bhuvō nāyakē śāsa(50)ti vasumatīṃ pitṛ(kāryēṣu[9]) vṛṣōtsargaḥ śaśinaḥ kanyātulārōhaṇaṃ (prasavēṣu) śūlavyāghātaciṃtā

[1] So also Hall's manuscripts A, B, C, H.
[2] Cf. *nirupadrutam* in Hall's manuscripts A, B, C, F, G, H.
[3] So also Hall's manuscripts C, D.
[4] Tel. ed. 61 and Grantha ed., *dhṛg*.
[5] Also in *Subhāṣitāvalī* 2631, reading *rasikō* for *hṛdayō* and *atyantaṃ spṛśati* for *atyarthaṃ vahati*.
[6] So also Hall's manuscript A, and the commentator Jagaddhara.
[7] Tel. ed. 61 and Grantha ed. omit *rājani*.
[8] So also Hall's manuscripts A, B.
[9] So also Hall's manuscripts D. H.

[dānacchēdaḥ karikapōlēṣu] dakṣiṇavāmakaraṇaṃ diṅ(niścayēṣu [1]) śarabhēdō dadhiṣu [126] śṛṃkhalābaṃdhō varṇagrathanāsu utprēkṣ(ākṣēpāv) {kāvya]alaṃkārēṣu lakṣadānacyutis sāyakānāṃ kvipāṃ sarvavināśaḥ kōśasaṃkōcaḥ kamalākarēṣu (na janēṣu) jāti(vi)hīnatā (mālāsu na duṣkulē) śṛṃgārahāni[127]r jaratkariṣu na janēṣu durvarṇayōgaḥ (karṇikādiṣu) na kāminī[kānti [2]]ṣu gāṃdhāravicchēdō rāgēṣu na pāuravanitāsu (mūrchādhigamō (51) gānēṣu na prajāsu karmā)bhāvō nīcasēvakēṣu na pari(dhānēṣu [3]) malināṃbaratvaṃ niśāsu na janēṣu [128] calarāgatā gītēṣu na vidagdhēṣu vṛṣahānir nidhuvanavilāsu na pāurēṣu bhaṃguratvaṃ rāgavikṛtiṣu na cittēṣu anaṃgatā kāmadēvē na parijanē [4] mārāgamō yāuvan(ōdgamēṣu) na prakṛtiṣu dvijāghātaḥ suratēṣu na prajāsu raśanābaṃdhō ratikalahēṣu na dānānumati[129]ṣu adhara(rāgatā) taruṇīṣu na parijanēṣu (kṛṃtanam) alakēṣu [5] na puraṃdhrīṣu nistriṃśatvam (asiṣu) na (manassu) karavāḷanāśō (yōdhēṣu na janapadēṣu) param [6] (ēvaṃ vyavasthitaṃ. tasya [7] ca 'bhūd ēvaṃbhūtasya rājñō) (52) mahiṣī diggaja[kapōla]mada(rēkhē) 'vā 'naṃditāḷiganā [130] pārvatī 'va sukumārā (caṃdrarēkhālaṃkṛtā ca vanarājir iva navamālikōdbhāsitā sacitrakānanā ca apsarassaṃhatir iva saṃhatasukēśī samaṃjughōṣā ca) sarvāṃtaḥpurapradhānabhūtā anaṃgavatī nāma [8]. tayōś ca madhyamōpāṃtē vayasi vartamānayōḥ katham api dāivavaśāt tribhuvanavilōbhanīyākṛtiḥ pulōmatanayē 'vā 'naṃditasahasranētrā (mērugirimēkhalē 'va sujātarūpā śaranniśē 'vō 'llasattārakā satpariṣad ivā 'cchidradvijapaṅktibhūṣitā rākṣasakulaśrīr iva mālyavatsukēśaśōbhitā) tanayā ('bhūd) vāsavadattā nāma. atha sā rāvaṇabhuja(vana [9]) ivō 'l(lasitagōtrē [10] viṃdhyācala iva ma(53)danālaṃkṛtē pārāvāra iva saṃjātalāvaṇyē naṃdanavana iva sadākalpa [11] śō-

[1] So also Hall's manuscripts C, D, E, G, H.
[2] Hall's manuscripts D, F also omit *kānti*.
[3] So also Hall's manuscripts A, B, C, D, E, G, H.
[4] Trichinopoly ed. and Srirangam text, *parijanēṣu*.
[5] Trichinopoly ed., *kamalēṣu*.
[6] Tel. ed. 61 and Grantha ed., *paramam*.
[7] So also Hall's manuscripts A, B, C, D, E, F, and the commentator Narasiṃha.
[8] Grantha ed., *anaṃgavatīnāmā*.
[9] So also Hall's manuscripts A, B, C, D.
[10] So also Hall's manuscripts A, B, C, F.
[11] Tel. ed. 61 and Grantha ed., *kalpaka*.

bhitē pavana iva sumanōharē[1]) pariṇāmam upayāty api (yāuvanē) pariṇayaparāṅmukhī tasthāu. [131] (athāi) "kadā[2] [tu] vijṛmbhamāṇasahakārakōrakanikurumbanipatitamadhukaramālāmadakalajhaṃkāra(huṃkāra[3]) janitapathika[janasañ[4]]jvaraḥ kōmaḷamalayamārutōddhūtacūtaprasavarasāsvādakaṣāyakaṃṭhakalakaṃṭha(kuhakuhārava[5])bharitasakaladiṅmukhaḥ vikacakamalaṣaṃḍa(ni)līyamāna[132]mattakaḷahaṃsakulakōlāhalamukharita[sakala]sarōvaraḥ parabhṛta(kharatrōṭi)kōṭipāṭita[6](pāṭalī)kuṭmala[vṛnta]vivaravinirgatamadhudhārāsāraśīkara[kaṇa]nikara(samārabdha)dakṣiṇasamīraṇa(māravāraṇa)vraṇitapathika[jana]vadhūhṛdayaḥ madhumadamuditakāminī(mukhakamala)gaṃḍūṣaśīdhu(sēvana)puḷakitavakuḷaḥ madana(raya)paravaśavilāsinītulākōṭivikaṭacaṭulacaraṇāraviṃda(54)[manda]prahāraprahṛṣṭakaṃkēḷitaruśataḥ prati(dinam) aślīlaprāya(vāihāsika)gīyamānagītaśravaṇōtsukaṣidgajanaprārabdhaca[133]rcarīgītākarṇana(mādyad)anēkapathika(janaḥ) durjana iva satāmarasaḥ duṣkula iva jātihīnaḥ rāvaṇa ivā 'pītalōhitapalāśaśata(sēvyamānaḥ) mahāśṛṃgārī 'va sugaṃdha(vāhaḥ) surājē 'va samṛddhaku[134]valayaḥ vāstavika iva [vi]vardhitasukhāśaḥ satkavikāvya(pra)baṃdha ivā ('nava)baddhatuhinaḥ satpuruṣa iva dōṣānubaṃdharahitaḥ kāivarta iva [ā[7]]baddharājīvōtpala(jālaḥ) samṛddhakāsāra[śakuni]sārtha ivā ('naṃdita)[135]ma(55)ruvakaḥ śakra ivē 'ṃdrāṇī(rucirah mahādhīr) ivā 'dharīkṛtadamanakaḥ ṣidga ivā 'mlānasubhagaḥ vasaṃtakāla ājagāma. [136] atidūrapravṛddhēna madhunā jagati kō vā na vi(kriyēta) yad ati(muktō) munir api vicakāsa. kusumaśarasya navacūta(kusumabāṇa)mūlanilīnā madhukar(āvair vilikhitā nāmākṣarapaṅktir) iva rējē. vṛṃtavinirgatavi(kaca[8]-vicikilavivarē[9] kūjan) madhukarō makarakētōs tri[137]bhuvanavijaya[prayāṇa]śaṃkhadhvanim iva cakāra. navayāvakapaṃka-

[1] Cf. *vindhyācala iva madanādhiṣṭhitē pārāvāra iva sañjātalāvaṇyē madanavana iva sadā kalpataruṇābhinanditē pavana iva sumanōhāriṇi* in Hall's manuscripts B, C.

[2] Cf. *aṭhāi "kadā tu* in Hall's manuscript C.

[3] Cf. *madakalahuṃkāra* in Hall's manuscripts A, D, G.

[4] Hall's manuscripts C, G, H also omit *janasañ*.

[5] Tel. ed. 61 and Grantha ed., *kuhākuhārava*; Trichinopoly ed., *kuhakuhārāva*.

[6] Tel. ed. 61, *kharatrōṭipāṭita*; Grantha ed., *kharatrōṭitapāṭita*.

[7] Hall's manuscripts B, C also omit *ā*.

[8] So also Hall's manuscripts C, E, H.

[9] Cf. *vicakilavivaraguñjan* in Hall's manuscript C.

pallavita(vara)nūpura(raṇitaramaṇīya)taruṇīcaraṇaprahārānurāgavaśān navakisalayacchalēna tam (ēva[1]) rāgam udavahad aśōkaḥ. madhuramadhu[pari[2]]pūritakāminīmukhakamalagaṃḍūṣa(saṃgād[3]) i(56)va tadrasa(gaṃdham[4]) ātmakusumēṣu bibhrad vakuḷatarū rarāja. aṃtarāṃtarā nipatitamadhukaranikara(kimmīraḥ) kaṃkēḷigucchōrdhanirvāṇamanōbhavacitācakrānukārī pathikajana(citta)dāham uvāha. vikacavi(cikila)rājir aḷikulaśaba[138]lā (kalitēṃdranīlā) muktāvalī 'va madhuśriyō virurucē. virahiṇāṃ hṛdayamathanāya kusumaśarasya (śāṇa)cakram[5] iva nāgakēsarakusumam aśōbhata. pathikajanahṛdayamatsyaṃ gṛhītuṃ makarakētōḥ (pāḷāvalī[6]) 'va pāṭalī(kusumam) adṛśyata. kaṃdarpakēḷī[sampal]laṃpaṭalāṭīla[139]lāṭataṭa(lulitālakadhammilabhāra[7]-kusuma)parimaḷasamṛddhamadhurimaguṇaḥ kāmakalākalāpa(nipuṇa)karṇāṭasuṃdarī(suṃdara[8])stanakalaśa(yugaḷa)ghusṛṇadhūḷi(paṭala)parimaḷāmōdavāhī (raṇaraṇakarasitāparāṃta)kāṃtā[kuntalī]kuṃtalōl(lasita)saṃkrāṃtaparimaḷamiḷitāḷimālā(madhura)jhaṃkāraravamukharitanabhas(sthalaḥ) navayāuvan(ōddhata)kēraḷīkapōlapāḷīpatrāvaḷī[140]paricayacaturaḥ catuṣṣaṣṭikalākalāpavidagdhamugdha(57)(mukharamāḷavī)[nitambinī[9]]nitaṃbabiṃbasaṃvāhana(subhagaḥ) surata(pari)śramaparavaś(āṃdhrapuraṃdhrī[10])nīraṃdhrapīnapayōdharabhāranidāghajalakaṇanikara(śiśiraḥ) malaya(mārutō[11]) vavāu. atrāṃtarē vāsavadattāsakhījanāt vidita(sutā)bhiprāyaḥ śṛṃgāraśēkharas svasutāyāḥ svayaṃvarārtham aśēṣa(dharā)talabhājāṃ (rājaputrāṇām) ēkatra (mēḷanam) akarōt. tatō dagdhakṛṣṇ(āgarudhūpa)parimaḷāmōdamōhitamadhu(karamālā[12][141]bahuḷaghumaghumāyita[13]-rava)mukharita(digaṃtaraṃ) atirabhasahāsacchaṭ(āmōdaparimaḷi-

[1] So also Hall's manuscripts B, C, D, G, H.

[2] Hall's manuscripts A, B, C, D, F, G, H also omit *pari*.

[3] So also Hall's manuscripts B, C.

[4] Cf. *tatsamānagandham* in Hall's manuscripts A, B, C, F, G.

[5] Cf. *takrāṭacakram* in Hall's manuscripts A, B, and the commentator Narasiṃha.

[6] Trichinopoly ed., *jālāvalī*.

[7] Cf. *dhammillabhāra* in Hall's manuscript D.

[8] So also Hall's manuscripts A, B, D, E, F, G, H.

[9] Hall's manuscripts C, E, F, H also omit *nitambinī*.

[10] So also Hall's manuscripts C, F.

[11] So also Hall's manuscripts A, B, G, H.

[12] So also Hall's manuscripts A, B, G.

[13] So also Hall's manuscript F.

taṃ) anēkaparihāsa(kathā [1])lāpavidagdha(śṛṃgāra[142]maya [2])jana(nicaya)samākulaṃ dahyamāna(mahiṣākṣādisugaṃdhadravya)-sāurabhākṛṣṭapurōpavanaṣaṭpadakul[asam]ākulaṃ arjunasamaram iva naṃdighōṣamukharitadigaṃtaraṃ (nṛpāsthānam iva sarājōpahāraṃ tāpasāśramam iva vitānōdbhāsitaṃ triviṣṭapam iva sumanōlaṃkṛtaṃ) maṃcam ārurōha (varārōhā) vāsavadattā. tatra [ca [3]] kēcit kulāṃkurā iva vi(dita)nagaramaṃḍa(58)nāḥ [143] aparē pāṃḍavā iva (sadivyacakṣuṣaḥ [4]) kṛṣṇāguruparimilitāś (ca) anyē śaraddivasā iva [su [5]]dūrapravṛddh[asukh [6]]āśāḥ itarē (prahartum) udyatā [144] iva svabalārthinaḥ kēcid vyādhā iva śakunaśrāvakāḥ kēcid ākhēṭakā(saktā) iva rūpānusārapravṛttāḥ kēcit jāiminimatānusāriṇa iva tathāgatadhvaṃsinaḥ kēcit khaṃjanā iva (sāṃvatsarika)phaladarśinaḥ kēcit sumērupa(59)risarā iva kārtasvaramayāḥ kēcit [145] [vikaca [7]]kumudākarā iva bhāsvaddarśanamīlitāḥ kēcid dhārtarāṣṭrā [146] iva viśvarūpāvalōkanajanitēṃdrajāl(ādbhut [8])apratyayāḥ kēcid ātmani vāraṇabuddhyā balavaṃtō 'pi subāhāḥ kēcit pāṇigrahaṇārthinō [147] 'py asukaraṃ manyamānāḥ kēcid adharī(kṛtā [9]) (60) api sthirāḥ kēcit pāṃḍuputrā ivā 'kṣahṛdayājñānahṛtakṣamāḥ kēcit bṛhatkathānu(sāriṇa iva) guṇāḍhyāḥ kēcit tiryaggataya (iva) sugaṃdhavāhāḥ [148] kēcit kāuravasāinikā iva drōṇa(śāstra)sūcakāḥ kēcit (kāiravā)karā ivā 'sōḍhasūrabhāsaḥ (kṣaṇam ēvaṃ) sthitāḥ rājaputrāḥ. (sā ca kṣaṇēnāi "tān) ēkāikaśas sam(ā)[149]lōkya viraktahṛdayā (satī) tasmāt (karṇīrathād [10]) avatatāra. atha tasyām ēva rātrāu [svapnē] vālinam ivā 'ṃgadōpaśōbhitaṃ kuhū(mukham [11]) iva hārikaṃṭhaṃ kanakamṛgam iva rāmākarṣaṇanipuṇaṃ jaya[150]ṃtam iva vacanāmṛtānaṃditavṛddhaśravasaṃ kṛ(61)ṣṇam iva kam-

[1] So also Hall's manuscripts A, B, C, D, F, H.

[2] So also Hall's manuscripts A, B, C, D, F, H.

[3] Tel. ed. 61, Grantha ed., and Trichinopoly ed., *atra*; Hall's manuscripts D, E, F, G, H also omit *ca*.

[4] Cf. *divyacakṣuṣaḥ* in Hall's manuscripts A, B, H.

[5] Hall's manuscripts C, D, F also omit *su*.

[6] Hall's manuscripts A, B, H also omit *sukha*.

[7] Hall's manuscripts A, B, C, D, E, F, H also omit *vikaca*.

[8] So also Hall's manuscripts A, B, C, F, G, H.

[9] So also Hall's manuscripts A, B, C, H, and the commentator Jagaddhara.

[10] So also Hall's manuscripts C, F, H.

[11] So also Hall's manuscripts A, B, C, D, E, F, G, H, and the commentator Jagaddhara.

saharṣaṃ na kurvaṃtaṃ mahāmēgham iva vilasatkarakaṃ (samudram iva mahāsatvatējōyuktaṃ mālinyā kabarikayā tuṃgabhadrayā nāsikayā śōṇēnā 'dharēṇa narmadayā vācā gōdayā bhujayā svarvāhinyā kīrtyā ca puṇyasarinmayam iva) ādikaṃdaṃ (śṛṃgāra[1])pādapasya [ā[2]]rōhaṇagiriṃ (sakalaguṇaratna[3]-samūhasya[4]) prabhava(śāilaṃ) suṃdara(kaṃdarpa)kathānadīnāṃ surabhimāsaṃ vāidagdhyasahakārasya ādarśatalaṃ (sāuṃdaryasya prathamamūlaṃ) [151] vidyālatānāṃ svayaṃvarapatiṃ (sarasvatyāḥ[5]) spardhā(grahaṃ kīrtilakṣmyōḥ[5] mūla)gṛhaṃ śīlasaṃpadāṃ kōśa(gṛhaṃ) mahāsāuṃdarya(dhanasya) tribhuvana(ramaṇīyā)kṛtiṃ (kaṃcid) yuvānaṃ dadarśa., sa [ca] cintāmaṇināmnō rājñas tanayaḥ kaṃdarpakētur (iti) svapna ēva (tan)nāmādikam (aśṛṇōt). anaṃtaram ahō prajāpatē rūpa(62)nirmāṇakāuśalaṃ [idaṃ] manyē svasyāi "va [152] nāipuṇyasyāi ("katra) darśanōtsukamanasā (vēdhasā) jagattrayasama(vāya)rūpaparamāṇūn ādāya viracitō 'yam (iti) anyathā katham ivā 'sya kāṃtiviśēṣa īdṛśō bhavati. vṛthāi 'va damayaṃtī naḷasya kṛtē [153] (vanē) [vāsa]vāiśasam [av]āpa. mudhāi 'vē 'ṃdumatī mahiṣy apy ajānurāgiṇī babhūva. (vi)phalam ēva duṣyaṃtasya kṛtē (durvāsasaś śāpam anubabhūva śakuṃtaḷā). nirarthakam (ēva[6]) madanamaṃjarī[7] naravāhanadattaṃ cakamē. [154] niṣkāraṇam ēva (mērugirinitaṃbē ūrugarima[8]nirjita)raṃbhā raṃbhā naḷakūbaram acīkamata[9]. (vyartham) ēva dhūmōrṇā (svayaṃ)svayaṃvarārtham (āgatēṣu dēvagaṇēṣu) [155] dharmarājam (ācakāṃkṣē[10]. ṛddhis tu niṣprayōjanam ēva gaṃdharvayakṣēṣu kubēram āsasāda. ahētukam ēva pulōmatanayā dēvēṃdrāsaktacittā babhūva). iti bahuvidhaṃ (ciṃtayitvā) viraha(63)murmur(āgni)madhyam adhirūḍhē 'va (madanadāvā)gniśikhākabaḷitē 'va (va-

[1] So also Hall's manuscripts A, B, C, D, F, G, H.
[2] Hall's manuscripts A, B, C, D, F, H also omit *ā*.
[3] So also Hall's manuscripts A, B, C, D, F, G, H.
[4] So also Hall's manuscript D.
[5] So also Hall's manuscripts A, B, C, D, E, F, G, H.
[6] So also Hall's manuscript D. [7] Trichinopoly ed., *madanamañjukā*.
[8] So also Hall's manuscripts C, D, G, H.
[9] Tel. ed. 61, Grantha ed., and Hall's manuscript E have *acakamata*.
[10] Srirangam text, Trichinopoly ed., Hall's manuscripts A, E, F, G, H, and the commentator Jagaddhara have *ācakāṅkṣa*.

saṃta)kālāgni(śikhāgṛhītē 'va dakṣiṇamāruta)rudrapāvakagrastē 'va (unmāda)pātāḷa(gṛhaṃ) praviṣṭē 'va śūnyakaraṇagrāmē ('va[1] vartamānā) hṛdayē (vi)likhitam iva utkīrṇam iva pratyuptam iva kīlitam iva nigaḷitam iva vajra(sāra)ghaṭitam iva asthipaṃjara-praviṣṭam iva (majjārasaśabaḷitam iva marmāṃtarasthitam) iva prāṇaparītam iva aṃtarātmāna[156]m adhiṣṭhitam iva rudhir(ā-śayē[2]) dravībhūtam iva palalasaṃvibhaktam iva kaṃdarpakē-tum manyamānā unmattē 'vā ('ṃdhē 'va) badhirē 'va mūkē 'va śūnyē 'va nirast(ēṃdriya)grāmē 'va mūrchāgṛhītē 'va grahagrastē 'va yāuvanasāgara(taraḷa)taraṃgaparaṃparā(parītē) 'va rāgaraj-jubhiḥ (parivāritē[3]) 'va kaṃdarpakusumabāṇāiḥ kīlitē 'va śṛṃgā-rabhāvanāviṣa(rasa[4])(64)ghūrṇitē 'va rūpaparibhāvanāśalya(kī-litē) 'va malayānilāpahṛtajīvitē 'va (bhavaṃtī sā[5] hā priyē) sakhy anaṃgalēkhē vitara hṛdayē mē pāṇipadmaṃ dussahō 'yaṃ vira-hasaṃtāpaḥ mugdhē madana[157]maṃjari siṃcā ('ṃgāni) caṃ-dana(vāriṇā) saraḷē vasaṃtasēnē saṃvṛṇu kēśapāśaṃ taraḷē ta-raṃgavati vikirā ('ṃgēṣu kāitaka)dhūḷiṃ vāmē madanamālini vījaya śāi(vālakalāpēna) capalē citra(rēkhē vicitrapaṭē[6] vilikha) citta(cōraṃ) janaṃ (bhāmini) vilāsavati (vikṣipā[7] 'vayavēṣu) muktācūrṇanikaraṃ rāgiṇi rāgalēkhē sthagaya naḷinīdaḷa(nica-yēna) payōdharabhāraṃ (su[8])kāṃtē kāṃtimati (maṃdaṃ) maṃ-dam[9] apanaya bāṣpabiṃdūn (yūthikē yūthikālaṃkṛtē saṃcāraya kadaḷīdaḷatāḷavṛṃtēnā "rdravātān) [158] ēhi bhagavati nidrē anugṛhāṇa māṃ dhig iṃdriyāir aparāiḥ kim iti lōcanamayāny ēva (na kṛtāny aṃgāni) vidhinā bhagavan kusumāyudha (tavā[10]) 'yam aṃjalir [tē] anu(vaśō) bhava bhāvavati (mā)dṛśē janē [159] malayānila surata(mahōtsava[11])dīkṣāgurō vaha yath(ēṣṭam) apa-gatā mama prāṇā iti bahuvidhaṃ bhāṣamāṇā (vāsavadattā) sa-

[1] So also Hall's manuscripts B, E, F, H.
[2] Cf. *rudhirāśayadravī* in Hall's manuscripts C, H.
[3] So also Hall's manuscript F.
[4] Cf. *śṛṅgārarasabhāvana* in Hall's manuscripts D, G, H.
[5] Tel. ed. 61, Grantha ed., and Srirangam text omit *sā*.
[6] Trichinopoly ed. and Srirangam text, *citrapaṭē*.
[7] So also Hall's manuscripts A, B, C, F, H.
[8] So also Hall's manuscripts A, B, C, D, F, H.
[9] Cf. *mandamanda* in Hall's manuscripts A, C, D, F, G, H
[10] Cf. *añjalis tavā 'nucarō* in Hall's manuscripts C, D
[11] So also Hall's manuscript D.

khījanēna samaṃ mumūrca. (sapadi) parijana(prayatnāt gṛhītajīvā) [satī[1]] kṣaṇam atiśiśiraghanasāraras(ākul)animnagā[kula]-puḷinē kṣaṇam atituhinamalayajarasasaritparisarē kṣaṇam (atilōhitakanakāraviṃdakadaṃba)parivāritasaras(ta(65)ṭīcaṃdana)-[160]viṭapicchāyāsu kṣaṇam anilōl(lasita)daḷēṣu kadaḷīkānanēṣu kṣaṇaṃ kusuma(pravāḷa)śayyāsu kṣaṇaṃ naḷinīdaḷa(prastarēṣu kṣaṇaṃ tuṣārasaṃghātaśiśiritaśilātalēṣu parijanēna[2] nīyamānā) praḷayakālōditadvādaśaravikiraṇakalāpatīvravirah(ānaladahyamānā) atikṛśa(prāṇām) iva tanuṃ bibhratī (sā 'balā) maṃda-(maṃdam) āṃdōḷita[161]dugdhasiṃdhutaraḷataraṃgacchaṭādhavaḷahāsacchuritādharapallavaṃ tanmukhāraviṃdaṃ dvijakulam iva śrutipraṇayitadīkṣaṇayugaḷaṃ sahajasurabhimukhaparimaḷ(āmōdam[3]) āghrātukāmē 'va [su]dūravinirgatā (tan)nāsāvaṃśalakṣmīḥ kaḷaṃkamuktēṃdukalā(kalāpakōmaḷapiyyūṣa[4])phēna-[paṭala]pāṃḍurā[5] (tad)dvijapaṅktiḥ [tad a]dṛṣṭacaram anaṃgam (atiśāyi[6]tadrūpaṃ) dhanyāni tāni sthānāni[7] tē [ca] janapadāḥ (puṇyāḥ tāni) nāmākṣarāṇi [ca[8]] [162] sukṛtabhāṃji yāny amunā pariṣkṛtānī 'ti muhur muhur [pari]bhāvayaṃtī [dikṣu vidikṣu] (vi)likhitam iva nabhasi [utkīrṇam iva vi]lōcanē pratibiṃbitam iva citra-(paṭē[9]) purōdarśitam iva[10] (tam) itas tatō vilōkayaṃtī vyatiṣṭhata. atha tasyās (tamālikā nāma śārikā) tat(priya)sakhībhis (samaṃ samā[11])lōcya kaṃdarpakētu(bhāvam) ā[163]kalayituṃ (prēṣitā). (sā 'pi) mayā [ēva] sārdham (āgatā) 'trāi "va tarōr adhastāt tiṣṭhatī 'ty uktvā virarāma. atha (tac chrutvā[12] kaṃdarpakētus) saharṣaṃ (sam)utthāya tamālikām (ā(66)hūya) viditavṛttāṃtāṃ akarōt. sā (tasmāi) kṛtapraṇāmā [makarandāya] patrikām upānayat. atha (makaraṃdas) tām (ādāya) svayam ēvā 'vācayat.

[1] Hall's manuscripts C, D, H also omit *satī*.

[2] So also Hall's manuscript D.

[3] So also Hall's manuscripts A, B, D, E, F, G, H.

[4] So also Hall's manuscripts A, B, C, E, G, H.

[5] Tel. ed. 61 and Grantha ed., *pāṃḍarā*.

[6] Srirangam text and Trichinopoly ed., *adṛṣṭacaram anaṅgātiśāyi*.

[7] Srirangam text and Trichinopoly ed., *tāni dhanyāni sthānāni*.

[8] Hall's manuscripts E, G also omit *ca*.

[9] So also Hall's manuscript D.

[10] Trichinopoly ed., *pratibimbitam iva lōcanē purōdarśitam iva citrapaṭē*.

[11] So also Hall's manuscripts A, B, D.

[12] So also Hall's manuscript D.

[164] pratyakṣadṛṣṭabhāvā 'py asthirahṛdayā hi kāminī bhavati
svapnānubhūtabhāvā dṛḍhayati na pratyayaṃ yuvatiḥ.

tac chrutvā kaṃdarpakētur amṛtārṇava(ni)magna(m) iva sarvānaṃdānām uparivartamāna(m ivā "tmānaṃ manyamānō[1] maṃdamaṃdam[2]) utthāya prasāritabāhuyugaḷas tamālikām ā(liliṃgē). [atha] tayāi "va (ca) sārdhaṃ kiṃ karōti kiṃ vadati katham āsta ityādi sakalaṃ vāsavadattāvṛttāntaṃ (sa) pṛcchan [tatra tāṃ niśāṃ] (taṃ) divasaṃ [api] (tatrāi "vā) 'tivāhya (tasmāt pradēśāt tayā sahō[3] 'ccacāla sasuhṛt kaṃdarpakētuḥ). [165] atrāṃtarē bhagavān api marīcimālī [taṃ] vṛttāṃtam (imaṃ) kathayitum (iva) madhyama[4]lōkam avatatāra. atha vāsaratāmracūḍacūḍācakrākāraḥ cakravāka(hṛdaya[5])saṃkrāmitasaṃtāpatayē 'va maṃdimānam udvahann (astagiri)maṃdārastabakasuṃdaraḥ siṃdūra(rājiraṃjita[6])surarājakuṃbhikuṃbhavibhramaṃ bibhrāṇaḥ tāṃḍavacaṃḍavēgōcchalitadhūrjaṭijaṭājūṭa(makuṭavikaṭabaddha[7])baṃdhura[vi[166]kaṭa]vāsukibhōgamaṇitāṭaṃkasanābhimaṇḍalaḥ saṃdhyā(sīmaṃtinī[8])sa(67)rasayāvaka(patra[9])cāruḥ vāruṇīvāravilāsinī[aruṇa[10]]maṇikuṃḍalakāntiḥ kālakaravāḷa(saṃchinna)vāsaramahiṣaskaṃdhacakrākāraḥ [167] (madhura)madhu(pūrṇaṃ kapālam) iva (gagana)kapālinaḥ amlānakusumastabaka iva nabhaśśriyaḥ (puṣpastabaka iva) gaganāśōka(tarōḥ) [iva] kanaka[maya[11]]darpaṇa iva pratīcīvilāsinyāḥ (bhadra iva vāruṇīsaṃgataḥ sarāgaś ca durvidagdha iva parityaktavasuḥ saviṣādaś ca śākya iva raktāṃśukadharaḥ sūrir iva saṃjñōpētaḥ) bhagavān dinamaṇir (aparākūpāra)payasi taraḷataraṃgavēgōcchalitavidru-

[1] Cf. *parivartamānam ātmānaṃ manyamānō* in Hall's manuscript D.

[2] So also Hall's manuscripts A, B.

[3] So also Hall's manuscript D.

[4] Trichinopoly ed. and Srirangam text, *madhyamaṃ*.

[5] So also Hall's manuscript F.

[6] Cf. *sindūrarañjita* in Hall's manuscripts A, B.

[7] Cf. *jūṭamukuṭakōṭibandha* in Hall's manuscript D.

[8] Cf. *sāirandhrī* in Hall's manuscript F, and the variant reading *purandhrī* recorded by Śivarāma.

[9] Cf. *paṭacāru* in Hall's manuscripts B, C, H, and the commentator Jagaddhara; also *paṭṭacāru* in manuscript D, and the commentator Narasiṃha.

[10] Hall's manuscripts B, C, D, H also omit *aruṇa*.

[11] Hall's manuscripts A, B, C, D, F, H also omit *maya*.

mavitapākrtir mamajja. (tataḥ[1]) kramēṇa [ca] [168] rajō[vi[2]]-luṭhitōtthitakulāyārthi [paraspara] kalahavikalakalaviṃkakulaka-lakalavācālaśikharēṣu śikhariṣu vasati(sā[3])kāṃkṣēṣu dhvāṃkṣēṣu anavaratadahyamānakāl(āgaru)dhūpaparimaḷōdgārēṣu vāsāgāra-(jālavivarēṣu) dūrvāṃcitataṭinītaṭaniviṣṭa(gōṣṭhī[4])vidagdhajana-prastūyamāna [kāvya[5]] kathāśravaṇōtsukaśiśujanakalakala(ravōt-kupitasamṛddhēṣu) vṛddhēṣu ālōlikātaraḷarasanābhiḥ kathita(ba-hu)kathābhir jaratībhir a(68)tilaghu[169]kara(tāḍana[6])janita (su-khābhir[7] anugatē[8]) śiśayiṣamāṇē śiśujanē viracitakaṃdarpamu-drāsu kṣudrāsu kāmukajanānubadhyamānadāsījanavividhāślīla-(vacaś)śrutivirasī(kṛtāsu[9] kāminīṣu) saṃdhyāvaṃdanōpaviṣṭēṣu śiṣṭēṣu rōmaṃthamaṃtharakuraṃga(kuṭuṃbā)dhyāsyamānamra-diṣṭhagōṣṭhīnapṛṣṭhāsv araṇyasthalīṣu nidrā(vidrāṇa)drōṇa(kāka)-kula(kalila[10])kulāyēṣu (grāmatarunicayēṣu) [170] kāpēyavikalaka-pikula(kalilēṣv) āśrama(drumēṣu kalakalavikalabakakulēṣv ārā-mataruṣu) nirjigamiṣati jarattarukōṭarakuṭīrakuṭuṃbini kāuśika-kulē timiratarjananirgatāsu dahanapraviṣṭadinakara(śākhāsv[11]) iva [pra[12]]sphurantīṣu dīpa(śikhāsu[13]) mukharitadhanuṣi varṣati śaranikaram [anavaratam] aśēṣa(sāṃsār[171]ika)śēmuṣīmuṣi ma-karadhvajē surat(ākalpāraṃbha[14])śōbhini śaṃbhaḷībhāṣitabhāji bhajati bhūṣāṃ bhujiṣyājanē sāiraṃdhrībadhyamānaraśan(ākalpa)-jalpāka(jaghanāsu[15]) janīṣu viśrāṃtakathā(69)nubaṃdha[172]tayā pravartamāna(kathaka[16])janagṛhagamanatvarēṣu catvarēṣu samā-(sādita)kukkuṭēṣu (kirātajana)niṣkuṭēsu kṛtayaṣṭisamārōhaṇēṣu

[1] So also Hall's manuscript D, and the commentator Narasiṃha.
[2] Hall's manuscript C also omits *vi*.
[3] So also Hall's manuscripts A, B, C, D, E, F, G, H.
[4] Cf. *nibaddhagōṣṭhīkavidagdha* in Hall's manuscripts A, B, C, D, E, F, G, H.
[5] Hall's manuscript D also omits *kāvya*.
[6] So also Hall's manuscripts A, B, C, D, F, G, H.
[7] So also Hall's manuscripts B, C, F.
[8] So also Hall's manuscripts A, B, C, E, F, G, H.
[9] Cf. *kṛtēṣu* in Hall's manuscript D.
[10] So also Hall's manuscripts C, D, H, and the commentator Jagaddhara.
[11] So also Hall's manuscripts A, B, C, D.
[12] Hall's manuscripts A, B, C, D, G, H also omit *pra*.
[13] So also Hall's manuscript A. [14] So also Hall's manuscripts A, B, C, D, F, H.
[15] So also Hall's manuscripts A, B, C, D, F, G, H.
[16] So also Hall's manuscripts A, B, C, D, E, F, G, H, and the commentator Jagaddhara.

barhiṇēṣu vihitasaṃdhyāsamayavyavasthēṣu gṛhasthēṣu (svapati) saṃkōcōdaṃcad(ucca[1])kēsarakōṭisaṃkaṭakuśēśay(ōdara)kōṭarakuṭīra(kuṭila)śāyini ṣaṭcaraṇacakrē ['tha] anēnāi ("va pathā) bhagavatā (bhāsvatā) [samā]gaṃtavyam iti (sarvataḥ) paṭṭamayāir vasanāir [iva] maṇikuṭṭimāḷir iva viracitā varuṇēna (ravēḥ) [173] kāla(karavāḷa)kṛttasya divasamahiṣasya rudhiradhārē 'va vidrumalatē 'va (caramā)rṇavasya raktakamalinī 'va gagana(taṭākasya) kāṃcana(kētur[2]) iva kaṃdarpa(rathasya) maṃjiṣṭhārāgāruṇapatākē 'va gaganaharmya(sthalasya) lakṣmīr iva svayaṃvara[pari[3]]-gṛhītapītāṃbarā bhikṣukī 'va tārānu(rāga)raktāṃbaradhāriṇī (vārayōṣid iva pallavānuraktā kāminī 'va kālēyātāmrapayō(70)-dharā babhur iva kapilatārakā[4]) bhagavatī saṃdhyā samadṛśyata. (tataḥ) kṣaṇēna [ca] kṣaṇad(ānu)rāga[racanā]caturāsu (vēśyāsv iva saṃdhyāśiṣyāsv iva sphuraṃtīṣu dīpalēkhāsu) [174] tulādhāraśūnyāyāṃ paṇya(vīdhikāyām) iva divi [ghana]ghaṭamānadaḷapuṭāsu puṭakinīṣu[5] timiraprati(hatēṣv ivē 'tas tataḥ) paribhramatsu kamalasarasi madhukara(nikarēṣu) vikalakurarīrutacchalēna [175] ravivirahavidhurāsu vilapaṃtīṣv iva sarōjinīṣu (pratiphalitasaṃdhyārāgarajyamānasalilasthitāsu pativināśahṛtpīḍayā dahanapraviṣṭāsv iva kamalinīṣu) gaṇaka iva nakṣatrasūcakē pradōṣē harakaṃtha[kāṇḍa]kāḷimasanābhi dāityabala[176]m iva pra(kaṭita[6])tārakaṃ bhāratasamaram iva vardhamānōlūkakalakalaṃ dṛṣṭadyumnavīryam iva kuṃṭhitadrōṇapra(bhavaṃ) naṃdana[vana[7]]m iva saṃcaratkāuśikaṃ kṛṣṇavartma(jvalanam) iva (ni)khilakāṣṭhāpahārakaṃ sagarbham iva [177] ghanatarapāṣāṇa(karkaśāsu) giritaṭīṣu sacakṣur iva supta(prabuddha)siṃhanayana(cchavi)cchaṭākapilēṣu sānuṣu sajīvam iva tamōmaṇibhiḥ saṃvardhitam ivā 'gnihōtradhūma(rēkhābhiḥ) māṃsaḷitam iva kāminīkēśa[pāśa]saṃskāra[aguru](dhūpa)paṭalāiḥ u(71)ddīpitam

[1] So also Hall's manuscripts C, D, F. [2] So also Hall's manuscript D.

[3] Hall's manuscripts A, B, D, H also omit *pari*; Tel. ed. 61, Grantha ed., and Hall's manuscripts C, F have *svayaṃgṛhīta*.

[4] So also Hall's manuscript D, except *kālēyaka* for *kālēya*, and omitting *kāminī 'va*.

[5] Tel. ed. 61 and Grantha ed., *puṭikinīṣu*.

[6] Cf. *prakaṭa* in Hall's manuscripts D, F.

[7] Hall's manuscripts B, F, H also omit *vana*.

iva ghanaṭara(nīla)madhukara[178](paṭalāiḥ mēcakitam iva[1]) pēcakikapōla(gaḷita)dānadhārāśīkarāiḥ puṃjīkṛtam iva vitatatamāla-(kānana[2]cchaṭā)cchāyāsu (ni)līyamānam iva kajjala(rasa[3])śyāma-bhōgibhōgēṣu prāvaraṇam iva rajanīpāṃsulāyāḥ palitāuṣadham iva vṛddhavāra(yōṣitāṃ) apatyam iva rajanyāḥ suhṛd iva [179] kalikālasya mitram iva durjana(hṛdayānāṃ[4]) bāuddha(siddhāṃ-tam[5]) iva pratyakṣadravyam apahnuvānaṃ [timiraṃ vyajṛmbhata] muditam iva [ati[6]]mattamātaṃga(gaṃḍhasthalē) phalitam ivā 'tisāṃdra(bahuḷa)cchada(vitata[7])tamāla(kānana[8]sphuṭapāṭavōtkaṭavi-śaṃkaṭānēkaviṭapiviṭapōtkaṭa[9]sphuṭakusumapuṭapihita[10]padaṣaṭ-padāvalīṣu[11]pari)sphuritam iva [atikānta]kāṃtā[jana]ghanatara-kēśa[pāśa[12]]saṃhatāu (unmīlitam) ivē 'ṃdranīla[maṇi]raśmibhiḥ ati[180]śayamāṃsaḷitam ivā 'vaṭa(taṭēṣu) sāṭōpam ivā[13] [sphuṭa-pāṭavōtkaṭaprakaṭaviśaṅkaṭakuṭajaviṭapōtkaṭavinaṭitaṣaṭpadāliṣu] ('ti)ghanataraghōraghasmaraviṣadharabhōga(bhāsuramada)bhara-matta[14]daṃtidaṃta[181]dyutitarjana(jarjharitatamaṃ [tamaḥ] divākarōdayāraṃbhaṇam) iva saṃkucat(kuvalayaṃ asatāṃ ma-hattvam iva tiraskṛtasakalāṃtaraṃ nimīlannīlōtpalavyājaracitāṃ-jaliputēna namad ivā "gatāṃ) tamīṃ (timiram arājata. atha) kṣaṇēn(āi "va) saṃdhyātāṃḍava(ḍaṃbarō)cchalitamahānaṭa(72)-jaṭājūṭakūṭakuṭila(skhalana)vivartitajahnukanyāvāridhārābiṃdava iva (pra)kīrṇāḥ dur(bharadharaṇī)bhāra[bhara]bhugnabhīmadiṅ-[matta[15]]mātaṃga(gaṃḍa)maṃḍala(vi)mukta[182]ṣīkaracchaṭā iva (tatāḥ[16]) atidavīyōnabha(sthala[17])bhramaṇakhinna(raviturаṃgamā-

[1] So also Hall's manuscripts A, D, F.
[2] So also Hall's manuscripts B, C, D, E, F, G, H.
[3] So also Hall's manuscripts A, B, C, D, F.
[4] So also Hall's manuscripts C, D, F.
[5] So also Hall's manuscripts A, B, C, D, E, G, H.
[6] Hall's manuscripts A, B, C also omit *ati*.
[7] So also Hall's manuscripts A, B, C, F, G, H.
[8] Trichinopoly ed. *kānanē sāṭōpam iva*.
[9] Cf. *śaṅkaṭānēkaviṭapōtkaṭaviṭapi* in Hall's manuscript D.
[10] Trichinopoly ed., *nihita*.
[11] Hall's manuscripts C, D, G, H, and the commentators Jagaddhara and Narasiṃha also have *āvalīṣu*.
[12] Hall's manuscripts D, E, H also omit *pāśa*.
[13] Trichinopoly ed. omits *sāṭōpam iva*.
[14] Trichinopoly ed., *bhāsuraṃ matta*.
[15] Hall's manuscripts A, B, C, D, F, G, H also omit *matta*.
[16] So also Hall's manuscript D.
[17] So also Hall's manuscripts C, D, G, H.

syavivarāṃta)phēnastabakā iva (viśīrṇāḥ [1]) gaganamahāsaraḥ kumuda(saṃdōha)saṃdēha(dāyīnaḥ) viśvaṃ gaṇayatō [vi]dhātuś śaśikaṭhinīkhaṃḍēna tamōmaṣīśyāmē ajina iva (viyati [2]) saṃsārasyātiśūnyatvāt śūnyabiṃdava iva vi(likhitāḥ) jagattrayavi(jigīṣā)vinirgatasya makarakētōḥ rati[183]kara[tala]vikīrṇā (iva lājāṃjalayaḥ [3] guḷikā)straguḷikā iva (vikṣiptāḥ) puṣpa(dhanuṣaḥ) viyadaṃburāśiphēnastabakā iva (vitatāḥ) rativiracitā gagan(āṃkaṇē) ātarpaṇapañcāṃguḷaya iva vikīrṇāḥ vyōma(tala)lakṣmīhāramuktānikarā iva (vicchinnāḥ harakōpānaladagdhakāma [4])citācakrād [5] vātyā(vēśaviprakīrṇāḥ) kāmakīkasa[184]khaṃḍā iva timirōdgama[dhūma]dhūmaḷasaṃdhyānalaparitaptagagana(mahānasa)sthālī[kaṭāha]bharjyamāna(sphuṭita)lāj(ānukārās [6] tārā) vyarājaṃta. tābhiś (śvitrī) 'va viyad aśōbhata. (dīrghatar)ōcchvāsaracanākulaṃ (saṃ [7])ślēṣavaktra(cakra)ghaṭanāpaṭu sat(kāvya)viracanam iva ca(73)kravākamithunam atī[185]vā 'khidyata. kamalinī[vana]saṃcaraṇalagnamakaraṃdabiṃdusandōhalubdhamugdhamukharamadhukaramālāśabalagātraṃ kālapāśēnē 'va (mūrtimad)rāmaśāpēnē ('vā) "kṛṣyamāṇaṃ cakravākamithunaṃ vijaghaṭē. ravivirahavidhurāyāḥ [186] kamalinyā hṛdayam iva dvidhā papāṭa cakravākamithunaṃ. āgamiṣyatō himakaradayitasya pārśvē saṃcaraṃtī kumudinyāḥ bhramaramālā dūtī 'vā 'lakṣyata. tārakā(nayanajalabiṃdu)vyājād astaṃgatasya divākara(dayitasya) śōkād iva [sthūlāśrubindubhiḥ [8]] kakubhō vyarudan. bhāsvatō nijadayitasya virahād abhinavakiṃjalkarājivyājēna (śōkānala)murmurō [iva] (naḷina)kōśahṛdayē jajvāla. (tatō) raviraśmi(davāgni [9] bhasmīkṛta)[187]nabhōvanamaṣīrāśir iva śrutivacanam iva (kṣapita [10])digaṃbaradarśanaṃ (kṛṣṇam api tiraskṛtaviśvarūpabhā-

[1] Cf. *śīrṇā* in Hall's manuscript B.

[2] So also Hall's manuscripts A, B, C, D, F, G, H.

[3] Cf. *vikīrṇā lājāñjalaya* in Hall's manuscript D.

[4] So also Hall's manuscripts C, D.

[5] Trichinopoly ed., *cakrāc candrād*.

[6] Cf. *sphuṭitalājabījānukārā* in Hall's manuscripts B, C, F, H, and the commentator Jagaddhara.

[7] So also Hall's manuscript D, and the commentators Jagaddhara and Narasiṃha.

[8] Hall's manuscripts D, E, H also omit *sthūlāśrubindubhiḥ*.

[9] So also Hall's manuscripts B, C, G.

[10] Cf. *kṣata* in Hall's manuscripts A, F, H.

va[1]viśēṣaṃ) sadyō drāvita(rājatapaṭadravapravāha) iva śārvaram aṃdhakāraṃ [vy]ajṛmbhata. (atha) kṣaṇēna [ca] kṣaṇadārāja(ka-'nyākaṃtuka iva) kaṃdarpakanakadarpaṇa[2] (iva) udayagiribālama-ṃdārapuṣpastabaka (iva) prācī(mahiḷā(74)lalāmalalāṭa[3]taṭaghaṭita-baṃdhūkakusumatilaka)[188]cakrākāraḥ kanakakuṃḍalam iva nabhaśśriyaḥ (dig)vadhūprasādhikāhastasrastālaktaka(piṃḍa[4]) iva gaganasāudha(talaśātakuṃbha)kuṃbha iva prasthāna(maṃgaḷa)-kalaśa iva (makarakētōs tribhuvanavijayāiṣiṇaḥ) [kandarpakārta-svaratūṇamukhakāntitaskaraḥ prācyaśāilaśikharāgraprarūḍhaja-pākusumacchaviḥ svacchakuṅkumapiṇḍapūrṇa[189]pātram iva niśāvilāsinyāḥ] kuṃkumāruṇ[āik]astanakalaśa ivā "khaṃḍalāśā-ṃganāyāḥ (garuḍa) iva hariṇādhiṣṭhitaḥ rāma iva lakṣmaṇānvitaḥ (vānarēṃdra ivā 'nuraktatāraḥ vṛṣabha iva rōhiṇīpriyaḥ) surājē 'va raktamaṃḍalaḥ (mṛdukarasahitaś ca jāṃbavān iva ṛkṣapari-vṛtaḥ) rajanīpatir udayam āsasāda. [tataḥ] kāminīhṛdayasaṃkrā-mita iva (cakrā)ṃganā(nayanayugaḷa)pīta[190] iva raktakumuda-kōś(ā)līḍha iva kṣīṇatāṃ (gataḥ) kṣaṇadā(karagatō) rāgaḥ. ana-ṃtaraṃ śarvarīvrajāṃganāviṣkṛta(nūtana)navanītasvastika iva (mṛgacchāyā)mudrita[mukura[5]] ivā ("darśaḥ) śvētātapatram iva makarakētōḥ daṃta(pāḷī)cakram iva viyanmahā(khaḍgasya) śvē-tacāmaram iva madana[191]mahārājasya (bāla)puḷinam iva niśā-yamunāyāḥ sphāṭikaliṃgam iva gaganamahātāpasasya aṃḍam iva kālōragasya kaṃbur iva nabhōmahārṇa(75)vasya cāityam iva [madanāridagdhasya makarakētōś citācakram iva] (kāl)āṃgāraśa-baḷaṃ (bhavanētrāgnidagdhasya) saṃkalpajanmanaḥ (puṃḍarīkam iva gaganagāmigaṃgāyāḥ phēnasaṃcaya iva gaganamahārṇa-vasya) pāradapiṃḍam iva (gagana)dhātuvādinaḥ rājatakalaśa iva dūrvāpravāḷaśabaḷō (manōbhavābhiṣēkasya[6] śvētacakram iva) ka[192]ṃdarpa(rathasya cūḍāmaṇir ivō 'dayagirināgarājasya śvē-tapārāvata ivā 'ṃbaramahāprāsādasya gaganasariddhāutakuṃbha-sthalam ivāi "rāvatasya) bhagnaśṛṃgapurāṇa(gōmuṃḍam) khamda

[1] So also Hall's manuscripts D, F. [2] Trichinopoly ed., *darpaṇam*.

[3] Cf. *prācīmahilālalāṭa* in Hall's manuscript D.

[4] So also Hall's manuscript D.

[5] Hall's manuscripts A, B, C, D, E, F, H, and the commentator Jagaddhara also omit *mukura*.

[6] So also Hall's manuscript D.

iva (tārā)śvētagōdhūmaśālinō nabhaḥkṣētrasya malayajapiṃḍa(pāṃḍu)rājata(tālavṛṃtam) iva siddhāṃganāhastasrastaṃ (kṣīṇarāgō bhagavān uḍu)patir ujjagāma. [193] yaś ca puṃḍarīkaṃ (lōka)lōcanamadhukarāṇāṃ śayanīyasāikataṃ [iva[1]] citta(rāja[2])haṃsānāṃ sphāṭikavyajanaṃ virahavahnīnāṃ śvētaśāṇacakraṃ [194] manmathasāyakānāṃ. atrāṃtarē 'bhisārikāsārtha(prēṣitānāṃ[3]) [195] priyatamān[4] prati dūtīnāṃ dvyarthās [sērṣyāḥ] saprapaṃcā vi(hāra)[196]bhaṃgurās (saṃ)vādā babhūvuḥ. tathāhi a(76)vastrīkṛtam ātmānaṃ [197] nā "kalayasi tattvataḥ kāṃta. prastara iva krūrō 'si na cā "karṣaka[198]cuṃbakadrāvakēṣv ēkō 'si bhrāmakō 'si paraṃ kitava. dharmārthānya[199]prayuktaḥ kṣēpaṇika iva mudhā vāhitataravāris tvam asi. sakhēdam iva (tāṃ) manasā ciṃtayasi dur(labhāṃ) [janaṃ]. (77) satvasāra(cittō) yō ripu[200]maṃḍalāgratō nirvṛtim upētya tiṣṭhati. sa khalu vīraḥ prati[201]pakṣasya yas saṃprahārataḥ kuṃjarān nayati. dhṛtōrukaravāḷasaṃca[202]yō 'pi paramakāṃḍa ēva saṃpatan mahāpadaṃ vigrahē(78)ṇa labhatē. [203] rājasēna (rājasē narahitō) rahitō dhruvaṃ. (asta)viśāradā [vi]śāradābhraviśadā viśadātmanīna(mahimāna)mahimānarakṣaṇakṣamā kṣamā[204]tilaka dhīratādhīratā manasi (bhūtā) 'bhūtatābhūtatā (ca) vacasi. sā 'ha sēna [205] sā 'hasēna kamalā (kamalālayā yayā) 'jitā sā tvadarpaṇā darpaṇākāravimalāśayā śayābja[vi[5]]nirjitakisala(79)yā salayā[206]ṃguḷir (iva) vibhramēṇa vibhramēṇa [prati]gavākṣaśalākāvivaraṃ (prati)vilōkayaṃtī [207] [vi](lōkayaṃtritavināśā vinā śāpam anubhavati) duḥkhāni. jīvanāyaka jīvanāya (kam iva) nā ("śrayati[6]) subhagaṃ. anyā[208]stā 'vadā 'satām (aham ēva) dāsatāṃ puratō bhajāmi māitryatō māitry atō [209] 'stu. aṃjasā ratas sārataḥ kim api kaṃdarpakaṃ darpakaṃ na (cēt) tanōṣi viśēṣatō (viśēṣataḥ sthiram[7]) ēva maraṇaṃ. śaṭhadhiyāṃ śōdhana ya(80)śōdhana [210] prēmahāryā mahāryā (samā sō[8]) 'tkaṭākṣāiḥ kaṭākṣāir āvi-

[1] Hall's manuscripts A, B, C, D, E, F also omit *iva*.
[2] So also Hall's manuscripts C, F, G.
[3] So also Hall's manuscripts A, B, C, F, G, H.
[4] Tel. ed. 61 and Grantha ed., *priyatamā*.
[5] Hall's manuscripts A, B, C, D, F also omit *vi*.
[6] So also Hall's manuscripts C, G.
[7] Tel. ed. 61 and Grantha ed., *viśēṣatasthiram*.
[8] Cf. *samāsamō* in Hall's manuscripts C, D, F, H.

rbhūtadāsyā 'stadāsyāḥ parijanāḥ. kamalākṛtinārīṇāṃ kamalākṛti nā 'rīṇāṃ [211] bhavatā mukhaṃ ca malinitaṃ. viśvasya viśvasya vyava(sthāṃ) samāsādyāsamāsā ('dyā) 'nēka(kālaṃ[1]) saṃgīta(rasika)tanuṣē tanuṣēkam (anaṃgasya) puṣpēṣupuṣpēṣu rujā tarasā jātarasā maṃdākṣamaṃ(81)dā kṣaṇam (api) [212] bhramaṃtī muhyati. kā madhurā 'dharēṇa kāmadhurādharēṇa (yuktā) rajō(rāja)viśēṣakēṇa viśēṣakēṇa mukhēṃdunā tava hṛdi lagnā [213] (mṛdimā)karēṇa karēṇa svēdabiṃdupayōdharēṇa payōdharēṇa vakṣaḥphalakāṃcanēna jitā 'nāvilakāṃcanēna. kāmadāruṇa (82) madāruṇanētrā smaramayaṃ (rasamayaṃtaṃ bhavaṃtam) adayaṃ madayaṃtī param akam itāraṃ [214] param akamitāraṃ vāṃchati hāriṇā hā 'riṇā stanakuṃbhēna hāriṇā 'kṣirucihāriṇā cakṣuṣā [hāriṇā] (ca[2]). anaṃtaraṃ dugdhārṇava(nimagnam) iva (sphāṭika)gṛhapraviṣṭam iva śvētadvīpa(niviṣṭam) [215] iva jagad āmumudē. (tataḥ) kramēṇa ca[3] vighaṭamānadaḷapuṭakumudakānanakōśamakaraṃdabiṃdusaṃdōha(sāṃdraniṣyaṃdāsvāda[4]mada)mudita[mugdha]madhukarakulakala(rava)mukharitadig(aṃtarē[5]) caṃdrikāpānabharālasacakōrakāminībhir abhinaṃdit(āgamē) suratabhara[pariśrama[6]]khinnapuḷi[216]ṃdarājasuṃdarīsvēdajalakaṇikā(83)pahāriṇi pra(vāti[7]) sāyaṃtanē tanīyasi niśāniśvāsanibhē nabhasvati kaṃdarpakētus tamālikāmakaraṃdasahāyō vāsavadattā[janaka]nagaram ayāsīt. atha (sa praviśya) kaṭakāika(dēśē vinihitam) [abhraṃlihaśikharēṇa sudhādhavalēnāi "kāntaraniviṣṭakanakamuktāmarakatapadmarāgaśakalēna vāsavadattā[217]darśanārtham avasthitadēvatāgaṇēnē 'va śālavalayēna parigatam] (anilōllasita)nabhastaru(kusuma[8])maṃjarībhir iva tarjayaṃtībhir iva gagana(pura[9])śriyaṃ patākābhir upaśōbhamānaṃ kanakaśilāpaṭṭ(āṃkaṇa)prasṛtābhiḥ karpūrakuṃkumacaṃdanāilālavaṃga[gandhōdaka]parimaḷavāhinībhiḥ [vāhinībhir ajñāta](taṭanikaṭa-

[1] So also Hall's manuscript D, and the commentator Narasiṃha.
[2] So also Hall's manuscripts A, B.
[3] Trichinopoly ed. omits *ca*.
[4] So also Hall's manuscript C.
[5] So also Hall's manuscripts A, B, C, E, F, G.
[6] Hall's manuscripts A, B, C, D, F, H also omit *pariśrama*.
[7] So also Hall's manuscripts A, B, C, D, F, G.
[8] So also Hall's manuscripts B, C.
[9] So also Hall's manuscripts A, B, C, D, F, G.

sphaṭikaśilā[1])sukhaniṣaṇṇanidrāya[218]mān(ōjjāta)prāsāda(śvēta[2])-pārāvatābhiḥ prabhraśyattaṭa[nikaṭa]viṭapi(suma)stabakitasalilābhiḥ anavaratamajjadunmajjad[mada[3]]yuvati[jana]ghanajaghan(āsphālanōcchvasita[4])śīkaranikarasnapita(tīra[5])vēdikābhiḥ karpūrapūra[viracita]puḷina(talaniṣaṇṇa[6])ninadānumīyamāna(rājahaṃsābhiḥ) vika[219]canīlōtpala[kānana]darśita(kāraṃḍava)cakravākatimiraśaṃkābhiḥ (yuvatībhir) iva supayōdharābhiḥ sugrīvayuddha-(vṛttibhir) iva kīlālasnapitakuṃbhakarṇābhiḥ sāgarakūlabhūmibhir iva suṃdarīpā(84)daparā[220]gaśabalābhiḥ [nava]nṛpaticittavṛttibhir iva (kulyāyamānakariṇībhiḥ nadībhir) upaśōbhitaṃ śikharagatamuktājālavyājēna purayuvati[jana]darśan[akutūhal]āgataṃ tārāgaṇam ivō 'dvahadbhiḥ upāṃta[221]nilīnābhiḥ kācakalaśākṛtim udvahaṃtībhiḥ śikhi(saṃhatībhir) udbhāsitāiḥ prāsādāir (upaśōbhamānaṃ) [kvacid] anavaratadahyamānakṛṣṇ(āgarudhūpa[7]maṃḍalāiḥ) darśitākālajalada(sannāhaṃ[8]) kvacid [ati[9]]gaṃbhīramurajaravāhūta(samada)nīlakaṃṭhaṃ śāyaṃtanasamayam iva patitalōkalōcanaṃ janakayajñasthānam iva dār(ōtsukita[10])[222]rāmaṃ (mānuṣam[11]) ivā 'bhinaṃditasurataṃ (araṇyam ivā 'nēkasālaśōbhitaṃ[12]) nidhānam iva kāutukasya (āsthānam) iva śṛṃgārasya kula(graham) iva (sakalavibhramāṇāṃ) saṃkētasthāna[223]m iva sāuṃdaryasya vāsavadattābhavanaṃ bhavanaṃdanaprabhāvō dada(85)rśa. dravasi drava(siddhēr agaditā[13]) capalā capalāyatē kim ēṣā [224] stabakas taba karṇataḥ patitō 'yaṃ. surēkhē (sukapōlarēkhē) surayā [citā[14]] surayā(citā[15]) śrīs tvam asi. (mattē) kalahē

[1] So also Hall's manuscript D.

[2] So also Hall's manuscripts B, C.

[3] Hall's manuscripts A, B, C, F, H also omit *mada*.

[4] Hall's manuscripts A, B, C, E, F, H also have *ucchvasita*.

[5] So also Hall's manuscripts A, D, G.

[6] So also Hall's manuscripts A, B, C, D, F, G, H.

[7] Hall's manuscripts A, B, D, F, H also have *dhūpa*, and manuscripts C, E, G *dhūpadhūma*.

[8] Cf. *utsāhaṃ* in Hall's manuscript D.

[9] Hall's manuscripts A, B, C, D, E, F, H also omit *ati*.

[10] So also Hall's manuscripts A, B, C, D, F, G, H, and the commentator Narasiṃha.

[11] So also Hall's manuscripts A, B, C, E, F, G, H.

[12] Cf. *kāntāram ivā 'nēkaśālōpaśōbhitaṃ* in Hall's manuscript D.

[13] Cf. *nigaditē* in Hall's manuscripts A, C, D, F.

[14] Hall's manuscripts A, B, D, F, H also omit *citā*.

[15] So also Hall's manuscripts A, B, C, D, E, F, G, H.

kalahēma(kāṃcī)dāmakvaṇitāiḥ smaram ivā "hvayasi. malayē malayēpsitaṃ (kuru) dṛśāi 'vā 'dhigatā 'si. kalikē [225] kalikētum (imaṃ) [mukharāṃ muñca mēkhalāṃ] śṛṇumaḥ kalavallakī(vi)-rutaṃ mēkhalā mē khalā na bhavati tvam ēva mukharatayā [mu]kharatayā ca. trapa(86)tē 'tra (patēyam iti nāga)kusúmōpa-(hārēṣu[1] skhalaṃtī 'yam). tava kāitavakāir alaṃ (kalilō niśvāsāir) vēpathur ēvā "śayaṃ vyanakti. vahatī 'va hatīr anaṃga[226]lē-khē (tava vapuḥ) smarasāyakānāṃ tava (ca hāralatā vihitā vihi-tāya) tē. (utkalikē tavō) 'tkalikā(bahuḷē) vadanē vada nētra(payō-jakāṃtē) kim upamānam i[227]ṃdur apy upayāti. vasatī 'va sa-tīvratē tava hṛdi kō 'pi śatadhā śatadhārasārā vācas tavā 'nubhū-tāḥ. (kēraḷikē[2] raḷitē) karakākarakāḷamēghakhaṃḍatulām (upa-yāty[3]) ulla(87)sitōtphullamallikā(mālāhārī tava) kuṃtalakalāpaḥ [tava yāti[4]]. (kuṃtaḷikē[5] kuṃtaḷālaṃkṛtē na ca) puragōpura(gāu-carāḥ) śrūyaṃtē (saṃ)gītadhvanayaḥ. kim iva kalpayasi kṣaṇam īkṣaṇamīlanād (asi[6] caṭula[228]caṭulaṃpaṭasakhījanā 'si. suratē suratē) stanatā stanatāḍanēṣu yat sāukhyaṃ [tal[7]]labdhaṃ sma-ratā smaratāpanōdanaṃ (tadā kēna viyuktā[8]) 'si. kim (ucyatē[9]) mahatō mahatō [dayitō[10]] dayitaḥ [229] smarati sma ratipriyaṃ tava kāuśalaṃ. navani(88)(śātana)kharāṇāṃ nakharāṇāṃ [vraṇaḥ] smarajanyāṃ sma rajanyāṃ kurutē (kurutēna) rujaṃ. [kiṃ] tē[11] lō-canābhyāṃ lōcanābhyāṃ (phalitā)khilajanēkṣaṇadēśaḥ kṣaṇadēśaḥ [230] kin na pīyatē. priyasakhi madanamālini (mālini biṃbādha-rasaṃgatyāgēcchayā) virāgaṃ kuru madhumadāruṇamāḷavīkapō-la(kōmalalōladaḷa)maṃḍalatayā latayā (kō viśēṣas tvayā). kura-[231]ṃgikē kalpaya kuraṃga(śābēbhyaś[12]) śaṣpāṅkuraṃ. kiśōrikē kāra(89)ya (kiśōraṃ) pratyavēkṣāṃ. taraḷikē taraḷaya kṛṣṇ(āga-ru)dhūpapaṭalaṃ. karpūrikē (pāṃsulaya) karpūradhūḷibhiḥ payō-

[1] So also Hall's manuscripts A, C, D, and the commentator Jagaddhara.
[2] So also Hall's manuscripts A, B, C, D, E, F, G.
[3] So also Hall's manuscript H. [4] Hall's manuscript H also omits *tava yāti*.
[5] So also Hall's manuscripts A, B, C, D, E, F, G.
[6] Trichinopoly ed., *ayi*. [7] Hall's manuscripts D, E, G also omit *tal*.
[8] Hall's manuscript D and the commentator Narasiṃha also have *viyuktā*.
[9] Tel. ed. 61 and Grantha ed., *ucyasē*.
[10] Hall's manuscripts B, D, G also omit the first *dayitō*.
[11] Srirangam text and Trichinopoly ed., *tava*.
[12] Tel. ed. 61 and Grantha ed., *śākhōbhyaś*.

dharabhāraṃ. mātaṃgikē mānaya mātaṃgaśiśu(dhāvanaṃ). śaśilēkhē (vi)likha lalāṭapaṭṭē śaśi(rēkhāṃ). kētakikē saṃkētaya kētakī(maṃḍapadōhaḷaṃ). śaku[232]nikē dēhi krīḍāśakunibhya āhāraṃ. madanamaṃjari (maṃjīraya latāmaṃḍapaṃ. kadaḷikē vidaḷaya) kadaḷīgṛhaṃ. śṛṃgāramaṃjari [saṅ]kalpaya śṛṃgāra(racanāṃ[1]. saṃjīvanikē[2]) vitara jīvaṃjīvakamithunāya (marīci[3])pallavaṃ. pallavikē pallavaya karpūradhūḷibhiḥ kṛtrimakētakīkānanaṃ. sahakāramaṃjari (sammārjaya śramōdakabiṃdūn) sahakāra(sāurabha)vyajanavātēna. madanalēkhē (vi)likha madanalēkhaṃ malayānilasya. [233] (makarikē makarāṃkaśōbhitē) dēhi mṛṇāḷāṃkuraṃ rājahaṃsa(śābēbhyaḥ). vilāsavati vilāsaya (90) mayūra(kiśōrakaṃ). tamālikē (lēpaya) malayajarasēna bhavanavāṭaṃ. kāṃcanikē vikira (kastūrikā[4])dravaṃ kāṃcanamaṃḍapikāyāṃ. pravāḷikē sēcaya (ghu)sṛṇarasēna [bāla]pravāḷakānanaṃ. ity anyōnyaṃ praṇayapēśalāḥ pramadā(janānām) ālāpakathāś śṛṇvan kaṃdarpakētuḥ makaraṃdēna (samaṃ tad bhavanaṃ[5]) [manasy ahō bhavanānām atiśāyi sāundaryam ahō śṛṅgārakalākēlikāuśalaṃ tathāhy ayaṃ tatkālalīlābahalaviralavimala[234]mālavīdaśanakāntikāntidantidantaghaṭitō maṇḍapō 'sāv api kanakaśalākāvinirmitayantrapañjarasaṃyataḥ krīḍāśuka ityādi paricintayan] praviśya vyākaraṇēnē 'va saraktapādēna (mahā)bhāratēnē 'va suparvaṇā rāmāyaṇēnē 'va suṃdarakāṃḍacāruṇā [235] jaṃghāyugaḷēna virājamānāṃ caṃdōvicitim iva bhrājamānatanumadhyāṃ nakṣatravidyām iva gaṇanīyahastaśravaṇāṃ nyāya(vidyām) ivō 'ddyōtakarasvarūpāṃ (satkavikāvyaracanām) ivā 'laṃkāra(prasā(91)dhitāṃ[6]) upaniṣa[236]dam iva (sānaṃdāṃ raviprabhām iva lōkam) uddyōtayaṃtīṃ dvijakulasthitim iva cārucaraṇāṃ viṃdhyagiriśriyam iva sunitaṃbāṃ (rōhiṇīm) iva gurukaḷatratayō 'paśōbhitāṃ śatakōṭi(mūrtim[7]) iva muṣṭigrāhya[tanu[8]]madhyāṃ priyaṃguśyāmāsakhīm iva priyadarśanāṃ brahmadattamahiṣīm iva

[1] So also Hall's manuscripts D, E, G.
[2] So also Hall's manuscripts D, H.
[3] So also the commentator Narasiṃha; Trichinopoly ed. and Hall's manuscripts C, D, F, G, H have *marīca*.
[4] So also Hall's manuscripts F, G, H.
[5] Hall's manuscripts A, D also have *tad bhavanaṃ*.
[6] Cf. *prasādhikām* in Hall's manuscript D.
[7] So also Hall's manuscript A.
[8] Hall's manuscripts D, E also omit *tanu*.

sōmaprabhāṃ [237] diggajakarēṇukām ivā 'nupamāṃ (rēvām) iva (śarmadāṃ) tamālapatraprasādhitāṃ (ca) aśvatarakanyām iva madālasāṃ vāsavadattāṃ dadarśa. atha tāṃ [prīti]visphāritēna cakṣuṣā pibataḥ (92) kaṃdarpakētōḥ jahāra cētanāṃ mūrchā[vēgaḥ]. tam (anu) vāsavadattā mumūrcha. atha makaraṃdasakhījana(prayatnāt) labdhasaṃjñāv (ētāv) ēkāsanam alaṃcakratuḥ. [238] (atha[1]) vāsavadattāyāḥ prāṇēbhyō 'pi garīyasī (sakhī[2]) kalāvatī nāma kaṃdarpakētum uvāca. āryaputra nā 'yaṃ visraṃbha(kathānām[3]) avasaraḥ (atō[4]) laghutaram ēvā ('bhidhīyatē[5]). tvatkṛtē yā 'nayā (yātanā) 'nubhūtā sā yadi nabhaḥ patrāyatē sāgarō [239] (mēḷāmaṃdāyatē) brahmā[yatē] (lipikārāyatē bhujaṃgapatir[6] vā kathakāyatē tathā) 'py anēkāir yugasahasrāir abhilikhyatē (vā na) vā. tvayā (ca) rājyam ujjhitaṃ. kiṃ bahunā 'tmā ('syās) saṃkaṭē samārōpitaḥ [ēva[7]]. (yāi) 'ṣā 'smatsvāmiduhitā [pitrā] (prabhātāyāṃ[8] [240] śarv.ryāṃ pitrā) yāuvanāti(krama[9])śaṃkinā haṭhēna vidyādharacakravartinō vijayakētōḥ putrāya puṣpakētavē pāṇi(grahaṇāya) dātavyē "ti (niścitā[10]). anayā (cā 'smābhis saha sammaṃtryā) "lōcitaṃ adya yadi taṃ janam ādāya (nā "gacchati tamālikā) tadā 'vaśyam ēvā ("śrayāśa āśrayitavya) iti. [tad asyāḥ sukṛtavaśēna mahābhāgē 'māṃ bhūmim anuprāptaḥ.] tad atra yat sāṃpratam tatra bhavān ēva pramāṇam ity uktvā virarāma. atha kaṃdarpakētur (api) bhītabhīta iva (praṇayā[11])naṃd(āmṛta[12])-sāgaralaharībhir āpluta iva [bhuvanatrayarājyābhiṣikta iva] vāsava[241]dattayā saha sammaṃtrya makaraṃdaṃ (93) vārtānvēṣaṇāya tatrāi "va nagarē niyujya (bhujagēnē[13]) 'va sadāgatyabhimukhēna (saritpuḷinēnē 'va śuktiśōbhitēna viṃdhyavipinēnē 'va śrīvṛkṣalāṃchitēna haṃsēnē 'va mānasagatinā vanaspatinē "va skaṃdhaśōbhitēna vajrēṇē 'vē 'ṃdrāyudhēna[14]) manōjavanāmnā tura-

[1] So also Hall's manuscripts A, B.

[2] So also Hall's manuscript D.

[3] So also Hall's manuscripts D, E, H.

[4] So also Hall's manuscripts E, F.

[5] So also Hall's manuscripts E, F.

[6] Cf. *bhujagapatir* in Hall's manuscripts A, B, C, D, F, G.

[7] Hall's manuscripts D, H also omit *ēva*.

[8] So also Hall's manuscripts D, H, and the commentator Jagaddhara.

[9] Cf. *kramadōṣa* in Hall's manuscripts D, H.

[10] So also Hall's manuscript D.

[11] Cf. *sapraṇayama* in Hall's manuscripts A, B, C, D, F, G, H.

[12] So also Hall's manuscripts A, B, C, D, F, G.

[13] So also Hall's manuscripts C, D, E, F, G, H.

[14] Cf. *mahōdadhipulinēnē 'va śuktiśōbhitēna vindhyavipinēnē 'va śrīvṛkṣalāṅkṣitēna*

gēṇa tayā (vāsavadattayā) saha (purān niragāt[1]. tataḥ[2]) kramēṇa [ca] (gavyūtimātram adhvānaṃ gatvā nara[3])jāṃgalakabaḷan(ārthaṃ) miḷitaniśśaṃkakaṃkaku[242]lasaṃkulēna ardhadagdhacitācakrasimasimāyamāna (vasāvisra) vikaṭakaṭatṛṣṇācaṭulakaṭapūtanōttāla(tālu)ravabhīṣaṇēna śūlaśikharārōpitaśaṃkita[varṇa]karṇa(nāsā)cchēda(patita[4])rudhirapaṭala (patanaṭaṃkāritakarakōṭikarparakarāḷakōṇapanṛttatumulēna baṃbharāḷikēḷisaṃbhāra)bharitabhūmibhāga(bhībhatsēna) kaṭāgnidahyamāna(caṭula[5]caṭātkāra)-[243]nṛ(karōṭi)ṭaṃkāra(bhāiravēṇa vivṛtōlkāmukhamukhōjjvalitajvalanajvālājaṭilēna āṃtrataṃtukalilakapālaprālaṃba(94)ḍāmaraḍhākinīgaṇakṛtakuṇapavibhāgakōlāhalēna ārdrasirāracitavivāhamaṃgaḷapratisarapiśācamithunapradakṣiṇīkrīyamāṇacitāgninā[6]) śūlapāṇinē 'va kapālāvali[bhasma]śivā(bahubhūti)bhujaga(rājā)varuddhadēhēna puruṣātiśayēnē 'vā 'nēkamaṃḍalakṛtasēvēna (daṃḍakāraṇyēnē 'va kabaṃdhādhiṣṭhitēna cakravartinē 'vā 'nēkanarēṃdraparivṛtēna tridivēnē 'va saṃcaradbalāriṇā) śmaśānavāṭēna (nirgatya nimiṣa)mātrād ēvā 'nēkaśatayōjanam (adhvānaṃ gatvā punar api) praḷayakālavēḷām iva samuditārkasamūhāṃ nāga[244]-(rājya[7])sthitim ivā 'naṃtamūlāṃ sudharmām iva svacchaṃdasthita(95)kāuśikāṃ satpuruṣasēvām[8] iva [bahu[9]]śrīphalāḍhyāṃ bhāratasamarabhūmim iva dūraprarūḍhārjunāṃ pulōmakulasthitim iva sahasranētrōcit(ēṃdrāṇīṃ śūra)pāla[citta[10]]vṛttim iva (darśita[11])-gaṇikārikāṃ sajja[245]nasaṃpadam iva vikasitāśōkasaraḷapunnā-

varuṇahaṃsēnē 'va manasagalinā 'raṇyēnē 'va gaṇḍakaśōbhitēna vajrēṇē 'vē 'ndrāyudhēna in Hall's manuscript D.

[1] Hall's manuscripts A, B, C, F, H, and the commentator Narasiṃha also have *niragāt*.

[2] So also Hall's manuscript D.

[3] Hall's manuscript D also has *nara*; cf. *nava* in the commentator Narasiṃha.

[4] Cf. *chēdagala* in Hall's manuscript D.

[5] So also Hall's manuscripts E, G.

[6] Cf. *vivṛtōlkāmukhamukhōjjvalajjvalanajvālājālajaṭilēnā "ntratantraprōtakalitakapālakūṭapralambiprālambiḍāmaraḍākinīgaṇakṛtarūpavibhāgakōlāhalēnā "rdraśarācitavivāhamaṇḍalapratisarapiśācamithunapradakṣiṇīkriyamāṇacitācakrānalēna* in Hall's manuscript D; Srirangam text and Trichinopoly ed. also have *ḍakinī* and *kriyamāṇa*.

[7] So also Hall's manuscript D.

[8] Grantha ed., *sēvanam*.

[9] Hall's manuscripts A, B, C, D, F, G, H, and the commentators Narasiṃha and Jagaddhara also omit *bahu*.

[10] Hall's manuscripts A, B, F, G, H also omit *citta*.

[11] So also Hall's manuscript D.

gāṃ śiśujanalīlām iva kṛtadhātrīdhṛtiṃ kvacid rāghavacittavṛttim iva vāidēhī(mayāṃ) [246] kvacit kṣīrasamudramathanavēḷām ivō 'jjṛmbhamāṇāmṛtāṃ kvacin nārāyaṇa(mūrtim[1]) iva svacchaṃ(96)-dāparājitāṃ kvacid vālmīkisarasvatīm iva darśitēkṣvākuvaṃśāṃ (kvacil) laṃkām iva bahupalāśasēvitāṃ[2] (kvacid dhārtarāṣṭra)sēnām ivā 'rjunaśaranikaraparivāritāṃ (kvacin) nārāyaṇamūrtim iva bahurūpāṃ [247] (kvacit) sugrīvasēnām iva panasa(naḷa)kumudasēvitāṃ (kvacid) avidhavām iva siṃdūratilakabhūṣitāṃ pravāḷābharaṇāṃ ca (kvacit) kurusēnām[3] ivō 'lūkadrō[248]ṇaśakunisanāthāṃ dhārtarāṣṭr(āṃcitāṃ) ca amlā(97)najāti(vi)bhūṣitām api (viruddha[4])-vaṃśāṃ darśitābhayām api vibhīṣaṇāṃ satatahitapathyām api [249] pravṛddhagulmāṃ ṣaṭpadavyā(ptām) api dvipadānākulāṃ dvijakulabhūṣitām api (na)kulīnavaṃśāṃ viṃdhyāṭavīṃ (pra[5])vivēśa. (atrāṃtarē[6]) tayōr nidrām ādāya (niśā[7] 'jagāma. tataḥ) kramēṇa ca kāla(kāivartakēna) tamisrā(nāvaṃ) prakṣipya gaganamahāsara-(98)si sajīva[250](śaphara)nikara iva [apa[8]]hriyamāṇē tārāgaṇē (saṃdhyā)raktāṃśuk[apaṭ]ē viṣamaprarūḍhabisalatāśara(yaṃtrā)-nugataśatapatrapustakasanāthē makaraṃdabiṃdusaṃdōhanirbharapānamattamadhukara[sāndramandra](maṃjuravāiḥ) svadharmam iva paṭhati vikacakamalākarabhikṣāu kṛṣīvalēnē 'va kālēna timirabīja(nikarēṣv) iva madhukarēṣu [kumudakṣētrēṣu] madhurasakardamitaparāgapaṃkēṣu ghanaghaṭamānadaḷa(puṭēṣu[9] kumudākarakṣētrēṣū) [bhramarēṣu vyājāt [251] paṅkajēṣū] 'pyamānēṣu rajōmurmurasanāthamadhukarapaṭala(dhūmā[10])nugatōddaṃḍapuṃḍarīkavyājād dhūpa[paṭala]m iva bhagavatē kiraṇamālinē prayacchaṃtyāṃ kamalinī(tāpasyāṃ[11]) rajanīvadhūkara[tala[12]]-dvayōcchalitapatatprabhātamusalāhatikṣatāṃtarē ulūkhala iva ca-

[1] So also Hall's manuscript E.

[2] Trichinopoly ed. omits *kvacil . . . °sēvitāṃ*.

[3] Trichinopoly ed. omits *iva panasa° . . . kurusēnām*.

[4] So also Hall's manuscripts A, B, C, E, F, G, H, and the commentators Jagaddhara and Narasiṃha.

[5] So also Hall's manuscripts A, B, C, D, F, G.

[6] So also Hall's manuscripts A, B, C, D, F, G, H, and the commentators Jagaddhara and Narasiṃha.

[7] So also Hall's manuscript D.

[8] Hall's manuscript C also omits *apa*.

[9] So also Hall's manuscripts A, C.

[10] So also Hall's manuscript A.

[11] Cf. *kamalinītapasvinyām* in Hall's manuscripts A, C, F.

[12] Hall's manuscripts D, H also omit *tala*.

ṃdra(maṃḍalē) khaṃḍana(vi[1])kīrṇēṣu [iva] taṃḍulēṣv (iva) tārā-
gaṇēṣu (ni[2])mīlatsu saṃdhyātāmramukhēna [iva] vāsaravānarēṇa
nabhastarum (āruhya) śākhābhya iva kaṃpitā(99)bhyō digbhyō
vikacaprasūna(nikara[3]) iva tārāgaṇē (phala ivē 'ṃdumaṃḍalē[4])
[ca ni]pata[252]ti tārā[gaṇaśāli]taṃḍula[5](śabaḷita)nabhō 'ṃgaṇaṃ
sphuradaruṇa(kiraṇa)cūḍā(cakra)cāruvadanē vāsarakṛkavākāu ca-
ritum avatarati mat(saṃgamād[6]) atipravṛddhō vāruṇī(saṃgamād)
dvijapatir ēṣa (patatī) 'ti hasanntyām ivā "khaṃḍal(āśāyāṃ) aru-
ṇakēsari(kharanakharapāta)nihatāṃdhakārakarīṃdrarudhiradhārā-
bhir ivō 'dayagiriśikhara(gāirika)nirjhara[dhāutadhātu]dhārābhir
iva (tvaṃgat)turaṃgakharakhurapuṭapāṭitapadmarāgacchaṭābhir
iva [253] [kēsarikaratalāhatamattamātaṅgōttamāṅgasaṅgaladasra-
prasāriṇībhir iva] udayācalakūṭakōṭiprarūḍhajapākusumakāṃti-
bhir iva (pūrvagiri[7]kēsaricaraṇatalāhatamattamātaṃgōttamāṃga-
vigaḷadasṛgdhārāsāriṇībhir iva) tribhuvanakārya(saṃpādanā[8]tura)-
rāgarasāir iva raktamaṃḍalē tārākumuda(vana[9])grahaṇāya prasā-
ritahasta iva kuṃkum(āruṇāiḥ kiraṇāiḥ kanakadarpaṇa[10] iva) prā-
cīvilāsinyāḥ pūrvācalabhōgīṃdraphaṇōpalē gaganēṃdranīlataru-
[kanaka][254]kisalayē nabhōnagara(prāgdvāra)kanaka(pūrṇa)ku-
ṃbhē taptalōhakuṃbhākārē prācī(kumārī[11])lalāṭataṭa(ghaṭitaku-
ṃkuma[12]tilaka)biṃdāu saṃdhyā(bāla[13])latāikakusu(100)mē maṃji-
ṣṭhā[rakta]paṭṭasūtra(piṃḍa)sadṛśē saṃdhy(āruṇasūtragrathita)-
prācī(vadhū[14]kāṃcī)kāṃcanadīnāracakra iva (kumāra iva saṃhṛta-
tārakē padmanābha ivō 'llasat[15]padmē adhvaga iva cchāyāpriyē
śakra iva gōpatāu udayagiri)dhāturāgāruṇadiggajapādatalānukāriṇi

[1] So also Hall's manuscript E. [2] So also Hall's manuscript D.
[3] Cf. *nicaya* in Hall's manuscript D.
[4] So also Hall's manuscripts D, E, and the commentator Jagaddhara.
[5] Cf. *tārāgaṇataṇḍula* in Hall's manuscripts A, B, C, D, F, G, H.
[6] So also Hall's manuscripts D, H
[7] So also Hall's manuscript D.
[8] Cf. *sampādanaprabhā* in Hall's manuscripts D, H.
[9] So also Hall's manuscript D.
[10] Hall's manuscript D also has *kanakadarpaṇe*.
[11] So also Hall's manuscript A.
[12] Cf. *taṭakuṅkumāmbubindāu* in Hall's manuscripts A, B, C, F, G.
[13] Cf. *sandhyāpravālalatā* in Hall's manuscripts E, H.
[14] Cf. *śacīvadhūkāñcana* in Hall's manuscript A.
[15] Tel. ed. 61, Grantha ed., and Srirangam text, *'llasita*.

(prabhūta)timirataskarē (sam)udayam ārōhati (bhagavati bhāsvati) maṃjiṣṭhā(nikara[1]) iva diggajēṣu mahābhārata[samarabhūmi]rudhirōdgāra iva kurukṣētrēṣu [255] sura(dhanuḥ)kāṃti(vi)lēpa iva jalada(cchadēṣu) kāṣāyapaṭa iva śākyāśrama(śākhāsu) kāusuṃbharāga iva dhvajapaṭapallavēṣu phalapāka iva karkaṃdhūṣu kuṃkuma[cchaṭā]rasa iva vyōmamahāsāudh(āṃgaṇē[2]) saṃcaradaruṇa(yavanikā)paṭa iva kāla(mahānaṭasya[3]) [bāla[4]]pravāḷa(bhāgā)ruṇē prasarati bālātapē kṣaṇēna [ca] cāṭucaṭulacakravākahṛdaya(kōśa)saṃtāpaharaṇād iva dahana(pratāpa)pravēśād iva dinanāthakāṃtōpal[ānal]asaṃgād ivō 'ṣṇimānam uṣṇaraśmēr āśrayati raśmisaṃcayē kaṃdarpakētus sarvarātrajāgaraṇa(vaśād) āhāraśūnya(paravaśa)śarīratayā niścētanō 'nēkayōjanaśa[256]t(ādhva)bhramaṇakhinnō vāsavadattayā 'py ēvaṃvidhayā saha latā(grahē) maṃdamārutāṃdōḷitakusumaparima(101)ḷalubdhamugdha(mukhara)paribhramatbhramarajhaṃkāramanōharē tatkāla(sulabhayā[5]) nidrayā gṛhītō niṣpaṃdakaraṇagrāmas suṣvāpa. tatō vaṇijī 'va prasāritāmbarē mahādāvānala iva sakalakāṣṭhōddīpini (kalpavṛkṣa iva sarvāśāprasādhakē) pataṃgamaṃḍalē (madhyaṃ nabhassthalasyā[6]) 'rūḍhē [katham api] kaṃdarpakētuḥ (prabuddhaḥ[7]) priyayā vinākṛtaṃ latā(graham) avalōkya (cō) 'tthāya [257] [ca] tata itō dattadṛṣṭiḥ kṣaṇaṃ (viṭapiṣu) kṣaṇaṃ latāṃtarēṣu kṣaṇaṃ [taruśikharēṣu kṣaṇaṃ] (adhaḥ)kūpēṣu kṣaṇam (ūrdhvataruśikharēṣu) kṣaṇaṃ śuṣkaparṇarāśiṣu kṣaṇam ākāśa(talēṣu) kṣaṇaṃ dikṣu (kṣaṇaṃ[8]) vidikṣu ca bhramann anavarata[virahānala[9]]dahyamānahṛdayō vilalāpa. (hā) priyē vāsavadattē dēhi mē darśanaṃ [258] (kṛtaṃ) parihāsēna aṃtarhitā 'si tvatkṛtē yāni [mayā] duḥkhāny anubhūtāni tēṣāṃ tvam ēva pramāṇaṃ. hā priya(sakha[10]) makaraṃda paśyē ('daṃ) dāivadurvilasitaṃ kiṃ (pūrvaṃ mayā kṛtam anavadātaṃ) karma. ahō (vipākō niyatēḥ) ahō duratikramā kālagatiḥ ahō grahāṇām

[1] Tel. ed. 61 and Grantha ed. omit *nikarā*.
[2] So also Hall's manuscript B.
[3] Cf. *kālanaṭakasya* in Hall's manuscript D.
[4] Hall's manuscripts D, E, H also omit *bāla*.
[5] So also Hall's manuscripts D, E.
[6] Cf. *nabhōmadhyam* in Hall's manuscript E.
[7] Cf. *prāptabōdhaḥ* in Hall's manuscripts E, H.
[8] So also Hall's manuscript B.
[9] Hall's manuscripts A, C, E, F, G, H also omit *virahānala*.
[10] So also Hall's manuscripts A, B, C, E, F, G.

atikaṭu kaṭākṣa(pātanaṃ[1]) ahō visa(dṛśatā) gurujanāśiṣāṃ ahō dussvapnānāṃ durnimittānāṃ ca (phalaṃ) sarvathā na (kaścid[2]) agōcarō [259] (bhavitavyānāṃ). kiṃ na samyag āgamitā (vidyā) kiṃ [na] yathāvad (anārādhitā) guravaḥ kin nō 'pāsitā vahnayaḥ [kim adhikṣiptā bhūdēvāḥ[3]] kin na pradakṣiṇīkṛtās surabhayaḥ kin na kṛtaṃ [260] (śaraṇyēṣv) abhayaṃ. (102) iti bahuvidhaṃ vilapan (maraṇēcchuḥ[4]) dakṣiṇēna kānanaṃ nirgatya navya(naḷa)-naḷadanaḷinīnicuḷa[picula](vidaḷa)vakuḷa(ciribilvabahuḷēna[5] pracura-viracitavividhō)ṭajakuṭajaruddhōpakaṃṭhēna sōtkaṃṭhabhṛṃga-[261]rāja[rasitasundara]suṃdarī(kṛtāsvāda)vitata(cūtavratatī)vrātāvaraṇa[taruṇa]varuṇa[6](taru)skaṃdhasannaddhabhṛṃga(gōḷēna) gōlāṃgūlabhagnagaḷanmadhu[ccha[262]tramadhu]paṭalarasāsāra-(śīkara)siktatarutalēna (pravṛddha[7]nārikēḷakaṃkēḷirājatāḷītālatamāla[8])hiṃtālapunnāgakēsara(nāgakēsaraghanasārēṇa) mallikā(kētakī)kōvidār(ārkaparṇajaṃbū)bī[263]japūrajaṃbīra[jambū]gulmagahanēna (pavanasaṃvāhitānēkapanasaviṭapiviṭapēna) [apratyūha]dātyūha(kuhakuhārāva)bharitanadī(taṭanikuṃjapuṃjēna) puṃjit(ōt)kaṃṭha kalakaṃ(103)ṭhādhyāsit[ōddām]asahakārapallavēna [capalakulāya]kukkuṭakuṭuṃbasaṃ(vāsitō)tkaṭ(ānēka)viṭapēna kōrakanikuruṃbarōmāṃcitakuravakarājinā raktāśōkapallavalāvaṇya(vi)lipyamānadaśadiśā pravikasitakēsara(kusuma[9])rajōvisara-(dhūsaritaparisarēṇa) parāga(puṃja)piṃjara(siṃduvāra[10]rajyamāna)madhukaramaṃjuśiṃjitajanitajanamudā (lavaṃgacaṃpakamadhūkakṛta.nāla[11]lōdhrakarṇikārakadaṃbakadaṃbakēna) madajalamēcakita(gaṃḍakāṣa)mucukuṃda[ska[264]ndha]kāṃḍa(kathyamāna[12])niśśaṃkakarikaṭa[13][vikaṭa]kaṃḍūtinā katipayadivasaprasū-

[1] Cf. *patanam* in Hall's manuscripts C, D, E, F.
[2] So also Hall's manuscripts A, B, D, E, G, H.
[3] Hall's manuscripts A, B, C, D, E, F, G, H also omit *kim adhikṣiptā bhūdēvāḥ*.
[4] So also Hall's manuscript D.
[5] Hall's manuscripts C, D, G also have *bahulēna*.
[6] Tel. ed. 61 and Grantha ed., *vāruṇa*.
[7] Tel. ed. 61 and Grantha ed. omit *pravṛddha*.
[8] Cf. *nārikēlakarakēlirājatālītāla* in Hall's manuscript D.
[9] Cf. *pravikasitakusumakēsara* in Hall's manuscripts A, B.
[10] So also Hall's manuscript A.
[11] Tel. ed. 61 and Grantha ed., *madhūkatamāla*.
[12] Cf. *mathyamāna* in Hall's manuscripts A, B, F.
[13] Tel. ed. 61 and Grantha ed., *niśśaṃkakaraṭa*.

cakukkuṭī(kuṭī[1])kṛta[kuṭaja]kōṭarēna caṭakasaṃcāryamāṇacaṭulavācāṭacāṭakāirakriyamāṇacāṭunā sahacarī(sahacaraṇacuṃcura)cakōra(caṃcunā) śāilēya(sugaṃdhi)śilātalasu[265]khaśayita(śaśaśiśurāśinā) śēphālikāśiphāvivaravisrabdhavartamāna(gāudhēya)rāśinā nirātaṃkaraṃku(nikarēṇa) nirākulanakula[kula]kēḷinā kalakōkilakulakabaḷita(cūta)kalikōdgamēna sahakārārāmarōmaṃthāyamāna(camara)yūthēna śravaṇahārisa(nīḍa[2])girinitaṃbanirjharanināda(śravaṇōtsukanidrānaṃda[3])maṃdāyamānakarikulakarṇatāḷaduṃdubhi(dhvaninā) samāsannakinnarīgīta(śravaṇaramamāṇa)ruruvisarēṇa [266] (kuhari(104)ta)haridrādravarajyamānavarāhapōtapōtrapāḷinā guṃjā(kuṃja[4]puṃjaguhijāhakajātēna[5] daṃśa)daṃśanakupita(kapi[6])pōta(pēṭacapēṭaka[7])pāṭita(pāṭalīpuṭakīṭasaṃghēna) kuliśaśikharakharanakharapracayapracaṃḍacapēṭ(ā)pāṭitamattamātaṃga(mada)cchaṭācchuritacārukēsara(bhara)bhāsurakēsarikadaṃbēna mahāsāgarakacchōpāṃtēna katipayadūram (adhvānaṃ[8]) gatvā aticapala(vāripracayaprahataprapātatayā) tāṃḍa[267]vōddaṃḍa(dōṣṣaṃḍa[9])khaṃḍaparaśuviḍaṃbanāpaṃḍitaṃ vāruṇī[10]-vijayapatākābhir iva śēṣakulanirmōka[mañju]maṃjarībhir iva (sudhāsahacarībhir iva jyōtsnāsahōdarībhir iva) śaśāṃka(maṃḍala)paramāṇu(saṃtatībhir) iva lakṣmīlīlā(darpaṇadhāriṇībhir) iva jaladēvatā(kuca[11])caṃdana(dhārātarpaṇa)vicchittibhir iva phēnarājibhir upāṃta(ramaṇīyaṃ) aparam iva gagana(talam) avan(ītalam) avatīrṇaṃ [arṇava](acchajalā)ducchalacchīkara(nikarēṇa) nabhaścarān muktāphalāir iva vilōbhayaṃtaṃ abhayābhyarthanāgatānēka(pakṣati)kṣitidharabharitakukṣibhāgaṃ sagarasuta(visarasamud)khātaṃ (vārijātamukhōdbhāsitapārijātaṃ) abhijātamaṇiratnākaraṃ kari(105)makara[ku[268]la]saṃkulaṃ (śakuni)kulakaba-

[1] So also Hall's manuscript C, and the commentator Jagaddhara.

[2] So also Hall's manuscripts C, D.

[3] Hall's manuscripts A, B, C, D, F, G also have *nidrānanda.*

[4] So also Hall's manuscripts A, B, C, E, F, G, H; cf. *guñjāpuñjakuñja* in Hall's manuscript D.

[5] Hall's manuscripts D, E, F also have *jāhakajātēna.*

[6] So also Hall's manuscripts C, D.

[7] Hall's manuscript D also has *capēṭaka*.

[8] Cf. *katipayādhvānaṃ* in Hall's manuscript E.

[9] Cf. *dōḥkhaṇḍa* in Hall's manuscripts A, C, D, E, F.

[10] Srirangam text and Trichinopoly ed., *vāruṇa.*

[11] So also Hall's manuscripts B, C, F.

ḷanābhilāṣasaṃcarannakracakraṃ (stimitatimi)timiṃgilakulaṃ (kadaḷīvanavāṭa) viluḷit (āilā) lavalīlavaṃga (mātuluṃga[1]) gulma (gahanaṃ) ūrmimāruta(marmaritataralatarō) ttāla (tāḷi[2] vanacarita[3]) jalamānuṣamithunamṛdita[salila]puḷinabālaśāivālaṃ pravāḷāṃkurakōṭipāṭitamukhakhinnaśaṃkhanakha (mukharakharaśikharavi) likhitataṭa(rēkhaṃ) khagēśvaragōtrapatrarathapaṭalakalilasalilaṃ adyā 'py anirmuktamaṃdaramathanasaṃskāram ivā "vartabhrāṃtibhiḥ sāpa[269]smāram iva (sitaphēnasaṃcayāiḥ) sasurā(gaṃdham) ivāi ("lāparimaḷāiḥ saghōṣam) iva garjitāiḥ sakhēdam iva (nāganiśvāsāiḥ) sabhru(bhaṃgam[4]) iva taraṃgāiḥ sālānastaṃbham iva rāmasētunā kuṃbhīnasīkukṣim iva lavaṇōtpattisthānaṃ vyākaraṇam iva [vitata[5]]strīnadīkṛtyabahuḷaṃ rājakulam iva dṛśyamānamahāpātraṃ hastibaṃdham iva vārigatānēkanā[270]ga(106)mucyamāna(śūt)kāraṃ viśvāmitraputravargam iva aṃbhōja(cāru)matsyōpaśōbhitaṃ satpuruṣam iva gōtr(ātiśayaṃ) sādhum ivā 'cyutasthitiramaṇīyaṃ sunṛ(patim[6]) iva sajjanakramakaraṃ kṛtamanyum iva karatōyāpluta[271]mukhaṃ virahiṇam iva caṃdanōdakasiktaṃ vilāsinam iva narmadānugataṃ (rāśim iva samīnakuḷīraṃ śṛṃgāriṇam ivā 'nēkamuktālaṃkṛtaṃ) uddhṛtakālakūṭam api prakaṭitaviṣarāśiṃ ativṛddham api suṃdarī[pari]vṛt(ōp[7])akaṃṭhaṃ (107) surōtpattisthānam apy asurādhiṣṭhitaṃ jala[272][ni]dhim apaśyat. aciṃtayac ca ahō mē kṛtāpakārēṇā 'pi vidhinā upakṛtir ēva kṛtā yad ayaṃ lōcanagōcaratāṃ (gatas) samudraḥ tad atra dēhaṃ (tyajāmi) [priyāvirahāgniṃ nirvāpayāmi]. yady apy anāturasyā ("tma[8])tyāgō na vihitaḥ tathā 'pi (khalu naḥ kāryaṃ) na [khalu] sarvas (sarvaṃ[9]) kāryam (ēva) karōty [ity[10]] asārē saṃsārē. kēna kin [273] (nāma[11]) na kṛtaṃ. tathāhi gurudāra(hara-

[1] So also Hall's manuscripts E, F, H, and the commentator Jagaddhara.
[2] Srirangam text and Trichinopoly ed., *tālī*.
[3] Hall's manuscript D also has *carita*.
[4] So also Hall's manuscripts A, D, E.
[5] Hall's manuscripts A, B, C, F, G, H also omit *vitata*.
[6] So also Hall's manuscripts A, B, C, E, F, G.
[7] Cf. *parivṛtōpakaṇṭham* in Tel. ed. 61, Grantha ed., and Hall's manuscripts B, E.
[8] So also Hall's manuscripts C, D.
[9] So also Hall's manuscripts C, D.
[10] Trichinopoly ed., *iha*.
[11] So also Hall's manuscripts C, D, H.

ṇaṃ[1]) dvijarājō 'karōt. purūravā brāhmaṇadhanatṛṣṇayā vinanāśa. nahuṣaś (śakra)kaḷatra(dōhaḷī bhujaṃgatām ayāsīt). yayātiḥ (kṛtapurōhitasutā)pāṇigrahaṇaḥ [274] papāta. sudyumnaḥ strīmaya (ēvā) 'bhavat. sōmakasya prakhyātā (jagati[2]) jaṃtuvadhanirghṛṇatā. purukutsaḥ kutsita (ēvā 'bhavat). kuvalayāśvō 'śva[275]tarakannyām api (jagāma). nṛgaḥ kṛkalāsatām agamat. (naḷaḥ kalinā 'bhibhūtaḥ.) saṃvaraṇō mitraduhitari viklabatām (agamat). [276] daśarathaḥ (abhī)ṣṭarāmōnmādēna mṛtyum avāpa. kārtavīryō [gō]brāhmaṇapīḍayā paṃcatvam ayāsīt. [yudhiṣṭhiraḥ samaraśirasi satyam utsasarja.] (śaṃtanur[3]) ativyasanāt (vanē[4]) vilalāpa. (tad) itthaṃ nā 'sty (ēva jagaty) akaḷaṃkaḥ kō 'pi. tad aham api dēham (utsṛ(108)jāmī) 'ty (ēvaṃ) vi[277]ciṃtya kurara[khara]nakharaśikharakhaṃḍita(pṛthuḷa[5])pṛthurōma-[bilamaviralaśakulakula]śalka(saṃkulaṃ[6] saṃkalita)jalanakula(kulō[7])ccāra(śāraṃ) krōṣṭukulōtsṛṣṭavikaṭakarkaṭakarparaparaṃparāparigata(prāṃtaṃ[8] atitaraḷa)jalarayaluḷitacaṭulaśapharakulakabaḷanakṛtamatinibhṛtabakaśakuninivaha(bahu)dhavaḷitaparisaraṃ aticapalajalakapikulaviharaṇa(tulira[9])salilakaṇa[278]nikara(parimiḷanaśiśiritatamālatalaṃ anudina)nipatadatitaruṇa[vana]mahiṣagavalaśikhara(vi)likhitaviṣamataṭaṃ anavaratacaradasitamukhacaraṇavihaga(vara)nivaha(madhukara)ninada(mukharita)himakara(kiraṇanikara) [279]rucirajalamanuja(gaṇa)śayanamṛdita(taṭadharaṇī)talaṃ ati(bahuḷa)mada[jala]śabaḷa(kaṭa[10])taṭakari[vara]śatanipatitamadhukara(nikaraṃ[11]) atijavanapavanavidhutajala(vighaṭana)nipatita(phaṇi)gaṇaparigataparisaraṃ jalanidhi(jalagata)bhujaganirmuktanirmōkapaṭṭaṃ [iva] darpaṇam iva vasuṃdharāyāḥ sphaṭikakuṭṭimam iva varuṇasya (kamalavanam iva sapadmarāgaṃ vanapra-

[1] So also Hall's manuscripts, A, B, C, D, F, G, H.

[2] So also Hall's manuscript D.

[3] So also Hall's manuscripts A, C, F, H.

[4] So also Hall's manuscripts A, F, H.

[5] So also Hall's manuscripts B, D.

[6] So also Hall's manuscripts A, B, C, D, E, F, H, and the commentators Jagaddhara and Narasiṃha.

[7] So also Hall's manuscripts A, B, C, D, E, F, G, H, and the commentator Narasiṃha.

[8] So also Hall's manuscripts B, C, D, F, G, H.

[9] Tel. ed. 61, Grantha ed., Trichinopoly ed., and Srirangam text, *tulita*.

[10] This reading is also recorded by Śivarāma, *ad loc.*

[11] So also Hall's manuscripts A, B, F.

dēśam iva savidrumalataṃ kātaram[1] iva sadaraṃ viṣṇum ivā 'nēkamuktōpētaṃ) puḷina(talam) āsasāda. tataḥ kṛtasnānādi(sakalakṛtyō jalanidhi)jalam avataritum ārēbhē śarīratyāgāya. atha sānugrahēṣu grāhēṣu nirmatsarē(109)ṣu matsyēṣu akṣudrēṣu kṣudr(āṃḍēṣu anicchēṣu) [280] kacchapēṣu akrūrēṣu nakrēṣu abhayaṃkarēṣu makarēṣu amārēṣu (śiṃśumārēṣu ākāśāt[2]) sarasvatī samudacarat. ārya kaṃdarpakētō punar api tava (priyāsamāgamō) bhaviṣyaty acirēṇa tad virama maraṇavyavasāyād iti. (sō 'pi) tad upaśrutya maraṇ(āraṃbhād) virarāma[3]. [punaḥ priyayā śamāgamēcchayā śarīrasthitihētum āhāraṃ cikīrṣur mahāsāgarakacchōpāntabhuvaṃ jagāma.] atha tata itaḥ paribhraman phalamūlādinā vanē (vartayan[4]) [kiyantaṃ] kālam (anēkaṃ) nināya [kandarpakētuḥ]. ēkadā (tu[5]) katipaya(divasā[6])pagamē kākaḷīgāyana ivō [281] ('pasamṛddha[7])nimnagānadaḥ (sāyaṃtana)samaya iva nartitanīlakaṃṭhaḥ kumāramayūra iva (samārūḍha)śarajanmā [mahā]tapasvī 'va praśamitarajaḥ prasaraḥtāpasa iva dhṛtajaladakarakaḥ praḷayakāla iva darśitānēkataraṇivibhramaḥ nirupa(drava)kānana(pra[8])dēśa iva ghanōt(sē[282]kita)sāraṃgaḥ rēvatīkarapallava iva halidhṛ(110)tikaraḥ (laṃkēśvara iva samēghanādaḥ viṃdhya iva ghanaśyāmaḥ[9] sam)ājagāma varṣāsamayaḥ. (vi)bhinna[mēgha]nīlōtpalakānana(nīlē) krīḍāsarasī 'va nabhasi smarasya (kanaka)ratna(nāur) iva jalada(kāla)lakṣmīmātaṃgakanyānartanarajju[283]r iva nabhassāudhatōraṇa(ratna)mālikē 'va pravasatā nidāgha(kālakāṃtēna dyustrī)payōdharē datt[ā smaraṇāy[10]](anakhapad)āvalir iva gaganalakṣmī(baṃdhura)raśanāmālē 'va nabhōmaṃdāra[taru[11]]suṃdarakalik[āmāl]ē 'va ratinakhamārjanaratna(śilā)śalākē 'va ratna(śaktir) iva[12] (vilāsayaṣṭir iva) kusu-

[1] Trichinopoly ed., *kāntāram.*

[2] So also Hall's manuscripts A, B, D, F, H.

[3] Cf. *virarāma maraṇārambhāt* in Hall's manuscripts C, D, E.

[4] So also Hall's manuscripts C, D, F, H.

[5] So also Hall's manuscripts C, D, E, H.

[6] So also Hall's manuscripts A, B, F, H.

[7] Cf. *samṛddha* in Hall's manuscripts A, B, C, D, E, F, G, H, Trichinopoly ed., and Srirangam text.

[8] So also Hall's manuscripts F, G.

[9] Cf. *rāvaṇa iva samēghanādō vindhyagirir iva saghana* in Hall's manuscript C.

[10] Hall's manuscripts C, D, E, F also omit *smaraṇāya.*

[11] Hall's manuscripts C, D, E, G, H also omit *taru.*

[12] Trichinopoly ed. omits *ratnaśaktir iva.*

ma[1]kētōr iṃdradhanurlatā rarāja. ati(tṛṣṇā)vēga[ni]pītajala(ni)dhijalaśaṃkhamālāṃ [iva] ba[284]lākācchalād udvamann (iva) adṛśyata jala(dharanikaraḥ). pītaharitāiḥ (kṛṣṇakēdārikāgōṣṭhīṣu) samutpatadbhiḥ (jātuṣa[2]durōdarāir) iva dardura(śiśukāir) nayadyūtāir iva cikrīḍa (vidyutā samaṃ[3] ghanakālakāṃtaḥ). ravidīpa(kajjaḷitamēgha)nikaṣōpalē [iva] mēghasamaya(svarṇa)kāra(gharṣitasvarṇarēkhē) 'va (taṭid) aśōbhata. virahiṇāṃ hṛdayaṃ (vidāritum) [285] karapatram iva (kṛtaṃ) kusumāyudhasya (krū(111)ra[4]kāitaka)cchadam (abhāsata). [jaladadāruṇi lōlataḍillatākarapatradāritē pavanavēganirdhūtāś cūrṇacayā iva jalarēṇavō babhuḥ.] vicchinnadigvadhūhāramuktā(nikarā) iva kharapavanavēga(bhramitā) ghana(ghaṭā)ghaṭṭanasaṃcūrṇitatārānikarā iva tribhuvanavijigīṣōr makaradhvajasya prasthānalājāṃjalaya iva karakā vyarājaṃta. (navaśāḍvalaṃ sēṃdrakōpamahīmahilāyā lākṣārasāṃkitaṃ stanōttarīyam ivā 'lakṣyata. mēghakuṃbhasalilāiḥ pṛthivīnāyikāṃ snāpayitvā prāvṛṭcēṭikāyāṃ gatāyāṃ svaçcham aṃbaraṃ darśayaṃtī śaraccēṭikā samājagāma[5].) anaṃtaraṃ (sukhaṃjanē) nirbhara[286](bhara[6])dvājadvijavācāṭa(viṭapi)viṭapē (paṭutaraprabhāprabhātō 'd)bhrāṃtaśukakulakaḷama(kēdāra)pravēśit(āvēśa)rājahaṃsē kaṃsārātidēhadyutidyutalē haṃsa(kula[7])tulita(rājaj[8])jalamuci sāṃdrīkṛt(ēṃdumahasi) kāmuka(jana[287]mudita)[madhura]madhutṛṇavīrudhi (sarasa[9])sārasarasitasārakāsārē [śōbhana[10]]kaśērukaṃdalubdhapōtripōtrōd(ghātasarasataṭabhāga)cakitacātakē [sañcaranmatsyaputrikāpatripaṭalamadhuradhvanivihitamudi kadarthitakadambē kambudviṣi prasṛtabisa-

[1] Trichinopoly ed., *makara*.

[2] Hall's manuscripts A, B, D, F, H, and the commentator Jagaddhara also have *jātuṣa*; cf. the reading *jātuṣāir* recorded by Śivarāma, *ad loc.*

[3] So also Hall's manuscripts C, E, and the commentator Jagaddhara.

[4] Trichinopoly ed., *krūraṃ*.

[5] Cf. *navaśādvalaṃ sēndragōpaṃ mahīmahilāyāḥ śukaśyāmalaṃ lakṣarasalāñchitastanōttarīyam ivā 'lakṣyata. mēghakummasalilāiḥ pṛthivīnāyikāṃ snapayitvā prāvṛṭcēṣṭāṅgatāyāṃ tataḥ svaccham ambaraṃ darśayantī śarannadī samājagāma* in Hall's manuscript C; Trichinopoly ed. also has *śādvalaṃ* and *kōpaṃ*.

[6] So also Hall's manuscripts C, F.

[7] So also Hall's manuscripts, A, B, D, H.

[8] So also Hall's manuscripts A, B, D, E, F, G, H.

[9] So also Hall's manuscript D.

[10] Hall's manuscripts A, C, D, E, F, H also omit *śōbhana*.

prasūnē] viratavāridē [288] tārataratārakē (vāruṇītilaka)caṃdramasi (svādurasāvilē) sphurita[1]śaphara[cakra]kabaḷananibhṛta(narukabakāḷikē) mūkamaṃḍūkamaṃḍalē saṃkōcitakaṃcukini kāṃcanacchēdagāura(gōdhūmaka)śāliśālini (ut)krōśa(112)dutkrōśē surabhi[gandhi[2]]sāugaṃdhikagaṃdha(hāriṇihariṇāśvadaradaḷita)kumudāmōdini [kāumudīkṛtamudi nirbarhabarhiṇi niḥkūjatkōyaṣṭikē dhṛtadhārtarāṣṭrē hṛṣṭakalamagōpikāgītasukhitamṛgayūthē kathīkṛtayūthikē mlāyamānamālatīmukulē bandhūkabāndhavē sañjātasujātakē visūtritasāutrāmadhanuṣi smērakāśmīrarajaḥ[289]puñjapiñjaritadaśadiśi vikasvarakamalē] śaratsamayārambhē (vijṛmbhamāṇē) kaṃdarpakētus (tata itaḥ) paribhraman (kāṃcic chilāmaya)putrikāṃ dṛṣṭvā [kāutukēna mōhēna śōkāvēgēna mama priyānukāriṇī 'ti] karēṇa pasparśa. atha sā (dṛṣṭa)mātrāi ('va) śilā[sva]bhāvam utsṛjya [punar[3]] vāsavadattāsvarūpaṃ (pra)pēdē. tām (ava)lōkya kaṃdarpakētuḥ [amṛtārṇavamagna iva] su(dṛḍham) āliṃgya (priyē vāsavadattē kim ētad iti) papraccha. (sā pratyuvāca.) āryaputra apuṇyāyā (maṃdabhāgyāyā mama) kṛtē mahābhāgō [290] (bhavān utsṛṣṭa)rājya ēkākī (paribhraman)jana[4] iva (avāṅmānasa)gōcaraṃ duḥkham anubabhūva. [atha[5]] upavāsādinā (tṛṣāturē bhavati nidrāśāṃtē[6] prathamaprabuddhā 'haṃ bhavataḥ phalamūlādikam[7] āhariṣyāmī) 'ti viciṃtya phal(ādy)anvēṣaṇāya (vanē nalvamātram) agacchaṃ. (atha) kṣaṇēna [ca] tarugulm(āṃtaritaṃ) [kriyamāṇakāyamānikanikētanaṃ viracya[291]mānēśvaragṛham avatāryamāṇakaṇṭhārakam ārabhyamāṇapaṭakuṭīkaṃ vyavasthāpyamānavēśyānivēśaṃ śrūyamāṇaturagahrēṣāśataṃ vādyamānaviśramaḍhakkāśatapuṣkaram anviṣyamāṇasvādusalilāśayam uddi[292]śyamānavipaṇikētuvaṃśaṃ] sēnā(nivēśaṃ dṛṣṭvā) kim ayaṃ mamā ("karṣaṇāya tāta[8])vyūhas samāyātaḥ āhōsvid āryaputra(vyūha) iti (ciṃtayaṃtīm)

[1] Trichinopoly ed., *svādurasāvikalasphurita°*.
[2] Hall's manuscripts A, D, H also omit *gandhi*.
[3] Hall's manuscripts D, H also omit *punar*.
[4] Srirangam text and Trichinopoly ed., *paribhraman prākṛtajana*.
[5] Hall's manuscripts A, B, D also omit *atha*.
[6] Cf. *nidrāntē* in Hall's manuscript D.
[7] Cf. *phalamūlādikam* in Hall's manuscripts C, D.
[8] So also Hall's manuscripts E, F.

māṃ [prati] cārakathit(ōdaṃtō dūrāt kirātasēnāpatir dhāvati sma). tatō ('nyaḥ) kirātasēnāpatiḥ tādṛśa ēva (tathābhūtayā sēnayā) 'nvitō (mṛgayāṃ) gataḥ[1] sō 'pi (tac chrutvā dhāvati sma. [293] athāi "kāmiṣalubdhayōr gṛdhrayōr iva tayōr yuddham āsit.) tataḥ (prabhṛti) [prati]śarāsāradurdina(sthagita)dinakarakiraṇē raṇa[294]karmaviśārada(karadūr[2])ōtkṣipta(khaḍga[3]dhā(113)rādaḷita)subhaṭ(āśliṣyamāṇavidyādharī)vibhramē samaradarśan(āgata)-saṃcaradanēkanabhaścaracāraṇa(caraṇaprakaraviracitatōraṇa)cakravāḷē [vētālasamākrāntaskandhakabandhacakrakriyamāṇacārupracārē[4]] (carac)cārubhaṭakhaḍgakhaṃḍita(dvipapada)samāpta-(piśācikā)ka[295]rṇōlūkhal(ābharaṇē) kāutuk(ākṛṣṭajana[5]samudvalannāṃdikē) kāṃdiśīkabhīruṇi (praskannaklībajanē raṇōdyatajitakāśini[6]) raṇakhalē (sṛgālikā)sṛgālaprārthanīyēṣv āmiṣapiṃḍēṣv iva jihmagadaṣṭēṣv iva (śvitradurbhagēṣv iva) śarīrēṣu (nāsthāṃ) kalayaṃtas samaṃ (dviṣatāṃ) dhanuṣāṃ ca jīv(ākarṣaṇaṃ[7]) yōdhāś cakruḥ. (tatra) tyāgina iva dānavaṃtō mārgaṇasaṃpātaṃ (sahaṃtaḥ) samṛddhavilāsina iva śṛṃgār(ōp)aśōbhitāḥ sahēma-(kakṣyāś) ca sadarāmā iva kadaḷīrājitāḥ sadvijāś ca niśā(nivahā[8]) iva nakṣatramālōpaśōbhitāḥ (śarad)divasā [296] iva (sam)ullasat(padmāḥ) mahāmṛgā babhuḥ. ut(kupitā) iva kṣamām muṃcaṃtaḥ payōdhaya ivā "varta(śōbhinaḥ) sōrmayaś ca udyān(ōd)dēśā iva samallikākṣāḥ (kulāla)gṛhā ivā 'bhinavabhāṃḍa(bhāriṇaḥ) ratnākarā iva sadēvamaṇayaḥ lēkhā iva sēṃdra(vṛddhayaḥ kṣībā iva pāna(114)bhūṣitāḥ) turaṃ(gamā) [ca] virējuḥ[9]. karṇābhyāṃ śrutapar(āpavādā)bhyāṃ khalōdayasādhuvipattisākṣibhyām akṣibhyāṃ (asthānē 'pi namatā mūrdhnā kīrtayatā cā 'kīrtanīyān āsyēna ca viyuktō) 'haṃ (diṣṭyē[10]) 'ti harṣād iva (ciraṃ nanarta) kabaṃdhaḥ. tataḥ [kṛta[11]](parihāsakēnē) 'va cakṣuḥ pidadhatā

[1] Trichinopoly ed., *mṛgayārtham āgataḥ.*

[2] Cf. *dviradakaradūrōtkṣipta* in Hall's manuscript C and *dviradakaradūratarōtkṣipta* in Hall's manuscripts D, H.

[3] Hall's manuscripts C, D also have *khaḍga.*

[4] Hall's manuscripts E, F, H also omit *vētāla°* . . . *°pracāre.*

[5] Trichinopoly ed. omits *kāutukākṛṣṭajana.*

[6] Cf. *praskannaklībajanē janōp ḍhanajitakāśini* in Hall's manuscript C.

[7] So also Hall's manuscripts A, B, C, D.

[8] So also Hall's manuscripts C, D, E, F, G, H.

[9] Trichinopoly ed., *rējuḥ.*

[10] So also Hall's manuscript A, and the commentator Jagaddhara.

[11] Hall's manuscripts C, G also omit *kṛta.*

parāpavādaśravaṇa[297]bhīruṇē 'va śrōtravṛttiṃ sthagayatā sōnmādēnē 'va vāyuvēgavikṣiptēna[1] palitaṃkaraṇēnē 'va surayōṣitāṃ aṃdhaṃkaraṇēnē 'va yōdhānāṃ timirēṇē 'va samarapradōṣasya patitēnē 'va vimuktagōtrēṇa (kunṛpatinē 'va nakṣatrapathagāminā kṛtakalahēnē 'va kṛtadhūmyārucinā rājasēnē 'va vyavahitasatvēna avinītēnē 'vō 'ddhatēna asajjanēnē 'va pihitasatpathēna[2]) raṇajēna (rajōjātēna vijijṛmbhē[3]. anaṃtaraṃ ca nārāyaṇa iva) [rāvaṇavadham akarōt] kaścit [kṛṣṇa iva] narakacchēdam akārṣīt. kaścid bāuddhasiddhāṃta iva kṣapitaśrutivacanadarśanō 'bhavat. kaścit kṣapaṇaka iva kaṭāvṛta(vigrahō 'bhavat). kaścit (surāpa iva papāta[4]. kaścit suyōdhana iva śaṃkitōrubhaṃgaḥ sarōjalaṃ) vivēśa. kaścit śaratalpa(śayyā[5])gataḥ bhīṣma iva [298] (gatāyuś ciraṃ) śvasann āsīt. kaścit karṇa iva (viklababhūtāṃgaḥ[6]) śaktimōkṣaṇam akarōt. (kaści(115)d rāghava iva rāvaṇavadham akarōt.) tatō vi(hasta)dhvajapaṭaṃ patatpatākaṃ (vyūhacāribhaṭakaṃpitakhaḍgadhēnukaṃ tat samastam ubhayaṃ mithō jagāma hananaṃ) sāinyaṃ[7]. (tataś ca) yasyā "śramas tēna muninā puṣpādikam ādāyā "gatēna[8] (yōgadṛśā[9]) pratipannavṛttāṃtēna tvatkṛtē mamā 'yam āśramō bhagna (iti[10] kupitēna[11]) śilā[299](mayā putrikā[12]) bhavē 'ti śaptā ("smy) ahaṃ. (tataḥ) kṣaṇēn(āi "vē 'yaṃ varākī) bahuduḥkham (anubhavatī 'ty anugrahād āryaputrakaruṇayā ca sa munir yācyamāna[13]) āryaputra(hasta)sparś(āvadhikaṃ) śāp[ānt]am akarōt. tataḥ kaṃdarpakētuḥ (śrutavṛttāṃtēna) samāgatēna makaraṃdēna (tayā) vāsavadattayā ca [300] (samaṃ[14])

[1] Tel. ed. 61 and Grantha ed., *nikṣiptēna.*

[2] Cf. *kunṛpatinē 'va nakṣatrapathagāminā kaliṅgēnē 'va kṛtadhāumyārucinā rājasēnē 'va vyavahitasattvēna vinītēnē 'vā 'samuddhatēnā 'sajjanēnē 'va hatāntarēṇa* in Hall's manuscript C.

[3] Cf. *vijajṛmbhē* in Hall's manuscript D, Tel. ed. 61, Grantha ed., Trichinopoly ed., and Srirangam text.

[4] Cf. *kaścit surāpadvija iva papāta* in Hall's manuscript B.

[5] Cf. *talpaśayō* in Hall's manuscripts A, B, D, E, F, G, H, and the commentator Jagaddhara.

[6] Cf. *viklavībhūta°* in Hall's manuscript D.

[7] Cf. *tat samastam ihāśramē mithō nidhanaṃ jagāma sāinyam* in Hall's manuscript D and *tataḥ samastasāinyam anyōnyaṃ nidhanam avāpa* in Hall's manuscripts A, B.

[8] Tel. ed. 61 and Grantha ed., *ādāya gatēna.*

[9] So also Hall's manuscript C.

[10] So also Hall's manuscripts C, D.

[11] Tel. ed. 61 and Grantha ed., *kōpitēna.*

[12] So also Hall's manuscripts A, B.

[13] Cf. *varākī "va bahuduḥkham anubhavatī 'ti karuṇākṛṣṭō munir* in Hall's manuscript D.

[14] So also Hall's manuscript A.

svapuraṃ (pāṭalīputraṃ) gatvā [yathā[1]]hṛdayābhilaṣitāni (suralōkadurlabhāni[2]) sukhāni (tābhyāṃ sahā) 'nubhavan kālam (anēkaṃ) nināya[3].

(sarasvatīdattavaraprasādaś cakrē subaṃdhus sujanāikabaṃdhuḥ
pratyakṣaraślēṣamayaprapaṃcavinyāsavāidagdhyanidhiṃ prabaṃdhaṃ.
kavīnām agaḷad darpō nūnaṃ[4] vāsavadattayā
śaktyē "va pāṃḍuputrāṇāṃ gatayā karṇagōcaraṃ[5].

iti śrīkavisārvabhāumasubaṃdhuviracitā
vāsavadattā samāptā[6].)

[1] Hall's manuscripts C, D, E, F, G also omit *yathā*.
[2] Cf. *suratasukhāni* in Hall's manuscripts A, B, C, D, E, F, G.
[3] Tel. ed. 61 and Grantha ed. add *iti vāsavadattākhyō graṃthas samāptaḥ*.
[4] Tel. ed. 61 and Grantha ed., *nityaṃ*.
[5] Srirangam text and Trichinopoly ed. omit this interpolation from the *Harṣacarita*.
[6] Trichinopoly ed., *sampūrṇā*; Tel. ed. 61 and Grantha ed., *vāsavadattā savyākhyā samāptā*; Srirangam text, *iti vāsavadattā samāptā*; cf. *ākhyāyikā* in Hall's manuscripts A, B, C, D, E, F, G, H.

BIBLIOGRAPHY

In the following bibliography of the *Vāsavadattā* mere allusions to Subandhu and his romance in the general histories of Sanskrit literature are intentionally omitted.

Manuscripts.

Aufrecht, *Catalogus Catalogorum*, 1. 566, 726; 2. 133–134, 224; 3. 120, Leipzig, 1891–1903.

Editions.

The Vásavadattá, a Romance by Subandhu; Accompanied by Śivaráma Tripáṭhin's Perpetual Gloss, entitled Darpaṇa. Edited by Fitzedward Hall, M.A. Dēvanāgarī script. 56+300+6 pp. Baptist Mission Press, Calcutta, 1859 [*Bibliotheca Indica*, old series, Nos. 116, 130, 148].

śrīhayagrīvāya namaḥ. śrīmatā subandhunāmnā mahākavinā viracitē 'yaṃ vāsavadattākhyā mahākhyāyikā śrīpaccappapāṭhaśālāyāṃ saṃskṛtāndhrōpādhyāyēna viṃjīmūrukṛṣṇamācāryēṇa śōdhitā ōgguṭūruvēṇugōpālanāyakēna sūryalōkamudrākṣaraśālāyāṃ mudritā 'sīt 1861 saṃvatsarē ḍēsaṃbarē mārsitithiḥ. Telugu script. 126 pp. (2 pp. with 22 distichs in honour of Hayagrīva [Viṣṇu], 1 p. of *kōśas* used in the commentary, 4 pp. of summary of story, 119 pp. of text and commentary).[1]

śubham astu. śrīmannikhilasurēṃdrādivaṃditapādakamalaśrīvāgdēvīdattavaraprasādēna subaṃdhunāmnā kavikulasārvabhāumēna viracitaḥ vāsavadattākhyaḥ caṃpūprabaṃdhō 'yaṃ dhīmatām arthaparijñānāya vyākhyānēna sākaṃ madhurasubbhāśāstriṇā saṃśōdhyapariṣkṛtaḥ jñānasūryōdayamudrākṣaraśālāyāṃ tadadhikāriṇā bhuvanagiri raṃgayyaśēṭṭināmnā vāiśyacūḍāmaṇinā mudrākṣarāir mudrayitvā prakaṭīkṛtas san bhuvivijayatētarāṃ 1862 saṃvatsaraṃ yēpral nēla 19 tēdi. Telugu script. 115+1 pp. (the last page occupied by a *Rahasyatrayakārika*). [For the transcription of this edition see above, pp. 145–195.][2]

śrīhayagrīvāya namaḥ. śrīmatā subandhunāmnā mahākavinā viracitē 'yaṃ vāsavadattākhyā mahākhyāyikā vāvillarāmasvāmiśāstriṇā sarasvatitiruvēṃkaṭācāryēṇa ca samyak pariṣkṛtā śrīmaccannapuryābharaṇāyamānāyāṃ hindubhāṣāsaṃjīvinīmudrākṣaraśālāyām ōggulūruvēṇugōpālanāyakaprabhṛtibhir ētanmudrākṣaraśālāsāmājikāiḥ mudritā satī vijayatētarām. [Device containing the name of the press in English, Telugu, Grantha,

[1] A copy is possessed by the Library of the India Office, London.

[2] Copies may be found in the Library of the India Office, London, and in my own possession.

and Dēvanāgarī characters, and, in English, 'S. Thiruvengadacharuloo, V. Ramasawmy Saustry, O. Vanoogopaloo. N. and Co.'] *1870 saṃ janvari.* Grantha script. 134 pp. (1 p. of *kōśas* used in the commentary, 1 p. of names of officials, etc., of the press, 4 pp. of summary of story, 128 pp. of text and commentary).[1]

vāsavadattā mahākavisubandhuviracitā tripāṭhiśivarāmaracitadarpaṇākhyaṭīkāsahitā vi. ē. upādhidhāriṇā śrījīvānandavidyāsāgarabhaṭṭācāryyēṇa saṃskṛtā. kalikātāyām kāvyaprakāśayantrē mudritā. ī° 1874. Dēvanāgarī script. 154 pp. (3d ed., 132 pp., Gōvardhana Press, Calcutta, 1907.)[2]

Vāsavadattā of Subandhu. Edited with a Critical Commentary by T. V. Srinivasachariar (Sarasvata — Saranga), Senior Sanskrit Pandit, St. Joseph's College, Trichinopoly, and an English Introduction by Mr. G. Kasturiranga Aiyangar, M.A., Lecturer, Maharaja's College, Mysore. Dēvanāgarī script. 6+17+160 pp. St. Joseph's College Press, Trichinopoly, 1906.

Vasavadatta with Commentary by Pandit R. V. Krishnamachariar (Abhinava Bhatta Bana). Dēvanāgarī script. 5+66+359 pp. Sri Vani Vilas Press, Srirangam, 1906–1908.

Translations.

Vāsabdattā. Translated into Bangālī by Madun Mohun Tarkālaṅkār. n. p., 1837. [The sole reference to this version which I have been able to find is that by Zenker, *Bibliotheca orientalis*, 2. 319, Leipzig, 1861. It was inaccessible to Hall, though he knew that it was said to exist (Introd., p. 49).]

Hall (Introd., p. 29) states that his epitome of the *Vāsavadattā* (*ib.* pp. 29–43) was 'abridged from a literal version which was first prepared of the entire story.' The subsequent fortunes of this manuscript translation are unknown to me, and even Mr. Richard Hall, of Wickham Market, Suffolk, the son of Fitzedward Hall, has thus far been unable to trace it (letter of Nov. 27, 1908). The value of this rendering by the first editor of the romance, could it be found, would be too obvious to require further emphasis.

Adaptations.

Madanamōhana Tarkālaṅkāra, *Vāsavadattā*. A Love Tale, in Verse. In Bangālī. 5+258 pp. Calcutta, 1863.[3]

[1] A copy is possessed by the Library of the India Office, London.

[2] I have thus far been unable to ascertain the date, pagination, and press of the second edition.

[3] A copy is possessed by the Library of the India Office, London.

Jayagōpāla Gōsvāmī, *Vāsavadattā*. A Tale Adapted from the Sanskrit Romance of Subandhu. In Bangālī. 85 pp. Calcutta, 1861.[1]

Vāmana Dājī Ōk, *Vāsavadattā Kathāsāra*. An Abridged Version of *Vāsavadattā*, a Sanskrit Romance by Subandhu. In Marāṭhī. 4 + 24 pp. Bombay, 1889.[1]

M. T. Narasimhiengar, *The Vasavadatta-Kathasara, with Two Appendices useful to Candidates preparing for University Examinations*. In 132 Sanskrit verses. 1 + 36 pp. Srirangam, 1907.

STUDIES.

Cartellieri, 'Das Mahābhārata bei Subandhu und Bāṇa,' in *WZKM*. 13. 57–74.

Cartellieri, 'Subandhu and Bāṇa,' in *WZKM*. 1. 115–132.

Colebrooke, *Miscellaneous Essays*, ed. E. B. Cowell, 2. 121–122, London, 1873. Contains a brief outline of the plot of the *Vāsavadattā*.

Gray, 'The Hindu Romance,' in *Princeton University Bulletin*, 13. 99–100. A brief outline of the story of the *Vāsavadattā*.

Gray, 'Lexicographical Addenda to the St. Petersburg Lexicons from the Vāsavadattā of Subandhu,' in *ZDMG*. 60. 355–368.

Gray, 'Literary Studies on the Sanskrit Novel,' in *WZKM*. 18. 39–58: 'The Sanskrit Novel and the Arabian Nights,' pp. 39–48; 'The Sanskrit Novel and the Sanskrit Drama,' pp. 48–54; 'Reincarnation as a Novelistic Device,' pp. 54–58.

Gray, 'Śivarāma's Commentary on the Vāsavadattā,' in *JAOS*. 24. 57–63.

Manning, *Ancient and Mediaeval India*, 2. 344–346, London, 1869. A brief outline of the plot of the *Vāsavadattā*.

Mazumdar, 'Who were the Kaṅkas?' in *JRAS*. 1907, pp. 406–408.

Śāstrī, 'Some Notes on the Dates of Subandhu and Diṅ-nāga,' in *JRASBe*. 1. 253–255.

Stréhly, 'Un Roman indien. Vāsavadattā de Soubandhou,' in *Revue politique et littéraire*, 44. 305–311: outline of the story of the *Vāsavadattā*, pp. 305–308; translation of the introductory stanzas, p. 308; translation of Kandarpakētu's dream, pp. 308–311.

Telang, 'Subandhu and Kumārila,' in *JRASBo*. 18. 147–167.

Thomas, 'Subandhu and Bāṇa,' in *WZKM*. 12. 21–33.

Weber, 'Die Vāsavadattā des Subandhu,' in *Indische Streifen*, 1. 369–386, Berlin, 1868. A revised and enlarged reprint from *ZDMG*. 8. 530–538.

Zachariae, 'Bruchstücke alter Verse in der Vāsavadattā,' in *Gurupūjākaumudī, Festgabe zum fünfzigjährigen Doctorjubiläum Albrecht Weber*, pp. 38–40, Leipzig, 1896.

[1] A copy is possessed by the Library of the British Museum.

LEXICOGRAPHICAL APPENDIX

The following list of words and meanings occurring in the *Vāsavadattā*, which the St. Petersburg Sanskrit dictionaries either omit altogether [1] or cite only from native lexicographers, is condensed from my 'Lexicographical Addenda to the St. Petersburg Lexicons from the Vāsavadattā of Subandhu' (*ZDMG.* 60. 355–368), and is, at the same time, supplemented by the material from the Madras edition of 1862 (which was then unknown to me) and the Srirangam edition of 1906–1908, which appeared subsequently to the study just mentioned.[2] The Hall, Madras, and Srirangam texts are here denoted by the letters H, M, and S respectively, but the latter two are cited only when they present words or meanings not found in the edition of Hall. An asterisk (*) prefixed to a word or meaning denotes that the St. Petersburg dictionaries cite only from Sanskrit lexicographers, and a small circle (°) similarly prefixed implies that the word or meaning in question is entirely omitted by the St. Petersburg lexicons. The numbers within the parentheses refer to pages and lines respectively of the editions employed.

a

**a* (H 113, 1): Viṣṇu.[3]

aṃśuka (M 67, 6; S 212, 1): °ray, beam of light.

[1] It should be noted in this connexion that a complete index to the *Vāsavadattā* was prepared by Aufrecht and placed for a time at the disposal of Böhtlingk, who excerpted from it what he deemed most important for his dictionary (*Sanskrit-Wörterbuch in kürzerer Fassung*, 5. Introd., p. 1, St. Petersburg, 1884).

[2] Similar lists of words and meanings supplementary to those given in the St. Petersburg lexicons have recently been prepared by Meyer for the *Kuṭṭanīmata* and *Samayamātṛkā* (in his *Altindische Schelmenbücher*, 2. 151–156, Leipzig, 1903), by Schmidt for Appayyadīkṣita's *Kuvalayānandakārikā* in his translation of the work (p. 147, Leipzig, 1907), by Jahn for the *Saurapurāṇa* (*Das Saurapurāṇa*, pp. 194–195, Strassburg, 1908), by Schmidt and Hertel for Amitagati's *Subhāṣitasandōha* (*ZDMG.* 59. 266–267), by Schmidt for Rāma's *Manmathōnmathana* (*ZDMG.* 63. 411), by Oster for the *Bhōjaprabandha* (in his *Die Rezensionen des Bhojaprabandha*, pp. 15–17, Darmstadt, 1911), by myself for Rājaśēkhara's *Viddhaśālabhañjikā* (*JAOS.* 27. 7), and by Hertel for Hemacandra's *Pariśiṣṭaparvan* (*ZDMG.* 62. 361–369) and the *Pañcaṭantra* (*Pañcatantra*, ed. Hertel, pp. 291–295, Cambridge, Mass., 1908). By far the most important collection in the present connexion, however, is Thomas's 'Two Lists of Words from Bāṇa's Harṣacarita,' in *JRAS.* 1899, pp. 485–517, a list closely analogous to the one here presented from the *Vāsavadattā*. A similar study of the lexicography of Bāṇa's *Kādambarī* is still a *desideratum*.

[3] Professor Otto Franke (card of Oct. 14, 1906) kindly calls my attention to *Bhagavadgīta*, 10. 33, where Kṛṣṇa (Viṣṇu) says: *akṣarāṇām akārō 'smi*, 'of letters I am the A.'

akīrtaṇīya (M 114, 3; S 354, 6): °unpraiseworthy.

akṣa (H 72, 3): °conduct.

**agaru* (M 57, 6; 67, 10; 84, 5; 89, 1; S 213, 4; 287, 4; 298, 4): *Amyris Agallocha*, aloes-wood (also in *Pañcatantra*, 46, 5).

agādha (H 24, 2): °free from greed.

°*agranthin* (H 113, 2): pure-hearted.

agrēsara (H 23, 3): °friend.

aṅkaṇa (M 72, 9; 83, 5; S 283, 4): °court (faulty writing for *aṅgaṇa*).

acakra (H 112, 2): °without guile.

ajāpāla (H 111, 1): (1) *goatherd; (2) °elder brother of Rāma; (3) °clinging to passion.

°*añc* + *ava* [*avāñcant*] (H 172, 3): to bend down.

añcana (H 213, 2): °going, movement.

°*atitanīyastā* (H 46, 1): excessive thinness.

atimuktata (H 136, 2): (1) °completely emancipated; (2) **Gaertnera racemosa*, Roxb., a beautiful and hardy creeper, distinguished for the fragrance and beauty of its blossoms.

anaṅgatā (H 128, 2): °lack of allegiance.

°*anatimaya* (M 9, 2): (1) without *timi*-fishes; (2) unbending.

ananta (H 13, 1): °many.

°*anahibhaya* (S 32, 2): (1) having no fear of one's subjects; (2) having no fear of serpents (cf. **ahibhaya*: fear of one's subjects).

°*anubandhatā* (H 171, 3): series.

anubandhin (H 147, 2): °author of a book.

andhaṅkaraṇa (H 297, 2): °cause of blindness.

°*apadarśana* (H 76, 1): deprived of sight.

aparājitā (H 246, 2): **Clitoria ternatea*, Linn., a cultivated flowering plant, chiefly blue and white in colour.

°*abhūtatā* (H 204, 1): untruth

amāra (H 280, 1): °not murderous.

°*ambaratva* (H 127, 3): (1) cloudiness; (2) clothing.

ambhōja (M 106, 1; S 335, 2): °name of a son of Viśvamitra.

°*ambhōjacāmara* (H 270, 1): *Blyxa octandra*, Linn., an aquatic, grass-like plant, with large, white blossoms.

°*amradiman* (H 213, 1): hardness.

amlāna (H 135, 2; 248, 1): **Gomphraena globosa*, Linn., globe-amaranth.

arkaparṇa (M 102, 7): **Asclepias gigantea*, Willd., a large, ramous shrub.

°*ardh* + *upasam* [*upasamṛddha*] (M 109, 7): to be constant, to last.

ardhacandra (H 89, 1): *eye in the plume of a peacock.

**ardhaśaphara* (H 99, 2): demi-carp, a sort of fish of uncertain identification.

°*arpaka* (H 53, 3): causing to go, delivering over, yielding.

°*avakōṭa* (H 99, 1): crane.

avadhika (M 115, 8; S 357, 5): °having as a limit, up to, until.

avalōpana (H 72, 3): °sunset.

avaśyāya (H 23, 1): *pride.

°*avastrīkṛta* (H 196, 1): (1) wile of an evil woman; (2) made a miserable woman.

**avīcī* (M 46, 1; S. 136, 3): a certain hell.

asaṅkhya (H 112, 1): °weapon, arrow.

°*asitamukha* (H 278, 3): a variety of white goose with black head and legs.

°*astimita* (H 268, 1): restless, tremulous.

°*ahasa* (H 33, 1): sorrow.

**ahituṇḍika* (M 6, 6; S 26, 1): snake catcher, snake charmer.

°*ahimakara* (H 278, 3): sun.

ā

ākarṣaka (H 197, 1): °attractive to women.

°*āghrātuka* (H 161, 3): breathing forth.

āḍambara (H 181, 3): *beginning, commencement.

ātarpaṇa (H 183, 3; 267, 3): °pigment, cosmetic.

ātmaghōṣa (H 74, 1): °self-praise.

ānanda (M 91, 1): °Brāhma.

ārikā (H 244, 4): °recourse, summons.

°*āvirbhūti* (H 66, 1): manifestation.

āśā (H 13, 2): °west.

āśrayāśa (H 28, 2; 70. 5): (1) °longing for hermitages; (2) °refuge-devouring.

i

°*itar* (H 213, 3): going to, attaining, possessing.

°*indrakōpa* (M 111, 4): cochineal (faulty writing for *indragōpa*).

indrajālin (H 67, 1): °enchanting, bewitching.

°*indravṛddhi* (M 113, 14): sort of horse (cf. **indravṛddhika*: sort of horse).

**indrāṇikā* (H 244, 3): (1) °wife of Indra; (2) °*Asparagus racemosus*, Willd., racemose asparagus.

indrāṇī (H 114, 3; 135, 1): (1) *mode of coitus (cf. Schmidt, *Beiträge* *zur indischen Erotik*, pp. 530–531, 564, 570, Leipzig, 1902); (2) * *Vitex negundo*, Linn., a small tree.

u

**uccatāla* (H 102, 4): °lofty height.

uccāiḥśravas (H 73, 1): °deaf.

ujjvala (M 40, 3; S 121, 2): *passion, love.

utkalikā (M 86, 4; S 294, 1): °name of a girl.

**utkuṭa* (M 36, 4): °sort of fish.

utpala (H 42, 4; 134, 3): (1) *fleshless; (2) °sort of fish of uncertain identification.

°*utsēkita* (M 109, 11; S 344, 1): proud, haughty.

**uddaṇḍapāla* (H 99, 3): sort of fish of uncertain identification.

°*uddaṇḍavāla* (M 37, 6; S 112, 5): sort of fish of uncertain identification (variant spelling of the preceding word).

udrōka (H 24, 2): °light on an elevated place.

ullalana (S 168, 3): °act of swinging.

ē

°*ēkabandhu* (H 9, 1): only brother.

k

ka (H 77, 2): *hair.

**kaṃsārāti* (H 286, 2): [illegible]

kaccha (M 36, 4): °bristle.

kañcukin (H 288, 3): *serpent (also in *Harṣacarita*, 108, 11).

kaṭa (H 242, 1; 297, 8): *corpse (cf. Zachariae, *Beiträge zur indischen Lexicographie*, p. 34, Berlin, 1883, and especially Zupitza, *Die germanischen Gutturale*, p. 107, Berlin, 1896).

kaṭaka (H 216, 4): *capital, metropolis.

°*kaṭapala* (H 75, 2): (1) flesh of a corpse; (2) breaking of an agreement.

kaṇṭaka (H 18, 1): °informer, tell-tale.

°*kathakāy* [*kathakāyatē*] (M 92, 7; S 306, 5): to become a narrator.

kadalikā (M 89, 6; S 300, 1): °name of a girl.

**kadalī* (H 295, 6): banner borne on an elephant.

kanaka (M 64, 17; S 199, 1): * *Butea frondosa*, *dhak*-tree.

°*kapika* (H 266, 2): monkey.

kabandha (H 42, 3; 101, 3): *water.

°*kabarikā* (M 61, 2; S 186, 1): hair.

kamala (H 205, 1): °receptacle of bliss (*ka*: joy + **mal(l)a*: receptacle).

karaka (H 150, 2): *hand.

karaṇa (H 125, 4): °cleavage.

**kartana* (H 129, 1): spinning (cf. *kṛntana* below).

karpara (H 277, 3): *skull.

°*karma* (M 51, 1): silk (cf. *kṛmi*: worm).

**kalakaṇṭha* (H 131, 3; 263, 2): *Eudynamis orientalis*, koel, Indian cuckoo.

kalatratā (H 236, 2): °possession of hips and loins (cf *kalatra*: hips, *pudenda*, *Kuṭṭanīmata*, 295).

**kalāṅkura* (H 142, 4): name of a man.

kaliṅga (S 355, 7): *fork-tailed shrike.

kānta (H 267, 1): °destroyer of bliss (*ka*: joy + *anta*: end).

kāntāra (H 23, 3): °famine.

kālēya (M 69, 11; S 222, 2): (1) *saffron; (2) *liver.

kāvyā (H 12, 2): *epithet of a female demon.

kāṣṭha (H 176, 3): °eminence, prosperity.

°*kimmīra* (M 56, 2): variegated (Prakritism for *kirmīra*).

**kīlāla* (H 219, 2): water.

ku (H 201, 1): °wife.

kuñja (M 36, 4; S 109, 2): *jaw (cf. Zachariae, *Beiträge zur indischen Lexikographie*, p. 32, Berlin, 1883).

kuñjara (H 201, 1): *hair.

kuṭīkṛta (M 103, 7; S 329, 5): °crooked.

°*kup + ud* [*utkupita*] (M 67, 12; 113, 11; S 354, 1): to be angry.

**kuruta* (M 88, 1; S 296, 3): °unseemly noise.

°*kulagraha* (M 84, 9): palace (Prakritism for *kulagṛha*).

°*kuhakuhārāva* (M 102, 9; Trichinopoly ed., 83, 5): confused noise.

°*kuhākuhārava* (Tel. ed. 61, 58, 8; Grantha ed., 58, 5): confused noise (variant spelling of the preceding word).

**kuhūmukha* (M 60, 7; S 185, 1): *Eudynamis orientalis*, koel, Indian cuckoo.

°*kṛkalāsatā* (H 275, 1): lizardhood.

kṛti (H 210, 2): °wealth (cf. Zachariae, *op. cit.* p. 33, on *kṛta*: fruit, reward).

kṛntana (M 51, 6): °spinning (cf. **kartana* above).

kṛṣṇavartman (H 28, 2; 176, 3): *rascally.

°*kētakikā* (H 231, 5): name of a girl.

°*kēdārikākōṣṭikā* (H 284, 2): enclosure of a field.

°*kōkapriyatamā* (H 53, 3): female of the *Cascara rutila*, Pallas, the Brahminy or ruddy duck.

**kōṇapa* (M 93, 9): °sort of demon (faulty writing for *kāuṇapa*).

**krakacacchada* (H 285, 1): *Pandanus odoratissimus*, Linn., screw-pine.

kṣaṇa (H 173, 5; 229, 3): °night.

kṣaṇadēśa (H 229, 3): °husband.

°*kṣīṇatarā* (H 56, 3): extreme emaciation.

kṣudrā (H 169, 2): *courtesan (also in *Kuṭṭanīmata*, 439).

**kṣudrāṇḍa* (M 109, 1): shoal of fish.

kh

**khagēśvara* (H 268, 6): °Garuḍa.

khaṇḍābhra (H 114, 2): *sort of erotic bite (cf. Schmidt, *Beiträge zur indischen Erotik*, pp. 504–505, Leipzig, 1902).

°*kharatā* (M 85, 6; S 293, 1): roughness.

kharma (H 127, 2): *courage, manhood.

g

**gaṇanīya* (H 235, 2): that should be reckoned.

**gaṇikārikā* (H 244, 4): *Premna spinosa*, Roxb., a small tree.

gaṇḍa (S 309, 1): (1) *stud in a horse's trappings; (2) *rhinoceros.

°*garghaṇa* (Grantha ed., 48, 12): rubbing (variant spelling of °*gharghaṇa*, M 45, 4).

°*gal*+*sam* [*saṅgalant*] (H 253, 1): to drip.

**gāṇikya* (M 40, 2; S 121, 2): group of courtesans.

gāndhāra (H 127, 2): *minium, red lead used as a cosmetic.

**gāmuka* (S 348, 4): °traveller.

guṇa (H 15, 1): *Bhīma.

°*gulmatā* (H 93, 1): (1) bushiness; (2) spleenfulness.

**guhin* (M 104, 2): forest.

gōcaratā (H 272, 2): °range.

gōdā (M 61, 3; S 186, 2): °earth-giving.

gōdhūmaka (M 111, 15): °wheat.

gōpati (M 100, 3; S 323, 2): *epithet of Indra.

gōpāla (M 41, 5; S 125, 1): °eloquent.

gāudhēya (M 103, 11): *lizard.

**gāudhēra* (H 265, 2): lizard (variant spelling of the preceding word).

gāurika (H 88, 2; 89, 3): °ruddy.

gh

ghaṇṭāravā (H 106, 2): *a variety of *Crotularia*.

ghanasāra (H 262, 2): *a sort of tree

°*gharghaṇa* (M 45, 4): rubbing (variant spelling of °*garghaṇa*, Grantha ed., 48, 12).

°*ghā* + *ud* [*udghāta*] (M 111, 12): to dig up (faulty writing for *khā* + *ud*).

°*ghātanīya* (H 293, 1): to be killed.

°*ghumughumāyita* (Trichinopoly ed., 90, 3): humming.

c

°*caṭātkāra* (M 93, 11; S 311, 2): crackling noise (variant spelling of **caṭatkāra*).

candrarēkhā (M 52, 1; S 150, 2): °golden diadem.

capalā (H 223, 2): °name of a girl.

capalāy [*capalāyati*] (H 223, 2): °to tremble.

caraṇa (H 278, 3): °ray, beam of light.

**cāturikā* (H 57, 2): °pillow, cushion.

cāraṇa (H 264, 3): °passage.

°*cāribhaṭa* (M 115, 2; S 356, 8): soldier (variant spelling of °*cārubhaṭa*).

cāru (M 106, 1; S 335, 2): °name of a son of Viśvamitra.

°*cārubhaṭa* (H 43, 1; 294, 4): (1) a sort of fish of uncertain identification; (2) soldier (variant spelling of °*cāribhaṭa*).

citra (M 52, 2; S 150, 3): **Jonesia Asoca*, *ushoka*-tree.

citraka (M 52, 2; S 150, 3): *sectarial mark on the forehead.

cirajīvin (H 120, 6): probably **Terminalia tormentosa*, Roxb., *saj*-tree.

°*cuñcura* (M 103, 9; S 329, 6): eager, desirous.

cumbaka (H 198, 1) *addicted to kissing.

ch

chattra (H 44, 3): probably **Asclepias acida*, Roxb., soma-plant.

j

jaghanya (H 77, 1): **membrum virile*.

°*jarjharita* (M 17, 9): broken, shattered (variant spelling of *jharjharita*).

**jalanakula* (H 277, 2): otter.

°*jalamanuja* (H 279, 1): merman.

jīvā (H 295, 4): *bow-string.

jh

°*jhaṇātkāra* (M 20, 7; S 63, 3): jingle (variant spelling of *jhaṇatkāra*).

ṭ

°*ṭaṅkārin* (S 310, 4): hissing (cf. *ṭāṅkarin*: making the sound *ṭā*, in *Harṣacarita*, 161, 3).

ḍ

°*ḍī + samud* [*samuḍḍīyamāna, samuḍḍayamāna*] (M 18, 1; S 55, 1): to fly up together.

ḍh

°*ḍhākinī* (M 94, 1): sort of female demon (variant spelling of *ḍākinī*).

t

taṭā (H 218, 4): °proximity.

°*taṭit* (M 110, 12): lightning (faulty spelling for *taḍit*).

**tata* (H 77, 2): °sound of the lute and similar instruments.

tathāgata (H 114, 3): (1) °homely; (2) °customary.

°*tithin* (H 111, 2): lover.

°*tiryaggatin* (H 147, 3): (1) going in crooked ways; (2) breeze, wind.

tulādhāra (H 174, 1): *merchant (cf. *tulādhara*: merchant, *Samayamātṛkā*, 7. 21; 8. 45).

°*tulira* (M 108, 5): meaning unknown (H *lulita*; S *tulita*).

**trōṭi* (M 53, 8; S 154, 3): beak.

d

**da* (H 199, 1): wife.

°*dattakapāṭa* (H 65, 5): with closed doors.

damanaka (H 39, 2; 135, 1): (1) °hero, champion; (2) °foe.

darpaka (H 53, 3; 209, 1): °burning.

dahana (H 28, 2): °consumer, destroyer.

dānavant (H 295, 5): °shedding ichor (also in *Harṣacarita*, 200, 18).

dāra (H 221, 5): °love (cf. *dārikā*: courtesan, *Subhāṣitasaṃdōha*, 24. 14).

dāsī (H 169, 2): *courtesan.

divyacakṣu (H 143, 1): (1) °Kṛṣṇa; (2) *blind.

°*duratikramatā* (S 326, 3): state of being hard to overcome.

duḥśasana (H 20, 2): °evil instruction.

°*dyusṛṇa* (H 233, 4): *Crocus sativus*, Linn., common saffron (faulty spelling for *ghusṛṇa*; cf. Zachariae in *KZ*. 27. 577 [card of Professor Zachariae, June 14, 1910]).

°*dravas* (H 223, 2): running, course.

**drāvaka* (H 198, 1): (1) magnet; (2) causing to run.

drōṇa (H 148, 1; 169, 5; 176. 2; 247, 2): *crow (also in *Harṣacarita*, 89, 12).

**drōṇakāka* (M 68, 5; S 216, 1): raven.

dvijapati (H 252, 3): *moon.

dvijārājan (H 273, 1): °Brāhman of superior excellence.
dvyartha (H 195, 1): °uncertain, hesitating.

dh

°*dhūmyā* (S 355, 7): fork-tailed shrike (misprint for **dhūmyāṭa*?).
dhṛtarāṣṭra (H 15, 1): °ruler of a kingdom.

n

nagaramaṇḍana (H 142, 4): °adornment of a city.
°*natimant* (H 181, 2): bowed, bent.
nada (H 91, 3): °sound, noise.
nadīna (H 25, 1): °lord of rivers, ocean (also in *Pariśiṣṭaparvan*, 7. 138).
nandighōṣa (H 142, 2): *name of Arjuna's chariot (cf. Zachariae, *Beiträge zur indischen Lexikographie*, p. 40, Berlin, 1883).
nabhaścara (H 267, 6): *bird.
nabhōga (H 23, 3): °god, deity.
naya (H 284, 2): *sort of game, chess (?) or backgammon (?) (cf. Thomas, 'The Indian Game of Chess,' in *ZDMG*. 53. 364).
°*narakṣaṇa* (M 78, 3; S 264, 1): destruction.
°*naruka* (M 111, 14): vulture.
narmada (H 271, 1): *jester, buffoon.
nava (H 27, 3): *praise, glory.
navaka (H 7, 4): (1) °despised; (2) °unknown.
nāndika (M 113, 4): °shout of praise.
**nāndīka* (H 295, 1): °possessed of laudations.
**nārikēli* (S 137, 6): cocoanut-tree.
nāstikatā (H 18, 1): °poverty.
nirṛti (H 122, 3): °devoid of envy.
°*nirbarha* (H 288, 5): with fallen or drooping plumes.
°*nirlakṣa* (S 80, 4): aimless.
niśātana (M 88, 1): °paring, sharpening.
°*nistriṃśatva* (H 129, 2): (1) swordship; (2) cruelty.
nyagrōdha (H 104, 3): °underbrush.

p

°*pañcāṅgulaya* (H 183, 3): handful.
°*paṭakuṭīka* (H 291, 1): tent.
°*paṭuprabha* (H 286, 1): beautiful.
°*paṇyavīdhikā* (M 70, 3): shop (faulty writing for *paṇyavīthikā*).
pattraratha (H 42, 3): °arrow.

°*pattrikā* (S 205, 1): leaf letter.

pathya (H 248, 2): °health.

padma (M 113, 11; S 353, 5): °drop of water.

°*payōja* (M 86, 5; S 294, 1): lotus.

°*paraṇḍaka* (M 23, 16): barrier to separate elephants (misprint for *varaṇḍaka*?).

°*parimalay* [*parimalaya*] (H 233, 2): to perfume

°*parihāsaka* (M 114, 4; S 355, 3): smiling.

°*paruvakā* (M 22, 8; S 69, 4): casket.

palala (H 156, 1): *flesh, meat.

palāśa (H 133, 2; 246, 3): *demon.

pallava (H 38, 4; 114, 3): (1) *love; (2) *paramour.

pallavita (H 137, 1): *reddened.

°*pāṃsulay* [*pāṃsulaya*] (M 89, 2): to make dusty.

pātra (H 47, 3): °body.

°*pālāvalī* (M 56, 7): fishhook.

pāli (H 139, 5; 190, 5): (1) *beautiful (at the end of compounds); (2) °hilt of a sword.

puṇḍarīka (H 42, 4): *white parasol.

puṣpakētu (H 111, 2): °mass of flowers.

°*pūrvatana* (M 8, 2): former, ancient.

**pēcakin* (H 178, 1): elephant.

pēla (M 104, 2): *open hand with outstretched fingers.

°*pracayatā* (H 266, 6): mass, quantity.

°*prapātatā* (M 104, 6; S 331, 6): state of having a shore (cf. *prapāta*: *shore).

prabāla (H 114, 2; 247, 2): °long hair.

°*pravālamaṇi* (H 114, 2): sort of erotic bite (cf. Schmidt, *Beiträge zur indischen Erotik*, pp. 502–503, Leipzig, 1902).

prasūna (M 27, 2; S 84, 2): *fruit.

ph

°*phalatā* (H 258, 5): fruition.

b

bandhura (H 165, 5): *undiform, wavelike.

balāri (M 94, 5): °owl (cf. *kākavāirin*, *vāyasāntaka*: owl, foe of crows).

bahulatā (H 88, 3): °blackness.'

**bāha* (H 146, 2): arm (cf. Zachariae, *Beiträge zur indischen Lexikographie*, p. 57, Berlin, 1883).

bh

°*bhaṅguratva* (H 128, 2): (1) break; (2) crookedness.
bhadra (H 94, 2): **Cyperus rotundus*, Linn., galangal.
°*bhībhatsa* (M 93, 10): loathsome (faulty writing for *bībhatsa*).
bhīru (H 295, 2): *jackal.
°*bhujaṅgatā* (H 273, 2): (1) serpenthood; (2) profligacy (also in *Harṣacarita*, 88, 2).
°*bhujaṅgapati* (M 92, 7): prince of serpents, the cosmic serpent Śēṣa.
bhujiṣyā (H 171, 2): *courtesan (also in *Kuṭṭanīmata*, 332, 420).
bhuvana (H 32, 1; S 301, 5): (1) *water; (2) *house, palace.
°*bhūtatā* (H 204, 1): truth.
bhṛṅgarājan (H 260, 3): *sort of large bee.
°*bhramaṇaka* (M 28, 2; S 86, 3): wandering, roaming about.
bhramara (H 40, 1): (1) *lover; (2) °curl on the forehead.
bhrāmaka (H 198, 1): (1) *magnet; (2) °seducer of women.

m

ma (H 224, 3): *Śiva.
**makarāṅka* (M 89, 11; S 300, 6): Kāma, the god of love.
makarikā (M 89, 11; S 300, 5): °name of a girl.
°*mañjīray* [*mañjīraya*] (H 89, 6; S 299, 4): to anklet it, hasten, go.
mañjughōṣā (M 52, 3; S 150, 4): *name of an Apsaras.
maṇḍalāgra (H 200, 1): *crooked sword.
matsarā (H 72, 2): *fly.
matsya (M 106, 2; S 335, 3): °name of a son of Viśvamitra.
°*matsyaputrikā* (H 287, 3): sort of bird.
madana (H 87, 2): **Datura metel*, Roxb., white thorn-apple.
madanaśalaka (H 106, 4): *aphrodisiac.
°*madayant* (H 213, 3): intoxicated.
°*madhuśriya* (H 139, 1): vernal beauty.
marīci (M 89, 8): °black pepper.
maruvaka (H 135, 1): (1) probably **Ocimum basilicum*, Linn., common basil; (2) *crane from the district of Maru.
marman (H 112, 1): °secret, mystery.
malaya (H 224, 3): (1) °love; (2) °moon.
mallanāga (H 89, 1): °sort of elephant.
mahātapasvin (H 281, 2): °great ascetic.
**mahānaṭa* (H 181, 3): Śiva (cf. Zachariae, *Beiträge zur indischen Lexikographie*, p. 68, Berlin, 1883).
**mahiṣākṣa* (M 57, 9; S 172, 1): sort of bdellium.

°*mā* (H 122, 5; 211, 1; M 78, 2; S 264. 1): (1) Lakṣmī; (2) utter, entire.

°*māṃsalay* [*māṃsalita*] (H 177, 3): to make stout or strong.

°*mātaṅgikā* (H 231, 3): name of a girl.

mānuṣyaka (H 222, 1): *multitude of men.

mālaya (H 23, 2): °red lotus.

mukta (H 89, 1): °missile.

muktā (M 106, 5; S 336, 2): *courtesan.

muktāmaya (H 35, 2): °free from disease.

mud + *ā* [*āmumudē*] (H 215, 1): °to rejoice exceedingly.

muni (H 136, 2): **Mangifera indica*, Linn., mango-tree.

°*mūrchāgṛhīta* (H 156, 3): seized with faintness.

**mṛtyuphala* (H 91, 3): fruit of the *Trichosanthes palmata*, Roxb.. or of the *Musa sapientum*, Willd.

°*mṛdiman* (M 81, 3): softness.

°*mēlāmandāy* [*mēlāmandāyatē*] (M 92, 7): to become an inkwell (denominative from **mēlāmandā*: inkwell).

**mradiṣṭha* (H 169, 4): softest, very soft.

y

yantraṇa (H 136, 3): (1) °feather-guard on an arrow; (2) *protection.

yavasa (H 77, 2): °skill.

r

**ra* (H 213, 3): fire, heat.

raktamaṇḍalatā (H 230, 3): (1) °state of having a red disc; (2) °state of possessing devoted adherents.

°*rajōrājan* (M 81, 2; S 275, 1): Kāma, the god of

°*ralita* (M 86, 7): beautiful (by-form of *lalita*).

°*rasamayant* (M 82, 1): (1) delightful; (2) full of desire.

°*rāgatā* (H 128, 1): (1) a certain musical mode; (2) affection, love.

rāgitā (H 129, 1): °redness.

rājasa (H 203, 1): °passionateness.

°*rājā* (M 57, 11; S 172, 4): parched grain (by-form of *lājā* for the sake of paronomasia).

ripu (H 199, 2): °cowife.

ruṇḍa (M 23, 15): °staff of a balance.

rūpa (H 144, 2): *wild beast.

l

lamba (M 41, 2; S 124, 1): °section of a book (abbreviation of *lambaka*; cf. Lacôte, *Essai sur Guṇāḍhya et la Bṛhatkathā*, pp. 220–221, Paris, 1908).

laya (H 224, 3): °house.

lāsaka (H 55, 1): *peacock.

°*lipikārāy* [*lipikārāyate*] (M 92, 7; S 306, 5): to become a scribe.

V

°*val*+*samud* [*samudvalan*] (M 113, 4): to rise up together.

**vāri* (H 199, 1): speech, eloquence.

vāruṇī (H 267, 1): °water.

vāstuka (S 158, 2): °inhabitant of a city.

vikaca (H 64, 3): °the planet Venus.

**vicikila* (M 55, 5; 56, 4; S 164, 1; 166, 3): *Jasminum Sambac*, Arabian jasmine (variant spelling of *vicakila*).

vidagdha (H 128, 1): °libertine.

vidyādhara (H 14, 3): °receptacle of wisdom.

°*vinirmōka* (M 20, 8; S 63, 3): liberation, emancipation.

°*vimalīkṛta* (M 3, 6): cleansed.

virāma (H 22, 1): °absence of Rāma.

vilāsin (H 115, 3): *serpent (cf. Zachariae, *Beiträge zur indischen Lexikographie*, p. 30, Berlin, 1883).

°*vilōkayant* (H 207, 1): solitary.

viṣāda (M 67, 5; S 212, 1): °cloud.

viṣēśaka (H 212, 2): °without auspicious signs.

°*visadṛśatā* (M 101, 14): inequality, unlikeness.

vīratara (H 112, 1): *arrow (cf. Zachariae, *op. cit.* p. 76).

°*vāihāsika* (M 54, 1; S 156, 1): buffoon, jester.

Ś

śakuna (H 144, 1): °festal song, Holi song.

°*śaṅkitakarṇa* (M 93, 8): thief.

śaraṇa (H 260, 1): °refugee.

°*śarmadā* (M 91, 6): name of a river (faulty writing for *narmadā*).

śalāka (H 55, 1): **maina* bird.

śālabhañjikā (H 110, 1): °a Vidyādharī (less probably, a class of heroine; see Lacôte, *Essai sur Guṇāḍhya et la Bṛhatkathā*, pp. 222–225, Paris, 1908).

°*śikharagatasūryācandramastā* (H 90, 1): state of having the sun and the moon on the summit.

°*śikharatā* (H 85, 3): state of having a peak.

śikharin (H 168, 2): *tree.

°*śīthu* (Trichinopoly ed., 84, 3): spirituous liquor (faulty writing for *śidhu*, *sīdhu*).

°*śūrapāla* (M 95, 3; S 314, 3): name of a certain Vāiśya.
śōdhana (H 209, 2): °teacher.
śyāmā (M 18, 8; S 58, 1): °night (also in *Kalāvilāsakāvya*, 1. 33; see Meyer, *Altindische Schelmenbücher*, 2. 155, Leipzig, 1903).
śravas (H 150, 1): *ear.
°*śvitray* [*śvitrita*] (H 184, 4): to make leprous.
**śvētarōcis* (M 25, 2; S 77, 2): moon.

ṣaṭpada (H 249, 1): *louse.

sa (H 296, 4): *lord.
saṃślēṣa (M 72, 15): °paronomasia.
°*saṅgrahīti* (M 6, 5): capture, seizure.
°*sañjīvanikā* (M 89, 7; S 300, 2): name of a girl.
satpatha (M 43, 3; 114, 10; S 130, 1; 355, 9): °path of the planets.
sad + samā [*samāsādita*] (H 12, 1): °to uphold.
°*sadārāma* (H 295, 6): goodly garden.
sanīḍa (M 103, 13; S 330, 5): *neighbouring, near.
sant (S 303, 3): °Brāhma.
°*santāpatā* (H 165, 3): grief, sorrow.
sandhyārāga (H 58, 4): *sort of redness, red lead.
saprapañca (H 195, 1): °full of innuendo.
**samāsādya* (H 211, 2): attainable, desirable (cf. *sad* + *samā* above).
samudaya (M 100, 5; S 323, 4): *rising (of the sun).
°*sammōhinī* (M 25, 7): confusion.
°*sāgaraśāyin* (H 13, 1): Nārāyaṇa.
°*sitatva* (H 197, 1): bondage.
sindūra (H 247, 2): *a sort of tree.
°*sugandhavāha* (H 147, 3): (1) bearing perfume; (2) goodly breeze.
sumukha (H 34, 1): *learned, wise.
suratā (M 87, 4; S 295, 6): °name of a girl.
surasundarī (H 42, 3): °a sort of fish.
sūri (M 67, 6; S 212, 2): *sun.
°*sūryātmajā* (M 45, 10; S 135, 4): the River Yamunā (Jumna).
sṛgāla (H 29, 2): °coward.
°*sāutrāma* (H 288, 8): relating to Sutrāman (Indra).
strīmaya (H 274, 1): °loving women, addicted to women.
**sthapuṭay* [*sthapuṭita*] (M 37, 8; S 113, 2): to make uneven.

h

haṃsa (H 36, 1; 113, 1): (1) °slaying, murderous; (2) °pure.

hārikaṇṭha (H 149, 4): (1) *possessed of a sweet note; (2) *handsome neck.

hārin (H 214, 2): °wrathful.

hāsa (M 19, 2): °a certain *rāga*, or musical mode.

°*himānin* (H 23, 2): snowy.

Here also may be noted five verb-forms supplementary to Whitney's *Roots, Verb-Forms, and Primary Derivatives of the Sanskrit Language* (Leipzig, 1887): *itar* (H 213, 3), primary derivative from *i*: to go (cf. Lindner, *Altindische Nominalbildung*, pp. 72–75, Jena, 1878) [not in]; *acīkamata* (H 154, 1), aorist of *kam*: to love [only Brāhmaṇas cited for this form]; *acakāṅkṣat* (H 155, 1), aorist of *kāṅkṣ*: to desire [only lexicographers cited for this form]; *papāṭa* (H 186, 1), perfect of *paṭ*: to burst [not in]; and *haṃsa* (H 36, 1), primary derivative from *han*: to kill (cf. Lindner, *op. cit.* pp. 110–111) [not in].